SOVIET POLICIES IN CHINA, 1917–1924

SOVIET POLICIES IN CHINA, 1917–1924

Soviet Policies in China

1917-1924

By ALLEN S. WHITING

STANFORD UNIVERSITY PRESS   STANFORD, CALIFORNIA

**THE TRANSLITERATION SYSTEM USED
IS BASED ON THE LIBRARY OF CONGRESS SYSTEM
WITH SOME MODIFICATIONS**

Stanford University Press
Stanford, California
Copyright © 1953 Columbia University Press, New York
L.C. 68-12335
Printed in the United States of America
First published in 1954 by Columbia University Press
Reissued in 1968 by Stanford University Press

Acknowledgments

No single paragraph can do justice to the contributions and criticisms made by various individuals during the course of this study. The initial impetus to the writer's interest in Sino-Soviet relations came from Professor Knight Biggerstaff, whose vital concern with all matters Chinese has been a genuine inspiration. The careful, patient, and scholarly guidance of Professor Philip E. Mosely has nursed the research and writing from a limited seminar paper to a detailed dissertation. Whatever merit this study may have is a result of his rigorous training and precision. Consultations with Professors Nathaniel Peffer, Franklin L. Ho, and C. Martin Wilbur provided many insights from their long, intimate experience in China. Informal conversations with David Munford, Conrad Brandt, and Harold Isaacs offered criticisms which have proven most valuable. Louis Fischer and Robert C. North were kind enough to allow me use of their personal papers, some of which are published herein for the first time. Of particular importance was Mr. Fischer's file of the correspondence exchanged between Leo Karakhan and Sun Yat-sen, secured directly from Karakhan during Mr. Fischer's reportorial days in the Soviet Union. Dr. Tsui Shu-chin read part of the manuscript while the author was in Taiwan. Mr. Chang Kuo-t'ao was consulted on other portions in Hong Kong.

The scholar is helpless without the constant cooperation of the

kind and thoughtful librarian, and my sincere appreciation
to those who helped me at the New York Public Library,
Library of Congress, the libraries of Harvard, Columbia, and t
University of California (Berkeley), and the Hoover Library c
War and Revolution. Financial assistance was granted through th
Richard Watson Gilder Fellowship which I held during 1949–50
at Columbia University, and the Area Research Fellowship which
was granted me by the Social Science Research Council in 1951.
Of course, none of these organizations or individuals bear responsibility for the views expressed herein. Finally, I pay the
inevitably understated respects to my wife for her criticisms
and encouragement.

A. S. W.

Contents

SOVIET POLICIES IN CHINA, 1917–1924

SOVIET POLICIES IN CHINA 1917-1924

Introduction

TWO mighty revolutionary streams have merged their currents. The Russian and the Chinese revolutions, starting from widely separated sources, have swelled the tide of Communism to the point of overflow, threatening to engulf all surrounding nations. So dynamic has this process been that both Marxist and non-Marxist writers have tended to view the 1950 Sino-Soviet Alliance as the inevitable outcome of historical forces. An examination of the pre-1917 record does not support this analysis, however. China suffered humiliation and exploitation at the hands of Tsarist Russia during the nineteenth century, just as she suffered at the hands of the other major world powers. Russian troops occupied Chinese territory after the Boxer Uprising in 1900, being dislodged only under direct pressure from the Western nations and Japan. Russian economic penetration of North Manchuria by means of the Chinese Eastern Railway carved out a sphere of interest in China's richest mineral and food-producing area. Secret treaties concluded between Russia and Japan before and during World War I divided North China between them in typical imperialistic manner. Russian actions down to 1917 inflamed the same hatred and antiforeign prejudices among the Chinese people that other imperialist nations encountered. There was no reason to expect the new China, struggling to throw off the inferiority of a "backward" country, to regard Russia any differently from Japan, Great Britain, or France.

Bolshevik Russia, like Tsarist Russia, had little incentive to woo China in the chaotic days of 1917; far richer prizes lay to the west. European industry with its millions of highly skilled workers and advanced techniques was the Promised Land for world revolution according to Karl Marx. To the east, the so-called Republic of China was a sorry successor to the Chinese Empire of old. With the collapse of the Manchu dynasty in 1911, six years of military rule and anarchy prevailed in the Middle Kingdom. While Sun Yat-sen, the recognized leader of the Chinese revolution, cast about for combinations of intellectuals who could lead the Republic, Yuan Shih-kai exploited the Peking government for personal and political gain. After his abandonment of parliamentary procedures, Yuan embarked upon a short-lived monarchical restoration with himself as emperor. His passing from the scene in 1916 only compounded confusion, capped by China's entry into World War I in 1917. Largely because of this move, dissident elements withdrew from the Peking government, set up a rival regime in Canton, and completed the splitting of China. Hostile groups of war lords vied for power in various areas, supported in some instances by foreign money and material. Accompanying this political ferment were economic problems of appalling magnitude. China's industry, such at it was, lay primarily in the hands of foreign owners. Except for the thin façade of urbanization spread along the foreign-dominated coast, China lacked the basic network of communications and transportation so vital for modernization. Its proletariat was counted by thousands, in contrast with the several hundred millions of peasants eking out a living among poverty, starvation, and disease. The dramatic impact of Western influence on nearby Japan had highlighted the disintegration of China's traditional Confucian society. If so chaotic a country offered promise for Bolshevik agitators in 1917, it was a promise clouded by problems greater in scope than those within Russia itself.

On the face of it, then, many factors opposed alliance of these two nations, torn by upheaval and embittered by past grievances. Yet far removed as China may have been from the perspective of orthodox Marxists, Lenin and his followers embarked on a dual policy, weaving diplomatic and revolutionary activity so as to fashion a new pattern of Russian power in the Far East. While retaining basic Tsarist gains in Manchuria and extending them in Outer Mongolia, Soviet Russia became the champion of new China, concluding the first so-called equal treaty between Peking and a major foreign power. While providing Sun Yat-sen's revolutionary Kuomintang party in Canton with men, money, and munitions, Russia nurtured a fledgling Chinese Communist Party that was destined to be the future ruler of the Middle Kingdom. Despite the obvious paradoxes of Soviet policy, its success during the early twenties laid the foundations of Sino-Soviet relations that were to become of increasing importance during the succeeding decades, culminating in the Sino-Soviet Alliance of 1950.

History is seldom the work of one man alone; particularly is this true of Sino-Soviet relations. Lenin's role as leader of the Bolshevik revolution shaped the thinking of many, yet as an individual he cannot be credited for all of the success or failure of Soviet policy in China since ill health removed him from active direction of that policy as early as 1922. Not until 1929 did Stalin emerge as undisputed head of the world Communist movement, and prior to 1924 he appears to have had no part in Far Eastern affairs. In the interim, many groups worked in Moscow, Peking, Shanghai, and Canton, often at cross-purposes. The twofold question arises: how did Soviet policy in China evolve, and what were the implications of that evolution for Soviet Russia's position in the Far East?

It is toward this basic question that the following study is directed. Beginning with an examination of Lenin's writings on China prior to 1917, it traces the shaping and reshaping of his ideas under the impact of the events of 1917 to 1920, the period of civil war, foreign intervention, and consolidation of Bolshevik power. As the most important public debate among world revolutionaries concerning Communist tactics in the Far East, the Second Congress of the Communist International (Comintern) receives detailed attention. Despite the adoption of theses designed to lay down the principles for all future policy, deep cleavages remained within the organization as revealed in a survey of Comintern writings and speeches for the subsequent period. These cleavages, revolving around such crucial points as cooperation with the bourgeoisie and development of an essentially peasant program instead of focusing on the proletariat, take on increasing significance in the writings of the People's Commissariat for Foreign Affairs (Narkomindel) and the Red International of Trade Unions (Profintern). The perplexing problems associated with applying Marxism to an agrarian society and with making revolutionary principles compatible with Soviet foreign policy are clearly illustrated in the Congress of Toilers of the Far East, held in 1922. While providing a case study in the formulation of policy, the Congress highlights problems which were to plague implementation of policy in the period of Communist-Kuomintang alliance, 1924 to 1927.

The second half of the study follows in detail the efforts of the Narkomindel to win recognition from the Chinese Republic while reasserting Russian influence in the sensitive border areas of Outer Mongolia and North Manchuria. Again a case study illustrates the complexity of Soviet ends and means, centered in the 1922 mission of Adolf Joffe in Peking. His propaganda efforts among influential Chinese, his intransigent notes to the Waichiao Pu, and his sudden coup in winning a formal entente with Sun Yat-sen provide many clues to the central question of the study. As a concluding section, the Karakhan mission embodies the culmination of Narkomindel and Comintern policies, formalized in the Sino-Soviet treaty of May 31, 1924, on the one hand, and, on the other, in the appointment of Michael Borodin as Soviet architect of a revised Kuomintang-Communist revolutionary movement. A chronology in Appendix A traces the principal events in Sino-Soviet relations during the period under review.

A word of explanation, or perhaps apology, is necessary concerning the detailed documentation in the text. It is the author's conviction that because of the language barrier, the elusiveness of materials, and the Soviet rewriting of history, extensive translations of important Russian documents should be included wherever possible. In connection with documentation, it is recognized that no study of diplomatic history, much less revolutionary conspiracy, can be definitive until archives are opened. However, an overwhelming mass of secondary material, most of it highly authoritative, confronts the scholar of early Soviet history. Struck by varying accounts in English of the Karakhan Manifesto of 1919, the author attempted to unravel the differing versions and found that only by reading all of the material written by Soviet publicists could the contradictions be resolved. Consequently, instead of trying to spot certain events and the documents concerning them, an extensive survey of Russian periodicals, pamphlets, and books was made. For events in China, every issue from 1917 to 1924 of *Millard's Review*, later the *China Weekly Review*, was examined. In addition, relevant issues of the *North China Herald* were searched. For Soviet statements, virtually every issue of *Izvestiia* published between November 7, 1917, and June 30, 1924, was read by the author, as was every issue of *Pravda* from November 7, 1917, to March 1, 1920. Other issues of *Pravda* came under examination with regard to important events, such as the Congress of Toilers of the Far East. In addition, the complete files of all Comintern, Narkomindel, and Profintern journals published between 1917 and 1924 were examined, as were many pamphlets and books, as well as speeches by Lenin, Zinoviev, Bukharin, and their associates.

From this conglomeration of material, three basic points emerge. First, it is hoped that the present study is as complete

a record of Soviet words and deeds concerning China from 1917
to 1924 as the available records permit. Diplomatic notes and
Marxist debates furnish few insights in and of themselves. However, unless their contents are accurately presented, analysis is
confounded from the very start. Thus textual criticism became as
important as documentary searching. By comparing every Russian version of the Karakhan Manifesto, whether in newspaper,
pamphlet, or book, a long-standing controversy over an important passage was finally resolved. Similarly, only by examining
every printed version of the Second Comintern Congress, including those in Russian, German, French, and English, was it
possible to piece together the full story of the debates surrounding Lenin's theses on Asian revolutions. In some instances it was
found that deletions or changes were intentional, as with the
Karakhan Manifesto. In others, they were the product of the
turbulent times on which the study centers. As noted by editors
of the English stenographic account of the Second Comintern
Congress:

There were only two German stenographers [present], one French,
and no English. . . . Alone the transcription from the shorthand notes
has claimed two months' time. By the time the work of editing com-
menced most of the delegates had already gone. It was found that the
text was in many places mutilated and that there were many omissions
. . . and finally, many speeches, particularly those delivered in English, were only in the German or French translation. . . . The translation into English was done by different people with varying mastery
of the language.[1]

In addition to historical accuracy, reviewing so wide an ex-
panse of material provides valuable insights into the type and
amount of information available to Soviet planners of policy for
China. To be sure, there is no certainty of how much additional
material was available at top levels in the Russian hierarchy, but
given the early Soviet propensity to publish voluminously on
everything except the most covert revolutionary activity, it is
probable that the amalgam of minuscule news items and lengthy

articles by Soviet Far Eastern experts provides a fair picture of what was before those in policy-making positions. Thus no reference to China, regardless of its size, was disregarded for this study, although of course not every item merited inclusion in the following pages.

Finally, when all of the material had been recorded as presented in the various sources, it was correlated according to attitudes concerning various factors in the Chinese revolution, such as the bourgeoisie, the peasantry, the proletariat, the intelligentsia, political groupings, and foreign powers. It is not the facts but the way in which men view them that conditions policy. With remarkable consistency, attitudes on each of these issues differed according to definite groups within the Comintern, and among the Comintern, the Narkomindel, and the Profintern. The antibourgeois interpretation of Comintern writers clashed sharply with the probourgeois views of Narkomindel scribes, with consequent effect upon the actions of those two groups in China. Far from being monolithic, the Soviet structure of the early twenties presents a fascinating picture of clash and conflict, rooted both in theoretical differences and in political intrigue.

It should be pointed out that this study has been undertaken, intermittently, over a period of five years. Mr. E. H. Carr saw the manuscript at mid-point, as acknowledged in the preface to his third volume of *The Bolshevik Revolution, 1917–1923.*[2] In the later stages of research, particularly while at the Hoover Library on War and Revolution in the summer of 1953, the author added to and revised some of his earlier material. Consequently, discrepancies exist between the study by Professor Carr and this work, some of which will be noted at the appropriate places.

I

Before November: Lenin on China

KARL MARX speculated on the role Russia might play in the world revolutionary movement, but he failed to foresee the turn of Fortune's wheel which made the backward colossus of Russia the fatherland of international Communism. The German economist developed a comprehensive criticism of the capitalistic system of his day. He made no effort to design a detailed blueprint of socialism. Marx repeatedly asserted, however, that the workers of the world would be led by the masses of oppressed proletariat in the most advanced industrial countries of western Europe. In actuality, it was the workers and peasants of backward Russia who first achieved the Socialist state, and their success was carried further in Asia by the peasant masses of China. All was done in the name of Marx, yet little remained of the original doctrine beyond his basic tenets of class warfare, economic determinism, and analysis of history in terms of the dialectical process.

It was not the first time that history had failed to vindicate the words of a prophet, and in accordance with precedent it was to be expected that a restatement of doctrine would be undertaken. Such was the self-appointed task of Vladimir Ilyich Lenin. Yet he too failed to appreciate fully the extent to which backward, nonindustrial Asia would become a mainstay of world revolution. The consequences of attempting revolution on the Communist pattern where the concentration of capital and the scale of industrial production fell far short of the conditions prescribed by Marx brought endless dilemmas to Soviet strategists. Lenin was more aware than his European colleagues of the political and economic significance of colonial areas for world capitalism. Nevertheless, prior to 1917 he developed no comprehensive theory of revolutionary tactics in Asia.

In the turbulent months following November 7, 1917, the Bolsheviks had sufficient troubles at home to keep them from focusing on events some 6,000 miles to the east. When Asian ferment later stirred their imagination with the glowing prospect of carrying the Communist banner on the rising tide of nationalism, Russian revolutionists turned to the legacy of Lenin for guidance and direction. They discovered that before the Russian revolution Lenin had written a scant dozen articles on China, so preoccupied was he with the prospects of revolution in Europe. To be sure, he was hampered somewhat by a dearth of reliable information, as he himself admitted in 1921: "I know nothing whatever about the rebels and revolutions of South China, except two or three articles of Sun Yat-sen and several books and newspaper articles which I read several years ago." [1] To a far greater extent, however, his lack of emphasis on the East resulted from the firm conviction, shared generally by European Socialists, that the immediate future of the proletarian revolution lay in Europe, particularly in Germany.

Lenin had turned his attention to China during the Boxer Uprising of 1900. This antiforeign outburst was responsible for the invasion of Peking by troops of the great powers and the subsequent imposition of an indemnity upon the decaying Manchu dynasty for damage suffered and for the cost of armed intervention. Lenin warned Russia that any predatory acts would earn for her the hatred of the Chinese people, levied against those who "used their vaunted civilization only for fraud, plunder, and violence." [2] Aside from noting that such acts were characteristic of countries with rapidly developing industrial economies, he made no further analysis at this time of economic motivations behind the international race for concessions in China.

Again in 1908, Lenin touched briefly on events in the Far East while summarizing the relationship between revolutions in Europe and in Asia. As in many of his later writings, he dealt in detail with developments in India, Persia, and Turkey, allotting comparatively little space to China. Aware of this shortcoming in his analysis, Lenin remarked:

It is impossible to say anything definite as yet concerning an actual movement in China—so little is known of it and such an abundance of revolts are led in different localities—but there is no doubt of the strong growth of the "new spirit" and of "European ideas" in China, especially since the Russo-Japanese war. Consequently the transition of advanced Chinese uprisings into a consciously democratic movement is inevitable.[3]

It is interesting to note that the "inevitability" referred to was apparently regarded by Lenin as the consequence of ideological forces rather than of economic development.

Although the downfall of the Manchus in 1911 was hailed by formal resolution at the Paris Conference of the Russian Social Democratic Workers' Party,[4] it was only in July, 1912, that Lenin came to grips with problems inherent in the Chinese revolution. Commenting on an article by Sun Yat-sen, the Bolshevik leader wrote his most detailed analysis of China prior to 1917.[5] Many questions were treated, questions which later rose again and again to plague Soviet policy-makers. The role of the Chinese bourgeoisie, the influence of nationalism, the question of leaping over the capitalist stage of development and of moving directly from feudalism[6] into socialism, the appalling peasant conditions —to these points Lenin directed his attention. In view of the importance which these issues later assumed, a detailed examination of his analysis is necessary.

Lenin attempted to sum up Sun Yat-sen's eclectic, rambling doctrine in one Russian word: *narodnichestvo*. To the Russian reader, this typified a romantic socialism, petit bourgeois in character and based on an agrarian reform program. While from a Marxist standpoint obvious criticisms were implicit in such a term, Lenin's estimation of Sun's political program emerged distinctly favorable. He praised the "truly democratic enthusiasm" in Sun's platform, as well as his courage and his faith in the people. "Before us there is a truly great ideology of a truly great people which not only laments its traditional bondage, not only dreams of freedom and equality, but also *fights* the traditional oppressors of China."

There followed a comparison which was to be repeated many times in the following years with varying emphasis. For Lenin, China was passing through Russia's 1905 stage of development; the bourgeoisie was leading the struggle as in eighteenth-century France. This reference was bound to call up a host of associations in the minds of his Russian audience. The turbulent events of 1904–5 had expressed growing resentment at Tsarist autocracy. Smoldering hatred of oppressive living conditions exploded in scattered, spontaneous uprisings. Strikes multiplied, peasant riots spread, and the leaders of the opposition demanded a constitutional regime. Political reforms were instituted but there was no overthrow of the existing order. Similarly in China, unrest was manifest and the immediate successors to the Manchus were unable to quell dissension. Despite the fact that the traditional political regime had been overthrown, no fundamental reorganization of either the political or the economic order had been achieved. The Chinese bourgeoisie had yet to consolidate its power.

Although Lenin admitted that one wing of the bourgeoisie was capable of treachery, as shown by Yuan Shih-kai's betrayal of Sun's principles, he declared: "The revolutionary-bourgeois democracy, headed by Sun Yat-sen, is correctly following the path of 'restoring' China by developing the most self-active, resolute, and daring peasant masses in the work of political and agrarian reform." Thus Lenin approved the formula of bourgeois leadership of the peasant revolution. The 1905 analogy seemed applicable, despite the absence of the industrial proletariat and its strike movement.

It was Sun's economic program that received Lenin's sharpest barbs. Sun advocated agrarian reform measures with the "completely reactionary dream" of "forestalling capitalism." Lenin agreed that such measures were necessary in China's backward, semifeudal condition but scoffed at the idea of avoiding capitalism through these steps. He noted that it was understandable for Chinese intellectuals to focus all their attention on destroying feudalism and economic oppression in China and that their "socialism," imported from the West, would naturally carry along with it the anticapitalist theme. However, he maintained that Sun's plan was nothing more than a single-tax doctrine which would eliminate absolute rent, allow greater adaptation of agriculture to marketing conditions, and thus pose precisely the most favorable conditions for a rapid capitalistic development. As Lenin put it,

In that is the dialectic of social conditions in China, that Chinese democrats, in true sympathy with socialism in Europe, translate it into reactionary theories, and *on the basis* of that reactionary theory of "forestalling" capitalism produce a purely-capitalist, maximum-capitalist agrarian program.[7]

Lenin prophesied that a fierce struggle would have to be waged by Chinese revolutionists against a coalition of monarchists, feudal landlords, and native clergy. His failure to list foreign imperialists as members of this coalition must have been due to an oversight. He entertained no sanguine illusions concerning the outcome of the struggle, and in his formula for the fight Lenin made his first reference to proletarian activity in China.

The more China is behind Europe and Japan, the more it is threatened with break-up and national corruption. "To renovate it" is possible only through the heroism of the revolutionary masses, capable of creating in the realm of politics a Chinese republic, in the agrarian realm—of securing through the nationalization of the soil the quickest capitalist progress.

Whether it will succeed—that is another question. Different countries in their bourgeois revolutions brought to life different levels of political and agrarian democratism, and in most varied combinations. It will be decided by the international situation and the corresponding social forces in China. . . .

Finally, as the numbers of Shanghais grow in China, so will the Chinese proletariat grow. It will probably form one or another Chinese Social Democratic workers' party, which, criticizing the petit-bourgeois utopianism and reactionary views of Sun Yat-sen, will certainly carefully distinguish, preserve, and develop the revolutionary-democratic core of his political and agrarian program.[8]

Thus Lenin sketched the outlines of his future policy in China as early as 1912. As embodied in his analysis, the main points were: (1) support the reformist bourgeoisie and Sun Yat-sen against monarchical and semifeudal groups; (2) develop the purely bourgeois revolution through an agrarian program; (3) speed the transition to capitalism; and (4) simultaneously encourage the emergence of a proletarian nucleus which would be on guard against and would improve upon the incorrect, petit-bourgeois aspects of Sun Yat-sen's program.

A few months after this article appeared, Lenin expanded his appraisal of the bourgeoisie. Describing the various political groupings in China, Lenin wrote of Sun's followers:

The "Nationalist Party" is the party which, for the most part, is more industrious, more progressive, and better developed in *South* China. The main stronghold of the "Nationalist Party" is the peasant mass. The leaders of it are the intelligentsia educated overseas. Chinese freedom was won through an alliance of peasant democrats and liberal bourgeoisie. Can the peasantry, not led by a proletarian party, retain its democratic position *against* the liberals, who only wait for a satisfactory time to move to the Right? This will be shown in the near future.[9]

Brilliant as were Lenin's analyses of European Socialist developments, he often erred in transferring analogies to Asia. There is almost no support for his claim that the "peasant mass" supported the Kuomintang in 1912. It is highly improbable that the 400 million peasants even knew of the Kuomintang's existence, much less that they backed its platform. This oversimplification of the alignment of forces in the Chinese revolutions was to cause considerable confusion among those who carefully studied Lenin's words in later years.

Lenin was by no means of one mind concerning the bourgeoisie, as shown by his somewhat qualified praise of its "liberal" elements. Events in China left little hope of a quick settlement of internal problems while Peking was ruled by a peculiar mixture of parliamentarianism and autocracy under Yuan Shih-kai. As one Soviet writer later remarked, the bourgeoisie was "still in diapers." Yet only six months after Lenin's caveat quoted above, he remarked encouragingly: "In Asia everywhere a mighty democratic movement is growing, broadening and strengthening. The bourgeoisie there is *still* going with the people against reaction." [10] Three years later, the exigencies of World War I forced Lenin to a more vigorous exposition of his views as he endeavored to win support among the badly fragmented Socialist groups of Europe. Stilling his previously expressed fears about the bourgeoisie, he called upon his fellow radicals to "render determined support to the more revolutionary elements in the bourgeois-democratic movement for national liberation in these countries [China, Persia, Turkey, etc.] and assist their rebellion—and if need be, their revolutionary war *against* the imperialist powers that oppress them." [11]

This quotation brings up the external aspect of the Chinese revolution: its relationship to the world anti-imperialist struggle. In discussing internal aspects of the Chinese revolution, Lenin had obvious difficulties in appraising the complex impact of Western ideas on the Confucian-oriented society. Far removed from the scene of events and having only limited information, he made errors which were compounded by a rigid class analysis of a highly fluid and amorphous upheaval. However, Lenin was on firmer ground in understanding the latent feelings of hostility against the West which were breaking to the surface among Asian peoples. Tsarist Russia had long been "a prison of nations" with many exploited Asian nationalities within its extensive frontiers. Their hatred of the Great Russians was well known to both critics of and apologists for the oppressive regime. Moreover, as a subject of "one of the most primitive, medieval, shamefully backward of the Asiatic governments," [12] Lenin had good cause to understand the reactions of those whom imperialism had exploited. As early as 1900, he had warned of the hatred that Russian imperialism would foment in China. In subsequent years he tried to awaken the Second International to the possibilities of bringing colonial resentment to a head in a vast movement against British, French, and Japanese imperialism. Lenin constantly emphasized the sheer mass of the Asian peoples who waited impatiently for dynamic leadership to bring them into action against their foreign exploiters. Striking at the narrow focus of his colleagues who saw only Europe and its immediate problems, Lenin repeatedly hammered his theme: "400 millions of backward Asiatics attained freedom [in the Chinese revolution], awakened to political life. One-fourth of the world's population crossed over, so to speak, from sleep to light, movement, and struggle." [13]

The Bolshevik leader depicted an unbroken chain of revolutions following from the 1905 uprising in Russia. Persia, Turkey, India, and China were linked together in the movement of backward peoples against their feudal and foreign oppressors. Later Soviet commentaries followed uncritically this schematic analysis, although it ignored basic differences in the internal developments of these countries. For Lenin, their common factor was the fundamental aim of nationalism—of independence. On the eve of World War I he discussed the problem of self-determination of peoples:

In Eastern Europe and in Asia the period of bourgeois-democratic revolutions began only in 1905. Revolutions in Russia, Persia, Turkey, China, the Balkan wars—there is the chain of world events of *our* period, of our "East." And only a blind man could fail to see in this chain of events the awakening of a *whole series* of bourgeois-democratic movements, aiming at the creation of national-independent and national-unified governments.[14]

By 1915, the role the Middle and Far Eastern peoples were to play in the over-all struggle with European capitalism had become clearer to Lenin. His platform advocated awakening the oppressed masses by the slogan of peace without annexations and with self-determination for all. This would force the issue on the great powers, and if they should refuse the demands,

we would systematically arouse to insurrection all the peoples now oppressed by the Great Russians, all the colonies and dependent countries in Asia (India, China, Persia, etc.). . . . There is no doubt that a victory of the proletariat in Russia would create unusually favorable conditions for the development of the revolution both in Asia and Europe.[15]

This program met violent opposition from fellow Marxists. Rosa Luxemburg denied Lenin's contention that a so-called national war could be supported by the proletariat, whose only interests were international in scope. Lenin met her challenge skillfully, exhorting Socialists to support wars of liberation where conditions permitted such support to be consistent with Socialist principles. He was careful to interject a warning that he could not provide a definite outline of these "conditions." However, his faith in Asia's future role in the anti-imperialist struggle was summarized more clearly in the following excerpt than at any other point:

National wars waged by colonial and semicolonial countries are not only possible but *inevitable* in the epoch of imperialism. The colonies and semicolonies (China, Turkey, Persia) have a population of nearly one billion, i.e., *more than half the population of the earth.* In these countries the movements for national liberation are either very strong already or are growing and maturing. Every war is a continuation of politics by other means. The national liberation policies of the colonies will *inevitably* be continued by national wars of the colonies *against* imperialism. Such wars *may* lead to an imperialist war between the present "Great" imperialist Powers or they may not; that depends on many circumstances . . . it would be ridiculous to guarantee that these circumstances will arise. . . .

National wars . . . are *progressive* and *revolutionary*, although, of course, what is needed for their success is either the combined efforts of an enormous number of the inhabitants of the oppressed countries (hundreds of millions in the examples we have taken of India and China), or a *particularly* favorable combination of circumstances in the international situation (for example, when the intervention of the imperialist Powers is paralyzed by exhaustion, by war, by their mutual antagonisms, etc.), or a *simultaneous* uprising of the proletariat of one of the Great Powers against the bourgeoisie (the latter case stands first in order from the standpoint of what is desirable and advantageous for the victory of the proletariat).[16]

Lenin had by now moved far from the ambivalent, if hostile, attitude of Marx toward self-determination. In raising nationalist aspirations to a new position of prominence in Bolshevik theory, Lenin demonstrated his skillful mixture of theoretical development and pragmatic politics. From the theoretical standpoint, national wars were "progressive" in areas "like China, Persia, Turkey and all colonies" where "bourgeois movements have either *hardly* begun or are far from having been completed." [17] National wars in these countries were "progressive" because "capitalism, awakening Asia, has aroused the nationalist movements there, the tendency of these movements is to create national governments in Asia, and the most favorable conditions for the development of capitalism are found in precisely such governments." [18] From the pragmatic approach, national wars were "progressive" because they would provide another avenue of attack against the capitalist center of Europe. This joining of the bourgeois revolutionary movements of Asia with the proletarian revolutionary movements of Europe marked Lenin's most radical departure from nineteenth-century Marxism and found its fullest exposition in his classic study, *Imperialism, the Highest Stage of Capitalism,* completed just before the Russian revolution. Without attempting to summarize the entire work, a few quotations will illustrate his thinking on the interrelation of Asian revolutions and European capitalism.

According to Lenin, the existence of surplus capital in highly industrialized countries necessitated the export of capital to backward areas in search of higher rates of profit. Cheap land, low wages, and abundant raw materials provided "super-profits" which had a twofold consequence. They increased the desire of the capitalists to exploit the backward peoples and they gave the capitalists funds with which to bribe the labor force of the more advanced industrial countries. This was Lenin's explanation for the lack of class solidarity and the willingness of European labor leaders to compromise their class interests for the sake of personal, group, or "national" interests. The race to secure concessions in backward areas had resulted in a complete division of the world among the capitalist powers by 1900. Imperialist tensions were inevitable as a result, as was the penetration of finance capital into "independent" countries. Thus Lenin classified backward countries into two groups, those traditionally defined as colonies, and the "semi-colonies" or nations whose independence was more or less fictitious. Persia, Turkey, and China fell into the latter category and were the scene of particularly intense rivalry and competition among the great powers. This struggle was motivated inexorably and solely by economic forces; of this he had no doubt, declaring: "The more developed capitalism, the more the need for raw materials is felt, the more bitter competition becomes, and the more feverishly the hunt for raw materials proceeds throughout the whole world, the more desperate becomes the struggle for the acquisition of colonies." [19]

Could the capitalist powers resolve their differences? Could a peaceful division of China into spheres of influence reconcile the struggle? Absolutely not, replied Lenin, "for there can be *no* other conceivable basis under capitalism for the division of spheres of influence, of interests, of colonies, etc., than a calculation of the *strength* of the participants in the division. . . . And the strength of these participants in the division does not change to an equal degree, for under capitalism the development of different undertakings, trusts, branches of industry, or countries cannot be *even*." [20]

It followed from this that conflict was inevitable in the Far East, and until his death almost eight years later, Lenin repeatedly predicted open warfare between Japan and America, arguing that "the partition of China is only beginning, and the struggle between Japan, U.S.A., etc., in connection therewith is continually gaining in intensity." [21] Thus the semicolonial countries were important not only as allies in the general struggle with world imperialism but as precipitating factors which would embroil the imperialist powers in conflicts among themselves, dividing the world imperialist "front."

There was no suggestion here or elsewhere that Lenin placed exclusive or even primary emphasis on the struggle in colonial and semicolonial countries. While the above excerpts have dealt solely with this problem, it must be remembered that Europe with its great industrial forces remained first on the agenda of Bolshevik strategy. Lenin called attention to the ferment in Asia, but he never gave it priority over European developments.

Lest it be thought that Lenin's advocacy of self-determination was bereft of all internationalist sentiments, attention should be given to his remarks of 1916, wherein he attempted to formulate the policy of advanced proletarian regimes to the emerging "nations" which were to arise throughout Asia. His remarks have double significance because they were addressed specifically to areas on the Russo-Chinese frontier which had long been a scene of Tsarist expansion. Lenin declared:

We Great Russian workers must demand that our government should get out of Mongolia, Turkestan, and Persia. . . . But does that mean that *we* proletarians *want* to be separated . . . from the Mongolian, or Turkestan, or Indian worker or peasant? Does it mean that *we* advise the masses of the toilers of the colonies to "separate" from the class-conscious European proletariat? Nothing of the kind. . . . We shall exert every effort to become friendly and to amalgamate with the Mongolians. . . . We shall strive to give the nations, which are more backward and more oppressed than we are, "unselfish cultural aid," to use the happy expression of the Polish Social-Democrats, i.e., we . . . shall help them on towards democracy and socialism.[22]

Lenin's words provide, in retrospect, an interesting anticipation of later Soviet policy in the pivotal area of Outer Mongolia.

The above selection of articles comprises almost the entire bulk of Lenin's pre-1917 references to China. He was first and foremost oriented toward Europe, despite his remark on one occasion: "Geographically, economically, and historically, Russia belongs not only to Europe, but also to Asia. . . . The Russian revolution [of 1905] gave rise to a movement throughout the whole of Asia." [23] Lenin's associates paid almost no attention to the Far East except for their consideration of Japan as an imperialist power. Only Zinoviev elaborated briefly on China's role in the anti-imperialist struggle, but his was merely an unhistorical, simplified analysis of the Taiping and Boxer uprisings.[24]

Reviewing the prerevolutionary theories of Lenin concerning Asia, one is struck by their fragmentary nature. He added surprisingly little to this collection after the revolution, and the Leninist cult has had to weave and reweave its meagre pattern of quotations in support of varying programs of action. A few basic points are clear, however. Lenin saw the possibility of revolutionary action against foreign capitalism in so-called semicolonial countries. He felt that only the bourgeoisie was capable of leading such action and that its success would turn primarily on arousing the millions of peasants to active participation. He had no illusions concerning the development of Marxism in the Far East. Blasting the "would-be socialist theories" of Sun Yat-sen, Lenin chided the Chinese leader for his "inimitable—one might say—virginal naiveté." [25] Despite the shortcomings in the backward countries, however, Lenin saw no alternative. Either the growing movements of bourgeois revolution in the semicolonial countries were to be supported by the world proletariat, or the entire anti-imperialist front might be seriously weakened. The

Second International had failed to carry its international sentiments beyond the rather limited confines of Europe. It had
ignored the contradictions in its position which attempted to
straddle the issue of colonial exploitation by European governments. Such was Lenin's indictment of his rivals in the world
Socialist movement. His new organization, the Third International, was not to repeat that serious mistake.

II

Revolution and Foreign Policy: 1917–1920

WITH the Bolshevik seizure of power on November 7, 1917, Lenin and his followers found themselves beset by a multitude of problems, precluding any theorizing on revolutions in Asia or policy in China. Not until the Second Congress of the Communist International in 1920 was Lenin to lead a heated public debate among fellow-revolutionaries, designed to thrash out an over-all policy on revolution in colonial and semicolonial countries. In the meantime, economic chaos, counterrevolution, and foreign intervention pressed the Bolsheviks from all sides. Hemmed into an area no larger than sixteenth-century Muscovy, the small, highly disciplined band of radicals extended its hold, first to European Russia and eventually into the Far Eastern stretches of the old Russian Empire. Almost from the start, two problems faced Lenin simultaneously: how to preserve the Socialist fatherland, and how to achieve the international revolution of the world proletariat. The two were necessarily interlinked and, at the start, not obviously contradictory. For the European revolution to succeed, its advance units in Petrograd and Moscow must survive the initial blows of counterrevolution and world imperialism. It was no time for abstract polemics. If the war with Germany could not be pursued, peace must be secured. If Germany's peace terms demanded a heavy price in terms of Russian territory, no matter. The all-important principle of Lenin's policy at this time remained to advance the world revolution; survival of Bolshevik power was deemed fundamental to that revolution.

Such, in brief, proved to be the rationale behind Lenin's acceptance of the Brest-Litovsk Treaty, concluded with Germany in March, 1918, after three months of intensive debate and soul-searching within the Bolshevik hierarchy. That expediency should dictate strategy in the fierce struggle for survival came as no surprise to hardened revolutionaries, accustomed to years of underground activity. However, that strategy should influence future theory was not foreseen at this time. Yet it was in this very period of civil war and foreign intervention that a crucial series of events transformed the Bolsheviks from revolutionists operating within Russia into Russian statesmen conducting world revolution. The shift in emphasis is of more than semantic significance. In it lies the clue to the conduct of Soviet foreign policy with respect not only to China but to the rest of the world. To be sure, so basic a transformation did not come at a single stroke, fixing an immutable course for all subsequent activities by the leaders of Soviet Russia. However, an examination of Soviet statements concerning China during the years 1917 to 1920 reveals a pattern which was to become increasingly applicable in other areas of Soviet foreign policy at a later date.

Appointment of Leon Trotsky as People's Commissar for Foreign Affairs and publication of the celebrated "Decree on Peace," November 8, 1917, launched the new regime in Petrograd into an avowedly revolutionary foreign policy. Far from considering themselves the heirs of Tsarist foreign policy, the Bolsheviks proclaimed a new doctrine, based on open diplomacy, nonannexation of territories, and the self-determination of peoples. As Trotsky himself remarked of his new position: "I will issue a few revolutionary proclamations to the peoples of the world and then shut up shop." [1] Two actions underscored Trotsky's disdainful attitude toward traditional diplomacy. On November 23, 1917, *Izvestiia* printed the first of a number of articles, disclosing the terms of the secret treaties concluded between Tsarist Russia and the Allies before and during World War I. On December 26, 1917, *Pravda* carried a governmental decree, signed by Lenin and Trotsky, allocating funds to "representatives abroad of the Commissariat for Foreign Affairs for the needs of the revolutionary movement." [2] Thus Lenin's twofold responsibility, to the Socialist fatherland and to the world revolution, were initially merged into a single agency with dual responsibility.

Russian readers received their first news of Chinese-Soviet relations on December 16, 1917, when *Izvestiia* told of difficulties on the Chinese Eastern Railway (CER) between local Chinese forces and the Harbin Soviet of Workers' and Soldiers' Deputies. [3] Denying "bourgeois press accounts" that Peking supported anti-Bolshevik activity, the account blamed the "Russian reactionary bourgeoisie in Harbin and the magnates of the CER." The 1,073 miles of track cutting across northern Manchuria linked Siberia with Vladivostok, principal Pacific port for Russia and vital terminus of the Trans-Siberian Railway. While construction and exploitation of this railroad was given originally to a Russo-Chinese Bank in 1896, [4] the line actually had become a vehicle for Tsarist economic penetration and colonization in North Manchuria. From the turn of the century, Russians had filled all strategic posts, including those of president and manager. The military, judicial, and municipal administration were Russian-controlled, carrying St. Petersburg's influence through Chinese territory in traditional imperialistic fashion.

Except for this isolated dispatch, little else was heard from Harbin where confusion reigned amidst clashes among Bolshevik, White Russian, and Chinese troops, aided and abetted by intervention from the foreign consular body. Local Bolsheviks had asserted responsibility for administration of the CER in November, attempting to replace General Horvath, former Tsarist official and appointee of the defunct Kerensky government. Although local Chinese and White Russian troops resisted the Bolsheviks successfully, sporadic outbreaks continued until finally the foreign consular officials in Harbin encouraged the dispatching of some 10,000 Chinese troops to the area.[5] Following conclusion of a four-point agreement between Horvath and the local Chinese Commander, Sze Shao-chang, Peking appointed Kuo Hsiang-hsi as president of the CER in January, 1918, formally asserting Chinese authority in place of the previous Russian control.[6] At the same time, Chinese customs offices opened in violation of the Russo-Chinese treaty of 1896.

Meanwhile, in Petrograd, initial contacts between the Narkomindel and the Chinese mission, headed by Minister Liu Tsin-chen, attempted to clarify relations between the two countries. In view of the disrupted communications between Peking and Petrograd, it is unlikely that Liu, appointed originally to the Tsarist government, maintained close contact at this time with the Waichiao Pu. This may explain his cautious but conciliatory statements of February, 1918. In a press statement, the Chinese mission declared that China was not "occupying" the CER zone but merely safeguarding "order and securing the safety of foreigners and Chinese." Such action was sanctioned not only by China's "sovereign right," since Harbin lay "in Chinese territory,"[7] but also by Article Five of the 1896 treaty. Placing all blame for disorders in Harbin on the *ancien régime*, the statement concluded: "The Chinese Republic, the sincere friend and close neighbor of Russia, wishes only to develop Russian democracy. . . . In fact, negotiations between the NKID [Narkomindel] and the Chinese Mission are taking place for the regulation of administration of the CER, and for the export of foodstuffs from Manchuria to Russia."

This additional item, the regulation of trade between Manchuria and Russia, raised an issue of extreme importance to those concerned with the future of the Russian Far East, for without supplies from Manchuria, much of the area would be sorely pressed for food. Despite an official declaration of the Chinese mission to the Narkomindel denying continuation of any embargo,[8] reports continued to fill the Russian press of a complete cessation of trade over the CER between Russia and Manchuria.[9] Deputy Commissar for Foreign Affairs Georgi Chicherin's request that the "striking contradictions" between Liu's assurances and Peking's actions[10] be immediately clarified reportedly brought a settlement "satisfactory for both parties." [11] However, it was clear that Peking was not master in its own house, and with conclusion of a military pact between Japan and China on March 25, 1918, joint Japanese-Chinese management of the CER placed Tokyo, with its avowed anti-Bolshevik policy, in the ascendancy.

With Peking apparently inclined toward a pro-Japanese orientation and Japanese troops already on former Russian soil as a result of Allied intervention in the Siberian civil war, further *pourparlers* in Petrograd held little promise for Sino-Soviet relations. Although Chicherin, now Commissar for Foreign Affairs, notified the Chinese mission in April that any negotiations between Peking and former Russian officials in China or Mongolia would be considered as interference in Russia's internal affairs, his remarks had no effect whatsoever and talks in Petrograd terminated.[12] Turning from private negotiations to public declarations, the Commissar for Foreign Affairs outlined the content of Soviet Russia's policy toward China in a speech before the Fifth Congress of Soviets, convened in July, 1918. In this, the first detailed report on Sino-Soviet relations since the November revolution, Chicherin advanced the following proposals:

We renounce the conquests of the Tsarist government in Manchuria and we restore the sovereign rights of China in this territory, in which lies the principal trade artery—the Chinese Eastern Railway . . . if part of the money invested in the construction of this railroad by the Russian people were repaid by China, China might buy it back without waiting for the term stipulated in the agreement violently imposed on her.

We recall from China all military consular guards. . . .

We agree to renounce all land-rights of our citizens in China, Mongolia, and Persia.

We are ready to renounce all indemnities. . . . We only desire that these millions of the people's money go toward the cultural development of the mass of the people and toward the matter of drawing together Eastern democracy with Russia.

. . . We are prepared, in event of the consequent agreement of China, to renounce those particular rights on part of the Chinese Eastern Railway, and to sell to Japan the southern branch of this railway.[13]

Here was a genuinely revolutionary program designed to kindle sympathy for Russia and to awaken the deep-burning resentment of the Chinese people against other imperialist powers who had been usurping China's sovereignty piecemeal for more than fifty years. Not only did it offer to cancel the Boxer Indemnity and to give up special privileges held by Russians in China, both points of dissatisfaction in China, but it stressed by repetition the problem of the Chinese Eastern Railway. Setting aside the provisions of the 1896 treaty which allowed China to receive the railroad free of charge in 1980 but prevented her from purchasing the line before 1940, Chicherin spoke only of partial compensation and implicitly renounced the extensive mining and lumber concessions developed along the right-of-way by Tsarist officials.[14]

To be sure, China had already moved to assert her claim in the CER six months previously. Chicherin's offer had little chance of acceptance, given the absence of diplomatic relations between the beleagured Soviet capital and all foreign countries. Were this the only statement made by Soviet spokesmen concerning the CER, it might be concluded that it was made in the desperation of the moment, but such was not the case. One year after Chicherin's speech before the Fifth Congress of Soviets, a prominent Far Eastern revolutionary, Vladimir Vilensky,[15] commented on China's bitter disappointment at the deference shown to Japan's claims at Versailles. Writing in *Izvestiia*, he outlined a tentative Soviet foreign policy toward China, including "transfer, by Russia, of the Chinese Eastern Railway." [16] He added that this could be made "with a light heart" in order to acquire a badly needed alliance with China.

The most dramatic presentation of Soviet proposals to China

concerning the Chinese Eastern Railway was the famous Karakhan Manifesto of July 25, 1919, issued by the Council of People's
Commissars (Sovnarkom). In a blanket address "to the Chinese
nation and the Governments of Southern and Northern China," [17]
this Sovnarkom document repeated the declarations of principle
made by Chicherin in mid-1918. Spelling out in detail Chicherin's
program, it declared: "The Soviet Government returns to the Chinese people without any kind of compensation the Chinese Eastern Railway, and all mining, gold, and forestry concessions which
were seized from them by the government of Tsars, that of Kerensky, and the outlaws Horvat, Semenov, Kolchak, the Russian generals, merchants, and capitalists."

This single sentence was unambiguous in its proposal to give
up the strategic CER and all the concessions therewith. It epitomized the "new revolutionary" Soviet policy toward China. Yet
for the following five years, this sentence was the focal point of
bitter controversy in Sino-Soviet negotiations. Its significance and
consequences merit close study at this point, in terms of its implications for Soviet foreign policy.

Curiously enough, no reference was made to the Karakhan
Manifesto in any Soviet newspaper until one month after it was
issued. Generally, official documents were published immediately
in these years, but the manifesto was held back and then released
in *Izvestiia* and *Pravda without* the above-quoted sentence.[18] In
March, 1920, Peking received a copy of the manifesto, translated
into French and forwarded by wire from Irkutsk. This relayed
version created a veritable sensation in China by its inclusion of
the explicit offer to give up the CER without compensation.[19] It
is important to note that the wire from Irkutsk was identical in
every respect with the version of the manifesto printed in a Soviet
pamphlet by Vladimir Vilensky, Sovnarkom expert on the Far
East. The Irkutsk version differed from that published in *Izvestiia*
of August 26, 1919, only by inclusion of the sentence on the CER
and a phrase referring to revolutionary self-determination.[20]

Shortly after receiving the Irkutsk wire, Peking reported a Bolshevik repudiation of the March, 1920, text and warned the provincial governors to handle the manifesto cautiously. "According to a telegram from Li Chia-ao, High Chinese Commissioner in Siberia, it has been learned by inquiry with the representatives of the Soviet Government that they had not issued such a note." [21] No Soviet source has referred to this alleged Bolshevik repudiation, and the official caveat received little circulation in China. In short, the Peking statement is difficult to validate, and as far as public opinion in China was concerned, it did nothing to offset the open jubilation over the unexpected generosity of Russia. [22]

Without anticipating the story of Sino-Soviet negotiations over the Chinese Eastern Railway, mention should be made here of the repeated insistence by such Bolshevik leaders as Leo Karakhan and Adolf Joffe that no such offer concerning the CER had *ever* been included in the 1919 manifesto. [23] The mystery was heightened in 1924 when an *Izvestiia* commentary on the Sino-Soviet treaty of that year made the first reference in the Russian press to the disputed passage. In an unusual footnote, Antonov-Ovseenko, celebrated leader of the November, 1917, assault on the Winter Palace and recently appointed to the Narkomindel, explained that the original Sovnarkom decree had been drawn up at a meeting of Chinese workers in Moscow and then had been arbitrarily re-edited there. [24] It is quite improbable that so important an official document should have been composed in such an impromptu manner. Even if the story were plausible, its veracity is doubtful because no meeting of Chinese workers was reported in the middle of 1919 except that at which the manifesto had been read, one month *after* it had been drafted. Moreover, it was an official Narkomindel representative, Voznesenskii, who read it at that time.

An entirely different explanation of the erroneous inclusion of the CER passage was offered six years later by a well-known Bolshevik commentator. V. P. Savvin charged that the Peking government had followed a text which had been "entirely distorted" by White Guardist and imperialist agents. [25] He conveniently overlooked the fact that only one sentence had been in dispute and ignored the account which had been given previously by Antonov-Ovseenko in *Izvestiia*.

It is now possible to reconstruct the events surrounding the mysterious manifesto and to pinpoint the shift in Soviet policy from a new, revolutionary diplomacy of self-denial to a traditional, nationalistic diplomacy of self-interest. Vilensky's pamphlet, with the text of the manifesto appended, including the offer to return the Chinese Eastern Railway without compensation, contains reliable internal evidence dating its time of composition. Reference is made by him to an American radio broadcast of July 21, 1919. The final section of the pamphlet, which preceded the text of the manifesto, has the closing words of his article, previously quoted, concerning a "possible program" for Soviet Russia in China. This article appeared in *Izvestiia* on July 26, 1919, the day after the manifesto was allegedly issued by the Sovnarkom. Vilensky is known to have left Moscow in late August to help in the counterattack against Kolchak, and since there is no reference in the body of the pamphlet to the important manifesto, it appears that the text was hastily appended to a previously planned work. It is not improbable that Vilensky himself took part in the manifesto's composition.

What explains the one-month delay in the *Izvestiia* release and the omission of the vital sentence? A glance at the course of events in Siberia is suggestive. Admiral Kolchak received qualified *de facto* recognition from the Allies as leader of the anti-Bolshevik forces in June, 1919. Japanese intervention in the Far Eastern provinces had exceeded all expectation. There seemed little hope of breaking the circle of foreign intervention, but actually the high tide of counterrevolution had been reached. On August 16, 1917, an appeal signed by Lenin and Kalinin called upon the Siberian population to assist in the final attack on Kolchak and declared null and void all decrees passed by the Kolchak regime.[26] By this time, Kolchak's retreat had carried him beyond Ekaterinburg into the Siberian stretches pregnant with peasant discontent from the oppressive counterrevolutionary measures. Another Red counterattack in October sent him reeling farther back, beyond Omsk. Thus the turn in battle coincided with the change in the Karakhan Manifesto. Between its initial drafting in July and its publication in late August, responsible officials realized that regaining a foothold in the Far East was now an actual possibility, to be treated more cautiously than in so sweeping a renunciation of the highly strategic railroad.

The Vilensky pamphlet remains as irrefutable evidence that one version of the Karakhan declaration to the Chinese people *did* completely renounce the privileges accorded Russia by the treaties of 1896, 1898, and 1901. It did agree to return the entire Chinese Eastern Railway without compensation. Why Yanson did not receive a "corrected" version in Irkutsk by March, 1920, remains a mystery. The disrupted state of communications fails to account completely for this part of the puzzle. Furthermore, it is not known who was responsible for the decision to withdraw the offer and subsequently to deny that it had ever been made. One thing is clear, however. By mid-1919, traditional Russian goals had reasserted themselves in curious juxtaposition with avowed revolutionary principles. The timing indicates that it was not the impact of revolutionary setbacks in Germany and Hungary which brought a new emphasis into Soviet foreign policy, but rather the impact of victories in the Russian civil war which worked a slow but perceptible transformation on Soviet pledges and practice. Defense of this Socialist fatherland appeared to take precedence over advancement of world revolution when the decision to renounce forever all "imperialistic" rights on the Chinese Eastern Railway was abandoned in favor of asserting Soviet Russia's legal heritage of this Tsarist concession in China's territory.

While China's civil strife had yet to erupt into the widespread warfare and terror that ripped Russia at this time, conditions were not propitious for careful consideration of Chicherin's magnanimous proposals. The collapse of the Manchu dynasty in 1911 has no parallel in modern history for the protracted chaos and confusion which followed. Whereas the French and Russian revolutions passed through brief periods of crisis and interregnum, China witnessed almost fifteen years of strife and dissension. The establishment of a central government under Chiang Kai-shek during the 1930's was the first systematic attempt to found a republican government in China. After the abortive effort of Yuan Shih-kai to restore the monarchy in 1915, Peking became the scene of a complex struggle for power, not between political parties, but between vested-interest groups of militarists, bureaucrats, and foreign agents. In mid-1917, the question of China's entry into World War I brought the crisis to a head. A clique of military leaders known as the Anfu group won control of Peking while Sun Yat-sen, together with ex-members of Parliament, set up a military government in Canton. The ex-parliamentarians claimed that their election under the 1912 constitution left them the sole legitimate government in China, but they actually had only nominal control over provinces in South China. Peking continued to enjoy formal recognition by the major powers of the world. Open hostilities between North and South drove Sun from Canton in May, 1918, when militarists gained control of the southern government and effected a peace with the northern group.

As a Chinese analyst of the Kuomintang has remarked, Sun's party "had practically ceased to exist after 1916," [27] and what little cohesiveness remained was built on personal loyalty to Sun. The handful of intellectuals around the venerable leader lacked military strength and had little ability to arouse the masses of peasants and soldiers. When the party was officially reconstituted in 1920, it remained a loosely organized secret society.

Had Soviet planners been only revolutionists, they would have bolstered the southern government at Canton and attacked the counterrevolutionary regime in Peking. Had they been only Russians, they would have sought to strengthen their position in North China and ignored the feeble efforts of Sun Yat-sen. However, they were both revolutionists and Russians. Soviet foreign policy freely mixed inflammatory propaganda with traditional diplomacy. In August, 1918, Commissar of Foreign Affairs Chicherin wrote a fervent letter to Sun, stressing the common aims of Russia and China.[28] Although the initiative in this correspondence apparently had come from Sun, who had written eariler hailing the Russian revolution, Chicherin went beyond a formal acknowledgment. He warned Sun that common enemies were trying to wreck the traditional friendship of the two countries and expressed confidence that the Russian and Chinese revolutions would follow the same path, hand in hand. "Our success is your success. Our ruin is your ruin."

Here is the first example of the familiar Leninist tactic of dual struggle applied to China: conduct legal and illegal activity simultaneously; work openly and underground. Chicherin's speech of July, 1918, proclaimed Russia's willingness to negotiate with the officially recognized government in Peking. In the same speech he expressed guarded hope that the rival government of South China would prove sympathetic to the Soviet viewpoint. In August he sent a personal message of encouragement to Sun Yat-sen, head of this regime in Canton. When writing to "honored teacher" Sun, Chicherin castigated the Peking government as a "creature of foreign bankers," yet it was Peking with whom he directed negotiations over four arduous years in order to conclude the Sino-Soviet treaty of 1924. The Bolshevik leaders were realistic. Sun was of little use to them while he remained merely a titular spokesman for intellectual cliques. However, the contact might prove useful one day, and a correspondence between Chicherin and Sun continued sporadically over the years.

The dual policy was implicit in the Karakhan Manifesto of 1919, addressed not only to the recognized government of the North but also to the rump parliament in the South. As will be seen, Soviet officials later recognized the risks of using identical channels for diplomatic and revolutionary activity, and efforts were made to separate the Comintern from the Narkomindel. In practice, the lines occasionally crossed, with embarrassing and sometimes disastrous results.

Chicherin's letter may have exaggerated the interdependence of the Chinese and the Russian revolutions because of respectful politeness to Sun, or from impulsive enthusiasm. Nevertheless, at least some support to this idea was given by those who endeavored to make Communists of Chinese workers who were in Russia when the civil war broke out there. As early as November, 1918, a Union for Liberation of the East offered courses in Moscow which featured Voznesenskii, among others, lecturing on "Contemporary China and Japan."[29] In January, 1919, a "Chinese Working Men's Association" in Moscow discussed sending propagandists to China with the help of Soviet authorities.[30] These groups were destined to play a negligible role compared with that of the new world revolutionary organization, the Third or Communist International. At its First Congress, held in March of that year, the Communist International welcomed two Chinese delegates "with consultative votes" representing a so-called Chinese Socialist Workers' Party.[31] In view of the civil war in the Russian Far East, it is probable that these "delegates" had not come from China, but, like many at the Congress, were handpicked from groups within Russia.

The Communist International was organized by Lenin and his followers as a counterweight to the Second International and what they saw as the dead hand of European Social Democracy. It was hardly a representative gathering, with many of the elected or designated delegates denied passports by their home governments and others merely appointed by Lenin and Zinoviev from radicals present in Russia at the time. While it was primarily concerned with Europe, the Comintern on one occasion gave the platform to Chinese spokesmen, showing some awareness of the necessity for building a genuinely world-wide organization. Warm sympathies for its aims were expressed by Lao Hsiu-chao, who claimed to speak on behalf of his millions of fellow countrymen struggling for freedom from the imperialist yoke. He praised Sun Yat-sen's leadership and contrasted the silent treatment which Kerensky had accorded Sun's congratulatory message to revolutionary Russia with Lenin's manifesto to the peoples of the East and Chicherin's friendly letter.[32]

Aside from Lao's brief appearance, few words were wasted on China. The Congress had little time and many resolutions to work out which were to raise the banner of revolution throughout Europe. The "Manifesto to the World Proletariat" showed the relative unimportance given Asia by lumping together the anti-British struggles in Ireland, Egypt, and India and the anti-Japanese fight in China. The manifesto claimed these battles were being waged "not only under the banner of national liberation, but have a more or less clearly expressed socialist character." [33] A Socialist Europe must assist the colonies with industrial techniques and political organization. The manifesto closed with typical Bolshevik fervor: "Colonial peoples of Africa and Asia! The hour of proletarian dictatorship in Europe signifies for you the hour of your liberation!"

While Communist leaders in Petrograd were taking the first limited steps toward an eventual merging of two revolutionary forces—China and Russia—Allied representatives at Versailles were honoring Japan's claims to German rights and concessions in China, as agreed to in secret treaties concluded during the war. Taken by themselves, the Comintern resolutions pertaining to Asia would have seemed utopian to many observers. Coupled with the dramatic impact in China of the Versailles decisions, these words took on added meaning for Bolshevik leaders. Divided China's common desire for removal of foreign privileges, particularly those of Japan, had manifested itself in a combined delegation to Versailles from Peking and Canton. President Woodrow Wilson alone fought vigorously but vainly for China's demand that spheres of influence be removed by common agreement. Resentment over the Versailles discussions exploded in the celebrated movement of May 4, 1919. Angry students in Peking,

through mass demonstrations, ignited the spark that set off a series of popular chain explosions. Speeches, strikes, and boycotts
ultimately forced the Peking cabinet to oust three allegedly pro-
Japanese members, while the Chinese delegation at Versailles refused to sign the treaty in response to the wave of indignation at
home. The fervor of the Comintern's manifesto did not seem entirely misplaced under such circumstances. Chinese nationalist
circles gained new hope as the potential strength of mass agitation was fully realized. The Comintern had fertile ground for
sowing its seeds of protest against the West.

Izvestiia's reaction to the May 4 demonstration was one of un-
bridled optimism, seeing it as a vehicle carrying Bolshevism to
new heights in Asia.[34] The writer, Voznesenskii, showed little understanding of Chinese society in his portrayal of alleged class
divisions to be exploited by Chinese workers returning from participation in the Russian revolution.[35] Ignoring the total absence
of mass peasant uprisings and the nascent stage of trade unions,
Voznesenskii claimed that the peasants were ripe for agitation by
the proletariat. China had already completed its "1905," its bourgeois revolution; it remained for the Chinese proletariat to seize
control. Now that Russia had set the example for Asia, the writer
held that imperialism was completely helpless.

Such misinformed utopianism found no support from Lenin,
however. Speaking before a November, 1919, gathering of Asian
Communists resident in Russia, the astute leader warned that exceedingly difficult problems lay in the path of Asian revolutionists.[36] They had no factory-trained proletariat as in European
Russia to bolster the forces of revolution. Instead, they faced
vast amorphous masses struggling to overthrow the remnants of
feudalism. Laying aside the traditional texts of Marxism, Lenin
admitted that "no single book" had the answers for Communists
in backward Asia; theory must be adapted to the individual problems of each country. He reiterated in specific manner his pre-
1917 theme, advising his listeners to base their action on "bourgeois nationalism, which is awakening these peoples and cannot

help awakening them, and which has historical justification." Of particular importance was the alliance of the world proletariat through the Communist International:

We see that they [the British, French, German proletariat] cannot win without the help of the working mass of the oppressed colonial peoples, especially the people of the East. We must report that a single vanguard cannot realize the transition to communism. *The task lies in awakening revolutionary activity, independence, and an organized mass of workers, regardless of what stage they are in, in translating original Communist studies, intended for Communists of more advanced countries, into the language of each people, and in accomplishing the practical problems which must be solved immediately* and joining in the general struggle with the proletariat of other countries.[37]

It would be dangerous to misunderstand Lenin's words, particularly those in the first half of this excerpt. Out of context they suggest a major shift in his thinking, which had always held Europe in general, and Germany in particular, as the crucial battleground of the world revolution. His next words, "the transition to communism," were crucial, however. They referred to a stage of development *after* the overthrow of European capitalism. The immediate goal was the overthrow of the existing order; the transition to communism was a later step. That Lenin was searching for a frame of reference other than orthodox Marxism is shown by the italicized portion above. Marx spoke of revolution in a highly industrialized society. Lenin advocated forming the revolutionary nucleus "regardless of what stage" the society might be experiencing. If theory demanded an industrial economy with an organized proletariat, so much the worse for theory. Here, represented by the Korean, Mongolian, and Central Asian faces before Lenin, was "the vast majority of the world's population"—a phrase used repeatedly by him—ready to assist in the overthrow of world imperialism. The problems lay in "translating" Western theory into Eastern practice.

Lenin was often forced to feel his way through the political problems raised by the March and November revolutions in Russia. He was willing to change overnight from support of the Provisional Government to opposition to it. For months he could call for a constituent assembly and then, when it was convened, turn it out if it no longer served his purposes. He has been accused of compromising and contradicting his many statements on theory and strategy, as well as of revising the concepts of Marx and Engels. That these accusations are valid is illustrated in the speech considered above. Yet herein lay one of the great strengths of Lenin. He was able to meet the exigencies of the moment with a formula based on his "scientific analysis" of the historical forces, while preserving power in the name of Bolshevism. His intuitive grasp of the necessary tactic to win against overwhelming odds was seldom wrong. When it was, as in the disastrous Red Army advance against Warsaw in the Russo-Polish war of 1920, he recognized his error and attempted to avoid repetition of it. While this flexibility of action was an asset for Lenin, it prevents discussing post-Leninist Soviet policy in terms of "what Lenin would have done." His speech to the Asian Communists illustrates the wide latitude he left for interpretation and implementation of his basic views.

In terms of revolutionary theory, then, Lenin was prepared to temper the orthodox, if enthusiastic, tendencies of his colleagues with respect to Asia. While stressing the need for developing revolutionary cadres in the Far East, he was loath to identify Asian tactics with those designed for Europe. Action in Asia was to be determined not only by the internal social and economic conditions but also by the international struggle in the Pacific. Seen from this perspective, Lenin's stress upon China becomes clearer. The certainty of imperialist conflict sometimes carried him into wishful thinking, as revealed in his firm belief in early 1920 that war was imminent between Japan and the United States. At this time he declared that the two powers were "on the verge of war," [38] that "there is no possibility of restraining this war." [39] To be sure, America's dissastisfaction over Japanese interpretation of the 1917 Lansing-Ishii Agreement as sanctioning extension of Japanese influence in Asia, the latent American-Japanese conflict at Versailles, and the open clash of interests during the Siberian intervention of 1918–20 all supported Lenin's views expressed earlier in *Imperialism, the Highest Stage of Capitalism* concerning the immediacy of war in the Pacific. In such a conflict, Lenin argued, Russia was a necessary ally for China since the Middle Kingdom could expect little disinterested help from Japan or America, regardless of which power won. Conversely, in the future, China would be a necessary ally for Russia since neither Japan nor America was as dependable or as dependent a partner. Within two years of Lenin's words, the Washington Conference was to bring Japan and America to a peaceful, if temporary, reconciliation of their conflicting interests in the Pacific. All powers remained free to maneuver diplomatically in China, and it was not until 1937 that both Russia and China were to find themselves dependent upon mutual help to slow the march of Japanese imperialism.

On the eve of the Second Comintern Congress, the first genuinely representative gathering of world Communism, Lenin held an interview with the Japanese journalist Fuse concerning the prospects for Communism in the East and West. Although this interview was not published in the Soviet Union until 1925, it merits attention as an indication of Lenin's thoughts in 1920. To the question, "Which has the greater possibility for Communism being carried into effect, the East or the West?" Lenin replied: "At the moment, real Communism can have success only in the West. However, the West lives at the expense of the East. European imperialist powers are enriched, mainly, on the Eastern colonies. But at the same time they arm and train their colonies as fighters. And thus the West is digging itself a grave in the East." [40]

III

The Second Comintern Congress

BY the summer of 1920, domestic and foreign events had taken a most encouraging turn for the Russian revolution. Three years of civil war and foreign intervention had ended successfully for the Bolsheviks. The Allied economic blockade had finally been lifted, and only in the Far East was Russian soil still occupied by hostile troops. Japan, taking advantage of American withdrawal from the Siberian intervention in April, 1920, extended its hold on Vladivostok, the Maritime Province, and Sakhalin Island. Washington's prompt and negative reaction augured well for Russian interests, however, regardless of the absence of relations between Soviet Russia and the United States. At the very least, it provided a counterweight to Japanese penetration in an area remote from Bolshevik control. At the very most, it could result in war between Japan and America which might weaken both to the advantage of Russia. Europe offered promise too, despite the violent smashing of Bela Kun's Red regime in Hungary and the shooting of the two outstanding German radicals, Rosa Luxemburg and Karl Liebknecht. These disappointments which had followed hard on the heels of the First Congress of the Communist International were offset by the sudden reversal in the Russo-Polish war, begun by the Poles in 1919, which now saw Polish forces reeling back before Warsaw under relentless attack by Red cavalrymen. If

Poland should become Communist, the German workers could join hands with their proletarian brethren to the east; the center of European capitalism would become the stronghold of world revolution. Within Russia, so-called War Communism with its worker-run factories and radical social measures was still a heady brew whose ill effects had yet to be fully felt.

In this charged atmosphere, radicals from the world over converged on the Uritsky Palace in Petrograd for the Second Congress of the Third International. No gigantic portraits of Lenin towered over the delegates. Bolshevik Russia's prestige was established in deeds, not in decorations. However, where prestige was insufficient to assure the hegemony of the Russian Communist Party in Comintern decisions, political maneuvers eliminated oppositional leaders from other European Communist parties. In the crowded hall, with clusters of Asian, African, and European delegates packed around a simple, unadorned platform, the patterns were hammered out that were to shape the future of the Communist International and of left-wing movements everywhere.

By any standard, the 1920 Congress is significant for understanding international Communism. Because of its heated debates and lengthy resolutions on revolution in Asia, it is doubly vital for this study. However, a word of caution is necessary. As with all political organizations, the word is less important than the deed. It is not the public pronunciamento that the historian scans as much as it is the inner-council meetings, the orders sent to subordinate groups, the constant interplay of personalities and politics. This vital material is denied the contemporary critic when he approaches the world Communist movement. He must rely upon printed records, subject to editing and re-editing. All is not mere speculation, however. The value of a "stenographic report" for a Comintern Congress lies in its points of emphasis, its omissions and revisions where they can be discovered. A subsequent examination of Soviet writings on China will show where the resolutions were mere window-dressing, where they were practical guides to action. In this light, the Second Comintern Congress may be examined for its contributions to the formulation of Communist strategy in Asia.

Lenin came to the Congress armed with a preliminary draft of resolutions on the national and colonial questions.[1] The events since 1917 had revealed the inadequacy of earlier theory concerning the revolutionary process in backward countries. The traditional distrust of the peasant in Marxist writings clashed with Bolshevik reliance upon a soldier-worker-peasant coalition against counter-revolution. The aspirations of the Ukrainians, the Transcaucasians, and other minority peoples to put into practice Lenin's slogan of self-determination clashed with Bolshevik strategy of reinforcing the periphery by control from the center. Lenin's own criticism of Sun Yat-sen for seeking to "forestall capitalism" clashed with the radical experiment of War Communism in Russia, that strange period lasting from 1918 to 1921, which introduced a state-organized barter system and semi-military factory legislation.

Starting with the March revolution, Bolsheviks in Russia had skipped nimbly, endeavoring to keep up with Lenin's rapid shifts in position. Confusion was constant as prerevolutionary theories were scrapped for revolutionary practices. With the enunciation of his "April Theses" in 1917, Lenin chose a new tactic in regard to the Kerensky regime.[2] Support for the Provisional Government rapidly changed to competition for power and finally culminated in open opposition. This left unsettled the entire problem of gauging the stages of revolution in terms of bourgeois and proletarian power. While in Europe the problem was not important since bourgeois governments had long since come to power, in Asia the tactical question of timing Communist support of the bourgeoisie was vital. The impact of the dramatic events of 1917 shaped much of Lenin's preliminary theses and influenced subsequent debates in the Comintern meetings.

For Marx, there had been no possibility of by-passing necessary stages of historical development. Marxism as a science claimed to uncover the laws of economic determinism. Thus the transi-

tions from feudalism to capitalism and from capitalism so socialism were inevitable. Their precise manner of development would
vary only according to the particular contradictions within each
society, the development of the production relationships, and the
ability of the ruling class to delay its inevitable overthrow by the
oppressed class. Lenin had been on firm Marxist ground in scoffing
at Sun's "naive" hope of "by-passing" capitalism. However, his
political revision of 1917 which declared the bourgeois revolution
completed in a matter of weeks was paralleled by the economic
revisions which introduced War Communism. The two steps were
inseparable, since, according to Marxist theory, the political superstructure reflected the economic foundations of the society.
With the completion of the bourgeois-capitalist stage, Russia began the proletarian-socialist stage. Of course, it was not to be so
simple, but by 1920, War Communism's radical measures had not
yet proved to be disastrous. The novelty of the innovations made
by workers in industrial discipline and factory management
gripped many Bolsheviks with a fanatical fervor for the "new
society."

It is not surprising that under these cumulative pressures Lenin's
preliminary theses on revolutions in colonial and semicolonial
countries showed some major revisions from his pre-1917 ideas,
although most of his points concerning relations with the bourgeoisie and the peasantry followed concepts suggested in his 1912
critique of Sun Yat-sen. It was in his search for new answers to
the old problems in backward areas without capital accumulation
and lacking an organized proletariat that Lenin elaborated the
concept of "leaping over" the capitalist stage of development. As
he explained to the Congress:

Can we recognize as correct the assertion that the capitalist stage
of development in a national economy is inevitable for those backward nations which are now liberating themselves and among which
a movement along the road of progress is now, after the war, observed?
We reply to this question in the negative. If the revolutionary victorious proletariat carries on a systematic propaganda among them, and

if the Soviet governments render them all the assistance they possibly can, it will be wrong to assume that the capitalist stage of development is inevitable for the backward nations.

We must not only form independent cadres of fighters, of Party organizations in all colonies and backward countries, we must not only carry on propaganda in favor of organizing peasant soviets and strive to adapt them to pre-capitalist conditions; the Communist International must lay down, and give the theoretical grounds for the proposition that, *with the aid of the proletariat of the most advanced countries*, the backward countries may pass to the Soviet system and, after passing through a definite stage of development, to Communism, without passing through the capitalist stage of development.[3]

Lenin's reference to "Soviet governments" and "the most advanced countries" in the plural was not accidental. The German revolution still held promise; the advancement of backward areas remained dependent upon the proletariat achieving power in Europe. This was the all-important proviso which kept Lenin's revision of previous statements from being a complete denial of everything he had said before.

Karl Radek supported Lenin's theses wholeheartedly on the floor of the Congress in the subsequent debates, but his speech made clearer the points of emphasis italicized above. Radek appreciated Lenin's concern over the revolutions in Asia and called the attention of the Congress to the "toiling masses of the East." He claimed that capitalism looked on the colonies not only as a source of economic succor but also as a reservoir of military strength. Thus, he warned, should the European proletariat ignore colonial revolutions, it might one day find itself faced with fighting colonial troops under the direction of their metropolitan capitalist leaders. At no point did Radek discuss the struggle for independence as an end in itself but continually referred to its significance for the European revolution. Moreover, while Radek advocated the use of propaganda and agitation among the Asian peoples in order to "spare them the suffering of capitalism," he made it clear that "the capitalist stage is not inevitable for every country" *if* Socialism triumphed in Great Britain, France, and

Germany.[4] What if the revolution were not successful in these countries? The record does not show that the question was raised. "Leaping over" the capitalist stage of development in backward countries was not discussed except in connection with aid from victorious Socialist countries of Europe. If this qualification kept Comintern analysis in some sort of Marxist lineage, it at the same time held out hope to the anticapitalist radicals of Asia that a short cut to Socialism was possible.[5]

Lenin's preliminary theses contained another twist of tactics, of more immediate importance for revolutionary tactics than the remoter question of economic theory. His reference to "organizing peasant soviets" stemmed directly from Russian experience wherein Bolshevik-peasant relations were of critical importance. Appalling starvation followed the collapse of marketing facilities and the transportation network, but discontent was increased immeasurably by open hostility and mutual suspicion between the peasants and their new proletariat rulers. After the happy period of land seizures was past, Soviet strategists were unable to convince the independent peasants that their welfare was intimately connected with raising and selling larger amounts of produce to the city, when virtually no goods could be purchased from the city with the inflated currency accumulated by the peasants.

Lenin sought to apply the lessons learned at considerable cost in the Russian revolution. Consequently he placed heavy emphasis on bringing the peasantry actively into the revolutions in Asia where "pre-capitalist relations still predominate, and therefore a purely proletarian movement is out of the question . . . there is almost no industrial proletariat."[6] While not omitting the proletariat from the struggle, Lenin gave high priority to peasant activity. His words succinctly and frankly phrased the dilemma of being Marxist and at the same time desirous of leading revolution in Asia. Without disavowing Marx's vehemently antipeasant prejudice, Lenin attempted to turn the eyes of the Comintern from the handful of workers in Asia to the millions of peasants living in poverty and oppression.[7] His words paralleled those of another

leading Bolshevik theoretician, Nicolai Bukharin, in a speech
made one month before the Second Congress. Speaking to a group
of Chinese workers living in Russia, Bukharin proposed two slogans on behalf of the Comintern which were to rally the masses
of Asia to the Red banner: "First, 'the fight against European
capitalism' which is clear to everyone. . . . Second, 'throw out
the estate owners.' *The aim, consequently, is an agrarian revolution.* You will be able to accomplish the rising of the masses
through this war cry, as the slogan 'seize the land from the estate
owners' is clear to everyone." [8]

Lenin incorporated the peasant problem into his preliminary
theses at another point, demanding "special assistance to the
peasant movement . . . to establish the closest possible alliance
between the Western European Communist proletariat, and the
revolutionary peasant movement in the East." [9] After discussion
in the commission which considered these proposals, the slightly
revised theses adopted by the Comintern Congress recommended
the formation of peasant soviets, "where possible." [10]

It is evident from Lenin's discussion of "leaping over" capitalism and his suggestions on forming peasant soviets that the Russian revolution was to be the guiding example for revolutions elsewhere. He noted this specifically in May, 1920: "At the present
moment of history the situation is precisely such that the Russian
model reveals to *all* countries something . . . of their near and
inevitable future." [11] Solutions successfully applied in Russia were
to be attempted elsewhere, even though the problems were quite
different in many cases.

Lenin's idea of incorporating the peasantry into the revolution
to so great a degree received mixed reaction from the delegates.
Some of his Russian colleagues remained sceptical of arousing the
peasants of Asia, but most were willing to agree that such a program was necessary. Considerable support for Lenin's proposal
came from the Asian delegates to the Congress. M. N. Roy, of
India, was chiefly concerned with the proletariat, but conceded
that in the agrarian program there could be no "purely Commu-

nist principles." [12] He advocated first advancing such "petit-bourgeois reformist points" as division of land. In connection with the formation of soviets "at the first opportunity" he referred to the aid of "Soviet republics in advanced countries." Roy was here echoing the thesis already put forth by Lenin and Radek that the Socialist revolution would take place in several European countries before Communist principles would be applied in backward areas.

Another Asian, Pak Dinshun, from Korea, seconded Lenin's emphasis on the peasantry. "The industrial proletariat . . . is too weak in Asia for us to cherish serious hopes of an early Communist revolution, but there is no doubt of the success of an agrarian revolution if we are able to grasp the immediate problem of the great bloody struggle." [13]

Acceptance by the Asian delegates of the agrarian theses contrasted with their hostility to Lenin's proposal for support of the native bourgeoisie in semicolonial countries. Developing a detailed order of battle in his preliminary theses, Lenin argued the steps to be taken wherever feudal or patriarchal economic conditions prevailed: "First, all the Communist Parties must assist the bourgeois-democratic liberation movement in these countries, and the primary duty of rendering the most active assistance rests upon the workers in those countries upon which the backward nation is dependent as a colony or financially." [14] This was in keeping with Lenin's views examined earlier as contained in his pre-1917 writings. His qualifications of such support were spelled out in greater detail in his theses of 1920 than previously. He was not offering a blank check, to be filled out according to the whim of bourgeois leaders. Lenin's theses warned:

The Communist International must support the bourgeois-democratic national movement in colonial and backward countries only on the condition that the elements of future proletarian parties existing in all backward countries, which are not merely Communist in name, shall be grouped together and trained to appreciate their special tasks, *viz.*, the tasks of fighting the bourgeois-democratic movement within their own nations; *the Communist International must enter into a temporary alliance with bourgeois democracy in colonial and backward countries, but must not merge with it,* and must unconditionally preserve the independence of the proletarian movement even in its most rudimentary form.[15]

In these two quotations lies the united front tactic, the most difficult problem to plague Marxists since the doctrine of "permanent revolution" was first enunciated in 1850 as a formal slogan.[16] The question posed by the united front is not: "Will the bourgeoisie work in the interest of the proletariat?" but rather: "When do the interests of the bourgeoisie and the proletariat conflict?" Under the principle of class warfare, the bourgeoisie can never be a permanent ally of the proletariat; its basic aim is to preserve and increase its own power, first at the expense of the feudal class, later at the expense of the proletarian class. However, before the semicolonial or colonial area can achieve independence and thereby gain the freedom to develop economically, it must oust the imperialist powers and smash its own ruling class which compromises with those powers. In this struggle the bourgeoisie and the proletarian-peasant classes can act together. Then the critical point arrives when the proletarian-peasant group must turn on its "allies" to advance its own interest at the expense of the bourgeoisie. The turbulent months of 1917 had seen Lenin shift ground rapidly from support of the Provisional Government, as implied in his pre-March writings, to open opposition to the bourgeois institutions of Kerensky. Events moved too swiftly for theory. The command, "Ally but do not merge; support but prepare to fight," justified any zigzag in policy but hardly served as a precise blueprint for action.

The debates of the Comintern failed to solve the problem, for a priori it is incapable of solution. If the united front is admittedly temporary in nature, then its duration is limited by the power relationships between the bourgeois and Communist leaders. No resolution can appoint the time and the place when shifts in power permit the overthrow of the bourgeois allies. The crucial question of timing the break became distorted later by the terms "left deviation" and "right opportunism." Any popular front movement was an uneasy relationship at best, a treacherous and temporary truce at worst.

In 1920, the united front appeared unpalatable to orthodox radicals. Lenin's theses came in for considerable debate in the small commission which considered them before submission for Congress approval. M. N. Roy heatedly attacked the very point calling for assistance to the "bourgeois-democratic liberation movement." [17] He argued that the term "bourgeois-democratic" was unclear and would mislead the comrades into supporting "every" reformist movement. To combat this tendency, Roy demanded that the Comintern's exclusive concern should be the development of a purely Communistic movement, and called for exclusion of Lenin's paragraph on this point.

Roy's proposal was rejected by the British delegate present, who argued that while a small Indian Communist Party could be easily smashed by England, a broad national-liberation movement could not be suppressed. Lenin also sharply reprimanded Roy, pointing to the support the Bolsheviks had rendered liberal groups while fighting Tsarist oppression. Lenin concluded with this statement: "The Hindu Communists are duty-bound to support the bourgeois-liberation movement without, however, merging with it." [18]

Roy was unwilling to let it rest at this and finally prevailed upon Lenin to reword the theses. Lenin agreed, changing his terminology without altering the meaning of the resolution.[19] As he explained later to the Congress, by replacing "bourgeois-democratic" with "national-revolutionary," he was contrasting a "reformist" with a "revolutionary" bourgeois movement that would "not hinder us in training and organizing the peasants and the broad mass of the exploited in a revolutionary spirit." [20] Lest it be thought that this indicated a change in the historical stage through which the revolutions in backward countries were passing, Lenin asserted flatly:

There is not the slightest doubt that every national movement can only be a bourgeois-democratic movement, for the bulk of the population in backward countries are peasants, who represent bourgeois-capitalist relations. It would be utopian to think that proletarian parties, if indeed they can arise in such countries [*sic*], could pursue Communist tactics and a Communist policy in these backward countries without having definite relations with the peasant movement and without effectively supporting it.[21]

Roy was not alone in his opposition to even temporary cooperation with the bourgeoisie. While Lenin's fundamental tactic was consistent with earlier statements by him, it had never been fully debated by so representative a group. On the floor of the Comintern Congress, a debate took place similar to that which had occurred in the commission. No Leninist cult had as yet developed, and in 1920 the Russian leader was still open to challenge from those who disagreed. Many European radicals regarded as anathema support for any bourgeois group. Such a policy, for them, was characteristic of their detested enemies, the "reformist" Socialists of the Second International. Serratti, an Italian Socialist, attacked the resolution on several points. He emphatically declared that "only full separation from the exploiters and the bourgeoisie will allow true class struggle."[22] A struggle for power within the Italian delegation over the degree to which the delegation would accept Russian domination had left Serratti in a precarious position, however, and the abuse heaped on him by those currying favor with Lenin brought discussion to a fever pitch. Roy leaped into the battle, accusing Serratti of having charged both Roy and Lenin with "counterrevolutionary" ideas. Serratti interrupted vainly in justified protest over this fantastic accusation. The Indian's denunciation showed the lengths to which he would go in maintaining unity with Lenin, his severest critic: "It is unscientific to distinguish any other kind of revolution [except "national" ones]. All revolutions are different stages of socialist revolutions. . . . He who thinks that supporting these peoples in their national struggle is reactionary is himself reactionary and speaks the language of imperialists."[23] Such violent words had a strange ring when sounded by Roy who, only a few days previously, had voiced Serratti's very objections to Lenin in the privacy of the commission debates!

At this point, Maring, a Dutch Communist who had had considerable revolutionary experience in Java and who later represented the Comintern in China, attempted to spread oil on the troubled waters. Sensing the serious implications of Serratti's criticisms and their possible effect on Comintern unity, he maintained that although there might be a theoretical difficulty in formulating the precise relationship between the bourgeois and the revolutionary movements in colonial areas, the issue was quite simple in practice: the two groups *had* to work together. According to Maring, anyone who denied this was a "doctrinaire-Marxist." [24] Thus he swept aside further debate, impatiently advising less talk and more action.

The issue was not settled quite so easily, however. Lenin was to hear criticism from still another quarter for having advocated cooperation with native bourgeois leaders. The Asian delegates who spoke on this issue were generally much closer to Roy's original stand than to Lenin's, although some presented their criticisms more subtly than had the Indian delegate. For instance, Sultan Zade, of Persia, approved support of bourgeois-democratic movements *except* where they were a decade or so old.[25] In such cases he feared that the bourgeoisie had already become counter-revolutionary and that only a purely Communistic movement could be supported safely. More violent was the dramatic statement of the Korean delegate, Pak Dinshun:

Admitting that the first stage of the revolution in the East will be the victory of the liberal bourgeoisie and the nationalistic intelligentsia, we should nevertheless now prepare our forces for the next stage, drawing from the depths of the peasant masses enslaved by the feudal regime, organized forces for an agrarian-social revolution. . . .

. . . We shall utilize their [nationalists for national-political liberation only] revolutionary spirit in combatting world capitalism and for the triumph of the social revolution in the whole world; but if the revolution demands it afterwards, we will know how to turn the

weapons against the "allies" of yesterday and the victory will undoubtedly be ours . . . *only social liberation can give the full guaranty of
freedom.*[26]

Such open denunciations of the bourgeoisie were ill-advised if
the Comintern was to win the confidence of the desired "allies"
for at least a temporary period. Virtually none of the Asian delegates expressed enthusiasm over joining hands with their bourgeois brethren. In the last analysis Lenin's views prevailed, yet
the differences of opinion were revealing and stood as a harbinger
of things to come. The complicated verbiage of the prolific resolutions served as a convenient screen, covering the conflict between Lenin's tactics for revolution and the Asians' hatred of those
they considered their native exploiters. With this conflict unresolved, the "united front" tactic in China faced not only suspicion
from the Right but confusion on the Left. This basic problem was
to prove decisive in the years 1924 to 1927.

One final issue caused Lenin and Roy to cross swords, with peculiar consequences. In the preparatory commission which met
prior to reporting Lenin's theses to the Congress, Roy insisted
that the Communist International accept as a fundamental principle the complete dependency of the revolutionary movement
in Europe upon the triumph of the revolutions in Asia.[27] The Indian argued that utter failure might strike the European Communist parties should they not understand that the main resources
of world capitalism flowed from Asia's exploited markets and raw
materials. Basing his stand on Lenin's statements quoted previously from *Imperialism* referring to the "super-profits" from semicolonial areas, Roy shifted the emphasis considerably. He held
that unless this source of lifeblood for world capitalism were cut
off by Asian revolutions, the European proletariat would be unable to defeat their exploiters. Consequently the sole task of the
Communist International was to foster revolutions in Asia.

Lenin accused Roy of "going too far"[28] and chided him for the
failure of India's five million workers and thirty-seven million
peasants to organize a Communist Party. While the Russian was

anxious to emphasize the importance of the colonial struggle, he was loath to tell his European comrades that their efforts were futile unless the amorphous masses of Asia first achieved *their* revolution. The revolutions in Asia were an important means of assistance to the revolution in Europe, but the quickest way of bringing capitalism to its knees was obviously by striking at its very stronghold, Western Europe. The Asian campaign was definitely a subsidiary action.

Roy refused to give in. He drafted a set of supplementary theses, including his own analysis of the manner in which capitalism held back economic development in colonial countries.[29] Once again the commission wrangled over words and phrases, but semantic battles were a familiar story to Lenin. Far more skilled than his adversary, he gradually removed the heart of Roy's supplementary theses without rejecting them *in toto*. Roy agreed to soften the tone of the sections which originally had made the future of the European proletariat unmistakably and solely dependent upon success in the colonial struggle. His revised theses simply stressed the importance of Asian revolts. After these critical alterations, Roy included a single sentence in his seventh section which was a virtual capitulation to Lenin's point on cooperation with the bourgeoisie: "For the overthrow of foreign capitalism, which is the first step toward revolution in the colonies, the cooperation of the bourgeois national revolutionary elements is useful." [30]

The commission closed on a note of harmony. Lenin had revised his wording, changing "bourgeois-democratic movements" to "national-revolutionary movements." Roy had softened the tone of his supplementary theses and had added a single sentence. Now Lenin could proceed to the floor of the Congress and permit Roy to present the supplementary theses with the confidence that Roy would not oppose him openly. The Russian strategist had given in on terminology in exchange for his opponent's compromise on essential tactics.

The Second Congress of the Communist International formally

adopted both Lenin's theses on national and colonial problems
and Roy's supplementary theses as revised in commission. The
vote was unanimous with only three abstentions, one of those
being Serratti.[31] He refused to support the acceptance of "contradictory" and "incompatible" sets of resolutions.[32] There was
no denying their conflicting emphasis, despite the commission revisions. Even more confusion must have resulted in the minds of
those who scanned the stenographic accounts for Comintern policy, because until 1934 an error had allowed Roy's *original*, un-
revised theses to be reprinted in both Russian and German and
widely distributed! [33]

This error was an important one insofar as it left the two sets
of theses more contradictory than they actually were after their
adoption. The prevalent version contained Roy's extreme phrasing on the priority of Asian revolutions over those in Europe and
omitted Lenin's crucial sentence advocating cooperation with
bourgeois elements. Since the mistake was not noticed until a
second edition of the stenographic account was prepared in 1934,
it is possible that Roy's supplementary theses actually received
little further attention from Lenin or any other Bolshevik leader
once the Congress had adjourned.[34] Certainly Roy's complaints
at subsequent congresses over alleged mishandling of Asian problems support this analysis. In any event, his resolutions merit attention both as an expression of Asian radical sentiment and as a
criticism which forced Lenin into a fuller exposition of his own
views. The adoption of both sets of theses by the Comintern provided ample ammunition for all sides during the furious polemics
of the mid-twenties.

Before closing this study of the Second Comintern Congress,
mention must be made of the Chinese delegate, Lao Hsiu-Chao.
His speech was surprisingly superficial, despite his appearance at
the First Congress in 1919. He admitted that Sun Yat-sen had
been driven from Canton by southern militarists, yet claimed:
"There is no doubt that the Southern Government has a great
chance to succeed." [35] After paying faint praise to the newly

arrived proletariat of China, Lao sounded the "really Marxist" slogans currently appearing in radical Chinese journals. Following Lenin's carefully worded theses, the slogans struck a somewhat dissonant note—"Who does not work does not eat" and "Replace the principle of nationalism and statism[36] with the principle of internationalism." If Lao's slogans were truly representative, they bespoke an elemental type of radicalism, far removed from the sophisticated theorizing of Lenin and his associates. Lao's amalgam of primitive Marxism, anarchism, and utopian socialism underscored Lenin's reproval of Roy for "going too far" in insisting on placing all hopes in purely Communistic movements in Asia. It would be many years before a skilled organization of professional revolutionaries could be developed in colonial and semicolonial countries.

While considerable attention was given to the problems of national and colonial issues, the bulk of the proceedings of the Second Comintern Congress dwelt on purely European problems. The eyes of the delegates were still fixed on the West. Europe remained, in their view, the citadel of capitalism to be assaulted by the proletarian shock troops. The millions in Asia were to form the vast reserve armies, striking at the enemy from the rear. Sooner than the Congress anticipated, the Western shock troops were to be weakened by internal splits, as in Italy, and broken by external attack, as in Germany. The consequent necessity of greater dependence on the Asian reserves made the 1920 Congress increasingly important in retrospect.

Yet what meaning did the 1920 theses have for China's revolution? Lenin attempted to revise Marx's blueprint for constructing the new order without changing the basic design. His new plans contained ambivalences and ambiguities, while erasures and revisions within the Congress further blurred the pattern for action. Now there was hope of "leaping over" capitalism and speeding the economic transition from feudalism to communism provided the revolution succeeded in Europe. Now there was to be full-scale support for the bourgeoisie in Asia provided such support did not obstruct development of an antibourgeois movement. Now there was to be major emphasis placed upon the peasant revolution provided it was led by the proletariat. Revisions such as these conflicted with the views of some delegates; the attendant provisions confused the views of others. The program was incomplete if its major points with respect to the peasantry and the bourgeoisie were to guide the revolution in Peking and Canton. Before examining the varying interpretations given the program by the Comintern, Narkomindel, and Profintern, let us turn to those two centers in China to survey the problems which Lenin's theses were designed to solve.

IV

The Chinese Puzzle

THE China of 1920 presented a confusing scene of social disintegration and upheaval. Western ideas had shaken the very foundations of the social and moral order which had held the Empire together for so many centuries. Yet these new ideas were not winning the universal acceptance so necessary to provide a stable successor to the *ancien régime*. The Manchu political structure had collapsed completely, leaving in its wake a nominal capital at Peking controlled by militarists, often under Japanese influence. The rest of the country was fragmentized into groups of provinces, run in an *ad hoc* fashion by war lords and provincial governors. Underlying the entire picture was the transitional economic pattern, shifting from a relatively immobile agrarian society to one surging with disruptive influences accompanying the introduction of industry and new trade patterns.

Perhaps the very turbulence and chaos of the first decade of the Chinese Republic makes any systematic study of the struggles for power and the economic disorder an impossibility. Certainly the bulk of Western writings of this period are largely descriptive, rather than analytical. Yet a brief review of the economic and political movements is in order if Soviet analyses are to be evaluated critically. Without attempting a definitive presentation, a quick sketch of influences and pressures in China will provide a better background for the Soviet writings which follow.

A statistical analysis of groups and movements in China has several limitations, not the least of which is the extreme unreliability of Chinese statistics. With no central government of any power and none of the Western respect for and reliance upon statistical data, much of the material available is fragmentary or based on very rough estimates. So basic an item as the population of China was not established by census, and reliable estimates vary by as much as fifty million.

A second limitation on a numerical analysis is more fundamental. In China, literacy and means of communication were at a premium. The bulk of the population seldom took part in political action for the simple reason that much of that action was centered in the pivotal areas of power—Peking, Shanghai, and Canton. Had the material means for such participation been at hand, Confucian principles would have provided another obstacle. Chinese society found passive acceptance of the *status quo* with all its attendant misery and economic uncertainties a means of stability. Peace rather than progress seemed a necessary choice in most instances. Dynasties might crumble and be replaced by new rulers, the Mandate of Heaven might be withdrawn from one group and bestowed upon another, but the gigantic mass of peasants expressed itself only sporadically, in local revolts for limited objectives. While this served as a brake on any broad political movement based on the people, it encouraged the relatively thin layer of intelligentsia and political activists to fight for new ideas and new techniques. Thus sheer numbers fail to show the disproportionate power that could be wielded by a well-organized group with discipline and purpose. Any analysis of political groupings in China must consider their qualitative as well as their quantitative strength.

Since the primary emphasis of Marxism is on the proletariat, it might be appropriate to examine this group first, although in China it ranked near the bottom in the scale of political power in 1920. Many influences worked against the development of trade union organization, influences which were deeply rooted in Chinese society.[1] The impoverished Chinese peasant was often unable to support himself and his family on his inadequate plot of land; migration to the city provided one salvation. Such migration was only temporary, however. Once he had accumulated some meagre savings, he would return to the village until the next crisis. This large floating labor reserve allowed the employer to exploit workers almost beyond the limits of human endurance. If any objected, there were many more who were willing to accept the employer's terms. The over-all economic poverty forced women and children into sweatshop conditions rivaling the worst period of the industrial expansion in western Europe and America.

A few statistics provide graphic illustration of workers' conditions. Ta Chen, a noted Chinese economist, reported in 1920 that while the price of rice had increased 90 percent between 1918 and 1920, wages had risen only 50 percent.[2] Even this wage increase found common workers in Shanghai textile mills earning only 40–50¢ (Mex.) for working twelve to fourteen hours a day.[3] Women and children earned 30¢ and 20¢ a day respectively.

Two years later, conditions were no better, as shown in a study by J. B. Tayler and W. T. Zung.[4] Reports of a government inquiry were published charging that young boys worked in glass factories at Hong Kong from six in the morning to eleven at night, receiving only one Chinese dollar plus food *per month*. A sampling of typical working days found that in machine industries a twelve-hour day was common, and many worked as much as fourteen and seventeen hours daily. In silk factories, the average was fourteen hours a day; in steel mills, figures varied between twelve and *eighteen* hours a day. It should be remembered that Sunday was not recognized as a rest day, while holidays were few and far between. This same study attempted to review wage rates, but here the data is inconclusive. Unskilled trades reported a 15–20¢ daily wage, and lower-grade railroad workers received 24–30¢ daily. The writers estimated that two meals of cooked grain with vegetables and beans cost approximately 15¢.

These figures suggest the small amount of purchasing power left to the labor force in China.

Chinese industrialists were not content with such exploitation of manpower. An extensive contract-labor system recruited workers, particularly for mines, wharfs, and railroad gangs. An official report compiled in June, 1923, by a group in Shanghai, found children under six years of age frequently working twelve-hour days in mills and factories.[5] These children had been hired through a contract-labor scheme. The contractor was paid by the factory according to the productivity of the workers, while he in turn paid the parents of the children a flat monthly fee. It was estimated that the profit per child averaged four dollars a month while the rate paid the parents was only two dollars a month. Where the contractor was eliminated as middleman, the employers often used an apprentice system which could engage extremely young hands for almost no pay and discharge them as they became older, replacing them with new youths from the countryside. The sheer mechanics of organizing labor effectively were almost impossible to accomplish in this environment.

Underlying the functional obstacles hampering trade union progress were sociological problems. Just as the worker remained a creature of the country rather than of the city, so he was a resident of a province rather than of a nation. This was partially a result of the innumerable language barriers, with different dialects preventing verbal communication between men from Shanghai and Canton, or Peking and Hankow. Moreover, much of the provincial consciousness lay rooted in the relatively important role played by local government in Chinese society, as contrasted with that of the distant rule in Peking.

In addition to the provincialism of the workers, there was the extensive family relationship. In sharp contrast with the independent, small family unit prevalent in Western society, China had developed family ties firmly embracing all related members in one group. The individual did not exist in a community; he existed in a family. His rights and obligations were directed toward filial ties rather than toward social or economic allegiances. As a consequence, nepotism and paternalism influenced Chinese industrial organization to a degree unparalleled in the West. Such paternalism beclouded whatever consciousness the worker might have had of himself and his fellows as an entity engaged in economic struggle with the employer.

In the face of such formidable obstacles, it is difficult to see how any organization of the Chinese proletariat could succeed, yet by 1920 a nucleus had been started. Ta Chen estimates that as of that year some 200,000 factory workers were organized, as were 185,000 laborers in the mining and railroad industries.[6] To be sure, a few factors encouraged the growth of labor organizations. One was the concentration of industry in a relatively compact area centering around the coastal cities. These were both hotbeds of anti-Western feelings and contact points with Western radical ideas. The ferment which was at work elsewhere in China had its effect on the exploited proletariat, as evidenced by the mushrooming of strikes and the widening circle of labor disturbances. While in many cases the work stoppages were spontaneous, *ad hoc* affairs and were not started by union organizers, their very existence held promise for future agitation. Ta Chen's tabulation of those engaged in strikes of all types, economic and political, includes 108,000 for 1921 and 139,050 for 1922.[7]

The movement of May 4, 1919, with its attendant strikes and boycotts, spurred the growth of organized labor as increasing numbers of students and intellectuals turned to practical application of the lessons learned from Western writings on socialism and liberalism. With the introduction of a simplified written language at this time, a veritable flood of translations appeared in China. Ideas in these Western studies merged with those of Chinese who were returning from all over the world in hope of building a "new China," of raising the living standard of the masses and eliminating all forms of exploitation. New concepts of rights and privileges emerged with the return of the large force of coolies that had been shipped to France in 1917 and 1918 as China's contribution to the World War. Although these men dug trenches and performed the most menial tasks, they saw a different attitude toward their well-being from that experienced in their homeland. In September, 1919, those who returned formed an association in Shanghai, while in Paris a Labor Federation for Chinese Workers in France boasted over six thousand members.

During 1920 and 1921, Marxist study groups, students' Socialist societies, and workers' clubs introduced organizational activity among the growing Chinese proletariat. The transition from traditional guilds to orthodox trade unions was difficult and slow. Sometimes the new organization sprang directly from the old, as with the Chinese Seamen's Philanthropic Society which became the Chinese Seamen's Union. In the Hong Kong mechanics' strike of 1920, a regular guild association won nation-wide attention by calling a demonstration of its nine thousand workers against British practices in that strategic city.

The year 1922 saw the Chinese labor movement take a significant step forward, although in relation to the rest of Chinese society, it could not yet be termed a force of prime importance. In January, the Chinese Seamen's Union called a strike in Hong Kong, protesting a pay raise given to better-paid foreign seamen but not to Chinese workers. The strike lasted for two months, enlisted the support of other labor groups, and included 50,000 workers at its peak.[8] Besides costing the fourteen shipping lines involved an estimated five million dollars, the strike paralyzed Hong Kong completely.

Optimism was short-lived, however. After some moderately successful strikes on the Peking-Hankow railroad during 1922, the unions on that line called a general organization meeting at Chengchow in February, 1923. The authorities tried to forbid the holding of the conference, and the strike which was called in protest involved some 20,000 workers. General Wu Pei-fu, then in control of the Peking regime, used armed force to smash the strike with serious consequences for the Chinese labor movement, particularly in North China.[9] All trade unions within Wu's jurisdiction were ordered closed, and many others were driven underground. In this nascent stage of development, such a blow was crippling to the organized proletariat in and around Peking.

Traditional Marxists had little hope of building a revolutionary base on these meagre proletarian foundations. Those who accepted Lenin's emphasis on the peasant revolution looked to the bulk of the Chinese population for support, yet there the situation was no brighter. Nearly 85 percent of the Chinese populace in 1920 was in the countryside, but this mighty mass moved slowly. Peasant uprisings in the nineteenth and twentieth centuries had been limited in nature, except for the dramatic Taiping Rebellion. There is no doubt that peasant unrest existed during this time, but it seldom crystallized into a "movement" as such.

For the agitator, the life of the peasant offered fertile ground. While landed estates seldom reached the proportions commonly found in eastern Europe, land holdings in South China were concentrated in the hands of a small group. Tenant farming was a serious problem everywhere because of the inability of the peasant to acquire capital. Usurious rates of interest coupled with a crushing burden of rent and taxes made life one of perpetual indebtedness. Starting with a pitifully small parcel of land, the peasant was forced to work the impoverished soil intensively. Whatever he raised had limited value, however, since transportation was prohibitive in cost and distribution was dependent upon a middleman who monopolized the market in his locality. During the Empire, famine and floods took their periodic toll, while after the collapse of the Manchus, soldiers and bandits increased the misery of the countryside.

The passivity of the peasant may be exaggerated because of insufficient study of peasant revolts in China, but generally it may be concluded that he had little stimulus to break the chains that bound him. Certainly the gap between the peasant masses and the intelligentsia common to most countries was very great in China. Suspicion of the city person and deep-seated superstitions made a populist movement based on an agrarian program difficult to achieve. The illiteracy, the clannishness, the fear of "foreign devils" and their ideas—all these factors kept the peasants a dark mass of ignorance and inertia. In numbers they definitely were the strongest group; in organized strength they were a neutral, if not a negative, factor in the struggle to reform China.

The intelligentsia formed the third group upon which the revolution could be based. Here the Bolsheviks had a much brighter prospect. The story of the Chinese reform movements from 1890 to 1911 and thereafter is a fascinating study of frustrated philosophers and inspired idealists. Japan's example was a stimulating lesson in Westernization, and many were the students from China who sojourned briefly in the Japanese islands prior to 1914. It was the experience of Versailles, however, which made the Chinese intellectuals realize that until their country could become modern, independent, and strong, it would remain a pawn in the international game of power politics. The protest movement of May 4, 1919, marked an important transition from thought to action. Many new periodicals appeared in the *pai-hua* form, adopting the spoken language as a written medium of expression. Western Socialists and educators brought new stimuli to Chinese students while a thin trickle of Marxist literature was encouraged through the growth of Communist nuclei in 1921 and 1922.

Debates in Chinese universities questioned the applicability of Western parliamentarianism to the needs of turbulent China. The influence of Western democratic thought had preceded radical socialism in China, but it suffered a crippling setback with the discrediting of parliamentary institutions in Peking. Corruption and venality sat hard with the idealists who envisioned the Chinese Republic in truly representative terms. A new political theory was at hand in Marxism, one which promised to eliminate the ills of bourgeois democracy. Disillusionment with democratic procedures in North China merged with anti-British resentment in Central and South China. Western aims and methods were often under attack. Japan's Twenty-one Demands were contrasted with the apparently disinterested policy of Soviet Russia. Curiosity over communism grew into genuine admiration as the Bolsheviks beat back foreign intervention, won their civil war, and set about on a program aimed at eliminating all forms of exploitation, foreign and domestic.

One fundamental weakness of the Chinese intelligentsia lay in its failure to develop a comprehensive doctrine of political and economic thought. Although the French, American, and Russian revolutions had all given birth to a new form of government based on theories peculiar to the problems of each particular people, no such process was evident in China. Whatever reaction to the *status quo* took place, it was primarily negative in character. The Kuomintang party under Sun Yat-sen attracted many intellectuals, but, until 1924, it lacked a positive, coherent program of political and economic reform. Canton became the focal point of Chinese liberal thought primarily because it appeared impossible to unify China under the war lords of the North. Sun himself was essentially eclectic in nature, borrowing from sources as varied as Marx and Lincoln in an exasperating series of experiments and failures. The period was not propitious for constitutionalism, yet the society was unwilling to accept dictatorship or monarchy. A prolonged civil war was the tragic result.

Last but certainly not least, the builders of "new China" had to consider the merchant class or bourgeoisie. Although weak in numbers, the compradores, bankers, small industrialists, and shop owners were able to bring considerable influence to bear in the strategic port cities. There was much to make them anti-Western in sentiment and hence a convenient aid in the Chinese revolution. This antagonism was seldom expressed in inflammatory resolutions, although it found an outlet in antiforeign boycott demonstrations. The impotence of the Peking government in 1918 and 1919 in coping with foreign rights and privileges in China brought much criticism from Shanghai business groups. Foreign control of Chinese customs worked unfavorably for Chinese products. British, French, and Japanese spheres of influence kept China divided among warring militarists, strangling internal trade. Foreign concessions stretching into China's richer regions along the foreign-controlled railroads sucked out mineral resources. Foreign loans and indemnity payments drained the government treasury and necessitated higher taxation. Foreign-owned enterprises, particularly textile mills, competed successfully with Chinese entrepreneurs.

While business-class elements feared the proclivity of Sun's followers toward a vague socialism, the merchants did not give support to Peking as a counterweight. They had little interest in the welfare of the proletariat and none in the peasantry, but they had more than ample cause to join forces with nationalist groups in the anti-imperialist struggle.

No discussion of 1920 China would be complete without mentioning the many political factions which rent the country asunder. There were no political parties in the Western sense of the term, although the Kuomintang could claim with some validity that it modeled itself on such organizations. It tried unsuccessfully to break away from the traditional pattern of secret societies that had prevailed in the country for so long, but the other groupings were purely opportunistic cliques, generally depending upon a particular militarist for their power.

The degree to which each faction was oriented toward a particular foreign power has never been investigated in a satisfactory manner, but certain general tendencies were evident. Japan's influence lay primarily in North China and particularly Manchuria, with Peking receiving special attention and pressure. Japan's efforts to turn China into a full-fledged vassal state during World War I were well known, and its hold was challenged in 1919 when three allegedly pro-Japanese cabinet members resigned under the impact of the May Fourth movement. When the group in power, known as the Anfu clique, was finally overthrown in 1920 by a coalition of generals, led by Chang Tso-lin and Wu Pei-fu, Japanese interests were temporarily forced into the background. However, Japan soon shifted ground and gave increasing support to the Manchurian war lord, Chang Tso-lin, and to the group known as the Chihli clique. Tuan Chi-jui, premier from 1917 to 1920, had suffered a temporary ouster from the Chihli group, but through adept maneuvering he was able to get into the good graces of Chang Tso-lin. At the same time, Tuan carried on negotiations with Sun Yat-sen, representing the Canton regime. With Tuan as the connecting link, an entente between Chang and Sun was not inconceivable. Such a move would have strengthened Japan's hand in China, because if Sun and Chang were to join hands, the unification of China under Japanese influence would be well under way. Wu Pei-fu was unwilling to countenance this, however. He opposed Japanese penetration for several reasons, not the least of which was his personal rivalry with Chang. Open warfare broke out between the two war lords in 1921, leading to Chang's defeat in 1922.

Wu Pei-fu's victory brought a shift in power, and many of Sun's followers from the "old Parliament" left Canton for Peking. Li Yuan-hung was placed in the presidency by Wu, and a period of comparative peace prevailed. However, the war lord was no constitutionalist; at best he might be termed an enlightened militarist who remained fairly free of foreign control. His ruthless smashing of the railroad strike in 1923 showed his unwillingness to tolerate any group which might disturb his regime. Restoring "internal order and stability" in this fashion, he also headed off possible intervention by British and French forces.

By 1923, a *modus vivendi* saw the Three Eastern Provinces, or Manchuria, under Chang Tso-lin's sway. Peking and its surrounding provinces were administered by Wu, while Sun's "Southern Republic" held an area in South China. No formal agreement or fixed boundaries separated these spheres of power, nor were they administered as autonomous units recognizing any single central point of over-all control. Lesser war lords, such as Yen Hsi-shan, ruled single provinces, while Shanghai was dominated primarily by its large foreign concessions.[10]

The Kuomintang was slow to slough off the inept methods which had hampered its activities in the past. Sun Yat-sen continued to trust to personal loyalties, despite his repeated disappointments along this line. He hoped sooner or later to combine the necessary forces which could defeat the war lords of North China. The betrayals he suffered were many; the victories he enjoyed were few. Although he was officially proclaimed "President of the Chinese Republic" in April, 1921, he had only nominal control over Kwangsi, Yunnan, Kweichow, Szechwan, and part of Hunan, and actual control only over Kwangtung province.[11] Canton, the major city of that province, was modernized in administration under the mayoralty of Sun Fo, son of the Kuomintang leader. However, the army gradually became a personal instrument of General Ch'en Chiung-ming, Sun's trusted governor. The Kuomintang remained a loose organization, personally loyal to Sun but lacking effective control over the Kwangtung government and having no power in the surrounding provinces. Ch'en engineered a *coup d'état* in June, 1922, which brought Sun's fortunes to a new low. Many of his former supporters now decided that Wu's regime in the North offered more stability if less democracy. It was only the dissatisfaction of other southern generals which gave Sun the troops with which to oust Ch'en by January, 1923. As one writer has commented, the Kuomintang had "no unity of purpose, no concentrated action. Too much stress had been laid by Sun Yat-sen on military action, and too little on political propaganda. . . . His forced affiliation with elements basically opposed to his ideals had resulted in compromises which were little conducive to his political standing in the country." [12]

Thus it can readily be seen that the complexities of the Chinese puzzle made it difficult to analyze, impossible to solve. While the world recognized Peking as the capital of China, the locus of power shifted from group to group as the fortunes of civil war and foreign intervention varied. The absence of central government permitted violence and chaos to sweep the long-suffering masses. The needs of China seemed obvious to all, yet the means were nowhere at hand.

V

Congress of Toilers of the Far East: 1922

AS IF the complexities of China's struggles were not enough of a handicap to political analysts in Moscow, a dearth of information in Russian journals impeded cogent analysis. There is no definite way of assessing the quantity or quality of information available at top levels of Soviet planning circles, but it is evident that disrupted communications during the civil war severely hampered the flow of information from China prior to 1920. As late as 1923, a writer for the magazine *Vostok* complained that "materials for judging this world-important problem [China] are exceedingly meagre for the student in Petrograd, and they are in every case limited to scattered articles appearing in odd issues of the Party press up to October 1922. However, even these scanty materials are diverse enough to communicate something to the reader, if one omits politics and limits oneself to the objective factors in contemporary Chinese life." [1] The winter of 1922–23 saw a marked increase in space given to the Middle Kingdom, coinciding with the prolonged efforts of the Narkomindel to win recognition from Peking. The writer's complaint over the lack of news on "politics" remained valid, however, and little compensation could be found in the statistical information sent in dispatches of Soviet journalists and political representatives. To be sure, their statistics agree with non-Russian sources, for the most part, and appear reasonably accurate. However, the accompanying analysis often suffered from insufficient background and a somewhat rigid Marxist preconception of what should be happening in China, rather than interpreting what was actually happening at the time. It is small wonder that Russian writers, faced with the intricacies of the social upheaval in China, often turned to facile interpretations of class warfare and inevitable revolutionary victory.

The resolutions adopted at the Second Comintern Congress provided only the skeletal framework for Soviet strategy. Translation of theory into practice took several years, during which time important modifications were introduced under the combined pressures of reports from agents in China and of events in Europe. These years saw a fledgling Communist Party in China grow to become a full partner of the Kuomintang. They also saw Lenin's illness remove him from an active role in the political arena. Personal and ideological schisms appeared which were to shake the ruling class of Russia for a decade to follow. Conclusions reached by factions within the Comintern were often opposed by spokesmen for the Profintern and the Narkomindel. Lenin's stress upon the peasant program was sometimes completely ignored; his insistence upon support of the Chinese bourgeoisie was openly challenged. Doubts were expressed concerning the ultimate success of the revolution in China, so overpowering were its problems. After an examination of various views held within the Comintern, a comparison with those advanced by other political organizations in Soviet Russia will reveal the major points of difference within the Soviet elite concerning the Chinese revolution.

More dramatic in appearance than in accomplishment, the First Congress of Peoples of the East followed close upon the heels of the Second Comintern Congress. Held at the vital oil center of Baku in September, 1920, it was designed by the Comintern leaders as an anti-British catalyst for the peoples of Egypt and the Middle East. Zinoviev whipped the colorful assemblage to a high pitch by calling for a "holy war" against

Great Britain and demanding that peasant-proletarian revolutions in Turkey, Persia, India, and China "can and must work directly toward a soviet structure." [2] He scoffed at the need for a capitalist stage of development in backward areas but failed to mention Lenin's qualification that "leaping over the capitalist stage of development" would depend upon the help of victorious Socialist revolutions in Europe. This was not the only point of difference between Zinoviev's proposals and the program Lenin had proposed only a few weeks previously at the Comintern Congress. While Lenin's focus had been chiefly centered on the effects of Japanese imperialism in China, Zinoviev blamed Britain for China's ills. In all fairness to the fiery orator, it should be noted that very little attention was given China per se at the meeting. He may have included China in the list of British victims more for convenience than any other reason. However, Zinoviev's strongly antibourgeois speeches clearly conflicted with Lenin's statements at the Comintern Congress calling for support of bourgeois-nationalist movements in the Middle East and Asia. There is no denying the fundamental contradictions between the two spokesmen in 1920.

Zinoviev's sentiments were reflected in the general anti-British, antibourgeois tone of subsequent Comintern literature. These militant attitudes characterized the writings current in the official Comintern publication, *Kommunisticheskii Internatsional.* Although the magazine occasionally printed views at variance with those of editors Zinoviev and Radek, it was usually a reliable guide to Comintern thinking. G. Safarov, writing on the revolution in Asia, cited with approval Roy's warnings against trusting the native bourgeoisie in India, Turkey, and Persia.[3] He argued that class interests knew no national boundaries; therefore it was inevitable that the propertied classes in backward countries would unite with foreign exploiters, just as oppressed peoples of Asia would unite with the revolutionary proletariat of Europe. Safarov ordered future proletarian parties in the East to "*struggle with the bourgeois-democratic movements within their nations.*" [4]

Here was an explicit clash with Lenin's basic tactic of cooperation with the bourgeoisie in the national-liberation struggle. The respective strengths of the proletariat and the bourgeoisie in China received no attention from Safarov, yet this factor alone precluded success for his policy. Nevertheless, he was consistent in this extreme position, to the point of seconding Roy's assertion that Asia was the *only* source of wealth for world capitalism. Safarov stated this assertion flatly, without enlarging upon it as had Roy at the Second Comintern Congress.

While Safarov was not alone in castigating the bourgeoisie, he had little support from other writers for his presentation of Asia as the Achilles' heel of world capitalism. Furthermore, few articles dealing with the Far East appeared in the Comintern journal, reflecting the scant attention given to China. Roy dwelled on this "shortcoming" of Comintern leadership with resentful criticism at the Third Comintern Congress of June, 1921. In his opening remarks he charged that the problems of the colonial revolutions had been consistently overlooked by the Communist International. When the debate on the report of the Eastern commission began, he noted bitterly: "I have been given five minutes for my speech [which] could not be given in an hour." [5] Roy seems to have been concerned here for his personal position as well as for the problems of revolution in colonial and semicolonial areas.

The proceedings of the Eastern commission supported Roy's criticisms to some extent. No European delegates were present and no resolutions were adopted. In the debate on the floor of the Congress, attention was drawn to these shortcomings and a representative of a so-called Chinese Communist Party, Chang Tai-lei, demanded that more attention be accorded the Chinese revolution.[6] Immediately a Middle Eastern delegate demanded that *his* country receive more attention, since it was the key to *both* China and India. Such narrow-minded provincialism was brushed aside by a Soviet spokesman who declared that the entire matter of colonial revolutions had been amply covered at the 1920 Congress.[7] In view of the current Communist difficulties in Germany and France, little time could be given strategy in Asia.

One exception to this rather cursory treatment of Asian issues was, interestingly enough, embodied in the speeches of Trotsky. As a prominent figure at the Congress, he dwelt at length on the interplay of crises in East and West, terming colonial industrialization one of the three primary sources of world revolution. In view of Trotsky's role in the polemics over the post-1926 course of events in China, his remarks bear quoting in full:

The basis for the liberation-struggle of the colonies is constituted in the peasant masses. But the peasants in their struggle need leadership. Such leadership used to be provided by the native bourgeoisie. The latter's struggle against foreign imperialist domination cannot, however, be either consistent or energetic inasmuch as the national bourgeoisie itself is intimately bound up with foreign capitalism and represents to a large degree an agency of foreign capital. Only the rise of a national proletariat strong enough numerically and capable of struggle can provide a real axis for the revolution. In comparison with the country's entire population, the size of the Indian proletariat is, of course, numerically small, but those who have grasped the meaning of the revolution's development in Russia will never fail to take into account that the proletariat's revolutionary role in the Oriental countries will far exceed its actual numerical strength. This applies not only to colonial countries like India, or semi-colonial countries like China, but also to Japan . . . for the peasantry of India and of China has no other possibility, no other center of concentration than the young proletariat capable of struggle.[8]

Trotsky's antibourgeois tone challenged Lenin's 1920 theses, but the challenge was not met publicly. The year 1921 was one of regrouping for the Bolshevik leaders, and it may well have been that Lenin was engrossed in more immediate problems than that of the Chinese bourgeoisie. His New Economic Policy had set aside the radical measures of War Communism in an effort to restore production to idle factories and to reverse the growing gap between the industrial and the agrarian sectors of the economy. Catastrophic famines obstructed his plans as did discontented Bolsheviks who saw the concessions to bourgeois principles as a betrayal of the revolution. Yet Lenin had no alternative but temporary retreat. In March, 1921, the mutiny of Red sailors at Kronstadt had brought to a head the latent dissatisfactions under the new regime. At the same time, the European Socialist movement was suffering from the splits which divided all radical groups as they debated the acceptance of Lenin's twenty-one points for entrance into the Third International. Moderate socialists refused to accept the conditions posed by the Bolshevik leader, on the grounds that such conditions would make them subservient to the Russian Communists and would perhaps limit the freedom of policy determination for all non-Russian parties. These problems crowded Asia from Comintern discussions, and the six months following the Third Congress saw little space given to China in *Kommunisticheskii Internatsional*.

Immediately following the Baku Congress, the Executive Committee of the Comintern, after hearing Japanese, Chinese, and Korean radicals, agreed to convene a parallel "Congress of Peoples of the Far East" in a Siberian city.[9] Subsequent crises in the European Communist movements, particularly in Germany, undoubtedly diverted the attention of the Comintern, as evidenced by the speeches of the Third Congress. However, with the announcement of the Washington Conference, scheduled for the fall of 1921, Soviet interest turned increasingly to the Far East. Narkomindel's immediately hostile reaction came as no surprise in view of the exclusion of Russia from a conference called to discuss such matters as the presence of Japanese troops on Russian soil and the Chinese Eastern Railway. The Commissariat's initial plan appears to have included convening a rival conference, as proposed by Vilensky on August 2, 1921.[10] Calling for an "East Asian Conference" of China, Mongolia, the Far Eastern Republic, and the RSFSR, he admitted that while it was not known how the non-Soviet countries would react to the Washington invitation, he presumed they would follow Russia's

lead of refusing to recognize America's proposals. China, of
course, accepted the invitation to attend the Washington meeting. In view of the probable subservience of the Far Eastern
Republic to Moscow at this time, Narkomindel ambivalence is
suggested by contrasting Vilensky's assurance the Far Eastern
Republic would refuse, with the later dispatching of a Republic
delegation to act as "observers" at Washington.[11]

Narkomindel's change of tactic paralleled new Comintern activity, resulting in the calling of a Congress of Toilers of the Far
East, at Moscow, January 21, 1922.[12] Held under Comintern
auspices, the Congress in one sense fulfilled Narkomindel hopes
by launching an unmitigated attack upon the Washington Conference. In another sense, however, it ran afoul of Narkomindel
policy, particularly with respect to Outer Mongolia. This dilemma, coupled with the deep schism between Lenin's 1920
position concerning the Chinese bourgeoisie and that of Comintern spokesmen, makes the Congress an excellent case study of
the problems confronting Soviet policies in China.

Although the Congress named Lenin, Zinoviev, Trotsky, and
Stalin as chairmen, only Zinoviev appeared on the platform.
Safarov and Roy won seats on the presidium, as did three Chinese
delegates, none of whom appear to have been in the top echelon
of the Chinese Communist Party.[13] Of particular interest was
the presence of a large Chinese delegation, dominated by young
intellectual radicals, and including a representative of the Kuomintang party—the first visitor to Russia so identified in the
Soviet press.[14] In addition, delegates from Japan, Korea, Mongolia, India, and Indonesia, together with Asians living in the
RSFSR, made up the 144 members of the Congress. Simultaneous
sessions were held separately for "revolutionary youth" and for
"toiling women" of the Far East, but these were definitely subsidiary in nature.[15]

Two issues provided the centers of controversy as far as Sino-
Soviet relations were concerned. The first, Bolshevik opinion on
the Chinese bourgeoisie in general, and the Kuomintang in par-

ticular, continued a debate long raging in Comintern circles. The second, Russian policy in Outer Mongolia, requires some explanation here, although the detailed account of events in that area will be dealt with later in the examination of Narkomindel activity in China. Suffice it to say that in mid-1921, Red Army units, together with Mongolian revolutionaries, ousted White Guard troops from Urga where they had attempted to set up a regime hostile to both Russia and China under the hegemony of Baron Ungern von Sternberg. Following this military action, a Provisional Revolutionary Government of Mongolia, formed on Russian soil and supported exclusively by Soviet assistance, declared itself the *de facto* government. Chinese resentment over Russian invasion of territory traditionally recognized as lying within the Manchu Empire failed to be soothed by Soviet assurances that the troops would be withdrawn as soon as the counterrevolution had been smashed.

Zinoviev's first lengthy speech to the Congress bracketed both issues. Concerning the Kuomintang, he remarked: "It must be regretfully observed that, according to our information (and I must admit that our information is very poor and fragmentary), there are some people among the active workers of the South China revolutionary movement, among the adherents of Sun Yat-sen . . . who, at times, are looking not unhopefully towards America, i.e., towards American capitalism." [16] As for Mongolia's future, Zinoviev coupled defiance with advice. Mongolia's "liberation" was due "to some small support rendered it by Soviet Russia—the Soviet Government will, of course, always be proud of any possibility to lend even feeble assistance to the most oppressed peoples." [17] While referring to the "autonomy" of Mongolia, Zinoviev warned: "It would be a very sad situation if, among the leaders of revolutionary South China, men should be found . . . so doctrinaire on the Mongolian problem as to put forward the question of returning Mongolia under Chinese rule . . . for as you give so you shall receive." [18] With this somewhat modified version of the golden rule, intended to illustrate China's need to cease its own imperialism if it would oust foreign imperialism, the Comintern spokesman suggested that China concern herself with Mongolia "only when the revolution will be completely victorious in China." Zinoviev ignored the fact that on November 5, 1921, Russian and Mongolian plenipotentiaries had concluded a treaty in Moscow which implied recognition of Outer Mongolia as a state wholly separate from the Chinese Republic. His involved handling of this matter stemmed from the problems inherent in simultaneously extending Russian control in Chinese territory, wooing Mongolian revolutionaries, and attempting to champion the cause of "revolutionary China" against "foreign imperialism."

In only one respect did Zinoviev take a more conservative position than is generally found in his speeches. Completely reversing his Baku optimism concerning the possibility of "leaping over" the capitalist stage of development, he now pointed out that "China, Korea, and Mongolia are not at fault because they have no industrial proletariat. They cannot immediately leap over several stages of development." [19] This must have come as an unpleasant surprise to those Asians who had followed his earlier flamboyant analysis, for it suggested that there was no short cut to the Communist society.

No argument with Zinoviev's remarks came from the Mongol delegates. Danzan, in his welcoming speech to the Congress, had already lamented Mongolia's suffering under the combined exploitation of Japan and China, concluding: "Thanks to the help of Soviet Russia and its heroic Red Army, Mongolia freed itself from the yoke of foreign exploitation. The liberation of Mongolia is proof of the fact that Soviet Russia is the only liberator of the working people of the East." [20] Such implicit criticism of China together with Zinoviev's direct rebuke of Sun Yat-sen's supporters brought the Kuomintang delegate, Tao, to the rostrum in the first public clash between Communist and Kuomintang representatives. [21]

In accordance with the agenda, three Chinese had spoken

after Zinoviev, none of whom had made any reference to Sun or to the Kuomintang. It is symbolic of the Congress's antipathy to the bourgeoisie that Tao was permitted to give a "supplementary report" only after a special request and floor vote. In the course of his prolonged accolade of Sun and the Kuomintang, Tao denied any pro-American tendencies at Canton, and as for Zinoviev's claim "that there are people who would wish to restore Mongolia to China, I do not think it possible. I know not the sources of Comrade Zinoviev's information, but I wish to think that Comrade Zinoviev was mistaken, for I never heard of such a thing." [22]

Tao was to feel the consequences of his directness in due time. If his previous position at the Congress had been an isolated one, he had done little to improve it. While the Russian delegation considered its response to Tao's challenge, Din Dib, speaking on behalf of revolutionary Mongolia, gave a lengthy diatribe against China's historical oppression of his people. Eschewing Zinoviev's reference to "autonomy," he declared: "The People's Revolutionary Party aims at the complete liberation of Mongolia. . . . In the domain of international relations, the Government of Free Mongolia concluded a treaty with Soviet Russia in November, 1921, which recognizes the sovereign rights of the State of Mongolia." [23] As for the Peking government, Din characterized it as "the reactionary bourgeois Chinese Republic—the so-called 'most democratic state of the East.'" In a postscript to his prepared speech, the Mongol delegate took note of Tao's comments on Mongolia, concluding: "We . . . sincerely and joyfully welcome the declaration made by Comrade Tao, the representative of the ruling party of China [*sic*], because we find therein the vindication of our hopes and aspirations . . . that Mongolia will find a common language with the workers of democratic China as it has with socialist Russia."

Rather than risk a direct clash between the head of the Comintern and a Kuomintang spokesman, with all that it might imply for the avowed policy of supporting bourgeois movements in Asia, the Russian delegation took another tack. Leaving rebuttal of Tao's remarks to a later speech by Safarov, Zinoviev welcomed the clarification made by the Kuomintang speaker, apologizing again for his "scanty information" on South China. Immediately thereafter the Comintern leader moved on to a new argument, implicitly prodding the Kuomintang to a more radical position. After declaring that South China might not be able to wait longer to amass its forces against the North, because of Allied support of Peking, Zinoviev made an impassioned appeal for the principle of peasants' soviets. "Those Chinese parties which consider themselves the true followers of democracy must discard the old democratic watchword . . . and must declare themselves in favor of the true people's power, the Soviet system, even in such places where these Soviets will be pre-eminently peasant Soviets." [24]

It remained for Safarov to assume the role of disciplinarian, both for the Kuomintang delegate and for the Chinese Communists present. First, he declared that Zinoviev had been "quite right in saying . . . certain circles politically connected, more or less, with the Government of South China [had] many American sympathizers." [25] Secondly, he urged the Chinese comrades to work among the peasant masses, advocating a single-tax program and nationalization of land. This was necessary because

The Chinese labor movement is still in swaddling clothes, and we know perfectly well that in the near future it cannot take the commanding position assumed by the Japanese workers. . . . At the same time we must state definitely that the Chinese workers must go independently on their own way, not linking their fate with any democratic party or with any bourgeois elements. We know perfectly well that in the immediate future there can be no sharp conflicts between us and these bourgeois democratic organizations . . . but if they should limit the development of proletarian class-consciousness, we shall oppose them completely.[26]

There was little left in Safarov's speech of Lenin's emphasis upon *supporting* bourgeois-liberation movements, and the entire address closely paralleled Safarov's earlier article in the Comintern journal wherein he had aligned himself wholeheartedly with Roy's antibourgeois attitude.

At this point the Korean delegate seconded Zinoviev's remarks, paraphrasing his reference "about some simple-minded South Chinese leaders who find it difficult to rid themselves of a sneaking regard for America. Comrade Tao, feeling offended, has replied [to the contrary]. . . . We cannot but welcome his remarks." [27] Such thinly veiled sarcasm prompted Tao to the rostrum a second time, now to challenge not only Zinoviev but Safarov as well. Answering Safarov's proposed program for the Chinese revolution, Tao declared: "These very ideas were laid down as a foundation by the Kuomintang twenty years ago. There are some differences to be sure, but on the whole these points fully coincide." [28] In a long, detailed defense of the Kuomintang, he expressed resentment on the Congress's according Japan first place in the Asian liberation movement and tempered his general "approval" of Safarov's speech with "regret" that he "did not make his report complete by inclusion of the Mongolian question."

A veritable storm broke around the head of the Kuomintang delegate as questions from the floor demanded the number of proletariat in the Kuomintang—Tao replied he did not know exactly—and for details on how the Kuomintang advocated land nationalization—Tao dodged by saying it was still too early to spell out the program. Kolokov, presiding officer, announced receipt of a note from the floor denying Tao's assertion that the Shanghai Industrial Workers' Union had Kuomintang affiliations and ruled further discussion out of order with the request that additional questions be answered at sectional conferences. In response to a query concerning this curtailment of Tao's time in contravention of the Congress's rules, Shumiatsky as secretary gave an ambiguous reply. The meeting adjourned until evening.[29]

At the next session Safarov returned to the attack in no uncertain terms. "We are not so naive as to imagine this Party [the Kuomintang] is a revolutionary communist party . . . as to be mistaken as to the origin of this Party." [30] Returning to the theme of the Second Comintern Congress, he agreed to "support any bourgeois-democratic movement in colonial and semicolonial countries as long as it is actually directed at the national liberation of the oppressed peoples, but of course we cannot call this movement exactly the same as one which is a proletarian movement." Moving from his general assault to more specific points, Safarov rebutted Tao's contention that the Kuomintang program resembled in any way that proposed by the Comintern. If Tao believed the Kuomintang had been advocating soviets for twenty years, "he is not well acquainted with the principles of the soviet system." As for land nationalization, why wait until all of China is won—do it now and set an example for the peasantry! [31] Even if Tao's points had theoretical validity, "It is not enough to advocate this program in a small circle of so-called educated society." In short, "I contradict Tao's statement." Safarov reiterated his demand for a three-point program in China: (1) organization and agitation so that the soviet system might gain roots among the masses, (2) struggle against imperialism, and (3) ousting of native usurers in the villages and bourgeoisie in the cities.

Safarov omitted nothing. He declared Mongolia outside the confines of his remarks because it was dominated by patriarchal cattle-raising, because the "right elements" were now in power there, and finally, because Zinoviev had said all there was to be said on this matter. As for Tao's jealousy of Japan's revolutionary role: "Without a proletariat movement in Japan, none of the Far Eastern countries can achieve their emancipation. . . . Japan is the best organized and strongest force. Organization is an outcome of industrial development and factory life." Safarov repeated his readiness to support the Chinese bourgeoisie, "bourgeois to the very marrow," but insisted on full independence for the Communist movement, warning the Kuomintang not to "substitute for its [the Kuomintang's] ideals, radical democratic ideals painted in Soviet colors." [32]

Tao's position was not an enviable one. Not only did he serve as the target of antibourgeois sentiments, but he heard no eulogy of Sun Yat-sen, no glowing descriptions of Canton and the southern government. The bitterness of Safarov's words may have been more revealing of Comintern feeling than had been intended, for the official summary of the Congress in the Comintern newssheet shifted the emphasis of discussion considerably:

Revolutionists must not adopt the false position that it is necessary to support only the proletarian movements in the colonies. . . . [The] linking up of the class-conscious proletariat with the eager revolutionary non-proletarian elements was not only laid down as an abstract demand, but was also worked out in all its details. The inclusion of the broad masses of the peasants was exhaustively treated, with consideration for the hegemony of the proletariat in the general revolutionary movement.[33]

This analysis conflicts with the day-to-day accounts of the Congress in the Soviet press, and was either an implied rebuke to Safarov or an attempt to conceal the fact that the Comintern leaders cared little for working with bourgeois groups, Lenin's theses to the contrary notwithstanding. This latter interpretation seems more probable in view of Zinoviev's remarks and considering the other obvious distortions in the summary. Nowhere had the Congress "exhaustively treated" the peasant issue. Except for slogans on a single tax and nationalization, the Comintern spoke of the Chinese peasantry in general terms. In many instances, open suspicion of the peasantry was voiced. Similarly, the Congress had wasted little breath on so-called "eager revolutionary non-proletarian elements." Zinoviev's grudging concession to Tao's criticisms was the only bouquet tossed in a "non-proletarian" direction.

The First Congress of Toilers of the Far East threw into sharp relief the gulf separating radical Communists from Kuomintang spokesmen.[34] No Lenin appeared at the meeting to bridge this gulf. Safarov's lip service to the Second Comintern Congress theses carried little conviction in view of his scathing attack on all Tao had said. Zinoviev's juggling of the Mongolian issue likewise did little to clear up the ambiguity of Soviet actions in that area, while the frankly anti-Chinese tirades of the Mongol delegates augured ill for revolutionary solidarity in the Far East.[35] Perhaps these factors impelled the Comintern to de-emphasize this Congress, as it had the earlier one at Baku. Indeed, the report to the Executive Committee consisted of a brief two-page summary on the Congress's activity, made by Safarov.[36] In the abridged Russian account of the Congress, references to Kuomintang-Comintern conflict were removed, but favorable references to Sun Yat-sen and the Chinese bourgeoisie were handled cautiously.[37] The First Congress of Toilers of the Far East portrayed in microcosm the basic dilemma facing Soviet policies in China, a dilemma that was to prove increasingly important after Lenin's death.

VI

Comintern Comments on China: 1922–1924

ZINOVIEV'S complaint that Comintern policy-makers were badly informed on South China is difficult to verify, but the readers of *Kommunisticheskii Internatsional* certainly had little to draw upon when discussing events in China. Before mid-1922, no detailed descriptions of Chinese social or political conditions appeared. All previous articles followed the pattern of general propaganda statements or Marxist analyses based on a priori assumptions. In August, 1922, the need for increased information about China at the time of Adolf Joffe's Narkomindel mission to Peking saw a shift in emphasis from Europe to Asia. Lengthy accounts appeared covering the Chinese trade union movement, the war-lord factions, and events in South China. No effort was made to gloss over the discouraging facts of the situation. On the contrary, the general antibourgeois slant of Comintern writers made Sun Yat-sen's prospects seem even darker than they actually were, bad as his political fortunes appeared at the time.

Maring, the Dutch revolutionist who had attempted to smooth over differences at the Second Comintern Congress concerning Lenin's proposed support for Asian bourgeois movements, contributed a lengthy, well-informed article to *Kommunisticheskii Internatsional* on South China.[1] Based on his personal contacts with both Sun Yat-sen and Chinese Communist leaders, Maring's analysis revealed serious obstacles in the path of the Chinese revolution.[2] Sharply critical of Sun's economic and political philosophy, he termed "naive" the hope that foreign powers would permit China to solve its internal problems without outside intervention. Maring noted that although the Kuomintang spoke words of socialism, it relied on means of militarism and failed to arouse the masses. His barbs were not reserved for Kuomintang leaders, however, as indicated in his attack upon the apathy of all Chinese intellectuals, "including even those who call themselves Marxists." As a corrective to their impotent inactivity, the Comintern spokesman advised the Chinese Communists to enter trade union work in South China, then under Kuomintang influence, in order to "shift the whole movement to the left."

The general tenor of Maring's article, while critical of the Kuomintang, focused on improving Communist relations with Sun Yat-sen in opposition to the many militarist cliques in China. Maring did not write antibourgeois strictures as did many of his Comintern colleagues; in this sense he followed his advice of the Second Congress and agreed with Lenin's theses. It is significant, however, that nowhere in his lengthy analysis did he stress Chinese peasant problems, but, on the contrary, paid particular attention to trade union activity. Only in this sense did Maring depart from Lenin's theses and remain in general agreement with other Comintern writers. His role as Comintern courier to the Chinese Communist Party in 1921–22 may explain why one part of Lenin's 1920 program received more implementation in China than did another during the early years.[3]

In view of Maring's remarks at the Second Comintern Congress, his articles in *Kommunisticheskii Internatsional,* and his efforts to bring the Chinese Communist Party into closer relation with the Kuomintang, there seems little doubt that he was a persistent advocate of Lenin's policy within the Comintern, as opposed to that of Zinoviev, Safarov, and Roy. All agreed that in general some support of bourgeois movements was necessary and that such support should not preclude a separate Communist Party with independent discipline and program. However, their difference in point of emphasis was crucial. Whereas Lenin and Maring continually stressed the positive features of Sun's regime, making the alliance as palatable and durable as possible and deprecating any speed-up of the Chinese revolution, Zinoviev, Safarov, and Roy featured the negative aspects of the Canton regime, constantly referring to the time when the Chinese bourgeoisie could be overthrown and smashed. For one group, it was "support but remain separate"; for the other, "remain separate but support—if necessary." [4]

In an anonymous report to the Executive Committee of the Comintern, made in August, 1922, a similarly pessimistic evaluation of the picture emerged from a review of the first year's activity of the Chinese Communist Party, 1921 to 1922. [5] The writer complained that because Chinese politics were controlled completely by foreign powers, "the social classes now in process of formation do not exercise any direct political influence." Sun Yat-sen's "important" movement had failed to arouse the peasants, but the Communists had also failed to develop an agrarian program "because of the complexity of their [the peasants'] situation." Workers in Shanghai were hampered by "ancient medieval conditions" and hence were unable to organize as successfully as in Canton. Responsibility for poor labor organization also rested with the Chinese Communist Party, because "our comrades have not yet succeeded in making contact with the working masses. They carry on a sectarian activity which they excuse by the pretext of illegality." With this rebuff, the Chinese Communists were advised to concentrate their activites in Canton, assisting in the struggle between "Southern liberals and Northern reactionaries." As for Peking, it was written off as a hopeless area, lacking the nucleus of a workers' movement, surrounded by backward peasants, and permeated with inactive intellectual Socialists. It was a discouraging picture presented to the Comintern leaders in 1922.

At this same time, an even more devastating analysis of condi-

tions was sent by I. Maisky from Harbin, sufficiently black to
dampen the most enthusiastic of revolutionary ardors. Each group
in China was covered with the blistering criticism characteristic
of Comintern columnists. The peasantry was characterized by
"crass ignorance, proverbial resignation, the influence of . . . religion which teaches . . . forbearance." [6] The proletariat numbered "two–three percent of the population . . . primarily
unskilled . . . little class-consciousness . . . not as yet an active
political force." The bourgeoisie remained "weak . . . still
largely provincial, has no consciousness of national interests
. . . politically passive." Chinese bureaucracy "has no political
character and is ready to serve anyone who is willing to pay it."
As for the military, the writer noted: "Indifference and passivity
are the chief characteristics of Chinese society, which means that
any active organized force can easily rule this country. In China,
this force is the army." Concluding with a description of foreign
intervention, all of China's confused political crosscurrents were
swept aside in the generalization, "We may say that there are no
purely Chinese movements in the political life of present-day
China."

Dangerous implications underlay the comment that "any active
organized force can easily rule this country," for it suggested that
a small, determined, highly disciplined group could seize power
without bothering with mass support or a popular uprising. The
putschist tactic was not unknown in Communist circles, and
Maisky's comment may have stirred the impatient imagination
of more than one radical reader. The sentence immediately following these words—"In China, this force is the army"—was
not lost upon Soviet strategists, as will be seen in the following
chapter. General Wu Pei-fu, war lord *extraordinaire,* was regarded by the Narkomindel with considerable favor as a pro-
spective ally in the Chinese revolution. Thus while the Communists did not pursue the suicidal tactic of attempting to seize
Peking by means of a conspiratorial *coup d'état,* they were not

so steeped in principles of class warfare as to ignore Maisky's remarks of "any active organized force."

The only encouraging event reported in Comintern pages in this early period was the Hong Kong mechanics' strike of 1922. In an outburst of resentment against British shipowners, more than nine thousand Chinese staged the first large-scale strike in South China. As grist for the anti-British propaganda mill, the strike was appropriately exploited by Comintern writers. Voitinskii, high in the Third International hierarchy, hailed the awakening of the proletariat in the struggle for national liberation.[7] Assistance had come from workers far from Hong Kong, showing the breakdown of provincial attitudes. Although the Kuomintang had also helped the strikers, the bourgeoisie "already lack the initiative in this struggle which they had held in 1919." Voitinskii refused to allow his readers to be misguided by Canton's sympathetic attitude toward the strike, claiming that the southern government had already revealed its truly antilabor policy in strikes directly prejudicial to Chinese bourgeois interests. As evidence, he cited the printers' strikes and the work stoppages in the salt mines, both of which had been broken by the Canton regime. Because of these actions the Congress of Trade Unions in Canton had refused to recognize Sun Yat-sen's government in May, 1922.[8] Voitinskii concluded that while the bourgeoisie was losing its grip on labor, the Chinese Communists were changing their "intellectual Marxist circles" into "genuine workers' organizations."

This single article struck a small note of hope against a chorus of pessimistic Comintern commentaries on China, and it was amid these discouraging descriptions of the Chinese revolution that the Fourth World Congress of the Communist International convened in November, 1922. Even more disturbing than events in Asia were those in Soviet Russia itself. Since the Third Congress, the first Party purge had rocked the Bolshevik hierarchy. It had failed to still discontent and criticism of the New Economic Policy, but it had shaken the confidence of many Communists who had previously felt free to debate Party policy within the limits prescribed by the 1919 Party statutes.[9] Just when strong leadership was most necessary, Lenin suffered a serious stroke on May 26, 1922. He recovered in the fall, but could no longer shoulder the burden of responsibility for the myriad problems confronting Soviet Russia. Commissar Chicherin was given increased power over foreign policy decisions. His last conference with Lenin on these matters concerned the preparations for the conference of Lausanne, scheduled to be held in the fall of 1922. Except for Lenin's instructions to the Russian delegation at the Moscow Disarmament Conference in late 1922, the architect of the Russian revolution took no further part in the formulation of foreign policy.[10] His inability to resolve differences among his colleagues concerning the Chinese revolution became more important as he withdrew from the scene.

In November, 1922, the Fourth Comintern Congress met in Moscow, providing the last full-scale debate on policy in China before Lenin's death in January, 1924.[11] It was not an auspicious moment for the Chinese Communist Party, which could claim only 300 members, of whom 180 had paid dues, in a county of some 400 million inhabitants.[12] Ch'en Tu-hsiu, celebrated Chinese scholar and founder of the Chinese Communist Party, attended the meeting, but all speeches were handled by another delegate, Liu Jen-ching.[13]

As Zinoviev remarked in his opening report, the past year had seen the establishment of "a more or less strong nucleus in Turkey, China, and Egypt. Of course, illusions are not nourished as a result—this is a very small nucleus."[14] Zinoviev's speech added nothing new to his previous utterances, claiming that the struggle in the world was twofold, to broaden the working-class movements and to lead "all liberating antibourgeois movements."[15] He stressed that while the colonial revolutions were neither communist nor socialist in character, they were still of "first-rate importance in the struggle against the capitalistic regime."

Bukharin made a few pointed comments, demanding that a "much larger place" be given the colonial problems and laying stress on the revolutionary reserves of the East.[16] However, it was Roy once again who seized the banner of colonial revolution and held it high. In a vigorous attack upon the failure of the European proletariat to provide the assistance which had been promised at the Second Comintern Congress, Roy charged his colleagues with indulging in uncritical generalizations on Asia, with ignoring the different levels of development of various countries. He classified colonial and semicolonial revolutions under three groupings, but failed to specify which countries fell in each classification. However, he was quite specific in his treatment of three major issues—the bourgeoisie, the role of imperialism in backward areas, and the peasantry. On all three points he introduced important revisions in his views as expressed in his supplementary theses of 1920, generally following the criticisms voiced by Lenin at that time.

Whereas previously Roy had demanded that the exclusive aim of the Communist International should be the establishment of Communist parties as antibourgeois cadres, now he declared:

We know that the national struggle cannot develop in the people a recognition of their political independence while the social structure and economy is tied up in a feudalistic-patriarchal system; while the bourgeoisie does not head the society, the national struggle cannot reveal all its revolutionary possibilities. Thus, in all these countries the national struggle is strengthened proportionate to the development of the bourgeoisie. Therefore, although we know that there is always the danger of a compromise of the colonial bourgeoisie with the imperialist bourgeoisie, we always must insist in principle that the bourgeois nationalist movement in colonial countries is objectively revolutionary and therefore has a right to our support." [17]

Roy's attitude was much more favorable toward the bourgeoisie than at any previous time, although he did not let this group escape without a warning on its limitations. The bourgeois struggle was "not class war, but war within one class," because it was directed merely against foreign imperialism and not against feudal remnants. When it came to discussing concrete ways to assist the bourgeoisie in its fight for independence while at the same time preparing for the overthrow of the bourgeoisie in the future proletarian-peasant revolution, Roy dodged the question. He apologized that "lack of time" prevented him from filling in such important details.

Roy's second change of heart concerned the role of imperialism in the economic development of colonial areas. Previously he had maintained that the European countries sought to restrict the advancement of colonial and semicolonial countries by driving them into an ever increasing dependency on agriculture. Now he termed such reasoning "mechanical" and chided those who supported it. As evidence to the contrary, he claimed that Britain had encouraged industry in India because she could no longer maintain superiority over European competitors on the strength of British industry alone. Britain hoped to find new markets in Indian industry for its production of capital goods, and, according to Roy, the increased purchasing power of Indian workers was expected to multiply immeasurably the demand for such consumer goods as cotton clothing.

Roy's third revision of his earlier theses concerned the problem of the peasantry. Although he had always given a perfunctory nod to the "joining" of the peasant and proletarian revolutions, he had never attached much importance to the countryside. Now Roy described vividly how vast masses of peasants and workers could "tear the land from the hands of the present leaders." [18] The peoples of the backward countries would rise against imperialistic capitalists and native feudalists simultaneously. Roy's shift of emphasis from proletariat to peasantry was not a temporary one. In 1927 he was to figure prominently in the effort to press upon the Chinese Communist Party the adoption of a policy of peasant armies and of village soviets.

Thus were the differences between Lenin and Roy appreciably lessened by 1922. Roy was not yet in full agreement with Lenin's views on these three fundamental points. The Indian radical seemed to parrot the Russian leader rather than develop detailed bases for his new views. This tendency was evident in his remark, "We can well utilize the bourgeois-revolutionary parties." [19] While advocating a united front in which Communist parties were to attain control, Roy did not make clear the absolute necessity of such a tactic, as had Lenin. On the contrary, his wording suggested that such a tactic might be advantageous but it might also be discarded in favor of something else.

Much more revealing and explicit was the declaration of the Chinese speaker on this very point of bourgeois collaboration. Liu Jen-ching called for the joining of the Kuomintang and Communist movements, not merely on grounds of "utility," but through sheer necessity. Substantiating Zinoviev's earlier comments about the "nucleus" which then represented the total strength of the Chinese Communist Party, Liu warned:

If we do not join this party [Kuomintang] we shall remain isolated; we shall preach a Communism which is certainly a great ideal but which the masses cannot follow. The masses would rather follow the petit-bourgeois party, which would use them for its own purposes. If we do join the party we shall be able to show the masses that we favor revolutionary democracy, but that for us, revolutionary democracy is only a means to an end. Furthermore, we shall be able to point out, that while we fight for the still far-distant goal, we can still work for the everyday demands of the masses. We can rally the masses around us and split the Kuomintang.[20]

Put bluntly, Liu's words admitted that the Chinese Communist Party would remain a mere splinter group, incapable of winning mass support for its Marxist program unless it "joined" the Kuomintang. Yet how literal was the "joining" to be? Lenin's words spoke of "support" for the bourgeois-liberation movements in Asia. The tactic of forming a "bloc without" permitted complete separation yet cooperation between the bourgeois and proletarian parties. Marxist analysis described political parties as representative of differing economic classes; thus, separation of the

Communist and the Kuomintang membership was the logical theoretical tactic. Liu's words, however, permitted a different interpretation based on a logical practical tactic. By joining the Kuomintang as members, forming a "bloc within," the Communists could
gain control of the only organization capable of attracting mass
support, and at the same time they could prepare for the eventual
destruction of the bourgeois leadership in the Chinese revolution.
No Marxist reasoning is presented by Liu; his approach is purely
pragmatic.

Liu's words broached a new interpretation of Lenin's 1920
theses, at least for the Comintern at large. Within the higher
echelons of the world revolutionary organization, however, the
policy had been discussed for some time. As early as August,
1922, Maring overrode the objections of Ch'en Tu-hsiu and advised the Chinese Communists to join the Kuomintang as individuals while keeping intact a separate Chinese Communist
Party organization.[21] Maring's advice aroused sharp opposition
within the Chinese Communist Party, paralleling the hostility
Lenin experienced when advocating support for the bourgeoisie,
and accounts differ as to the degree of pressure exerted to win
acceptance in China of Comintern strategy. That the policy was
presented to the Congress as something to be discussed and debated even though, unknown to most delegates, it was already
operative, testifies to the deep resistance of the Comintern against
working with bourgeois groups. Even Roy was unable to still
his suspicions of the bourgeoisie, as noted in his remarks preceding Liu's speech: "This united front . . . cannot be organized
under the leadership of a bourgeois party." [22]

It remained for Karl Radek to apply the oratorical whip to the
reluctant comrades. Addressing himself directly to the Chinese
delegates, he chided them for failing "to associate themselves
with the working masses. . . . Many of our comrades out there
locked themselves up in their studies and studied Marx and Lenin
as they had once studied Confucius." [23] Lest they think his two-
point program of organizing workers and improving relations

with "the revolutionary bourgeoisie" was all-inclusive, Radek advised the Chinese Communist Party to go "not only to the workers, but also to the peasant masses." [24] This word of warning might have sufficed to guide the Asian organizations had it not been offset by the Comintern statements already referred to which deprecated the revolutionary potentialities of the peasantry and which praised those shown by the proletariat.

Radek's following words were highly significant for Communists in Europe as well as Asia. The majority of delegates to the Fourth Congress were Western radicals to whom the inability of the German workers to raise the Red flag had come as a bitter disappointment. If the financial chaos and political turmoil of 1922 was unable to spawn a proletarian revolution in Germany, what could be expected in Great Britain and France where stabilizing forces were in the ascendancy? Yet the Third International was loath to give up its revolutionary hopes in Europe and to turn elsewhere to tasks of far greater complexity and of far less promise. Radek's challenge at this point was more than mere exhortation. It signaled a new emphasis in Comintern policy, a shift of Communist efforts from West to East:

Comrades, the world situation at the time of the Second Congress was entirely different. The majority of delegates then counted on the immediate appearance of revolutions in the West; now we are in a period of gathering revolutionary strength. We must activate this tendency in the countries of the East. . . . Therefore the slogan of this Congress must be: to the long-suffering masses of the East! . . . We must be not only the nucleus of the future workers' party but also must become the true people's [*narodnyi*] party in the East.[25]

In the light of subsequent world history, these words carry a prophetic ring.

Many pages of resolutions were adopted by the Fourth Congress of the Third International, including endless repetition and elaboration of the fundamental 1920 theses on Asian revolutions. Communism brought neither brevity nor clarity into political propaganda, and in this it shares at least one sin in common with bourgeois political movements. Only a few particulars in the resolutions need be mentioned here.

Intricate verbal formulae were concocted in an effort to solve new problems with old theorems. When a wholly unorthodox situation was faced, as in Outer Mongolia where Lamaist priests and native princes formed a small but effective ruling class over a nomadic people, particularly novel "Marxist" resolutions resulted:

Only where the feudal-patriarchal tenor of life has not yet deteriorated so as to completely separate the native aristocracy from the mass of the people, as with the nomads and semi-nomads, can the representatives of these groups appear as active leaders in the struggle with imperialist violence (Mesopotamia, Morocco, Mongolia).[26]

Another section devoted completely to agrarian revolutions omitted all reference to China. It seems highly improbable that this was accidental, particularly in view of the detailed treatment given to India, Persia, and Egypt, as well as the listing of countries to which the resolution presumably applied. Whatever may have been the reason for China's omission from the agrarian thesis, the net result was to place all emphasis upon the newborn Chinese proletariat, despite the words of Bukharin and Radek advocating the contrary.

Where China was specifically mentioned, the resolutions were couched in a cautious, and toward the bourgeoisie, hostile, tone. Such was the warning to all Asian Communists to guard against political groups which "exploit the moral-political authority of Soviet Russia . . . and clothe their bourgeois-democratic tendencies in socialist and communist form . . . (state socialism proposed by several representatives of the Kuomintang Party in China)."[27] The Bolsheviks were not going to let any group in China ride to power on the coattails, as it were, of Russia's success simply by claiming friendship and admiration of the Russian revolution. There were other dangers against which the Chinese Communists were warned. They were to be on the alert for possible "bargains between bourgeois nationalism and one of several hostile imperialist powers." Russian strategists had much to fear from such "bargaining." At the very least, it would increase the non-Russian influences shaping a new China. At the worst, it might result in the complete exclusion of Soviet ideas and ideology.

Had the Comintern resolution stopped here, it would have been clear and explicit. However, an additional section sanctioned such "bargains" with "imperialist powers" under circumstances so vague as to confuse rather than clarify tactics in Asia:

Recognizing the admissibility and necessity of partial and temporary compromises with the aim of getting respites in the revolutionary-liberation struggle with imperialism, the working class must with all its irreconcilability push against the efforts of obvious or hidden divisions of power between imperialists and native ruling classes in the aim of preserving the privileges of the latter classes.[28]

Here was Lenin's old concept of the *peredyshka,* the "breathing-spell." If the "temporary compromise" seemed to be a complete capitulation to the imperialist powers, as at Brest-Litovsk, it was to be regarded as merely a short-run tactic which would bring greater returns to the revolution in the future.

Given a group of Lenins in Asia, these resolutions might have been of real value. Since they were read by less sophisticated radicals, however, they meant all things to all men. Tactics were to be governed more by circumstances than by theory. Thus the Communist Party in Asian countries was advised to make "partial demands," embracing purely bourgeois aims, "as long as the relative strength at the present time does not allow it to realize its soviet program." The question of timing became all-important, since support of the bourgeois program was clearly to be a temporary policy, necessitated by the "relative strength" of the Chinese Communist Party compared with the Kuomintang. Rupture of the united front was to be determined solely by the balance of power within the temporary coalition.

These Comintern resolutions on the struggle in Asia show the difficulty of forecasting Communist action or interpreting Com-

munist thought simply by analyzing words and phrases taken
out of the body of literature and polemics which surrounded
them. The 1922 Congress formulated statements that permitted
development of a peasant program yet avoided making agrarian
reform a major point. The directives centering on propaganda
and agitation work among the masses did not exclude a resolution sanctioning alliances with war lords. Reasons for the eventual elimination of patriarchal and feudal princes were given as
well as excuses for permitting their existence.

One thing was missing from the elaborate pronunciamentos
of the Fourth Congress—a clear guide for revolutionary action in
China. As a result, oral directives conveyed by Comintern agents
were necessary to interpret the shadings and turnings of the
over-all line. This made the job of assessing ultimate responsibility for mistakes difficult, if not impossible, while increasing
the confusion that threatened to paralyze Communist efforts in
China.

After the Fourth Congress, the next significant Comintern
commentaries on China followed General Wu Pei-fu's move
against the railroad strikers in February, 1923. The suppression
of this strike on the Peking-Hankow line by mass executions had
far-reaching consequences for the Chinese proletariat. Communist leaders were aware that their Chinese comrades had played
a major role in the formation of the railroad workers' union and
accordingly bore much of the responsibility for calling the ill-
fated strike. This did not prevent Maring from assailing the
strike as a dismal failure.[29] The former Comintern agent in China
voiced a surprisingly un-Marxist lament, concluding that the
venture was disastrous on two counts. First, such mass murders
did nothing to advance the cause of the proletariat, because the
shootings went unreported outside of China and were only briefly
dealt with by Kuomintang papers within China. Secondly, Maring attacked Communist exploitation of the shootings through
ad hoc demonstrations, adding bitterly that even a general strike

"in sympathy" would not restore the martyrs to their families.

Maring's views smacked of "bourgeois sentimentality." No such weakness marked *Pravda's* treatment of the incident. In a lengthy report, accompanied by a blistering denunciation of the shooting from the Executive Committee of the Comintern, a Soviet analyst called for "a ruthless war against the imperialists and their Chinese allies." [30] Demanding "the independence of the proletariat, equally with the support of the bourgeoisie—without it, or against it," he showed an equivocal approach to the Kuomintang. Although he declared it to be "in class content not a bourgeois-led party, but predominantly a unification of petit-bourgeois linking elements, radical intelligentsia, and workers," the writer's many theses identified all Chinese bourgeoisie with war lords and imperialists. In Europe, the bourgeoisie had ousted feudalism and had led progressive forces; in Asia, the bourgeoisie was born of foreign money and remained dependent on it. The proletariat "has no illusions about class co-operation" was his pointed conclusion.

The entire question of the future of the Chinese proletariat, implicit in these articles, was handled with considerable detail at this time by Musin, a writer for *Novyi Vostok*. Complete with statistics on trade union development in China, his article traced the history of union activities in China without attempting to paint the picture in a rosy hue of optimism.[31] Musin vigorously attacked Wu Pei-fu and his alleged American support for the annihilation of the strikers. This action had smashed forever the illusions of the workers in Wu's "democracy." Although Musin asserted, "The Chinese working-movement is not broken," this was more of a gesture to the note of promise traditional in Communist writings than a confident conclusion to his article. For those who had accepted uncritically the comparison of 1922 China with 1905 Russia, he warned that backward conditions in Peking precluded any positive results similar to those achieved by the St. Petersburg uprising.

As though he immediately regretted the objectivity and cruel honesty of this article, Musin wrote a brief, superficial summary for the Comintern journal, surveying the effects of 1922 on the Chinese working class.[32] Perhaps it was written before the full story of the February fiasco was known in Russia, for it was thoroughly optimistic in tone and content. Far more characteristic of the Comintern outlook was a blunt analysis of conditions in China, published in an official handbook covering events in 1923. With scant regard for the efforts of the Chinese Communist Party, it concluded:

Since China is still going through the beginning stage of its capitalistic development, the Chinese proletariat still has not become a class which realizes its social significance. A workers' movement in the real sense of the term, represented by something more than sporadic outbursts, exists only in the South; but even here this movement is limited to the city of Canton. . . . The class-consciousness of the Chinese worker is still weakly developed.[33]

Thus the general theme of the Comintern remained consistent right up to Lenin's death in January, 1924. It emphasized Europe over Asia, it castigated the bourgeoisie generally and particularly in China, and it held little hope for the Chinese proletariat, none for the Chinese peasantry. Not all members of the Third International were of one mind on these points, and with respect to collaboration with the bourgeoisie, they ranged along a spectrum extending from complete, uncompromising opposition to bourgeois movements to united front tactics encouraging Communists to join the Kuomintang as full-fledged members. The largest group, judging from the pages of *Kommunisticheskii Internatsional*, polarized around the opposite end of the spectrum from that occupied by Lenin. How the schisms within the Comintern were reflected in other sectors of the Soviet elite remains to be examined in the following chapters.

VII

Other Voices: Narkomindel and Profintern

BEFORE comparing the less verbose views of the Narkomindel and the Profintern with the voluminous outpourings of the Comintern, it might be well to scan the occasional statements made by Soviet leaders which lacked organizational affiliation. Lenin, alone of the Bolsheviks, seemed always to tower above such connections, yet his writings on the Chinese revolution were few and far between from 1920 to 1924. His comments, considering his role as both theoretician and tactician, appear extended only when compared with the scanty references to China made by Bukharin, Trotsky, and Stalin. If Lenin enlarged upon his views in confidence to these or other Bolsheviks, such confidences were never made public nor where they referred to by the participants in later debates on China. One is forced to conclude that although illness limited much of Lenin's effectiveness during these years, he was actually unwilling to go beyond his 1920 theses on national and colonial problems. In China, the ceaseless machinations of military factions compounded confusion as Peking and Canton continued to tug in opposite directions. In Russia, party schisms and personality clashes loomed increasingly important as the ailing Lenin attempted to retain revolutionary objectives while restraining revolutionary practices. His New Economic Policy with its mixture of capitalism and state socialism brought disillusionment to many of his comrades. Questions of theory, so dear to the

heart of many revolutionaries, fell into disrepute before the on-
slaught of practice.

Small wonder that Lenin's infrequent references to China from
1920 to 1924 were little more than generalized exhortations, similar to many of his prerevolutionary statements. Not only did
China defy analysis, but analysis threatened to become a platform
for polemics as those afflicted with ambition competed for control
within the Soviet elite. Already aware of the conflict between
Trotsky and Stalin, Lenin lacked the energy or the power to resolve it before his death.

That Lenin was aware of internal opposition to his new emphasis on colonial and semicolonial countries is shown in an interesting aside included in a lengthy analysis of the Japanese threat
to China and the "inevitability" of war between Japan and the
United States.[1]

Not long ago the Communist International journal came out under the
slogan "Proletariat and oppressed peoples of the world, unite!" One
of the comrades asked: "When did the Central Committee order the
slogan be changed?" I actually cannot remember it. Of course, from the
viewpoint of the *Communist Manifesto* it is incorrect, but the *Communist Manifesto* was written in entirely different conditions; from
the viewpoint of today, it is correct. Relations have become strained.
All Germany stirs, all Asia stirs. . . . In China there is raging hatred
against the Japanese, also against the Americans.

Lenin's last public references to Asian revolutions continued to
stress the importance of the East. On *Pravda's* tenth anniversary,
Lenin hailed the national-liberation movements of India and
China, where 700 million people were experiencing Russia's
"1905."[2] His only qualification to this historical comparison was
that these countries, unlike Russia, required aid from external
sources in order to complete their "1905." A more detailed article appeared in March, 1923, less than a year before Lenin's
death. Here he attempted to redefine the situations in Europe
and Asia in view of what he saw as the temporary stabilization
of Western capitalism. The capitalist system had prolonged its
life in the West by exploiting the East; it had forestalled the Com-

munist revolution for the immediate future. Now the danger to international Communism lay in the capitalist division of the world on unequal lines, leaving Russia and Germany surrounded by a circle of predatory powers. Lenin held out hope for redressing the disproportionate division of power and accordingly fell back on his familiar emphasis on population rather than industrial production. He confidently predicted:

The outcome of the struggle depends in the end on the fact that Russia, India, China, etc. contain a mighty majority of the population. And precisely this majority of the population is, with unexpected rapidity in recent years, being drawn into the fight for its own freedom, so that in this sense there can be no doubt of the final outcome of the world struggle. In the sense the final victory of socialism is fully and unconditionally secured.[3]

It would be misleading to read too much into Lenin's last words on China to the effect that "the outcome of the struggle depends in the end" on the populations of Asia joining the world revolutionary movement. From a recapitulation of his varying views on China's role in the world revolution, it appears that Lenin's concept of this role never went beyond his views in *Imperialism*. Prior to 1917, Lenin expressed an interest in national movements of Asia, pointing to their similarities and asserting their connection with Russia's 1905 revolution. During World War I, he saw that self-determination would rend asunder the empires held by European capitalists and argued against Rosa Luxemburg for support of these national movements for independence. However, his writings prior to *Imperialism* do not formulate the consequences of revolutions in backward areas except in general terms. In *Imperialism*, Lenin pointed out the colonial and semicolonial countries as sources of "super-profits," funds which bribed the trade union leaders of Europe and prolonged the life of capitalism. At no point in this classic study nor in his subsequent statements did Lenin subscribe to the theory that merely by cutting off the source of raw materials and profits from these areas could the world proletariat overthrow world capitalism.

Lenin's debates with Roy and his insistence that Roy make certain changes in the supplementary theses are dramatic proof that Lenin refused to place revolutions in Asia first on the timetable of Communist strategy. In the terms of his familiar military terminology, the Asian peoples were to serve as the vast reserves for the world revolution. They were to weaken capitalism by denying it further areas of exploitation. This would hasten the triumph of the European proletariat but would not alone bring it about. When Lenin spoke of the "final victory of socialism" as being "fully and unconditionally secured," he was referring to the inability of counterrevolution to draw upon the colonies for troops. Thus the national-liberation movement would be an *additional* assurance that the victory of the world proletariat would be successful. Only by ignoring the previous decade of theorizing could these words be interpreted as indicating Lenin's conviction that colonial revolutions would bring victory to the world proletariat; these revolutions could only help to speed that final moment of victory.

Victory was promised, but when? "Tomorrow" meant one thing on the lips of Lenin, another on those of his successors. Lenin was a persistent person. If circumstances blocked him at one point, he was ready to look for a more favorable opportunity elsewhere. The approaches might be varied, but the goal remained the same. It was this single-mindedness of purpose which sustained him through the many changes in fortune from the small radical gatherings of the 1890's through exile in World War I to final victory within Russia from 1917 to 1924. Those who read his words about "the final victory of socialism" had the precedent of the past upon which to build their faith in the future. Their faith, however, rested largely on the tangible achievements of Lenin. With his death, a reassuring symbol and center of confidence was removed. Scattered as were his writings on Asia, they far outweighed in quantity and quality those of the other Bolshevik leaders. Viewed in this light, the differences of opinion on policy which were evident before his death were forced by circumstances to become centers for political controversy after the gifted leader passed from the scene.

In addition to Lenin, two other Bolshevik leaders have significance in and of themselves, aside from organizational affiliations. The first, Josef Stalin, had little to say on China, but in view of his later role in the Chinese revolution, his few remarks bear mention here. Stalin's Georgian origin, coupled with his lack of familiarity with Europe, helps to explain his concentration on nationality problems of Tsarist Russia and Central Asia, while his comrades continually looked westward for their revolutionary inspiration.[4] Prior to 1917, however, Stalin's focus centered exclusively on problems within the Russian border whenever he dealt with "Asian problems." One year after the revolution, in a lengthy review of the impact of the November events on nationality problems, he turned to the larger question near the very end of his article, remarking: "The oppressed colonies and semicolonies, looking with hope at Russia [are] already organizing their own soviets of deputies (India-China!)." [5]

Within a few weeks, Stalin again called his comrades' attention to the fact that while admittedly Europe was the primary area of struggle with world capitalism, there was still Asia "with its hundreds of millions, suffering under imperialism." [6] Following Lenin's familiar views, Stalin noted that while capitalists babbled about Europe, they never ceased thinking about China, India, and Persia, with their "inexhaustible reserves" of man power and resources. He concluded:

The task of Communism—to smash the centuries-old lethargy of the Asian peoples, to infect the workers and peasants of these countries with the liberating spirit of revolution, to raise them to struggle with imperialism and in this manner to deprive world imperialism of its "secure" rear line, of its "inexhaustible" reservoir. Without this there can be no thought of the final triumph of socialism, of complete victory over imperialism.

Stalin's last words here seem to anticipate those of Roy at the Second Comintern Congress, making success in Europe contin-

gent upon success in Asia. Aside from the ambiguity of the phrase
"the final triumph of socialism," it should be noted that Stalin's
words at this point appear more as propaganda than as sober reflections on theory. Writing as Commissar of Nationality Affairs
immediately after the First Congress of Moslem Communists,
held in Moscow, he made sweeping exhortations which were
quite in order, if admittedly overstated. Bolshevik orators traditionally told each audience that *it* held the key to the future
of the world proletariat, when generally the orators believed that
they *themselves* had the greatest possibility of leading the world
revolution to victory. Stalin does not seem to have repeated his
statement at any other point prior to Lenin's death.

Stalin's later references to "the East" were no more specific
than the above quotations and never referred to China directly
before 1924. In this he was in line with many Bolsheviks whose
interest in Asian affairs centered primarily on Central Asia. In
part this stemmed from Soviet preoccupation with winning control of the vast Moslem population living within the former borders of the Russian Empire but having little sympathy for Bolshevik ideology. In part it stemmed from the leading role Great
Britain assumed, not only in world imperialism, but also in foreign
intervention during the civil war. The logical counterattack lay
through Britain's sphere of influence in Turkey, Persia, and Afghanistan—even India, should the possibility arise. It would be
highly misleading to assume that all Soviet references to "Asia"
and "the East" during these years included China, even by implication. Particularly is this true of Stalin's writings.

The other leading Bolshevik concerned with Asian problems
was Nicolai Bukharin, prominent theoretician of the Russian
Communist Party. His most important address on political and
economic conditions in China was delivered at the Twelfth Party
Congress in 1923, one month after Lenin's final article, quoted
above. From the content of the speech, it appears likely that much
of it was worked out privately with the ailing Lenin. Certainly
the anti-British tone was that of Bukharin, but the emphasis upon

collaboration with the bourgeoisie and development of an agrarian policy in China smacked strongly of Lenin. With none of the customary cautious qualifications, Bukharin praised the forces of Sun Yat-sen, scolding his Russian comrades for their. defeatist scepticism over the Kuomintang's possibilities.[7] He refuted those who claimed that all political groupings in China were identical since all depended on military force, declaring: "In history this has not been and is not possible. This has never happened and this cannot be." Bukharin analyzed the all-inclusive character of Kuomintang principles which attracted all classes in China. His conclusions were identical with those drawn by Lenin in 1920. "In such a state of things, in a country whose petit-bourgeoisie exceeds ten times the petit-bourgeoisie of Russia, it would be unthinkable to break with the Kuomintang Party, at whose head stands Sun Yat-sen. On the contrary, the duty of communists is to form an all-revolutionary bloc." As with Lenin, the united front tactic was obligatory; no other course was possible. For Bukharin, "the revolutionary soil" in China had to be used as the Communists found it, not as they wished it to be.

Although Bukharin's statistics were inaccurate, his skillful outline of peasant conditions in China put many previous commentators to shame. There was no mistaking his meaning when he described the peasants as "the most powerful revolutionary stream in quantity . . . the gigantic reserve of revolutionary infantry." [8] His comrades might praise the "quality" of the Chinese proletariat, but the "quantity" which was vital to the revolution lay with the Chinese peasantry. Lenin could have found no quarrel here.

Bukharin closed his speech with a rapid survey of the years of foreign intervention in China and their catalytic effect on the revolutionary movements there. As always, his concise, schematic analysis showed the brilliant powers of organization at the command of one of the Bolsheviks' leading theoreticians. His descriptions of the petit-bourgeois forces at work in China coupled with his advice on the peasantry proved amazingly accurate considering the heavy burden of European problems which must have occupied his attention. In his final words, Bukharin returned once more to the theme of the united front in China. "That is the job of the Communists. The reserves are great; the significance colossal!"

NARKOMINDEL

Although the examination of Soviet diplomacy in China will take up the second half of this study, a review of Narkomindel writings at this point is necessary for a comparison of the differing theoretical views of leading groups within the Soviet hierarchy. In any society, divisions exist between civil and military authorities, and among civil authorities themselves. Conflicts of interest combine with conflicts of personality. Prestige rivalries are masked behind debates on policy and practice. All this was doubly true in Soviet Russia, where the leader's illness touched off an early jockeying for power among his followers. An added complication was the competition for policy determination between the Comintern and the Narkomindel. One was organized for conducting international revolutions; one was organized for conducting international relations. The Comintern was not an official representative of the Soviet government, yet its headquarters were in Moscow, its personnel were Russian-directed, and its agents often operated through accredited Soviet embassies abroad. The Narkomindel was not an instrument officially designated as the bearer of world revolution, yet Chicherin's 1918 letter to Sun Yat-sen showed his willingness to conduct negotiations with an avowedly revolutionary government in China. Similar unorthodox diplomatic activity was more openly displayed by Adolf Joffe in January, 1923, when he left Peking after fruitless negotiations as the accredited representative of Soviet Russia, to conclude an entente with Sun in Shanghai. Thus the lines of Comintern and Narkomindel activity repeatedly crossed, although a conscious effort was exerted by leaders in both organizations to keep them separate.

At first glance, few contradictions should have presented themselves. Both organizations claimed as basis for theory and action the same writings of Marx, Engles, and Lenin. Both organizations were avowedly promoting the interests of the world proletariat. The Comintern's main advantage lay in its ability to push aside the niceties of diplomacy and to ignore the similarity of strategic interest that linked Soviet Russia with Tsarist Russia. Had the Narkomindel followed its early pattern of conducting diplomacy through propaganda and eschewing all bourgeois techniques, differences in approach might have been eliminated. Once the Narkomindel decided to operate through secret negotiations, to debate about debts with creditor nations, and to seek formal recognition from bourgeois governments, it was compelled to drop its early revolutionary practices and to work under more restricted conditions. More than once Narkomindel officials were undoubtedly embarrassed by their Comintern colleagues, whose sweeping statements antagonized and often angered the very parties with whom the Narkomindel was negotiating.

Essentially, however, the contradictions that arose were more basic than those of approach; they involved contradictions of purpose. Strange wonders were worked on revolutionary Marxists once they became entrusted with Soviet Russia's foreign policy. The Communist International might work for the victory of the world proletariat tomorrow, but today found the world divided among bourgeois states and the struggle for survival demanded that Russia's position be safeguarded. The turn in policy on the Chinese Eastern Railway has already been described, showing how gestures to win sympathy abroad were on occasion scrapped in favor of actions to win control in territories adjacent to Russian soil.

As one instance of the impact of these differing means and ends, the attitude of the two groups concerning Great Britain might be cited. The anti-British orientation of the Comintern was amply evident in the speeches of Zinoviev, Roy, and others. British imperialism held millions of Asians in colonial subjugation. Winston Churchill epitomized to Soviet leaders the reactionary forces who had sought to strangle Bolshevism at its birth by foreign intervention. This line was pursued in China as elsewhere in the Middle and Far East. The Narkomindel, however, soft-pedaled anti-British progaganda in favor of a strongly anti-Japanese policy. *De facto* recognition from Britain had come as early as 1921. In China, British influence was rapidly being replaced by that of Japan. Lenin's strictures on Japanese imperialism, already mentioned, were seconded by Chicherin's warnings of imminent Japanese aggression in the Far East. Lenin commented hopefully in late 1920 that contradictions between Japan and America made a Pacific war "inevitable." [9] In such an event, it would be the task of Russian diplomacy to assure the exclusion of its nearest rival, Japan, from its weakest neighbor, China. There was little Marxist reasoning given for this choice of Japan instead of Britain as the archenemy, or for the choice of America instead of Japan as a possible ally in the Pacific. It was apparently dictated by the same motivations of self-interest that moved diplomats in all quarters of the globe.

Vladimir Vilensky was perhaps the most brilliant Narkomindel writer on the Far East; certainly he was the most experienced. His interpretation of America's role in world affairs contrasted sharply with that of Comintern spokesmen, notably Trotsky's at the Third Comintern Congress. Lenin's continual attack on Japanese imperialism in the Pacific, coupled with his prediction of a war between Nippon and America, implied relative harmlessness toward Russia of the latter power. In was clear that the only major power capable of forcing Japan to retreat from its Siberian adventure was the United States, and there was no denying the hostility to Japan evident in American intervention in that area during the civil war period.[10] Vilensky carried his interpretation of American policy in China to a much further point than had Lenin, however, with some astonishingly prophetic conclusions embodied in the course of several articles. Writing from Peking in anticipation of the Joffe mission in mid-1922, the Narkomindel commentator noted that whereas previously America had called itself the "defender of Chinese interests" while actually safeguarding its own position in China with respect to other powers, now she was moving toward "co-operation with Russia against Japan." [11] He hastened to add that this "co-operation" would not grow into a full-scale alliance because the United States still pursued a sphere-of-interest policy in China, but the implications of his earlier remark were clear. Such provocative speculation was not to be taken for granted, however, in view of the complete absence of diplomatic relations between the two countries and the exclusion of Russia from the Washington Conference of 1921–22.

This was not an isolated instance of partiality toward America. Vilensky pursued his theme in a lengthy piece for the Comintern magazine, specifically naming China's enemies as Great Britain, France, and Japan. China's friends included "Soviet Russia, Germany, and with some reservations, America. . . . China, Soviet Russia, Germany—that is the political scheme for the near future. America will join this grouping somewhat later." [12] Only one year previously, Trotsky had delivered a lengthy attack on American capitalism as the stronghold of world imperialism, yet here was Vilensky predicting that the two outcasts of international society, Russia and Germany, would join hands with the United States to help China against would-be plunderers.

Of course, Vilensky did not attribute America's participation in his grouping of China's friends to the same altruistic motives he attributed to Russia. On the contrary, American loans would be forthcoming to China only because American capitalists needed investments abroad to make use of their surplus capital. Furthermore, America would never supply China with the strong national army it needed because the West "fears the hour when China shows sufficient strength to escort her to the door." Vilensky's implication that this army would be provided by Soviet Russia will be discussed shortly. Here it is only necessary to note that he foresaw the single point of common interest which could bring Russia and America into cooperation in the Far East: Japanese aggression. He also suggested the single point of conflict

which could later split Russia and America apart: Chinese instability. While Japan remained a dominant threat in the Pacific,
Russia and America were in danger of being attacked in their
most vulnerable areas. While China remained dependent on outside help, Russia and America would compete for influence
within the Middle Kingdom. One could provide military aid; the
other could provide financial aid. Vilensky was confident that
eventually Russia's military assistance would supersede America's
financial assistance. If one makes allowance for his inability to
anticipate the rise of Fascism in Germany and its consequent
linking of that country with Japan, Vilensky's analysis was well
substantiated in the subsequent twenty-five years of Far Eastern
events.[13]

To conclude this analysis of Narkomindel views of other powers at work in China, mention must be made of a brief, unex-
plained twist in the approach to American actions. As happens
so frequently in Soviet policy, a drastic reversal of direction occurred for no apparent reason, suggesting that criticism from an
unknown quarter forced a recanting and rewriting of current analyses. Vilensky suddenly scrapped his "soft" approach toward the
United States on the fifth anniversary of the Russian revolution,
in 1922. Terming it Russia's duty to awaken the Asian peoples to
struggle against both Japanese imperialism and American capitalism, he held that American capitalism was the more dangerous
because it plundered and exploited China while masquerading as
a "friend" of "independent China."[14]

No significant event had taken place to cause an anti-American
outburst at this particular time, nor did this theme reappear in
Vilensky's writings. One possible explanation may lie in the frustrated efforts of Narkomindel officials who had been quietly test-
ing the ground for a *rapprochement* with the United States during 1922. Karl Radek expressed himself rather frankly on this
subject, but when Washington ignored or rejected these feelers,
they were withdrawn for the time being.[15] Vilensky's comments
remain as interesting evidence of Narkomindel hopes in 1922.

It might be expected that the Commissariat of Foreign Affairs would be concerned primarily with China's foreign relations, leaving her internal problems to the Comintern, but such was not the case. True, the Narkomindel wrote little on China in 1921, devoting its attention to the thorny problems of reparations, recognition, and debts. Germany and western Europe still occupied the spotlight. Its few commentaries on Sino-Soviet relations will be discussed in a later chapter covering the specific negotiations of the time. However, in 1922, several articles appeared, particularly by Vilensky, which give considerable insight into the Narkomindel's analysis of Chinese society and politics. Again there was considerable variance with Comintern views.

Vilensky's realism and his keen understanding of the facts brought forth clear but discouraging pictures of the Chinese revolution. On the situation of the peasants he was in agreement with his colleagues in the Third International. Only the greatest effort over a long period of time could bring this "extremely inert and immovable" mass into the revolutionary stream.[16] He admitted that some new rays of understanding might penetrate the thick wall of peasant ignorance by participation of peasants in war-lord armies which actually operated against their interests, but essentially this class held little promise for the Bolsheviks, according to Vilensky. In this, Vilensky differed with Lenin's views as expressed in 1920. It was the only difference revealed in his writings, however.

Vilensky dismissed the proletariat with even fewer words, noting that while it was "ripening," it would probably "go its way, differing greatly from the course of the revolutionary European proletariat." [17] Without elaborating on this "different" course, he merely asserted that the distant future belonged to the workers. The absence of any supporting proof left this conclusion without much conviction.

It was for the Chinese bourgeoisie that Vilensky reserved all his attention and praise, in sharp contradiction with writers of the Comintern but in full agreement with Lenin's theses on revolu-

tion in semicolonial countries. Vilensky pointed to the many fears
and limitations that had handicapped this class, admitting that
although the bourgeoisie should have been ready to seize power
in 1911, "it was still in diapers." However, in the following decade
it had developed a genuine class consciousness. Here Vilensky
took issue with a Comintern writer, Ivan Maisky, who had asserted that the Chinese bourgeois groups were unable to think in
terms beyond their own province.[18] The Narkomindel scribe held
that the situation was precisely the contrary, that a nationally
minded bourgeoisie was already evident in China. "The Chinese
bourgeoisie knows that the tomorrow in China belongs to it . . .
*the historical process is leading to the inevitable coming to power
of the Chinese bourgeoisie,* and consequently to what might be
called the completion of the bourgeois revolution in China." [19]

Vilensky was not alone in his sympathetic approach to the Chinese bourgeoisie. Moving from class analysis to political commentary, another Narkomindel writer, A. Khodorov, presented a
lengthy eulogy of Sun Yat-sen and the Canton government under
the Kuomintang administration.[20] Just as Vilensky's confident prediction of bourgeois supremacy was a far cry from the Comintern
diatribes against this class, so Khodorov's appraisal of the Kuomintang was quite opposite from the customary scepticism and
derision found in the writings of the Third International. He gave
special praise to General Ch'en Chiung-ming, Sun's military
leader, who had sent greetings to Lenin in May, 1920, on the
success of the Russian revolution.[21] Of course the Kuomintang
government was bourgeois in its reforms, wrote Khorodov, precisely because this was a bourgeois revolution which was forced
to clear the ground of feudal vestiges in order to build a capitalistic economy. In contrast, he described Peking, with its control
by war lords and foreign interests, as trying to restore China's
decadent past. His criticisms of Peking were undoubtedly sharp-
ened by the disappointing failure of two Soviet missions to win
official recognition for Russia from this "corrupt" and "decadent"
regime in North China.

Again a reversal of the prevailing line must be noted, though unlike Vilensky's change of attitude concerning America, this one can be readily explained. In mid-1922, news reached Moscow of an alleged attempt by Sun Yat-sen to form an alliance with Chang Tso-lin, the Manchurian war lord, against Wu Pei-fu, then in control of Peking. Khodorov did an about-face and submitted Sun to the most devastating criticism given by any Narkomindel correspondent. Lashing at the proposed Sun-Chang entente as an "unholy alliance," Khodorov charged the Kuomintang leader with "using the masses as cannon fodder" and characterized his policy as "adventurism, zigzags, petit-bourgeois hesitation, with the masses yet objectively against the masses." [22] The violence of this attack in contrast with his earlier high praise of Sun may be attributed to Russia's fear that should Sun allow himself to be duped into giving assistance to the Manchurian general, Japan would thereby gain admission into the stronghold of "new China"—the Kuomintang. Once Sun became dependent on such aid, it would be difficult to swing him away from Nippon. After it became clear that the possibility of a Sun-Chang understanding was past, a return to the former Narkomindel line of praising the Kuomintang was evident. No other Narkomindel articles before 1924 dealt in such harsh terms with the government of South China as did this one by Khodorov.

Khodorov, in the same article, proposed a program of action for the Kuomintang which corresponded surprisingly well to later events. Proceeding on the theory that the Kuomintang would remain relatively powerless without the coal and iron resources of Central and North China, he suggested three steps: (1) unite the South; (2) link up with Central China; and (3) conquer the North. Under this scheme, the capital of Kuomintang China would move from Canton to Hankow, and eventually to Peking.

By implication, Khodorov showed a preference for Wu Pei-fu over Chang Tso-lin; certainly his sharpest criticisms were reserved for the Manchurian war lord. Vilensky supported this preference at almost the same time when he wrote that although America had tried to gain a sphere of influence by controlling Wu, the general desired to build a united, independent China and had resisted external ties.[23] A few months later, Vilensky wrote his long article for the Comintern journal, which has already been cited, in which he listed America, Russia, and Germany as "friends" of China. Carrying the favorable references to Wu Pei-fu considerably further in 1922 than at any previous point, Vilensky gave the most systematic development of Narkomindel theory on China. Because of their far-reaching implications and their complete contradiction of views usually found in *Kommunisticheskii Internatsional*, the main points must be examined closely.

Vilensky took issue with the general antimilitarist Comintern line, stating flatly: "At the present moment, as real quantities in the political arena of China, there is the militarized mandarinate and the Chinese bourgeoisie. Only in the most recent times has the Chinese proletariat spoken for itself."[24] "No real parties" existed in China for Vilensky, except possibly the Kuomintang which bore some resemblance to the Social Revolutionaries of Tsarist Russia. Yet essentially the Kuomintang remained an amalgam of groupings with no agrarian program. It had failed to conduct propaganda, to build an organization, and to effect any party discipline. If these criticisms were at variance with Vilensky's earlier analysis in *Novyi Vostok* and presaged a cooling of his enthusiasm for Canton, the reason was immediately evident in his treatment of Wu Pei-fu.

Ignoring Sun Yat-sen completely, the Narkomindel commentator devoted his full attention to General Wu Pei-fu, "who even in the evaluation of the Chinese Communists is considered the best of the militarists." Lest this be construed as damning with faint praise, Vilensky went on to term Wu genuinely nationalistic and strongly opposed to those war lords serving foreign imperialists, i.e., Chang Tso-lin. Furthermore, Wu was under the "close" influence of liberal circles in China, even if admittedly he did stray from their ways occasionally.

Having neatly shifted his position from avowed support of Sun Yat-sen to a somewhat qualified recommendation of Wu Pei-fu, Vilensky then examined the various means at hand for the unification of China. Although the Chinese Communist Party would assuredly lead the proletariat in the distant future, it was "not yet significant." A similar passing reference to the peasantry, "on whose involvement the success of the revolution depends," carried little weight. Only one real hope remained for China's salvation—a national army. While America furnished China with capital, Russia could furnish China with military assistance. The leader of this unifying force would be none other than Wu Pei-fu. Such were the conclusions which necessarily followed from Vilensky's presentation, although they were not spelled out explicitly. It was too soon to reveal quite so clearly the shift from Lenin's "revolutionary cadres" of 1920 to an army under "the best militarist" in 1922, especially in the face of Comintern writings to the contrary.

Vilensky's handwriting on the wall became clearer as time passed and the implications of this new formulation of tactics in the Chinese revolution became evident. It did not spring from any rereading of Marx or new discoveries by Lenin. The Narkomindel desired to negotiate a treaty of recognition with the leading power in China, and that power happened to be Wu Pei-fu. Western writers have speculated at length upon Stalin's role in initiating a shift of emphasis from a mass revolution to the Red Army as the vehicle for Communism in China.[25] However, such a shift was evident long before Stalin's statements of 1925. Vilensky's theory was plainly dictated by necessity, and if Wu required Marxist garb for Russian readers, it would be provided for him, ill-fitting as it might appear. If any systematic theory was developed at this time concerning the use of armed force to win the victory in China, it was not evident in Narkomindel writings. On the contrary, the theory appears to have been worked out after the fact in an *ad hoc* manner. This is supported by Vilensky's press buildup preceding Joffe's unsuccessful mission of 1922–23.

The Narkomindel analyst interviewed Wu personally and reported favorably on his high praise of the Red Army.[26] The general's plans for uniting China on centralistic principles were quoted, as were the statements of Wu's secretary to the effect that the future combination would find China, Russia, and Germany together. This echoing of Vilensky's earlier prediction suggests his anxiety to make the interview completely palatable to his readers back home. The only word of caution was over an unfortunate tendency of this "best militarist" to join hands with heavy industrial interests in Central China.

Not all war lords enjoyed Vilensky's blessing, as shown in his next article which wrote off Chang Tso-lin as an agent of Japanese imperialism.[27] The Manchurian general was a threat to "Republican China"—meaning Wu Pei-fu, *not* Sun Yat-sen. This identification of Wu with republicanism was explicit in the final article of this series, one ostensibly devoted to Sun but actually returning to the initial figure of Wu.[28] While the Kuomintang leader was politely called "the hope of the revolution," his stature was considerably diminished by Vilensky's account of Sun's political failings. Sun remained "outside" class lines because of his inadequate program, and while he might one day become China's great leader, for the immediate future he lacked the power to be in command. In sharp contrast, Vilensky described Wu's strong bourgeois support, his shrewd use of Sun's former slogans, and his fairly widespread control. Thus underlying the Marxist analysis lay a policy of *Realpolitik*. The Narkomindel moved ahead with its efforts to win a favorable relationship with a recognized war lord who wielded considerable power.

Vilensky had now cleared the way for developing a theory of a "bourgeois revolution" in China revolving around Wu Pei-fu. The Sun-Joffe entente of January, 1923, passed without comment in the Soviet press, but at this time Vilensky wrote a favorable commentary on Sun and predicted an entente between Sun and Wu.[29] As a clear indication of where the locus of power lay, he described how Wu would appoint Sun as "president" in order to unify

China, but told how Wu would remain in control behind the scenes. There was no criticism of the militarist in this frank analysis; on the contrary, the inference was clear that such an arrangement would be highly satisfactory to all concerned.

The implications of Wu's ruthless smashing of the railroad strike in February, 1923, were highly embarrassing for the Narkomindel line. *Izvestiia* reacted accordingly by giving little space to the event and by ignoring "the best militarist" for over six months. This did not mean more than a temporary silence, however. The omission of news of Wu was as much a consequence of the complete breakdown of Soviet efforts to reach an agreement in Peking as of the railroad shootings. The pro-Wu theme was taken up again with the celebrated Karakhan mission to China in late 1923. Here Vilensky developed his concept of "the strategic center" of China, under control of Wu Pei-fu, and gave the fullest statement of Narkomindel hopes of developing influence in this center, asserting that it "has the most favorable position and possesses the greatest natural resources. It seems to us that China now faces the possibility of establishing a sufficiently firm bourgeois power which must set itself the task of consolidating the different parts of China into a single unit. . . . It must be presumed that in the coming years, this party [Wu] will hold power firmly in its hands." [30]

At this very moment, a key figure in Soviet strategy and ultimately prime mover in the Chinese revolution, Michael Borodin, was conferring with Sun Yat-sen in Canton. The two men were preparing a reorganization of the Kuomintang which was to carry the southern government on a victorious march against the war-lord forces of the North. Simultaneously, Leo Karakhan was in Peking, laying the groundwork for the Sino-Soviet treaty of 1924. As will be shown later, the two Russian representatives were fully informed as to each other's activities. [31] Here was the fulfillment of Lenin's familiar advice to pursue legal and illegal activity, to work with recognized government leaders and with those extralegal groups which could further Soviet aims. All was done in the name of Marx, including the analysis of Vilensky that Wu Pei-fu, an avowed militarist with demonstrated antiproletarian sentiments, deserved support as a base for the "firm bourgeois power" necessary to China. Such were the conflicting policies pursued in 1923–24.

Before considering the views of the third major Soviet group, the Profintern, two additional points of the Narkomindel's chief writer should be mentioned. Vilensky was not enthusiastic over the work of the Chinese Communist Party, as might have been anticipated from his general approach. Seldom did the Chinese comrades receive praise from his pen, and often they were conspicuously absent from his articles on contemporary China. At one point, Vilensky clearly implied that only under the pressure of events did the Chinese Communist Party move away from "intellectual sectarianism" toward active work among the proletariat.[32] In a recommendation which received no support from other Soviet writers, he advised the Chinese Communists to take part in parliamentary activity, in order to educate the masses and to strengthen the party's own position.[33]

Finally, it should be noted that Vilensky constantly emphasized the impossibility of "leaping over" the capitalist stage of development in China. His writings in 1922 and 1923 were much closer to Lenin's position on this matter than to that of Zinoviev and other Comintern spokesmen. To those who claimed that China lacked capital accumulation, Vilensky pointed to the wealth amassed by compradores, bankers, and war lords. However, he carefully refrained from estimating how much industrialization would be possible under capitalism in China and refused to predict the time or duration of this stage of economic development.

PROFINTERN

The Red International of Trade Unions was established in 1921 in an effort to win control of the vast labor movement in western Europe. Adherents of the old Second International joined with Western trade union leaders to form a rival international labor organization with its headquarters in Amsterdam. The two groups vied for power, and the early twenties saw both "internationals" concentrating their energies on internecine warfare that hampered, rather than helped, the cause of the world proletariat. European labor groups split in two, each part swearing loyalty to Amsterdam or Moscow but each determined to vanquish the other. Within Russia, the Profintern's star did not rise rapidly until after Lenin's death. Only after 1924 did the Bolshevik labor leaders enjoy a sudden burst of prestige and power in a short-lived period, ended by Stalin's drive against Tomsky and his supporters. However, as early as 1922 and 1923, the Profintern felt sufficiently strong to pursue its own policies, independent of the Comintern and the Narkomindel. Its writings on China are scanty when compared with those of the two larger organizations, but it is possible to perceive serious differences of opinion between the Profintern and the two larger groups with respect to Far Eastern revolutions.

Profintern writers expressed constant skepticism of China's prospects for proletarian development, and with considerable justification. The best-organized labor force in the world lay in western Europe, and resources for the struggle with "yellow Amsterdam" were slim enough considering the value of the prize, without diverting them to China. Furthermore, Profintern figures on developments in the Middle Kingdom accurately reflected the staggering problems facing trade union organizers in that country. It was one thing to debate abstractly whether the proletariat should lead the Chinese revolution or whether some other combination of forces should be supported. It was quite a different story to see the labor group's statistics which showed that only 2 million Chinese were industrial workers, of whom barely 300,000 were in any kind of trade union.[34] To describe this fledgling movement as a lever with which to move a mass of more than 400 million inhabitants seemed utopianism of the most bourgeois variety. Not only was the Chinese proletariat largely unorganized, but what little union activity there was took place chiefly among rail and ship workers. Light industry, the largest factor in the nonagricultural sector of the Chinese economy, had only 3 percent of its total labor force in trade unions.[35] Small wonder that the Profintern seldom waxed enthusiastic about events in China.

At its first congress in July, 1921, the Red International of Trade Unions gave one lone Chinese delegate a "consultative vote" but otherwise made scant reference to his homeland. A resolution virtually echoed the Second Comintern Congress, declaring that "the might of the European and American bourgeoisie depends on the backward Near and Far Eastern colonial countries." [36] However, the discussions gave little weight to this sentiment. Lozovsky, a leading spokesman, warned that the growing workers' movement in Asia was degenerating into racial hatred, pitting yellow against white, as it merged with the national-liberation struggle.[37] He demanded that the struggle be on a class basis, that the white and yellow and black proletariat join hands against their common exploiters—the capitalists of all nations. Thus still another voice was added to the antibourgeois chorus which continued to oppose Lenin's appeal for support of native bourgeois leaders in their fight for independence. Lozovsky concluded by warning his European comrades against falling into the pit of Western chauvinism through the use of such words as "backward" when referring to Asian peoples. This error would only lead to an incorrect Marxist outlook and alienate potential allies in the East.

In the first eleven issues of the Profintern's bimonthly journal, started in 1921, no mention was made of the Chinese proletariat. This was no accident, as shown by a hardheaded statement which appeared anonymously in the magazine late that year:

In spite of the general tendency of capitalistic development of China, capitalism is not now the characteristic organization of China, and capitalistic enterprises until now continue to remain only oases in a wide mass of artisan enterprises. In connection with this, the proletariat is only a highly insignificant percentage as compared with the remaining toiling masses of China—the peasantry on one hand and the artisans on the other.[38]

To emphasize his point, the writer described unceasing persecution of the labor movement by both the northern and southern governments. Its only salvation lay with the intellectuals of China, yet they persistently ignored the proletariat. In short, he foresaw a bourgeois seizure of power in the near future combined with a struggle against feudal remnants, but the day of the proletarian victory was definitely far off. Evidently the Profintern writers disagreed with Roy's optimistic descriptions of working-class developments in Asia.

The most complete exposition of Profintern theory came in a pamphlet, "China and Its Labor Movement," by Iu. Smurgis.[39] Showing considerable knowledge of the traditional social structure of China, the author analyzed the myriad forces which acted to keep the peasantry in a fatalistic torpor. "The Chinese village must undoubtedly awaken, but for the time being, there are no concrete facts as evidence of this awakening."[40] If these were harsh words, he found little to cheer his readers in the development of Chinese industry, concluding:

The history of the capitalistic development of China is too brief; roots linking contemporary China with its obsolete social institutions lie too deeply in the depths of the thousands of years of historical development, for the political and social overthrow necessary for the unbroken capitalistic development to be successfully completed in one decade. . . . China actually has not made its bourgeois revolution.

Lest his audience find such sweeping generalizations too vague, Smurgis followed with an excellent review of the deplorable labor conditions, the innumerable obstacles of language and of tradition, and the chaos resulting from the collapse of the Manchu dynasty. His conclusion was a sound one: the proletariat "still is unorganized and few in numbers . . . playing no role of any importance in the political struggle of today."

A vast array of evidence was produced by Smurgis to show the futility of ignoring conditions in China in order to pass resolutions on revolution. In this Profintern publication, Sun Yat-sen did not escape criticism, much of which was aimed at his electoral law that excluded the overwhelming majority of workers from the ballot through imposing literacy requirements. Unfortunately, neither the Chinese intelligentsia nor the Chinese Communists were facing up to the problems around them. As an example, Smurgis cited the Chinese journal *Communist* which had many articles on the Russian and European Communist parties, but which had virtually nothing on the Chinese workers' movement!

Taken as a whole, the pamphlet betrayed none of the errors common to those newly acquainted with China or to those who allowed revolutionary fervor to blur their vision. Its conclusions were as inescapable as the problems it raised. Arguing in orthodox Marxist terms, the pamphlet concluded that it was impossible to portray China as offering ground for anything more than a splinter-group Communist organization. In political and economic development, China was decades behind Russia. She offered discontent, strife, and explosive anti-Western sentiment. For the class struggle per se, however, China was most unpromising.

During the first half of 1922, no articles on China appeared in the Profintern's monthly publication. In March the appointment of several Chinese delegates to the Far Eastern Council of Trade Unions was announced, but otherwise the journal concerned itself with European trade union problems. Under these circumstances it is not surprising that when the Second Profintern Congress convened in 1922, Heller gave a pessimistic evaluation of the situation in China. His conclusion spoke for itself: "The working movement in China is extremely young and therefore cannot be regarded seriously as a revolutionary factor. However, it has brilliant prospects." [41] Despite the appointment of a representative of the Chinese Revolutionary Seamen to the presidium,[42] nothing more was said with reference to the Middle Kingdom. The resolutions which were adopted on colonial and semicolonial areas bore little resemblance to the fervent declarations of Roy and Zinoviev. A special blow was aimed at the bourgeoisie, including a vehement blast at the Kuomintang, claiming that the bourgeoisie

. . . all the time deceived the masses by the slogan of "the fight for independence," betraying the workers constantly, and directing the class-movement of the toilers into the channels of the national, democratic, emancipation movement against the rule of the invaders.

. . . While participating in the general nationalistic emancipationist struggle, the workers should take an independent position . . . exposing the hypocrisy, the faint-heartedness of the bourgeoisie and petit-bourgeoisie and their parties (the Kuomintang in China) and the insufficiency of their agrarian program.[43]

This unconciliatory policy had little in common with Vilensky's views in its attitude toward the Kuomintang. It stemmed not unnaturally from the deep-seated prejudice held by the majority of the Profintern members against all nonlabor parties. An anonymous article in the February, 1923, issue of the Profintern journal branded Sun Yat-sen an enemy of labor, despite Sun's avowed aim of helping the Chinese worker.[44] The article termed Sun's words sheer hypocrisy, designed to use the workers in his climb to power. This review of the strike movement in China completely contradicted Vilensky's assertion that only in South China did the proletariat have encouraging conditions for growth and that only under Kuomintang leadership could the bourgeois revolution advance the cause of the worker. It also ran counter to most of Lenin's writings, although admittedly the Russian leader had little to say during these years on Canton and its administration.

For the Profintern, the Chinese bourgeoisie was indissolubly linked with all antilabor forces, regardless of their manifestation. This was shown most clearly in its analysis of the February railway massacre, following a message from Russian workers to their Chinese comrades on International Workers' Day. While Vilensky built his theory of a bourgeois revolution hopefully around "the best militarist," the labor leaders did not hesitate to brand Wu Pei-fu together with the entire Chinese bourgeoisie as detested enemies of the proletariat.[45]

An incidental appearance by Roy at a meeting of the Profintern's central committee in mid-1923 apparently did nothing to focus attention on China, despite his diatribes at the Comintern congresses, since all of the Profintern's published discussion centered on metropolitan-held colonies.[46] In fact, Roy may very well have criticized the Chinese proletariat for its shortcomings and compared it unfavorably with India's trade union development. A pamphlet on trade unions in Asia appeared about this time by Heller, which noted that the Chinese proletariat was "much weaker, comparatively, than that of India." [47]

In one of the first instances of open interference in Profintern affairs from an outside quarter, Vilensky made an unprecedented appearance in the international labor journal in order to change the "incorrect" line of the organization.[48] The divergencies between Profintern views and those voiced in Comintern resolutions and Narkomindel analyses were so glaring as to suggest serious opposition to an active China policy from the trade union leaders. Their strictures against the Chinese peasantry and bourgeoisie boded ill for future efforts to build strong contacts with these groups. The debate had raged freely for three years, but now Karakhan and Borodin were moving swiftly in their assigned tasks of strengthening Soviet Russia's position on the diplomatic and revolutionary front. Serious problems threatened should the Profintern criticisms continue unchecked.

Vilensky did not spare the rod. He struck out at those "experts" on the Far East who ignored the reports of growing strikes in China but stressed only the dead heritage of China's past. Contradicting his own writings, the Narkomindel scribe asserted that trade union progress in China was no different from that in Europe and that Chinese labor organizations were growing with amazing speed in the face of many natural obstacles. His most severe criticism attacked those Profintern writers who had called for a fight with the Chinese bourgeoisie. For Vilensky, the bourgeoisie was the very group which, despite its lack of class consciousness, could best give experience to the working class. The true forces of revolution, the bourgeoisie and the proletariat, must be allied against the imperialists and the war lords. The only danger was that of American "Gomperism" corrupting the trade union policy, and this was definitely of minor importance.

Vilensky's faith that the "correct" line in China would succeed along the points he had presented may have been based on his knowledge of events currently taking place in Canton, information on Borodin's activities which was not available generally to Profintern circles. At any rate, his role was clearly that of a messenger, bringing the new policy to Profintern readers. It is significant that the shift came initially from a non-Profintern writer, thus avoiding the complications and embarrassments that might have arisen had one of the organization's leaders undertaken to correct the "errors" of his colleagues.

It was too late to solve problems merely by cutting off debate. Strategy could not be redefined by such simple methods. Within a month, Lenin was dead. The Kuomintang-Communist alliance was under way. Action in China was becoming more and more influenced by events in Russia as Borodin assumed a commanding position in the affairs of the Chinese revolution. It was imperative that some consensus be reached in Moscow among the various organizations responsible for determining Soviet policies toward the Chinese revolution. The Comintern was of two minds on the tactic to pursue: a minority stressed Lenin's 1920 theses concerning promulgation of a peasant program and support of the bourgeoisie, while a majority advocated a more extreme, traditional Marxist program based solely on the Chinese proletariat. The Narkomindel wrote encouragingly of the war-lord Wu Pei-fu and made little mention of the Chinese Communst Party. Profintern publicists were frankly sceptical of any positive program in China, particularly in view of the richer prizes to be won in western Europe. Sincere differences of opinion in 1920 and 1921 gradually crystallized intragroup factions. In the struggle for power between Trotsky and Stalin, many of these differences appeared to be merely polemical vehicles for attack and vilification. One thing is certain, however. That part of the Great Debates of 1925 to 1927 concerning China had its roots firmly embedded in the differences examined in these pages, differences which existed long before the struggle for power within the Soviet hierarchy began.

VIII

Heritage from the Past: Narkomindel in China

IF one turns from the profuse polemics concerning theoretical argumentation to the practical implementation of policy, it is readily apparent that it was within the Soviet foreign office, the Narkomindel, that the principal activity took place during the first seven years of the Bolshevik regime. Not only did Lenin, Trotsky, and Chicherin make foreign relations a cardinal point in their pronunciamentos directed at home and abroad, but from 1920 to 1924 Peking witnessed an almost unbroken series of efforts by Russian representatives to win recognition from China and to conclude a treaty of commerce. In contrast, the Comintern cautiously felt its way among the minuscule Marxist groupings in China, sending envoys with funds and advice for the nascent Chinese Communist Party, but playing a peripheral role at best in the Chinese revolution prior to 1924. While its activities will be examined in more detail later, the work of the Narkomindel provides the fullest picture of Soviet ends and means in China at this time.

Russian Far Eastern policy frequently attempted, during the nineteenth and early twentieth century, to alter the *status quo* favorably to its own interests. A policy of expansion at the expense of China was especially marked at the turn of the century when China's disintegration was sped by its defeat in the Sino-Japanese war of 1894–95 and by the deterioration of the Manchu dynasty. Japanese resistance to Russian expansion, bolstered by ambitions on the part of the Japanese themselves to gain a foothold on the Asian mainland, culminated in the Russo-Japanese war of 1904–5. Russia's defeat marked the end of its unilateral activity in the Far East. St. Petersburg had to seek the cooperation of Tokyo if it was to maintain spheres of influence in North China and Manchuria. Such was its policy from 1907 to 1916, concluding treaties both public and secret with Japan which defined respective areas of domination in the crumbling Chinese Empire.

Loath as the Bolsheviks may have been to accept the responsibilities left by their Tsarist predecessors, they could not ignore the consequences of this expansionist policy. In the first place, much of Siberia and all of the Maritime Province of Russia depended upon Manchuria for important foodstuffs. Acceptance of these territories as part of Russia brought with it the responsibility of providing for their development. Crucial to supplying them with produce was the Chinese Eastern Railway, cutting across Manchuria and exploited by the Tsarist regime as a means of dominating China's wealthiest region. Furthermore, this railroad linked the Trans-Siberian Railway with the vital Pacific port of Vladivostok. The twofold importance of the line found protection in Tsarist treaties concluded with both China and Japan, the first group based on China's financial paralysis, the second based on the willingness of two imperialistic powers to divide China between them. Neither set of treaties was recognized by the Bolsheviks in 1917. In fact, Narkomindel spokesmen specifically repudiated them as characteristic of capitalistic-imperialistic nations and unworthy of revolutionary-proletarian regimes. Yet the importance of supplying the Russian Far East with food and of assuring communication with Vladivostok remained. With no Russian influence in North Manchuria, Japanese hegemony seemed inevitable, given the fragmented state of China.

A second consequence of Tsarist policy was a tradition of strained relations with both China and Japan. Although Peking had welcomed Russian intervention after the Sino-Japanese war, it soon discovered that what Russia forced Japan to disgorge she was all too willing to swallow herself. Russian control of the CER became an established fact after 1901, and it was only the Japanese victory of 1905 which denied the Liaotung Peninsula area with strategic Port Arthur to St. Petersburg. In Outer Mongolia, Tsarist policy eschewed annexation and even opposed Mongol independence in 1911, but with the downfall of the Manchus, Russian influence in this area became paramount, replacing that of China. As for Tokyo, its collaboration with St. Petersburg had been an uneasy one at best. Never content with half a loaf, Japan's military leaders looked to complete domination of North China, excluding all foreign powers including Russia. World War I provided them with a golden opportunity to oust Germany from the Shantung Peninsula. The Bolshevik revolution with its consequent civil war and chaos offered a similar chance to establish a Japanese sphere of influence over the Maritime Province, Siberia, North Manchuria, and all of Mongolia. The Narkomindel had forsworn cooperation with Japan in its renunciation of secret treaties, yet it lacked the means to compete with Japan in maintaining Russia's position in the Far East.

Heightening the importance of this second problem was the vulnerable and confused nature of Russian frontiers in the area. Only the relatively short distance of the Amur River provided a clearly demarcated boundary between Russia and China, and this was no obstacle to invasion. The remainder of the extensive boundary running through Manchuria and Mongolia remained unmarked and unprotected. Counterrevolution and foreign intervention could cross at will between China and Russia, without interference from either Peking or Petrograd. After 1917, White Guard troops found refuge in both Manchuria and Mongolia, while Japanese forces established bases throughout the Russian Far East. Were it not for the presence of American troops as a restraining influence in the intervention period of 1919–20, Japan might well have extended its control over all of Siberia. Even after 1921, when the danger of hostile forces decreased markedly, Russian planners regarded the respite as temporary. So large an area of vulnerability, given the frustrated aspirations of Japanese militarists after their rebuff at the Washington Conference, demanded countermeasures from the new Bolshevik rulers.

Thus economic, political, and strategic consequences flowed from the Tsarist policy of establishing Russia as a Far Eastern power. History did not begin anew for the Bolsheviks; they entered upon it midstream with all three currents operative upon their course simultaneously. Yet they explicitly denied that these economic, political, and military factors, often lumped under the term "national interest," determined their course of action. The Bolsheviks introduced still another standard by which to measure their behavior. They claimed to found all foreign relations on revolutionary principles of diplomacy, essentially self-denying in contrast with Tsarist imperialism. Lenin and his followers challenged comparison of their ends and means with those of bourgeois-capitalist states. Thus they suffer the consequences of having their actions evaluated in terms of their words. Bolshevik policy pledged itself to principles of self-determination, nonannexation, open diplomacy, and businesslike relations with any power promising to refrain from interference in Soviet Russia's internal affairs. Furthermore, it declared its willingness to give up all privileges extorted from other nations by Tsarist Russia under unequal treaties. In the absence of an accepted norm of international relations in 1917, Lenin and his followers enunciated a standard which went far beyond that of Woodrow Wilson in sweeping aside traditional means of diplomacy.

For this reason, the first test to which Narkomindel policy in China may be put is its success or failure in measuring up to these avowed principles. It is not enough to say that China and Japan failed to pursue similar principles and thus Bolshevik negotiators were forced to act accordingly. They made no such reciprocity a condition for putting their principles into practice. Furthermore, they at no time dropped their claim to a morally superior foreign policy but continually invited comparison of their methods with those of other great powers.

As has been suggested, economic factors demanded that peaceful relations be established along the lengthy Sino-Soviet frontier. Trade statistics based on Chinese customs figures show the changing pattern of food imports from China to the Russian Far East during the decade 1913 to 1923. Tea, soya-beans, and bean cake had traditionally made up the bulk of this trade, providing China with an export balance in this area as much as nine times the size of her imports.[1] During World War I, European Russia was unable to supply its distant holdings, and imports from China accordingly rose to 135.98 percent of the 1913 figure. A shift to more essential foods was reflected in the position of tea on the import list, dropping from first to seventh place between 1913 and 1923, paralleled by a corresponding increase in the importance of soya-beans and wheat. In 1913, tea made up 17.2 percent of the imports from China; in 1920, soya-beans occupied primary importance, composing 15.2 percent of imports in this area.

The one-way pattern of trade with its dependence on Chinese goods worked to Russia's disadvantage during the chaotic years of revolution and civil war. While Chinese markets were able to shift elsewhere, no new source for these vital supplies was available to the Bolsheviks. Imports from China reached an all-time high in 1916, only to drop precipitously by 1918 to one quarter of the 1916 figure. In 1921, the total exchange of goods between Russia and China was a mere 35.94 percent of the 1913 base figure. These bare statistics give no indication of the suffering and disease which accompanied the stoppage in the flow of food to inhabitants of Siberia and the Maritime Province. To compound the misery, White Guard refugees and bandits plundered the countryside while Peking was unable and Tokyo unwilling to restore law and order. The few Russian traders who continued to ply their trade faced still greater problems in 1920 when the Chinese government withdrew recognition from Prince Kudashev, the Tsarist representative in Peking, and simultaneously wiped

out the protection given by Russian consular officials. The need
to re-establish normal relations with China was indeed pressing.

Pivotal in the entire economic picture was the Chinese Eastern
Railway. This line served both as a vital artery in supplying Russia's Far Eastern peoples with products of North China and Manchuria and as a vehicle for carrying goods to and from the thriv-
ing Pacific port of Vladivostok. Effective administration of the
railroad was of primary interest to Russia, even were its use as
a means of political penetration ignored. Tsarist officials had ma-
nipulated freight rates in order to divert traffic from the South
Manchurian Railway and its non-Russian terminus of Dairen.
During World War I, the situation was reversed and Japanese
authorities were able to shift the flow of commerce southward,
decreasing the shipments to Vladivostok. Partially because of this
enforced inactivity, reports in 1920 told of Vladivostok's decaying docks, empty warehouses, and rusting equipment. One alternative to such interference by Japanese and Russian agents with
the railroad's normal functioning would have been to allow China
to administer it completely. However, Peking's political and economic instability left the efficiency of Chinese administration
problematical, and Japan seemed determined to prevent a strong,
united, and independent China from becoming an actuality.

A second alternative would have been to abandon the Chinese
Eastern Railway to the vicissitudes of Chinese administration
while Russia increased the capacity and the facilities of the long
Amur route circling North Manchuria, connecting the Trans-
Siberian Railway with Vladivostok entirely within Russian territory. This would have had the liability of increased costs and
would have left unanswered the problem of how to guarantee
receipt of foodstuffs from Manchuria. However, it was the only
way to make certain that Russia did not encroach on Chinese
sovereignty, in accord with the doctrine given by Chicherin and
others as fundamental to Soviet foreign policy. This alternative
was apparently not seriously considered by Soviet policy-makers

in 1919, as it was never mentioned in any Russian writings on the problem during the period under study.[2]

Manchuria was not the only tension point in Sino-Russian relations. In Outer Mongolia, too, the Narkomindel was to play an important role, although in this instance economic factors were definitely subordinate to other motivations. The vast nomadic territory with its scattered population and low level of economic development had been a convenient but unattractive area for Tsarist penetration. During the nineteenth century it had served as a valuable buffer zone separating Russia and China. At a time when Russian colonists were pushing steadily outward in the Far East and in central Asia, Mongolia enjoyed an autonomous position in the Chinese Empire, remaining unmolested by either of its two great neighbors.[3] Russia was content to recognize Chinese suzerainty in an area which seemed more of a liability than an asset, considering its abundance of bandits and its dearth of rich resources. China, on the other hand, allowed the Mongolian society, with its Lamaist priests and native princes, to remain free of control from Peking, going so far as to prohibit Chinese colonization in the unsettled land in recognition of the *status quo* as established in the 1727 Treaty of Kiakhta.

Responsibility for disrupting this mutually beneficial arrangement is generally attributed to the Manchu rulers, although few studies have appeared in Western languages on this remote region. In 1906, a special office was set up in Peking to encourage colonization in Mongolia, paralleling the Chinese colonization of Manchuria which had been proceeding uninterruptedly since the middle of the nineteenth century. Unlike Manchuria, however, Mongolia presented problems of assimilation which the Chinese were unable to overcome. Deep antagonisms arose between the local populace and the foreigners from the south.[4] Increased burdens of taxation, land confiscation, and military service accompanied the arrival of Chinese officials, and were resented by the nomadic Mongols. Malpractices by Peking's representatives were frequent, and it was no surprise when the Mongols availed themselves of the opportunity provided by the fall of the Manchus in 1911 to proclaim Mongolia independent from China.

This Mongol action was not without precedent. In 1756 a group of Mongol chieftains had revolted against Chinese domination and offered themselves to St. Petersburg as a Russian protectorate.[5] The Tsarist government refused to take on this responsibility. Similarly, in 1911 a delegation of Mongol princes approached Russia for assistance against China and requested recognition for an independent state of "Mongolia." Paralleling its cautious role in the earlier situation, however, Russia did not exploit its opportunities to the fullest extent. That it would use this chance to halt further Chinese infiltration into the buffer area was to have been expected. However, there were definite limits to the support Tsarist Russia was willing to give the Mongols. Korostovets, Russian minister to Urga, enunciated his country's aim as "maintaining the autonomous regime, protecting her right to maintain a national army and her decision to permit neither the presence of Chinese troops on her territory nor the colonization of her land by the Chinese."[6] A Russo-Mongol protocol to this effect was signed in 1912, carrying with it no recognition of Mongolian independence. This important point was underscored in a Russo-Chinese treaty of 1913, essentially restoring Mongolia to its autonomous position of pre-1906. Neither Russian nor Chinese troops were to enter the region nor were the two powers to colonize it. The treaties of 1912 and 1913 were brought into full agreement by the tripartite Russian-Chinese-Mongolian treaty, signed at Kiakhta on June 7, 1915. Thus if Soviet Russia were to play an active role in Outer Mongolia, it would be following in the footsteps of its Tsarist predecessors, intervening in an area contiguous to Russian soil but possessing slight economic importance for Russia.

At the outbreak of the Russian revolution, relations with China were governed principally by treaties concerning the Chinese Eastern Railway and Outer Mongolia, in addition to those guaranteeing extraterritorial privileges to Russian citizens, providing for the indemnity paid by China for the Boxer Uprising in 1901, and permitting the stationing of Russian consular guards in China. The first of these agreements, that concerning the CER, was violated by Peking soon after the fall of the Provisional Government. Despite protests from the Russian Ambassador in Peking, Prince Kudashev, and from the Bolshevik Commissar for Foreign Affairs in Petrograd, Trotsky, Chinese officials took over administration of the railway in January, 1918. A warning from Peking to Russia "not to interfere" came on March 18, 1920, and the following day China officially completed the establishing of its control over the entire CER zone.[7]

Similar Chinese action in Outer Mongolia faced considerable local hostility but was facilitated by the complete breakdown of internal trade accompanying disrupted conditions on all sides. The influential sector of the populace which amassed its wealth through trading facilities preferred peace under Peking to chaos from the effects of the Russian civil war which threatened to spill over the unmarked frontiers. In a series of moves, Chinese authorities strengthened their control of the country's finances and increased their consular guards in direct violation of the 1915 treaty. Ataman Semenov, leader of anti-Bolshevik forces in Siberia, envisioned himself as founder of a new Mongol empire and hastened further action from Peking by his fantastic plans for a pan-Mongolian movement. In March, 1919, over Kudashev's futile protest, Chinese troops in Urga were increased beyond the limit of the Kiakhta agreement.[8] On July 20, the War Participation Bureau, formed originally to administer China's participation in World War I, was transformed into the Northwestern Frontier Defense Bureau and headed by the notorious General Hsü Shu-tseng. "Little Hsü," as he was better known, handled his assignment in Urga, the capital of Outer Mongolia, with a mailed fist. Bribes and intimidation were used to achieve his ends, increasing the hatred already latent among the populace.[9] One Chinese historian tells of Hsü's forty-eight hour ultimatum, backed by several thousand troops, ordering the Mongols to renounce their autonomy as well as all previous pacts concluded with Russia.[10] Under such circumstances the President of the Mongol Council of Ministers had little choice but to petition Peking obediently: "We, officials, princes, and lamas, hereby declare the abolition of the Autonomy of Outer Mongolia, and the restoration of the relations subsisting under the late Ch'ing Dynasty." [11] Paralleling the renunciation of autonomy, the President declared that all former treaties with Russia became "null and void automatically." As a practical consequence, Russian commercial enterprises were seized by Chinese and Mongols. Little Hsü had accomplished his mission of reasserting Peking's control in this outlying territory, though at a cost of alienating whatever sympathies for the Middle Kingdom may have been dormant among the Mongol population. His removal in mid-1920 after the fall of the Anfu clique in Peking was a tardy recognition of the harm caused by his predatory actions.[12]

An earlier chapter has discussed Soviet declarations made during this period concerning the Chinese Eastern Railway, foremost of which was the Karakhan Manifesto of July 25, 1919. Less publicity was given a similar statement on Outer Mongolia, issued the same year, which renounced all special privileges and concessions. In one paragraph a significant change in Russian policy was introduced:

Mongolia is a free country. . . . All power and law in this country must belong to the Mongolian people. Not a single foreigner has the right to interfere in the internal affairs of Mongolia. By overthrowing the 1913 agreement, Mongolia, as an independent country, has the right to carry on direct relations with all countries, without any interference on the part of Peking or Petrograd. The Soviet Government, publicly announcing this to the Mongolian people, offers immediate entry into diplomatic relations with the Russian people, and asks her to meet the representatives of the Red Army.[13]

This manifesto struck the same revolutionary note as did the original Karakhan Manifesto, drafted in the same period. There is no doubt of its intention to foster a complete break between Outer Mongolia and China. The words "free country" and "independent country," the offer to establish "diplomatic relations," and, above all, the complete absence of any reference to "Autonomous Mongolia"—the term consistently used in official Tsarist pronouncements—all point in the same direction. Tsarist policy specifically refused to recognize Mongolian independence; Bolshevik policy openly encouraged it. While this followed Lenin's principle of national self-determination, the initiative in the process of "determination" appears to have been Russian, rather than Mongolian. Since no contact between Red Army representatives and leaders of the "Mongol people" was reported at this time, no immediate clarification of Soviet policy emerged.

With civil war and foreign intervention raging along most of the vast Sino-Soviet frontier, the winter of 1919–20 saw only minimal contacts between the two countries. In February, 1920, local Chinese and Russian officials concluded talks at Amur and Kiangkow, in northernmost Manchuria, leading to the lifting of trade restrictions.[14] In April, *Izvestiia* gave prominent notice to a dispatch from Verkhne-Udinsk telling of an agreement concluded with Chinese representatives from Manchuria and Mongolia.[15] Either this report was unduly optimistic of the agreement's contents or the Chinese misrepresented their powers. However, it correctly reported negotiations simultaneously in progress between Chinese authorities in the distant province of Sinkiang and Communist officials of Tashkent, in Russian Turkestan. Sinkiang's desire to restore its profitable wool exports to Russia coincided with the latter's need to shut off Sinkiang as a haven for White Guard soldiers fleeing the Red Army. Accordingly, ten resolutions generally favorable to Sinkiang were agreed to by local Russian and Chinese negotiators in Ili on May 27, 1920.[16]

These instances of reconciliation were more separated in distance than in time, and their impression was distinctly favorable in Peking, where prior reports had characterized the Bolsheviks as renegades and rapists, caring little for the amenities of friendly relations with neighboring countries. It was in March, 1920, that the celebrated Karakhan Manifesto, offering to return the Chinese Eastern Railway without compensation, was made known in the Chinese capital. In this general climate of opinion, the Soviet leaders made a major effort to break down the barriers between themselves and the outside world by assisting in the formation of the Far Eastern Republic. This curious state, whose existence was officially proclaimed at a constitutional assembly in April, 1920, was little more than a buffer between Russia and Japan, but it served as a sounding board for the Bolsheviks through its agents abroad. Representatives of the Far Eastern Republic were admitted to conference halls which were closed to full-fledged Soviet representatives. Thus, at the Washington Conference in 1921, the Far Eastern Republic's spokesmen distributed materials concerning alleged Japanese intervention in Mongolia and assisted in bringing pressure to bear for complete withdrawal of Japanese troops from the Far Eastern provinces. While the Republic's existence was extinguished with its formal incorporation into the RSFSR in 1922, it had until then played an important role in bringing together representatives of the Russian and Chinese sides, as will be seen shortly.

These various events, all favorable from the Soviet point of view, coincided with a complete turnover in the Peking regime. A shift from open hostility against the Bolsheviks to an attitude of "friendly neutrality" took place in July, 1920, following the fall of the Anfu clique under the combined attacks of Generals Chang Tso-lin and Wu Pei-fu. Although the new cabinet was not fully independent of foreign influences, it was generally understood to be less dominated by Japanese interests than was its predecessor. Within a few weeks of taking power, the cabinet suspended payment of the Boxer Indemnity to the former Tsarist officials in China, with the announcement that the funds would be held for future settlement.[17] This was a relatively minor matter, but it had long nettled the Soviet leaders that representatives of the *ancien régime* should be supported by money which the Bolsheviks had gratuitously renounced in the Karakhan declaration. The only condition on their renunciation of the funds was that the money should serve to improve relations between the two countries. This condition could hardly be interpreted to include support for Kudashev and his staff.

General Chang Tso-lin, new power in Peking, played a complex role in mid-1920. It is easier to describe his actions than to explain the motivations behind them. For example, the contemporary Chinese press applauded him for allegedly plotting the overthrow of the pro-Japanese Anfu regime, yet only a few months later it castigated him for supposedly extending Japanese influence in the Three Eastern Provinces, or Manchuria. Documentary evidence seldom backed up these charges, but it appears that Chang was anxious to strengthen his own hand and would play off any group against another when it served his purpose. That this could redound to Russia's favor became evident as early as May, 1920. At that time Peking was held by strongly anti-Russian forces. Accordingly, the Manchurian war lord gave a cordial welcome to officials of a subsidiary of the Far Eastern Republic, the Verkhne-Udinsk government.[18] The Peking cabinet warned that this had no bearing whatsoever on Chinese-Russian relations and should not be misinterpreted as a resumption of those relations, but its future was short-lived. Chang's forces seized the capital by midsummer, and his mild flirtations with his northern neighbors continued, this time, perhaps, aimed at offsetting Japan's claim for influence. A delegation of three Westerners left Peking at Chang's direction to investigate conditions in the Far Eastern Republic.[19] The Republic had only shaky control over several districts and could not claim to be a unified state under a single government. Its position in relation to Soviet Russia was already evident, however, and Chang's mission encouraged Bolshevik leaders as a possible harbinger of Peking's shift from a Japanese orientation to a Russian one.

Vladimir Vilensky, then serving as representative for the RSFSR in the Far Eastern Republic, spoke with the investigating mission from Peking and emphasized the common interests of China and Russia against the aggressive designs of Japan.[20] After stressing the similar democratic aspirations of the two peoples, he referred to China's importance as a supplier of food for the Russian Far East. It was quite clear that the Far Eastern Republic was acting as an intermediary for Soviet Russia, and any doubt on this point was removed by Medvedev, president of the Provisional Government of Vladivostok. He informed the three investigators that Moscow's approval would have to be secured on all agreements concluded prior to a formalization of the relationship between Soviet Russia and the new-born Far Eastern Republic. Medvedev hastened to suggest that this approval could be facilitated by tripartite negotiations including all parties concerned. From this point he went into a lengthy discourse in which he asserted, on somewhat dubious grounds, that the Republic was successor to all the rights and privileges of Tsarist Russia in this area. However, he was willing to revise the old treaties and to give up both extraterritoriality and consular jurisdiction. It should be noted that the Far Eastern Republic still lacked a central government ruling a unified territory. Medvedev closed with a double-edged statement on the Chinese Eastern Railway, the first in a series of ambiguous declarations to be made by Russian spokesmen of varying rank:

The Republic repudiates in their entirety the imperialistic aims of the former Tsarist Government in the matter of the CER, particularly the scheme of colonization and Russification of Chinese territory in Manchuria through the agency of the railway. The Chinese Government must prevent reactionary elements from using Harbin and the headquarters of the railway as a base for counterrevolutionary moves, directed against the Provisional Government, particularly by Semenov's followers. Russia's financial and economic interests, with regard to the CER, must be maintained.[21]

This declaration, given in the presence of Vilensky, whose importance in the Narkomindel has already been noted, is significant because it was the first public reversal of the "hands-off" policy originally enunciated by Chicherin as covering all holdings outside Russian boundaries. At no point in Chicherin's speeches or in the earlier writings of Vilensky on the CER had it been suggested that "Russia's financial and economic interests" would have to be guaranteed by China before she could assume full control of the line. There was no doubt of Harbin's having become a meeting place of anti-Bolshevik groups, including penniless refugees as well as White Guard officers. However, the looseness of Medvedev's terms "reactionary elements" and "counterrevolutionary moves" left much room for future interpretation. Peking had removed General Horvath from his post in the CER administration after the fall of the White government at Omsk and had appointed Chinese directors to the positions vacated by the resignation of Kolchak and the death of Slauta.[22] These steps had been taken partially to increase Chinese control, partially to quiet Bolshevik charges of an allegedly hostile attitude in the CER zone. Both the alleged economic and security interests of Russia were to be considerably enlarged upon in future negotiations.

Meanwhile, another mission, this one from the Far Eastern government at Verkhne-Udinsk, was attempting to reach Peking. It had been well received in Manchuria in May, 1920, by Chang Tso-lin, but had to await the overthrow of the Anfu clique before it could proceed to the Chinese capital in late August. Led by its bearded chairman, M. I. Yurin, the delegation created quite a stir upon its arrival. Protests were sent to the Chinese Foreign Office, the Waichiao Pu, by both Japanese and French representatives. Peking was not to be caught off guard, however, and handled the delicate situation with considerable tact. The Chinese official who received Yurin emphasized that this step was wholly *un*official, while the Russian replied that his mission was simply to conclude a commercial agreement.[23] As a further assurance to the Western delegations in China that it would move slowly when dealing with quasi-official Soviet spokesmen, Peking requested that no formal talks take place until Yurin received full credentials from the other Far Eastern governments of Vladivostok, Amur, Zabaikalia, and Blagoveshchensk.

This circumspect behavior was characteristic of much of Peking's action at the time. Its internal power was limited, in the face of a rival government in Canton and with its own officials open to bribery and corruption. It could appeal neither to the progressive liberal elements, because of its decadent administration, nor to the strong reactionary elements, because of its pretense at parliamentary rule. Its foreign power was even weaker, for although Chinese officials maintained a courageous insistence on turning a new page in their diplomatic history, pressures from Japanese and French circles could not be ignored. Funds from Paris and Tokyo were crucial, and while China was anxious to conclude only so-called equal treaties, she was plagued with an impoverished treasury and a government whose actual survival was threatened with bankruptcy. Foreign powers had a strong club to wield when they protested any *rapprochement* between China and Russia.

For these reasons, negotiations between Peking and Moscow or Moscow's appointed spokesmen in the Far East resembled a shadow play much of the time. Statements of Chinese officials often served to screen actual negotiations, lest foreign powers object to a Sino-Soviet agreement. Peking's moves during these critical years can only be fully understood when official archives are available. However, it is possible, by careful study of press accounts of the negotiations and the official statements, to piece together the chain of events which culminated in the conclusion of the Sino-Soviet treaty of 1924.

Waichiao Pu officials often went to absurd lengths to assure their foreign critics that China would not act in advance of the West in recognizing the Bolshevik regime. Typical was the situation which arose when the ten resolutions concluded at Ili, in Sinkiang, came up for ratification in Peking at the same time that Yurin's mission was being received. As mentioned previously, these resolutions had been concluded months before, but the disrupted state of affairs with the change of cabinets precluded ratification prior to this time. The coincidence of events caused some alarm in foreign diplomatic circles, and an official statement was given summarizing the Waichiao Pu's stand:

In view of the contemplated or actual resumption of commercial intercourse with Russia by most of the powers of Europe and America, it behoves the Chinese Government to follow the tendency of recent international events, and to act in accordance with the attitude of her associates in the late war. In view of the chaos in Siberia and the inability of the old Russian official representatives in China to carry out the functions for which they are responsible, the adoption of some modus vivendi is immediately and urgently necessary to regulate to some extent the trade relations of the two countries, particularly along the frontiers, and to protect Chinese citizens and their interests in Siberia.[24]

Small wonder that Peking was unable to capture the imagination and support of those Chinese who felt that their country should cease to "follow the tendency" of the Western powers. Such an apology for so harmless an act as ratification of a local commercial treaty concluded in far-off Sinkiang revealed the timidity with which Chinese officials viewed their own prerogatives.

In this statement of justification, a significant hint of future action was given in the reference to the "old Russian officials" no longer able to carry out their proper functions. To be sure, Prince Kudashev's continued role as an accredited Tsarist official was no more anomalous than that played by Boris Bakhmatiev, who still represented the Russia of Kerensky's day in Washington. Nevertheless, on September 18, 1920, the Chinese Minister of Foreign Affairs suggested unofficially that Kudashev resign.[25] Five days later, a presidential mandate canceled recognition of all Tsarist representatives, and the Chinese Foreign Office announced that it would take over Russian concessions in trust until recognition of a Russian government was re-established.[26] This unilateral termination of the extraterritorial privileges protecting Russian nationals in China caused much confusion in the courts and aroused lengthy, involved protests by other foreign representatives who were unwilling to admit the legality of this precedent, much as they wanted to see Russia's position weakened in China. Peking's attempt to justify its actions in terminology similar to that of Western spokesmen made strange reading, in view of the events of the previous three years:

Since the outbreak of the Russian revolution, no government has been established in Russia to unite all political parties and fighting factions. In the circumstances there can hardly be any possibility of the political friendship between China and Russia being resumed. The Russian Minister and his subordinates and consuls from the old Russian government have lost their official status long since the outbreak of the Russian revolution. They cannot represent the Russia of today. . . . But the friendly relationship hitherto existing between the two countries in regard to the treatment of Russian citizens will be maintained. All respectable Russian citizens and their private property will be protected as usual, in this country, which will follow the footsteps of the Allied Powers and maintain a neutral attitude toward the political troubles in Russia.[27]

This document did little to improve Moscow-Peking relations, particularly with its reference to the "neutral attitude" of the Allied powers which was to serve as an example for Peking. Tangible results of such "neutrality" remained throughout the Russian countryside, ravaged by two years of civil war and occupation by foreign troops of thirteen nations. On the whole, however, the Bolshevik leaders had good cause for optimism in view of the "unofficial" reception given Yurin, the ratification of the Sinkiang treaty, and the withdrawal of recognition from Kudashev. Slowly but surely China was moving away from its hostile attitude and preparing the ground for increased contact with its northern neighbor.

Accordingly, Leo Karakhan drafted a second manifesto, closely paralleling that of July 26, 1919. The new declaration of policy, dated September 27, 1920, became the basis of all subsequent Soviet negotiations in China and was more carefully worded than its propagandistic predecessor.[28] Its diplomatic phraseology, its formal presentation of specific proposals, and its restrained wording all stood in contrast with the grandiloquent message of 1919. Even its salutation was corrected, omitting the reference to the southern government and addressing itself merely to "The Ministry of Foreign Affairs of the Chinese Republic."

The manifesto opened with a greeting to General Chang Shih-lin, allegedly in charge of a "military-diplomatic" mission to Moscow appointed by Peking. While the exact status of this individual was never made clear, it seems certain that he lacked plenipotentiary powers from the Chinese government.[29] This did not deter the Soviet leaders who, whether intentionally or mistakenly, gave him an official welcome and, on October 16, 1920, concluded an "agreement" granting free passage and consular rights for Chinese representatives on the basis of reciprocity.[30]

Following this greeting to Chang Shih-lin, the 1920 manifesto presented an eight-point program as a possible basis for further discussion between Russia and China. The opening paragraph categorically renounced an aggressive policy in China:

The Government of the Russian Socialist Federated Soviet Republic declares as void all the treaties concluded by the former Government of Russia with China, renounces all the annexations of Chinese territory, all the concessions in China, and returns to China free of charge and forever, all that was ravenously taken from her by the Tsar's Government, and by the Russian bourgeoisie.[31]

This generous statement of intentions was carefully qualified in the subsequent proposals. The most vital issue involved the future of the Chinese Eastern Railway, and here the draft agreement promised nothing concretely. The railway was to return to Chinese rule following a conference of China, Russia, and the Far Eastern Republic to draw up "the rules and regulations of exploitation . . . for the needs of the RSFSR." Obviously such "needs" might be narrowly or broadly defined. A minor proviso accompanied the offer to return the Boxer Indemnity, barring its later payment to any Russian persons or organizations claiming it "unlawfully." Property rights demanded by Soviet Russia were

limited to "all the buildings of the Embassy and consulates belonging to Russia in the territory of China as well as other
property and archives of the Embassy and consulates." A final
qualification lay in specific obligations which were to bind Peking
and to operate reciprocally upon Moscow. No such clauses had
been included in any published version of the 1919 manifesto.
Among these reciprocal obligations was the promise to return
all arms and persons seeking to overthrow the neighboring government. Each signatory was also to agree neither to tolerate nor
to render assistance to "private persons, groups, or organizations"
which carried on mutinous activities against the other party.
Little faith could have been placed in this proviso by either
party, although it was included in almost all treaties of recognition concluded between Soviet Russia and bourgeois powers.

Karakhan's 1920 manifesto fared little better at first than had
his 1919 declaration, despite his position as Deputy Commissar
for Foreign Affairs. Except for polite acknowledgment by Peking
upon receipt of the document, its proposals were officially
ignored.[32] The note of acknowledgment expressed a readiness to
negotiate on terms of equality, but no step was reported in
Peking which showed any intention of implementing this sentiment. It is difficult to understand exactly why this opportunity
to test the sincerity of Soviet proposals went unchallenged by
Chinese leaders. Certainly it was clear by early 1921 that whatever form of economy Russia might finally adopt, the Bolsheviks
were firmly in power and their bargaining strength regarding
China was continually improving. A comparison of the 1919 and
1920 Karakhan manifestoes would have suggested the gradual
stiffening that might take place in subsequent terms for negotiations. One possible explanation of Chinese inaction may have
been disagreement within the cabinet over the consequences to
China's relations with other powers if she made any move in
the direction of Moscow. Contemporary newspapers speculated
freely on warnings from foreign officials, particularly French

Minister Boppe.[33] French efforts centered on a *cordon sanitaire* around the Bolshevik menace. Moreover, a Russo-Chinese *rapprochement* threatened to jeopardize the Allies' extraterritorial privileges and commercial concessions. Russia's relinquishing such rights could only weaken the position of other powers in China. Finally, Japanese influence over Chang Tso-lin was reportedly increasing, and a return to the anti-Russian tone of the Anfu days was anticipated by competent observers.

Had the Waichiao Pu authorities full knowledge of Moscow's alternative tactic in China, they might have acted sooner to accept Karakhan's suggestion, rather than run the risk of throwing an ally into the arms of Sun Yat-sen. Only a month after the 1920 manifesto was dispatched to the Peking government, Chicherin wrote a flattering letter to Canton, strengthening his ties with the Kuomintang regime. Rumors coincidentally swept Peking, during the winter of 1920–21, that Sun had concluded an alliance with the Bolshevik leaders, conceding to all of their "exorbitant demands," and virtually passing control of the southern government over to Russia. These alarmist stories were probably inspired by anti-Kuomintang elements anxious to discredit Sun in the eyes of his fellow-citizens, but had Chicherin's letter been published in the Peking press, it would have given substantiation to the anti-Sun campaign. Writing in English, the Narkomindel leader declared:

Your country advances now resolutely, your people enter consciously the path of struggle against the world-suppressing yoke of imperialism. . . . Trade relations between us must be taken up immediately. No opportunity must be lost. Let China enter resolutely the path of good friendship with us.[34]

Chicherin's offer to open formal negotiations between Soviet Russia and Canton China cannot have been meant seriously, but he was too experienced a diplomat to miss an opportunity of appealing to Sun's susceptible ego. Chicherin's personal letter was wholly successful in this respect. Although Sun's reply was not written until August 28, 1921, it merits consideration at this point because of its information on communications between Soviet authorities and Sun during 1920–21.

Explaining that Chicherin's letter of October, 1920, had not reached Canton until June 14, 1921, via an "envoy" from Harbin, Sun wrote:

First of all, I must inform you that this is the first and only letter received by me from you or anyone in Soviet Russia. In the course of the past two years there have been several reports in the capitalist press concerning formal proposals allegedly made to me from Moscow. No such proposals have been communicated to me from Moscow. In case any of your colleagues has sent before or is now sending letters to me, please realize that I have not received one letter.[35]

The Kuomintang leader continued with a brief outline of recent events in China, claiming that Chang Tso-lin was clearly under orders from Japan. Chicherin's gesture of flattery was taken quite literally, as shown by Sun's comment that "trade relations" were impossible to effect between Russia and Kuomintang China, inasmuch as the two countries were completely separated by unfriendly territory. Apparently Sun ignored the sea route which would have allowed trade between Canton and Vladivostok. In obvious fear that Soviet negotiators might conclude an agreement with Peking and thereby damage his prestige, Sun warned:

Not before a fundamental purge [sic] is carried out in the capital— and this will be done when I get there—can Soviet Russia rely on the re-establishment of friendly relations with China. . . . Moscow must wait until I have finished with the reactionaries and counter-revolutionaries, who appear in every country the day after a creative revolution.

Sun's naive confidence reads in strange contrast with the derisive criticism of the Kuomintang filling the pages of the Comintern journal at this very time. Less than a year after this letter, Sun was to find himself ousted from Canton by General Ch'en Chiung-ming as the fortunes of the Kuomintang leader suffered another setback.

Sun's active role in bringing Soviet influence and advice to the Kuomintang is highlighted in his closing comments:

In the meantime, I would like to make personal contact with you and other friends in Moscow. I am extraordinarily interested in your work and in particular in the organization of your Soviets, your army, and education. I would like to know all that you and others can tell me of these matters, particularly about education. Like Moscow I would like to lay the foundation of the Chinese Revolution deeply in the minds of the younger generation—the workers of tomorrow.

With best wishes to you and to my friend Lenin, and to all those who have done so much for the cause of human freedom.

This request for information was not unusual for the Chinese revolutionist. He had searched in Japan, America, and England for ideas which could speed China's development. His recent rebuff from world investors had upset his plans for building a new China with the disinterested help of foreign capital. Russia was now the logical focus of his attention. That country had dramatically succeeded in throwing off the old order and forging ahead with the new, despite the concerted opposition of the great powers. It had renounced the predatory policies which forced China into a position of international inferiority, policies still pursued by the great powers. Sun's interest in Russia, then, was equal to that shown by the Russians in him. While Chicherin was active in maintaining his contact with Sun through correspondence, Sun Yat-sen, as early as August, 1921, expressed frank admiration for Soviet methods which he hoped might serve as models for the Kuomintang revolution. In view of later developments in the revolutions of the two nations, this mutual interest is highly significant.

Although China and Russia shared a frontier of several thousand miles, it was no easy matter for Chicherin to acknowledge Sun's request for information. Communication channels were tenuous enough for normal messages, but such highly confidential words could be sent only by courier. Chicherin's letter to Sun took eight months to be delivered; Sun's reply was sent by way of the Soviet trade mission in London! Narkomindel and Comintern representatives made sporadic contacts in China, but until recognition could be established, no regular channel for communication existed between Moscow and Peking or Canton. During 1920 and 1921, both Maring and Voitinskii, the latter as general secretary of the Far Eastern Bureau of the Comintern, visited centers of revolutionary activity in China, but it was to be several years before Sun's request could be fully met by Michael Borodin in 1924.[36]

The year 1920 was a transition year for Sino-Soviet relations. The change of rule in Peking coincided with new Russian efforts to establish contact with China. By the time Yurin had secured his credentials and was ready to take up formal negotiations in late 1920, the main points of Soviet policy in China had been established. While keeping a careful eye on developments in Canton, the Bolsheviks planned to pursue efforts to establish diplomatic relations with the accredited capital of China. Whatever might be the criticisms of the Comintern or the Profintern about the counterrevolutionary aspects of Peking, the Narkomindel was quick to realize that only Peking could sign a treaty of any weight. The second Karakhan Manifesto proposed a generous settlement with China on the nonessentials such as extraterritoriality, consular guards, and indemnities, while making it clear that the thorny problem of the Chinese Eastern Railway would be settled in quite a different manner. One major problem had been omitted. An area relatively dormant in 1920, Outer Mongolia, was soon to erupt with internecine warfare, causing Bolshevik moves of the most serious consequence for both China and Russia.

IX

First Attempts: The Yurin and Paikes Missions

WHILE Yurin was awaiting the credentials, necessary to begin negotiations, from the five groups comprising the Far Eastern Republic, China continued its piecemeal recovery of rights usurped by Tsarist Russia under "unequal" treaties. In a move of dubious legality, Peking concluded a "supplementary agreement" with the Russo-Asiatic Bank concerning the Chinese Eastern Railway. On October 2, 1920, this *émigré* group, then located in Paris, signed over effective control of the railway to Chinese administration. The Inter-Allied Technical Board, established in 1919 to bring order out of chaos in the CER zone, continued to supervise the activities of the line. Dr. C. C. Wang, Chinese member of this Board and a director of the CER, described the "supplementary agreement" as "merely temporary, subject to modification by negotiation upon establishment of a Russian Government, recognized by China and the Allies." [1] Despite these words, the agreement was generally regarded in Peking as a rebuff to Yurin's hopes for tripartite discussions on the CER.

Receipt in October of Yurin's credentials did not speed negotiations, and only sporadic conversations between Yurin and Dr. W. W. Yen, Chinese Foreign Minister, were reported in November and December. [2] The Waichiao Pu advanced several reasons for the delays, chief of which was alleged conversations between Khodorov and Chang Tso-lin in Mukden.[3] However, experienced observers concluded that Peking was acting slowly in response to advice from the French minister, as well as in hope of discovering Great Britain's imminent decision concerning recognition of the Far Eastern Republic.

While Peking seemed in no hurry to conclude an agreement, Yurin was quite anxious to terminate negotiations successfully. His government needed the prestige and the economic benefits that would follow a trade treaty with China. An alliance between China and the Far Eastern Republic might weaken Japan's position on the mainland, since China's orientation toward Russia would be furthered thereby. On November 30, 1920, Yurin attempted to bring negotiations to a head. In a lengthy note to the Chinese Foreign Office, he vowed to review more than fifty treaties and agreements which had been imposed unjustly upon China by the Tsarist regime, to eliminate all privileges which were not reciprocal in nature, and to define mutual relations "based entirely upon the principle of equal opportunity." [4] Elaborating upon the problem of the Chinese Eastern Railway, Yurin declared:

The interests, rights, and obligations of the two sides should be fully guaranteed in accordance with the principle of mutual justice. . . . Apart from this, due consideration must be attached to the question of surveying new routes as well as of improving railway and water transportation facilities with a view to animating the trade between the two countries.

In view of the weak economic condition of the Far Eastern Republic, Yurin's ambitious proposal to survey "new routes" was something of an overstatement. Enough of a problem lay in the "improving" of transportation facilities which had fallen into disuse and disrepair during years of civil war and maladministration. Nevertheless, Yurin was determined to prove his government's sincere intentions, and accompanied his note with an oral statement accepting Peking's four-point condition for the conclusion of a commercial pact:

(1) refrain from all political propaganda which is not suitable to the social institutions of China in Chinese territory;

(2) indemnify the Chinese merchants in Russia for all of their damages and losses incurred as a result of the revolution in Russia;

(3) protect effectively the life and property of Chinese residents in Russia and give them all facilities for travelling and trading and residing;

(4) settle all the outstanding incidents that took place on the Sinkiang frontier as well as in Zabaikal districts and take such action as to prevent a recurrence of them in the future.[5]

At this point Peking suddenly stiffened its approach. Despite Yurin's unqualified acceptance of these four points, he was served with a new set of demands which would have to be met before negotiations could continue. Included was a long list of damages allegedly suffered by Chinese residents in Russia, arising from the civil war period. Precisely at a time when Soviet plenipotentiaries were winning dramatic successes in negotiations with Persia and Afghanistan, a stalemate ensued in China which crippled Yurin's efforts for several months. The fault lay not with him, however, but with events in distant Outer Mongolia.

General Hsü and his troops in 1919–20 had done much to alienate the Mongols, but some effort was made by Peking after his ouster to ameliorate the situation. The attempt was short-lived, for in October, 1920, Baron Ungern von Sternberg, led a heterogeneous force of discontented Mongol princes, Buriat tribesmen, and White Russians in an attack upon Urga, the capital of Outer Mongolia.[6] This colorful adventurer, while defeated in his first attempt, ultimately enjoyed a brief period of success. It was highlighted by his confused sense of power and grandeur but had little significance in itself. Once his power was smashed, the Baron's movement left no impression on the trackless wastes, yet his brief appearance acted as a catalyst bringing into play other more far-reaching forces.

Ungern's initial assault on Urga threw the entire Mongolian situation into utter confusion. Vilensky reported on November 2 that local Chinese authorities in a Mongolian border town had appealed for help from the Far Eastern Republic and the RSFSR in driving Ungern back.[7] Vilensky's reaction, representative of at least one wing of Narkomindel, was flatly negative. Terming the Chinese fearful for their "imperialistic occupation of Mongolia," he followed a lengthy quote from the Soviet manifesto of 1919 to Mongolia with the assertion that Soviet Russia had no choice but to "recognize the complete independent freedom of Mongolia." Consequently, "We cannot interfere in the internal affairs of Mongolia"; the Mongolian people had sufficient strength to beat Ungern as they did any other oppressors.

The rapid deterioration of events in Mongolia scarcely bore out Vilensky's confident conclusion. Whatever took place within the inner councils of Narkomindel at this time, on November 11, the cautious policy was scrapped. In a formal note to the Chinese government, Chicherin outlined the threat posed to China, the Far Eastern Republic, and Soviet Russia by Ungern's activities:

Chinese troops in the vicinity of Urga were unable to defeat the White Guard bands which prevailed there, and therefore turned to our military commanders as well as to the military commanders of the Far Eastern Republic, with requests to render them help against these plundering gangs. The Soviet Government . . . is ready to render assistance to the Chinese troops for the destruction of the White bands in Urga. Corresponding orders have been given our troops. The Soviet Government declares at this time that its forces, going to Mongolia, appear there in the capacity of China's friends, and considering their task completed, they will immediately evacuate Chinese territory, as soon as the White Guard bands are destroyed.[8]

Before the Red Army could move into action, however, the Chinese prevailed and drove out Ungern. Chicherin's reaction was immediate. In a second note, of November 27, he recapitulated his earlier message:

Although we have not as yet, for reasons unknown to us, received any reply from the Chinese Government, we report with great pleasure that the Chinese armed forces succeeded in driving out the Semenov bands from Urga. . . . The Russian Republic, standing above all for the inviolability of foreign territory, finds it possible to hold back the appearance of its armed forces on Mongolian territory, being confident that the Chinese Government will take direct and energetic measures toward the complete and immediate liquidation of the plundering forces, hostile to Russia. . . . Our Government offers the Chinese Republic immediate military help in liquidating the anti-Russian counterrevolutionary bands, if . . . our help should appear necessary.[9]

Chicherin did not have long to wait for a reply to this message. Disavowing any local Chinese request for help, Peking moved to eliminate any excuse for Russian encroachments on Mongolian territory. In a strongly worded protest dispatched to the Chinese ambassador in London immediately upon receipt of Chicherin's message, China informed the Soviet leaders that no "aid" would be accepted from Russia, warning:

We consider it necessary to note that the crossing of the border by foreign troops violates the sovereignty subject to this country and that the indication on the first telegram that we requested help does not correspond to actuality. Though troops were dispatched and had been stopped, nevertheless the offer of military help in case of need remains, which we need not accept. We ask you to inform the Soviet representatives in England that the Chinese Government takes all necessary precautionary steps for the defense of Mongolian borders, and does not need foreign intervention.[10]

Peking's sharp note, relayed to Narkomindel, paralleled its sudden hostility toward Yurin. Had the Waichiao Pu known the full details of Russian moves, it might well have expelled the envoy altogether. Earlier in 1920, after months of conspiratorial activity in Urga apparently conducted among Mongol nationalists by Comintern agents, Soviet authorities organized a People's Revolutionary Party of Mongolia, on Russian soil.[11] As acknowledged in an official Narkomindel report the following year:

At this time, seeing the full impossibility of China's liquidating White bands and the robbing and wasting of their native land, members of the Mongolian national-revolutionary party and their supporters started to get ready in the territory of the Russian Republic for the coming struggle for freeing Mongolia and for winning her free autonomous political existence. . . . In October, 1920, a delegation of

the People's Revolutionary Party of Mongolia . . . in the name of the
Mongolian working people

appealed to Russia for military aid.[12]

Here was the Mongolian counterpart to the 1919 revision in
the Karakhan Manifesto concerning the Chinese Eastern Railway. Although the new Russian policy had been anticipated in
the 1919 declaration to the Mongolian people, Vilensky had
cited this manifesto in support of an essentially "hands-off"
policy, showing a cautious approach to an area admittedly within
Peking's jurisdiction. However, the activities of the Comintern,
spawning an independent Mongolian revolutionary movement,
meshed with the obvious threat to Russian security, bringing
Chicherin to the point of intervention. As in Manchuria, Soviet
policy began by renouncing all Russian interests gained by
Tsarist policy, but as in Manchuria, the course of events both
inside and outside Russia ultimately reversed the course of Soviet
policy. While the Narkomindel reference to "autonomous political existence" suggested a continuing recognition of Peking's
traditional suzerainty over the area, Comintern fostering of a
movement to "free" Mongolia would inevitably increase Russia's
influence in Urga, should the movement succeed. Vilensky's re-
jection of alleged Chinese requests for help, the orders to the
Red Army, countermanded within two weeks, and the encouragement of a "Mongolian national-revolutionary party" all show the
confused manner in which Russian policy was formulated and
carried out in this area.

Despite Chicherin's check on the Red Army, Moscow's interest
in Urga did not abate, much to Yurin's misfortune. On January
15, 1921, Karakhan dispatched a note to Peking congratulating
the Chinese on their victory over Ungern.[13] However, the com-
pliment was followed by a sharply critical passage alleging
mistreatment of a Russian cooperative, Tsentrosoiuz, in Urga.
Denying that Tsentrosoiuz was an agency of the Red Army, the
Deputy Commissar for Foreign Affairs condemned the reported
seizure of its fodder, valuables, and livestock. He argued that

since it was a genuine "cooperative, uniting large circles of Russian population," such acts of the Chinese government were actually "directed against the entire Russian populace." [14] In addition, Karakhan closed with a list of alleged border violations and river crossings into Russian Turkestan, terming such acts "hostile" and warning that they could "bring the most serious and undesirable consequences for both Russia and China." There was little similarity between the Karakhan of this *démarche* and the Karakhan of the 1919 and 1920 manifestoes.

Before Karakhan's criticisms could be considered, much less corrected, the *status quo* in Outer Mongolia was completely altered when Baron Ungern launched a second assault, taking Urga on February 2, 1921. The Chinese fled into the hills, an independent Mongol government was established under the nominal direction of the Living Buddha, while Ungern ruled from behind the scenes.[15] Although this new turn of events came as a blow to those in Peking who had been confident of their ability to control the situation, no time was lost in Russia in carrying out the plans which had been formulated for the earlier emergency of November, 1920. Reports appeared in the Moscow press of a "People's Revolutionary Army of Mongolia" which was created to unite Chinese, Mongols, and Russians in a liberation drive to Urga.[16] Soviet leaders made no secret of the fact that this army, eventually including troops of the Red Army and of the Far Eastern Republic, was organized on Soviet soil.[17]

The turbulent events of the spring of 1921 in Urga and Peking have never been completely clarified in Western studies, but it appears that discontent over Ungern's rule prompted the Living Buddha to seek aid from Peking at the same time that revolutionary Mongols were looking to Moscow for material support. China moved slowly; Urga fell in February and it was not until April that a conference of the leading Chinese political and military factions was called at Tientsin to discuss the Mongolian situation. At this time, Chang Tso-lin was made responsible for driving Ungern from Outer Mongolia. Chang's relationship with

Ungern requires further study, as does the problem of evaluating Japanese influence working simultaneously in Manchuria and Mongolia.[18] Whatever were the cross-threads of intrigue or intimidation, the fact remains that Chang Tso-lin took no decisive action against Baron Ungern von Sternberg.

Yurin's prestige in Peking fluctuated according to several factors, the most important of which was the situation in Urga. Soviet diplomatic pressure in December and January coincided with his inability to continue fruitful discussions with Dr. Yen. The absence of such pressure after Ungern's coup, coupled with the commissioning of Chang Tso-lin to restore China's rights, coincided with Yurin's winning a draft agreement from the Waichiao Pu. The Tientsin Conference and Yurin's new success both came in April, 1921. In addition to Mongolia, there was the world scene with its constant impact upon China. It should not be forgotten that Peking was anxious to "follow the tendency" of the other powers in dealing with Russian representatives. It could well afford to reach an understanding now, inasmuch as a Soviet-Persian treaty had been signed on February 26, a Soviet-Afghan treaty had been concluded on February 28, and, most significant, an Anglo-Russian trade agreement had been reached on March 16. Even the bitter enemies of Russian Bolshevism, the Poles, had concluded a treaty with Moscow on March 18.

Against this promising background, Yurin held an optimistic press conference while en route to Chita for consultation with his government. Disclosing the general terms of the draft agreement reached in Peking the previous month, he claimed it covered all problems including "the status of Russians in the Chinese Eastern Railway zone in connection with the abolition of extraterritoriality."[19] The Far Eastern Republic delegate was confident the proposals enjoyed support among "all classes of Chinese people." Yurin noted that while Japan's attitude was "more friendly" than before, French Minister Boppe continued to interfere with all efforts to bring about a reconciliation between China and Russia.

It was not France but Russia, however, who changed the course of events and ultimately upset Yurin's hopes before he could return to Peking. With no reference such as had been made in 1920 to alleged Chinese requests for help, Soviet troops crossed the Russo-Mongolian frontier in June, 1921, decisively defeating Ungern at Kiakhta and joining the Mongolian Revolutionary Army in Urga on July 7.[20] Execution of the vainglorious Baron after a trial in August brought to an end one of the final phases of the bloody civil war in the Far East. Thus a double threat to Russian security had been removed by force of Russian arms. The last outpost of troublesome White Guard activity had been liquidated, and the possibility of Japanese influence entering this peripheral area through Ungern or Chang Tso-lin had been temporarily eliminated. Of more far-reaching importance than these military victories, however, was the fact that Mongols were placed in power who owed their success almost wholly to Russia.

Soviet authorities must have anticipated the probable consequences in Peking of this move, particularly in view of China's negative reaction to the 1920 offer of "help" from the Red Army. Chicherin presented the Waichiao Pu with a *fait accompli* in a lengthy note of June 15, 1921, in sharp contrast with the Narkomindel messages of the previous November. Its importance for subsequent negotiations merits quoting it in full:

On June 15, the Russian Soviet Government, which during its entire existence has repeatedly given proofs of its desire to continue friendly relations with its neighbor, the Chinese Republic, declares now as one of the principles of its foreign policy the continuation of full respect for China's rights, and at the same time draws attention to the common enemy, Ungern, the leader of White-Guard bands now operating in Mongolia. His attacks on the armies of Soviet Russia and of the Far Eastern Republic developed into extensive military operations and forced Russian troops to cross the Mongolian frontier. Opposition to Ungern is to the interest of China, because by taking this task in hand the Russian Republic at the same time gives support to China, assisting her to crush these bands and maintain her authority.

The Russian Government categorically declares that only with this purpose did it take measures against the traitor Ungern; and likewise declares that when this purpose shall be fulfilled the troops will be withdrawn from Mongolia. By taking arms against Ungern the Russian Government confirms its friendly relations with its neighbor, China.[21]

The repeated references to "friendly relations" did not alter the significant fact that Russian troops were in Outer Mongolia but Chinese troops were not. Moscow had not troubled to inquire of Peking what plans the latter had for taking action in Mongolia, nor did the note propose joint occupation pending restoration of peace and order. China's reply was unequivocal. It asserted that Chang Tso-lin had been duly authorized to take appropriate steps against Ungern, that his means were ample to meet this end, and that Russian intervention could only be interpreted as a violation of China's sovereignty in Outer Mongolia.[22]

On the surface, Yurin's position remained unaltered. He was welcomed on his return to Peking, on July 25, by representatives of the president, of the cabinet, and of the foreign minister. However, his press statement frankly recognized the new element which had entered the picture: "I come to Peking partly to discuss with the Chinese Government the conclusion of a trade agreement *and the Mongolian situation,* and partly to renew my personal contact with the situation in China."[23] "The Mongolian situation" proved more than Yurin could surmount. His untenable situation became clear immediately, and on August 1 he quietly left Peking after having failed to recapture the favorable conditions of the previous spring.[24]

Soviet commentaries designed for home consumption show quite clearly the hopes that were placed upon the initial stages of Yurin's mission. At the very outset, Vilensky had linked the Chang Shih-lin group in Moscow and the withdrawal of recognition from Kudashev in Peking, predicting "a clear and decisive reply" to Soviet proposals of recognition and treaty revision.[25] When General Chang left Moscow, Chicherin issued an enthusiastic statement stressing Sino-Soviet friendship, and no less a figure than Lenin took the occasion to make commendatory references to Sun Yat-sen, somewhat ill-advisedly in view of Chang's alleged connection with the Peking regime.[26] In March, 1921, Vilensky hailed the establishment of trade relations with Great Britain as a harbinger of things to come in China.[27]

Russian readers received no advanced warning of the failure of Yurin's mission. On the contrary, continual assurances of success had been given by authoritative Narkomindel spokesmen. Khodorov was assigned the job of explaining Peking's hostility, and he did so with a vengeance that contrasted oddly with previous articles.[28] Calling the Chinese government a regime of "bureaucrats and minions of the Manchu dynasty," the writer analyzed the cabinet as being composed solely of Japanophiles and Russophobes. The Tientsin Conference of April, 1921, was described as a sheer struggle for power between Tsao Kun and Wu Pei-fu on one hand and Chang Tso-lin on the other, with the Manchurian war lord winning control over Inner Mongolia and the Three Eastern Provinces. According to Khodorov, Japan had astutely switched its support from the Anfu clique to Chang Tso-lin, and thus all of North China was a willing tool of Japanese imperialism. An interesting exception to this blanket indictment of the Peking regime was Khodorov's praise of Foreign Minister Yen as a genuine fighter for Chinese independence.

Of particular note were Khodorov's remarks on Mongolia, since the most important event of this entire year for Sino-Soviet relations had been the establishment of a Soviet protectorate in that area. He outlined the "Mongolian adventure" of the so-called Semenov–Chang Tso-lin–Japanese interests, concluding:

Mongolia—rear of Soviet Russia. Mongolia—bridgehead for organized force against the Far Eastern Republic. Mongolia—threat to Peking. Mongolia—inexhaustible source of coal, iron, and wool. . . . The Mongolian problem cannot be solved by means of a Chinese military expedition. There is not the slightest doubt of the striving of the Mongolian people for independence, securing friendly relations with China and Soviet Russia. . . . The real solution of the Mongolian problem lies in organizing the toiling masses of Mongolia.[29]

Here was a frank statement of Mongolia's immediate strategic and economic importance, and of Russia's means of securing her interests there. Not diplomacy in Peking but organization in Urga was to be "the real solution of the Mongolian problem." Yurin's failure was undoubtedly disappointing, but it was the calculated risk Moscow was willing to take in order to secure a position in Urga potentially greater than that ever attained by Russia in the past. The Bolsheviks did not create the situation in the far-off camp of Baron Ungern von Sternberg. However, they were quick to utilize the course of events in a manner made possible by the growing strength of Soviet forces in the Far East.

In another publication, this one by I. Maisky, published in 1921, a detailed analysis of the alternatives before Mongolia provided a different aspect of continuity between the past and Bolshevik policy.[30] As head of an economic expedition dispatched to northern Mongolia in 1919 by Tsentrosoiuz, Maisky produced a scholarly, detailed précis of some four hundred pages, complete with statistics and maps on the economic features of Mongolia. In his concluding remarks he asked, "Which way Autonomous Mongolia?" He dismissed the possibility of a "Great Mongolia" by declaring: "Naturally, each people, large or small, has full right to *cultural self-determination* . . . but cultural self-determination in no way requires . . . 'sovereignty' in the former sense of the word." [31] As for China, only "cultural stagnation and economic ruination" could come from that direction for Mongolia. From Russia, however, Mongolia could expect the "European cultural influence . . . cultural progress and economic prosperity."

Mongolia's significance for Russia was twofold. Economically, said Maisky, it could provide cattle and fodder in almost limitless quantities, while its mineral resources were most promising. Politically, it could provide a "neutral zone" between Russia and a newly militarized China. In outlining a veritable Point-Four program for bringing social, economic, and political progress to Mongolia under the socialist flag, Maisky sounded a theme familiar to nineteenth-century Russian expansionists. "Russia will not only be serving her own interest; she will at the same time be carrying out her natural historic mission. By its geographical position . . . Russia is the connecting link between two great continents—its head in Europe; its feet in Asia." For Asia generally, and Mongolia in particular, Russia was to be the "vanguard of European culture." Such was the vision of a prominent Soviet Far Eastern expert.

Yurin's failure was of little consequence in the long run, but his experiences served as an example for later Soviet negotiators faced with essentially the same problems as was the representative of the Far Eastern Republic. Three months after Yurin had left Peking, another Soviet mission was in the making, this one to be more authoritative in nature inasmuch as it was to represent Moscow directly.

As early as February 3, 1921, Moscow had been encouraged to establish channels for negotiation more direct than those of the Far Eastern Republic. On that date, a minor Chinese official, Chen Kuan-ping, arrived in the Russian capital with a report that "the Chinese Government in principle expressed agreement to the arrival of a Soviet representative." [32] Nothing more was heard from Peking, however, and the summer passed without any support for Chen's statement. Finally, on October 24, a telegram was received from Peking granting permission for a Russian trade delegation to enter China. On that same day, Alexander K. Paikes left Moscow as the first fully authorized representative of the Soviet Republic to negotiate with China. [33] Although innumerable references to his "trade delegation" were made at the time, it was no secret that he carried instructions concerning Outer Mongolia and the Chinese Eastern Railway. [34]

Yurin had encountered difficult problems as a result of Soviet moves in Urga, but events since his departure from Peking further complicated the picture for Paikes. In late July, the Provisional People's Revolutionary Government of Mongolia appealed to the RSFSR "not to evacuate part of the Soviet army from the boundaries of Mongolia until the moment of complete liquidation of the common enemy." [35] There is little reason to question the authenticity of this appeal which certainly had some precedent in the similar appeals in 1756 and 1911. Much of Mongol society had good cause to oppose the return of Chinese administration, for historical as well as financial reasons. Furthermore, Soviet help had already proved instrumental in driving out the forces of Ungern. To be sure, the appeal may have been a mere formality to serve as window-dressing for an understanding already arrived at between Red Army commanders and Mongol revolutionaries. In any case, it was simple for the Provisional Government to explain its need for Soviet forces in terms of the incomplete organization of the new administration and the possibility of dissident elements hiding in the remote parts of the country. The appeal closed by expressing confidence that "the mutual interests in liquidating the common enemy" would prompt favorable acceptance by Moscow.

Such confidence was well founded, as evidenced by Chicherin's prompt reply of August 10, 1921. In a remarkable document, the Narkomindel leader wove together the familiar pattern of elements well calculated to win the sympathy of an Asian people, including support for the revolutionary aspirations of the Mongols, assurance of Russia's disinterested assistance, and emphasis on the ever present threat of hostile elements in the Far East. The message stands as an example of the adroitness with which Bolshevik propaganda was used in Asia, characterized in this instance by the constant emphasis upon the "autonomy" of Mongolia while carefully omitting any reference to Chinese sovereignty or suzerainty:

The Russian Soviet Government in union with the Government of the Far Eastern Republic, ordering its troops hand in hand with the revolutionary army of the Provisional People's Government of Mongolia, struck the crushing blow at the common enemy—Tsarist general Ungern, who subjected the Mongolian people to unheard of misery and violence, violating the rights of autonomous Mongolia, at the same time threatening the security of Soviet Russia and perpetrating attacks on the territory of the fraternal Far Eastern Republic. *The appearance of Soviet troops on the territory of autonomous Mongolia has the sole aim of crushing the common enemy, of eliminating the constant danger which threatens Soviet territory, and of securing the free development and self-determination of autonomous Mongolia.*

Hailing the first steps of the People's Revolutionary Government of Mongolia on the path of building a new free structure in its country, freed from the enemy of both peoples, the Russian Government with deep satisfaction takes notice of the appeal to it by the People's Revolutionary Government of Mongolia, expressing the desire that Soviet forces not be withdrawn from Mongolian limits until the complete defeat of the common enemy. . . . The Russian Government declares that it fully realizes the serious situation and the mutual interests of Russia and Mongolia in liquidating the common enemy. *Firmly resolved to withdraw Soviet forces from the limits of autonomous Mongolia, bound to Soviet Russia only by the ties of mutually close friendship and common interests, as soon as the threat to the free development of the Mongolian people and to the security of the Russian Republic and to the Far Eastern Republic is removed, the Russian Government, in full agreement with the People's Revolutionary Government of Mongolia, declares that this moment has not yet arrived.* In response to the request of the People's Revolutionary Government of Mongolia, the Russian Government has decided to satisfy it in full.

The Russian Government is convinced that the combined forces of the two peoples, fighting against the force of Tsarist generals and against foreign exploitation and oppression, in the nearest future will completely secure the free development of the Mongolian people on the basis of its autonomy. As a result, the organized apparatus of people's revolutionary power in Mongolia will be completely established and erected on the lasting basis of people's revolutionary authority.[36]

Step by step Bolshevik statements were clarifying the content of the "new, revolutionary diplomacy," but it bore little resemblance to the principles enunciated so dramatically in 1917. The carefully worded notes to Peking of November, 1920, were replaced by the direct announcement of Soviet intervention in June, 1921. Then came the above reply to the appeal of the "autonomous" Mongolian government, sprinkled freely with such charged terms as "self-determination," "building a new free structure," and "fighting . . . against foreign exploitation and oppression." Under the circumstances, these phrases could only be directed against Chinese rule. The portions italicized above were sufficiently vague in wording to permit the presence of Red troops in Urga for an unspecified time.

A crucial decision now confronted the Narkomindel. It could continue guaranteeing the autonomy of Outer Mongolia by bringing pressure to bear on China whenever she violated that autonomy, concluding tripartite conventions similar to those of Tsarist days. Alternatively, Russia could leave its troops in the region, encouraging its complete separation from China and thereby turning a traditional sphere of interest into a thinly disguised protectorate. Its decision was soon evident. On September 1, 1921, the former Mongolian rulers abdicated in a formal edict, officially transferring power to the People's Revolutionary Government of Mongolia.[37] The new government's first move in foreign relations was, appropriately enough, a request to Moscow for further assistance. This note of September 10 asked not for troops but for diplomatic intervention which could restore relations between China and Mongolia on a "new" basis.[38] In an explanation of its request, the Mongol regime claimed that Russia was the best intermediary for this venture since, "convinced that you nourish no aggressive interests against the Mongolian people and its government's territory, China is attentive to your authoritative voice [*sic*] and offers of mediation."

Once again Chicherin did not disappoint the regime. He replied immediately on September 14, this time dropping all reference to "autonomy" and accepting the responsibilities offered by the Mongol authorities.

The Russian Government fully shares the conviction of the Mongolian People's Republic Government of the necessity of establishing peaceful and business-like relations between Mongolia and China. . . . Already repeatedly in the course of direct declarations to the Chinese Government and through the means of contact with them in relations with the Far Eastern Republic's representatives, the Russian Government has directed the proposal to the Chinese Government of opening negotiations in this matter. In the near future, the Russian Government expects to be in continuous relations with the Chinese Government through means of a trade delegation sent to them at Peking. . . . It hopes that the Chinese Government, on its part, will meet its proposal cordially which it puts forth in the capacity of intermediary with the aim of eliminating if possible the conflict between the governments of Mongolia and the Chinese Republic.[39]

By comparing this note with those preceding it, the final pattern of Soviet policy becomes clear. A new tone had emerged in Narkomindel documents referring to Outer Mongolia, implicitly accepting "the Mongolian People's Republic Government" as the *de facto* ruler of the territory and excluding any assertion of Chinese suzerainty or sovereignty. As the Mongol note had remarked, China was indeed "attentive" to Russia's "authoritative voice," but there was little likelihood that she would listen in a receptive manner.

One relatively minor matter, the destiny of Uriankhai or Tannu-Tuva, was influenced by events at this time. This area bordered on the extreme northwest of Outer Mongolia and had figured prominently in Tsarist expansion into the general region, becoming a protectorate of Russia in 1914.[40] At that time, aspirations of leading Mongols to link Uriankhai with their territory were politely but firmly rebuffed by Russia. In 1921, Red troops entered the area in pursuit of White Guards and to protect the many Russian inhabitants who had colonized the land in the previous decade. Chicherin followed the example of his Tsarist predecessors by definitely discouraging a move by the new independent Mongolian government to annex Uriankhai. Because this region in 1943 became incorporated into the RSFSR as the Tuvinian Autonomous Region, Chicherin's note of September 14, 1921, makes interesting reading:

. . . The Russian Government takes no rights for itself from the situation that in the Uriankhai territory are countless Russian settlers. It, however, considers it necessary to meet with the Uriankhai people and organs of its government administration in agreements on defense for the security and interest of these colonists, Russian workers, and peasants living in the Uriankhai *krai*, not in any event seeking by this to seize forcibly Uriankhai soil.[41]

Mongolia's significance in Sino-Soviet relations cannot be overemphasized, but its importance sprang from factors other than the customary desire of a nation, in this case China, to reassert control over an area which formerly lay within its historic boundaries. The Chinese populace had little cause to foster a deep-seated desire for the bleak, nomadic wilderness that made up much of that region. As has been noted previously, no Chinese colonization of any importance was permitted prior to 1906. However, the Chinese government had good reason to fear the blow to its prestige should its tenuous hold on the Mongol people become evident in China. In 1912, nationalist forces in China had made political capital of the Russo-Mongolian agreement, charging Yuan Shih-kai with betrayal of China's historic interests.[42] The Waichiao Pu offset this treaty with the pacts of 1913 and 1915, stilling criticism in China. In 1922 it was again an unstable regime in Peking, influenced by foreign pressures and internal splits, which was faced with possible Russian penetration in an area traditionally a part of the Manchu Empire. The Peking government could ill afford accusations of vacillation and compromise, particularly since its declared reason for not recognizing Russia was the weak, unstable character of the Bolshevik state.

Soviet policy-makers committed one of their few serious blunders at this time over this very sensitive issue. Alexander Paikes recognized the difficulties inherent in the obstacle which had defeated Yurin, and in his Harbin interview of December 10, 1921, he attempted to reassure Chinese readers as to Soviet intentions in Outer Mongolia:

China's dissatisfaction at our attitude on the Mongolia question is due to misunderstanding. Soviet Russia never had nor has it any aggressive designs. The advance of Soviet forces into Mongolian territory was imperative owing to the necessity of suppressing the threatening White Guard bandits, as the Chinese Government was not in a position to cope with them in spite of its promise. It goes without saying that our forces will be withdrawn as soon as the danger from organizations in Mongolia, which are hostile to Soviet Russia, is removed. There is no doubt that the Chinese Government, on learning our true intentions, will not doubt our sincerity, thereby facilitating the complete solution of the Mongolian question.[43]

Paikes's statement was given due prominence in the Peking press and indeed won favorable comment at that time.[44] However, it never appeared in the Soviet press, in contrast with the full publicity generally accorded all statements by Soviet representatives abroad. The reason is not difficult to discover. Russian readers had *already* learned that a "complete solution of the Mongolian question," as Paikes put it, had come from a Mongol-Soviet conference which met in Moscow on October 26, 1921.[45] On November 5, less than two weeks after the conference had convened and over a month before Paikes's press interview, a formal treaty was concluded between Soviet Russia and the People's Revolutionary Government of Mongolia which recognized the latter group as "the only legal government of Mongolia." While it might be argued that this did not give *de jure* recognition to the new republic, those unschooled in the niceties of international law assumed that it admitted the sovereign independence of the new regime. In the initial summary of the treaties, the Soviet press used identical terminology for the exchange of recognition, making no distinction between the juridical powers of the Soviet government and those of Mongolia.[46] Furthermore, it told of the agreement to exchange diplomatic representatives, to determine the border between the two countries, to grant most-favored-nations privileges to nationals of both signatories, to abolish extraterritorial rights for Russia, and to establish a new system of telegraph and postal communication. Given such terms, together with the general transition already present in Chicherin's notes, there was no reason to assume this **treaty** aimed at anything other than the establishment of an independent Mongolian government. Certainly later Narkomindel writers freely used the term *nezavisimi*—independent—when writing about Mongolia, although as will be seen, responsible officials intermittently employed the term "autonomous." [47] Unlike the Russo-Mongol treaty of 1912, no apparent opening remained for the subsequent establishment of Chinese participation in Mongol affairs.

The Soviet blunder lay not so much in the conclusion of the pact, for it was only the last in a series of steps of similar importance, but in the attempt to keep information of it from China. Why the Bolsheviks should have done this when a summary of the terms had already appeared in the leading Moscow daily remains a mystery. The fact remains that when reports of the agreement reached Peking, Paikes denied their validity upon direct questioning, shortly after his arrival in the capital.[48] On the one hand, it seems incredible that he should have been uninformed of so far-reaching a step. On the other hand, it must have been realized that sooner or later the truth would become known to the Chinese officials in the Waichiao Pu. This move was to cost Paikes dearly the following spring.

Paikes's denial sufficed for the immediate time, however. He turned to another issue in a public statement referring to the long-dormant matter of the Chinese Eastern Railway. Earlier, at Harbin, he had touched on this issue: "As to the Chinese Eastern Railway, the Soviet Government does not expect any obstacle in solving this question, as our government recognizes the sovereign rights of China over the railway as well as the entire railway zone. Of course, at the negotiations, the Soviet Government will consider the interests of the vast Russian working population in the zone." [49] Had he let the issue rest there, it would have remained sufficiently ambiguous to meet all the demands of Soviet policy in China, offering China her rights with one hand, and keeping the door open for Soviet pressure with the other. Paikes pursued the matter further, however, and on his arrival in Peking stated flatly that the more important part of his mission was the return of the CER to China *without com-pensation of any sort,* upon conditions guaranteeing that it would remain in Chinese hands.[50] Of course, he continued, Russia and particularly the Far Eastern Republic were economically inter-ested in maintaining an outlet to the Pacific over the railway. But this caveat received little attention, while the key words in his interview revived memories of the Karakhan Manifesto of 1919, as received by wire from Irkutsk. The reaction in the Peking press was immediate, as might have been expected. There is no reason to doubt the correctness of the reports of the interview, and yet again confusion arises from Paikes's words. Certainly this offer was never repeated at any other point in the prolonged negotiations in China, and both Joffe and Karakhan specifically denied that it had been made in 1919. It is possible that Paikes was laboring under a misunderstanding of Narkomindel direc-tives, but so gross a blunder seems incredible. The net effect of his statements on Outer Mongolia and the Chinese Eastern Rail-way was to create an illusion of conciliation in Soviet policy that was contrary to fact. When the facts were finally known in Peking, Paikes's position became wholly untenable.[51]

In the winter of 1921–22, as happened so frequently with So-viet negotiators in China, discussions were hampered under the impact of events thousands of miles away. The origin of the im-pact was different from before but the net result was the same. In Washington, the major powers with interests in the Pacific, ex-cluding, of course, Russia, were attempting to thrash out a *modus vivendi* on all outstanding problems, including "Sick Man" China with her Chinese Eastern Railway and "unequal" treaties. Peking hopefully stalled its talks with Russian representatives, awaiting the outcome of the decisions in America. Meanwhile, plenipoten-tiaries from the Far Eastern Republic vainly sought official recog-nition, and vocal Chinese circles voiced dissatisfaction with the Waichiao Pu, urging their government to accept the Bolshevik proposals to conclude new treaties of commerce and recogni-tion.[52] It should be remembered that these Chinese were taking

Paikes's words on the CER return without compensation at their face value. As for the Chinese Foreign Office, it continued to gamble on playing the same game at Washington that it had played at Versailles. It thought that by presenting a list of legitimate grievances to the great powers, moral force alone would suffice to cause a revision in the treaties which bound China's sovereignty and reduced her to an inferior legal and economic status. However, the great powers also played the game as at Versailles. China found the complex of international rivalries, vested interests, and mutual "understandings" too strong to allow any basic change in the *status quo*. If the chaotic conditions in China are considered, it is a credit to her delegations at both conferences that they were able, despite their political differences, to present their case so ably to the world.

Paikes's problems were numerous enough, but an added complication prevented him from capitalizing on China's keen disappointment over her treatment at Washington. Only a week after his arrival in the capital, Chang Tso-lin won new power through an overturn in the cabinet. Liang Shih-yi, accomplice to Yuan Shih-kai's ill-conceived restoration of the monarchy, headed the new group and was immediately accused of serving Japanese imperialism.[53] Wu Pei-fu was able to press this point to the extent of threatening civil war, forcing Liang's retirement from the scene in January, 1922. Following this, Acting Premier Dr. Yen attempted an uneasy interim rule, but it was soon shattered by open warfare between Wu and Chang in late April. Chang Tso-lin was badly defeated two weeks later, withdrawing to the Three Eastern Provinces and refusing to recognize the authority of Peking now held by Wu Pei-fu.

During this prolonged struggle for power, Paikes lacked a favorable atmosphere for negotiations. It is probable that some Japanese support for Chang made the situation even more difficult. In April when Vilensky left Moscow to help Paikes solve his many problems,[54] *Izvestiia* described China as a helpless tool in the hands of imperialistic capitalists, with Peking remaining a mere pawn among military cliques. However, *Izvestiia's* spirits should have been lifted by the victory of Wu Pei-fu in May, because as Vilensky had already noted, Wu was a more independent war lord than Chang. Wu's overtures to Canton held promise of peace between North and South. The most auspicious moment for a *rapprochement* between Russia and China since the Russian revolution appeared imminent. Now was Paikes's chance to succeed where Yurin had failed.

Almost immediately, the opportunity disappeared; the situation was completely reversed. In a note blistering with indignation, the Chinese Foreign Office notified Alexander Paikes on May 1, 1922, that it had received final verification of the Soviet-Mongol treaty, concluded in November, 1921:

> According to the recent report of General Li Yuan on the subject of the Russian-Mongol treaty, we asked you about this matter when you first arrived in Peking and you replied that it was entirely untrue. However, during a recent conversation with you, I again put the question to you, owing to the recent publication by the papers of the text of the treaty, and you admitted the truth of this report. . . .
>
> Now the Soviet Government has suddenly gone back on its own word and, secretly and without any right, concluded a treaty with Mongolia. Such action on the part of the Soviet Government is similar to the policy which the former Imperial Russian Government assumed toward China.
>
> It must be observed that Mongolia is a part of Chinese territory and, as such, has long been recognized by all countries. In secretly concluding a treaty with Mongolia, the Soviet Government has not only broken faith with its previous declarations but also violated all principles of justice.
>
> The Chinese Government finds it difficult to tolerate such an action, and therefore we solemnly lodge protest with you to the effect that any treaty secretly concluded between the Soviet Government and Mongolia will not be recognized by the Chinese Government.[55]

Paikes's position had been exposed completely by his own statements, as proved in the opening paragraph of this *démarche.*

His mission had exploded in his face. He beat a hasty retreat from Peking, so hasty that it went unreported in both the Russian and Chinese press.

In view of the absurdities inherent in Paikes's blunders, it is surprising that Russia's prestige in China did not suffer a fatal setback. That it managed to survive suggests the relative lack of weight the Mongolian imbroglio carried with the Chinese populace as compared with the more dramatic efforts of building China's prestige through removing the onerous burden of extraterritoriality. Of equal importance was the strengthening of psychological bonds between two revolutions struggling against a Western imperialism which was portrayed as exploiting Asian peoples everywhere. For the Narkomindel, Mongolia was of concrete importance, however, and it pursued its policy there vigorously. Following the *de facto* recognition of the new regime in Urga, Moscow gave an official reception to Count Tusha-gun Dava, on May 28, 1922, as representative of the revolutionary government.[56] In a subsequent interview, the Count expressed hope for further Soviet-Mongol agreements on matters relating to trade, finance, and communications.[57] As for his sentiments on the Middle Kingdom, they were summed up in two sentences: "No political, economic, or any other sort of agreements exist between China and Mongolia. Intercourse exists only in private trade with Chinese merchants as with other 'foreigners.'" For Count Dava, the main task was to create new and better relations with Soviet Russia.[58]

Until this time, Russia's interest in Outer Mongolia had been expressed primarily in terms of its political importance as a base, actual or potential, for hostile groups operating against the interests of Soviet Russia. Now additional factors were given in two significant articles throwing considerable light on the motivations behind the Narkomindel's persistent efforts to win control over this unmapped nomadic land possessing no railways and few roads. Ivan Maisky, perhaps the best-informed Russian writer on the area, contributed a lengthy essay to *Novyi Vostok* in which he discussed at length the economic potential of Outer Mongolia.[59] Despite the admittedly weak development of Mongolia's economy, he declared:

In the more or less distant future, extremely great industrial possibilities will open up, since the mineral wealth of Outer Mongolia is very great, from all appearances. Even the extremely fragmentary figures, which we are now in the process of gathering, on the geological structure of the country testify to the abundance of copper, iron, gold, and coal in the womb of the Mongolian plateau.[60]

Russians already had interests in this part of the Mongol economy, as the article noted, inasmuch as they controlled most of the mining and processing activity. The only industry owned independently by Mongolia—coal mining—was "directed by Russian engineers." With transportation between European and Far Eastern Russia in a highly disrupted state, the Soviet leaders had good reason to integrate the economy of Outer Mongolia with the needs of the distant Russian peoples.

Russian trade prospects were also hopeful, in contrast with recent years. Maisky reviewed the historical dominance of Chinese merchants over Russians and remarked that even in the "best days" of the past, 1911 to 1915, Russian traders had won only a third of the total market. By 1921, Chinese business interests held a near-monopoly in this aspect of the Mongolian economy. Now, however, the article concluded, China had been decisively expelled from Outer Mongolia and Russian trade should have a most promising future.

In the same issue of *Novyi Vostok*—the coincidence of publishing was not accidental—a frank summary of Russia's interest in Outer Mongolia was provided by a specialist in international law, S. Kotliarevsky:

Before the war, Mongolia was one of the few regions where Russia successfully faced up to competition in a foreign market. At the present time, Mongolia represents one of the richest countries in the world in terms of cattle-raising and livestock and its significance for the restoration of the Russian national economy can be very serious. . . . The

treaty of November 5 [1921] opens the possibility for a series of agreements on economics, transportation, etc., which in turn open the way
for Russian trade activity in Mongolia. . . . Traders will be the best
diplomats.[61]

The complete absence in both articles of any reference to a
purely Mongolian trade development struck a different note
from that sounded by Chicherin, who had written encouragingly
to Urga of "the free development of the independent Mongolian people."

The success enjoyed by Soviet Russia in this isolated sector of
the globe was not duplicated elsewhere in mid-1922. At both
Genoa and The Hague, Soviet diplomats had failed to win *de jure*
recognition, and the troublesome debts issues remained as far
from settlement as ever. The single victory in the West had been
the sensational signing of the Rapallo treaty, bringing together
formally two outcasts of international society, Russia and Germany. Although the pact was actually the culmination of several
years of discussions between groups operating behind the scenes
in both countries, it came as a profound shock to many Western
chancelleries.[62] Adolf A. Joffe, Soviet diplomatist *extraordinaire*,
was responsible for much of the negotiation preceding Rapallo.
For having audaciously mixed his diplomatic and revolutionary
activity in Germany in 1918, he had been expelled from that
country by the Kaiser's government. This diverted his efforts to
other channels, with the Rapallo treaty coming as the crowning
achievement. Now he was dispatched on a fresh assignment for
the Narkomindel, one that was to prove far more challenging
despite the weaker position of his protagonists. Joffe became the
second fully accredited Soviet negotiator to attempt a settling of
the differences between China and Russia. This next mission
brought to China one of the most skillful of Narkomindel diplo-
matists and one of the most gifted of propagandists. Yet even
Adolf Joffe was unable to resolve the problems which had stymied all Soviet efforts since 1917.

X

The Joffe Mission

AT first glance it might appear that Russia's diplomatic defeats
of 1922 turned the attention of the Narkomindel from West to
East in search of more promising areas of activity. The transfer
of Joffe from the hostile, anti-Bolshevik atmosphere of Europe
to the turbulent, revolutionary situation of Asia might be cited
as evidence in support of an analysis depicting Russian strategists
as consciously pushing first in one direction and then another.
Although such an analysis would have an element of truth in it,
it threatens to oversimplify Soviet foreign policy. Undoubtedly
there was a group within the Bolshevik hierarchy which felt that
the stabilization of capitalism in Europe made further efforts
there futile for the time being and urged concentration of energy
in Asia. This thesis was advanced by Radek at the Fourth Comintern Congress. Soviet policy operates like that of any nation,
seeking constantly to exploit the advantageous situations and to
skirt less favorable conditions. Because it is located both in Asia
and in Europe, Russia has often been blessed with a promising
development on one front to offset a disappointment on another.
Occasionally, as in the years 1917 to 1920, it has been faced with
acute pressure from both ends of its vast territory. However, in
view of the considerable Soviet efforts to win certain ends in
China from 1919 to 1922, it cannot be held that Joffe's appointment signaled a major shift of emphasis within the Narkomindel

from West to East. His trip to China simply indicated the persistent and serious concern which Russia placed on renewing its ties with China, thereby perhaps winning an influential position in the Chinese revolution.

Soviet commentaries generally stressed the chaotic political conditions in China when assessing the difficulties confronting Russian negotiators, but occasionally a few pointed criticisms were aimed at the Narkomindel. A. Ivin, an unusually objective and well-informed correspondent in Peking, compared Russia's understaffed delegations with the extensive groups working for Japan and America in the Middle Kingdom.[1] Stressing the importance of winning support in the Chinese press, he commented: "Such preparatory work is irrefutably of sufficient importance to require much energy and many different tactics." Ivin warned that victories on the diplomatic front should not be the only goal of Narkomindel representatives in Peking. Even if they should receive setbacks in negotiations, another aim needed to be met:

At the present, we should continue negotiations not only with the view of getting so-called tangible results, but also with the view of using them for getting into much closer contact with the Chinese people. . . . If we do not have public opinion on our side, we will meet great difficulty in solving both the Mongolian and the Chinese Eastern Railway questions.

Ivin's words were markedly perceptive, and Joffe's actions were to prove the wisdom of such advice. Moscow once again had high hopes in China, as evidenced by the extensive coverage of the new mission in Narkomindel reports, newspaper columns, and magazine articles. A veritable flood of propaganda statements came from Joffe and his staff. In short, it was the most fully reported of the four missions under study, and while its accomplishments were somewhat less than those of Leo Karakhan's mission in 1924, the abundance of materials provides an excellent case study of Soviet ends and means in Far Eastern foreign policy.

Moscow's optimism was not based solely on Joffe's proved ability; conditions in China had definitely taken a turn for the better. Wu Pei-fu had gradually consolidated his hold on Peking by winning support of moderate elements absent from the administration since 1917. General Ch'en Chiung-ming had ousted Sun from Canton, and while from a Communist viewpoint this boded evil, the *Realpolitik* of the Narkomindel recognized this as a step which made an understanding between South and North China more nearly possible. The old Parliament, illegally dissolved in 1917, had reassembled in Peking under a cabinet directed by the men who had so skillfully represented China at the Washington Conference. No fears of Japanese influence seemed justified under these auspicious circumstances. As for relations with Japan herself, there too some Russian hopes were entertained. From August, 1921, to April, 1922, conversations at Dairen between Soviet and Nipponese spokesmen had dragged on fruitlessly, but the main point of contention was removed when Japan announced her intention of withdrawing all forces from the Maritime Province. Clearly the Red star was no longer in a full eclipse in the Far East.

Adolf Joffe's initial statement in what proved to be an endless series of interviews during his stay in China came with his arrival in Harbin on August 9. Recognizing that many Chinese felt slighted by the general world focus on Europe, he stressed the importance of Sino-Soviet relations:

While the West is searching for outlets for economic and financial alliances, tossing about from one international conference to another, from one "witty" combination to another, from Genoa to The Hague, the East is accumulating strength and becoming more and more a powerful factor in international politics . . . the position which China is gaining every day in international politics indicates the necessity of establishing friendly relations between Russia and China on a basis of equality and strict observance of sovereignty between both parties. Soviet Russia is watching with great attentiveness the national struggle in China, since Soviet Russia is the only country which rejects all imperialistic policies.[2]

Joffe's reception in Peking on his arrival August 12 augured well for future negotiations. At a banquet attended by Dr. Tsai Yuan-pei, celebrated chancellor of National University, and Dr. Hu Shih, he was feted with warm expressions of admiration which he was quick to return together with a full measure of revolutionary sentiments for the Chinese intellectuals.[3] This "preparatory work" was precisely what Ivin had advised, and its success was reflected in the favorable tone adopted by the Peking press toward the Russian envoy.

Almost immediately, the Narkomindel representative had a series of informal interviews with the Chinese Minister of Foreign Affairs, Dr. Wellington Koo.[4] By September 2, Joffe was able to propose that full-scale negotiations be opened on the basis of the Karakhan manifestoes of 1919 and 1920, "with the aim of establishing between both countries friendly relations, co-ordinating those feelings which are maintained by both peoples in relations with each other."[5] Outside the halls of the Waichiao Pu, Joffe stated his goals more fully, making it clear in an interview that his was no mere "trade" delegation:

Trade agreements alone, without a resumption of normal diplomatic and consular relations do not—as has been proved by the experience of Britain—attain their end. It is quite easy to understand that solid firms or employers will not run the risk of doing business with a government which, from their viewpoint, is not a juridical power. *Moreover, that time is past, in my opinion, when the Workers' and Peasants' Government of Russia must needs have been satisfied with compromissary treaties instead of usual and commonly accepted ones.*[6]

This frank statement of Soviet Russia's increased bargaining strength carried a more ominous tone than that previously associated with Moscow's spokesmen in China, but it passed without comment in the press. Meanwhile, Dr. Koo showed no inclination to change the position of his government as given in his note of September 7 replying to Joffe's proposal. Despite the conciliatory tone of the statement, Soviet evacuation of Outer Mongolia was specifically demanded as a prerequisite for opening negotiations.[7] China was unwilling to give Russia the opportunity to use withdrawal of Red troops as a *quid pro quo* for recognition of Soviet Russia, or perhaps for fresh demands on the Chinese Eastern Railway. While the railway went unmentioned in Koo's reply, a significant warning was carried in his delicately worded sentence, "The Chinese Government hopes that the negotiators of both countries will carefully consider and decide all questions fully satisfactorily, in view of your proceeding entirely from the substance in the repeated declarations to China cited by you." Joffe may not have realized that by "repeated declarations" Koo was referring to the Irkutsk version of the 1919 manifesto as received in Peking in which the CER was offered to China without compensation.

At this stage of discussion, Joffe suddenly left for Changchun to represent Soviet Russia at a tripartite conference including the Far Eastern Republic and Japan. Thus the familiar tactic of playing one side against the other was used, frightening Peking with the spectre of a Russo-Japanese *rapprochement*. An interesting contrast is provided here with 1921 when Russian fears centered around the possibility that Japan would gain a foothold in the Chinese revolution through an entente between Chang Tso-lin and Sun Yat-sen. However, China had much sounder cause for alarm than had Soviet Russia. Japanese troops had begun evacuation of the Maritime Province on September 3. A settlement of outstanding differences between Russia and Japan might leave China to be carved like a melon, as agreed upon in the pre-1917 Russo-Japanese secret treaties.

Events at Changchun proved otherwise. The conference was premature. Soviet demands for a definite schedule of Japanese evacuation of northern Sakhalin were inflexibly opposed by counterdemands from Tokyo's representatives. Anxious concern in Peking changed to open relief when negotiations among the three non-Chinese powers meeting on Chinese territory collapsed. By September 25 it was evident that Joffe had suffered his first setback in the Far East. However, several significant statements made by him at this time indicated his confident outlook. The first, a sharp protest of September 21, concerned reports that China intended to use the Russian share of the Boxer Indemnity to guarantee short-term loans. Using this as an opportunity to expand his views on the Karakhan manifestoes, Joffe warned:

True, in its note of 1920 . . . the Russian Government renounced its share of indemnity for the Boxer Uprising, but first, it did this on condition that the Chinese Government under no circumstances would give remuneration to former Russian consuls or to any other persons or Russian organizations on this illegal pretense, and second, the above note was left unanswered on the part of the Chinese Government, and it is hardly possible to conceive that such a note, sent by a government with whom no juridical relations were established, could effect juridical consequences.[8]

This was only the first of many protests from Joffe to the Wai-chiao Pu. Covering various points, they grew increasingly belligerent when discussing the declarations of 1919 and 1920. His Chinese audience was quick to react to this threatening attitude, and considerable question arose over the sincerity of Soviet pronouncements.

On the same day, Joffe called Peking's attention to a proposed meeting in Harbin of the "so-called shareholders of the CER." [9] He expressed hope that such events would not be tolerated and asked to be notified of the steps planned to remedy the matter, adding: "The question of this railroad is undoubtedly one of the most important Russian-Chinese questions." Joffe's return to a problem which had been in the background for some time was paralleled in Soviet commentaries at this time. With Russian interests secure in the People's Revolutionary Government of Mongolia, it was natural that Bolshevik writings on Sino-Soviet relations should turn to the still unsettled issue of North Manchuria. A lengthy *Izvestiia* article in August referred to the Chinese Eastern Railway as "a legacy of the imperialist policy of Tsarist Russia," words almost identical with those later used by Joffe in Peking.[10] Reviewing pre-1917 policy in the railway zone, the writer lamented, "but now the results of this colonization activity are returning with consequences for Soviet Russia." His only expressed concern was the fate of the Russian families now caught without consular protection. Little mention was made of the military and economic factors influencing Russian interest in the CER. China's strategic needs were sketched in this article, as well as her inability to protect them from Japanese imperialism. In the light of later Soviet accusations of maladministration by Peking, it is interesting to find here a refutation of charges that the Chinese were unable to manage the railway. In fact, the writer held that the Chinese did no worse in this respect than the Russians. As for the estimated 400,000 Russians in the area, he concluded they would either have to be "integrally organized into the economy of Manchuria or else be forced to leave."

Vilensky contributed a short but puzzling bit to the story of Soviet statements on the CER when, in a contemporary review of Far Eastern affairs, he compared the Shantung railroad "of several hundred versts," for which Japan was demanding exorbitant payment, with "the Chinese Eastern Railway, of almost 2,000 versts, which Soviet Russia is returning to China without redemption." [11] Except for Vilensky's pamphlet of 1919, this was the only instance where a Soviet commentary, available to Moscow readers, stated the Narkomindel position in such generous terms.[12]

The most significant article on Sino-Soviet relations in the fall of 1922 appeared shortly after Joffe had returned to Peking from his abortive conference in Changchun. Mark Kazanin, writing in the official Narkomindel journal, presented a long, cautious analysis of the prospects in Peking. It was anything but optimistic.[13] Political turmoil in China, heightened by intrigue among the great powers, was relieved only by the presence of Wellington Koo, "young but experienced, known to Soviet diplomats." This favorable estimate was not shared by later Narkomindel writers who were to attack Koo bitterly. Kazanin went on to say that, if ordinary conditions were to prevail, the Chinese statesman would strive for an agreement with Russia within the limits already taken by European powers. Such was not to be the case, unfortunately, because

. . . conditions unfavorable for such decisive means of action exist: internal dissension and division of China, defection of Manchuria and Mongolia—main points, around which will turn the future treaty—all this forces China not to hurry and to await other, more favorable situations to begin negotiations. Of a political alliance with Russia, the striving for which might compel China to ignore temporary and minor interests, there can be no talk, inasmuch as territory uniting China and Russia is in the hands of Chang Tso-lin, and as a result, out of the control of Peking. At the head of the department of Russian affairs stands, as before, the former minister to the Tsar, Count Liu Tsin-chen, mistrustful and shortsighted in matters pertaining to Russia, and to an important degree obstructing the way of negotiations.[14]

Lest his readers think that Soviet representatives made no efforts to cope with these challenging circumstances, Kazanin reviewed at some length Joffe's dinners and receptions, contrasting the attacks these had brought Joffe from the foreign press with favorable Chinese reaction. After one reception given for the Russian by the chairman of the Chinese Parliament, thirty deputies had sent a petition to the government calling for immediate recognition of Soviet Russia to be followed by negotiations on other matters. But the Narkomindel scribe warned: "The first stage . . . lasting almost three weeks, gave no concrete results. . . . The treaty will be concluded not with the Chinese people, but with the Chinese Minister of Foreign Affairs."

With the stage thus set for his readers, Kazanin introduced a succinct statement of the issues at hand in Sino-Soviet relations: "They are briefly these: (1) trade treaty, (2) Mongolian question, and (3) the CER, or—making the last question broader—the Manchurian problem." The first matter, trade, was dismissed by him as having been amply covered in the Soviet renunciations of unequal rights, tariff privileges, and customs control. However, the other two deserved fuller treatment, and accordingly the following revealing analysis was made:

. . . Much more complicated is the question of Mongolia. . . . Chinese, in their arguments, tend to ignore completely the Mongolian Revolutionary Government. The question is very different and although in essence is immeasurably small, in comparison with the question of rapprochement with China, it awaits its solution.

Even more difficult and complicated is the question of the CER—to which are tied a whole bundle of political, military, and financial interests of a series of powers. Chinese consider the CER a legacy of the Tsarist aggressive policy, and since Soviet Russia has renounced such policies, want to receive the railroad back. . . . [While China focuses on the economic question] it entirely overlooks the political side of the question and the necessary guarantees. . . . The Chinese Minister of Foreign Affairs . . . will insist particularly on the buying-back of the CER from Russia.

All three questions are exceptionally important. But even more important for us must be the question of establishing definite mutual relations with China. The Chinese question—this is the basic question of our Eastern policy and should receive the maximum attention and good will, so that it may be solved in as friendly and as prompt a way as possible. Chinese sovereignty, which is beginning to be actually respected by imperialists, undoubtedly meets with full and unconditional recognition on the part of Soviet Russia.[15]

It was certainly difficult to reconcile the avowed recognition of "Chinese sovereignty" with the Soviet diplomatic record in Outer Mongolia. Similarly, the significant shift in emphasis from the *economic* importance of the Chinese Eastern Railway to the "political side of the question" raised serious doubts of the "good will" attending Soviet policy in the Far East. A clear-cut argument could be made for guaranteeing transit rights to Russia on the CER, and some reasonable plea might be allowed for non-discriminatory freight rates to cover Russian imports from Manchuria. However, the question of political influence could not be answered by written agreements. Chang Tso-lin was firmly astride the CER and his tendency to affiliate with Japanese interests was notorious. Only by direct Russian participation in the administration of this vital railway could a lasting settlement of the "political side" be made certain. Such a demand had not yet been voiced in Moscow or Peking, but it was certainly foreshadowed in the Kazanin article. Perhaps it was this knowledge of imminent Soviet action that made Kazanin pessimistic concerning the possibility of an immediate settlement in China.

Meanwhile, in Peking, Joffe sought to strengthen his position in the eyes of the Chinese populace so that added pressures might be brought to bear upon Koo and his associates to conclude negotiations favorable to Russia. His avowed desire, "to establish friendly and good relations between the Russian and Chinese peoples," [16] was manifested in the strikingly conciliatory tone Joffe used in public gatherings as compared with the firm hostility of his notes to the Waichiao Pu. On the one hand, his press releases continued to state Russia's exclusive aim as helping to build a strong China against the West. On the other hand, Joffe's note of October 14, 1922, protested to China over seven alleged cases of White Guard troops using northern Manchuria as a base for attacking territory of the Far Eastern Republic:

Not only are the Chinese authorities in northern Manchuria failing to hinder the White Guardist organizations, but they are even assisting the white bandits in their urge [*sic*] to deal a blow at the Russian people . . . [there is] irrefutable information confirming assistance rendered White bandits in northern Manchuria by the Chinese authorities.[17]

As noted previously, Soviet commentaries in Russia had admitted that northern Manchuria was entirely out of Peking's control, but it served Joffe's purpose to blame the Chinese Foreign Office for all acts committed under Chang Tso-lin's jurisdiction.

Dr. Koo did not long remain on the defensive. Joffe soon received several protests concerning reports of high taxation and overevaluation of Chinese goods in Outer Mongolia.[18] Levies and poll taxes had singled out Chinese merchants, while customs stations had practically halted trade by means of a 20 percent ad valorem tax on all exports from Mongolia. As a final blow, two thousand Chinese farmers, artisans, and merchants allegedly had been deported from Urga. In view of the obvious anti-Chinese sentiments of the Mongols and Russia's hope of winning a dominant position in Mongolia's profitable trade activity, discussed openly in Soviet journals, the charges probably had much validity. Joffe was not to be trapped so easily, however. He parried skillfully by denying that Russian military commanders held any responsibility in these matters and suggesting that the incidents be taken up directly with local Mongolian authorities.[19] The Russian repeated Chicherin's promise of the eventual withdrawal of Red troops but charged that White Guard elements were still using China as a base for attack against Soviet Russia. Although Peking attempted to meet this by issuing fresh orders for the disarming and expulsion of White bands fleeing across the border, Joffe refused to be pacified, continuing his protests and demanding Russian participation in the disarming and evacuation of the renegades.[20]

Notes flowed from the Russian mission in Peking like the mighty spring floods, each stronger than the last. Joffe returned to a central theme, the Chinese Eastern Railway, in a voluminous document of November 3, 1922.[21] Speaking of "the urgent necessity for immediate action," he proceeded to outline a case of mismanagement and corruption for which Chief Engineer Ostroumov was allegedly responsible. Ostroumov had been appointed by the Russo-Asiatic Bank in 1920 and was wholly unacceptable from the Soviet standpoint. In the course of this communication, a sharp note was sounded which clashed harshly with the earlier Karakhan manifestoes: "As a matter of fact, the Russian Government alone has the right practically to interfere, being more than any other Government concerned with the future of this railroad, since it was built with the Russian people's funds [sic] and is Russian property until Russia, of her own free will, decides to confer elsewhere her right of ownership." It was French loans, raised in the 1890's, which had passed through the Tsarist treasury, becoming Russian roubles en route, and which had ultimately financed the original construction of the CER. Their classification as "Russian people's funds" was pure sophistry, as both Peking and Moscow must have realized. Furthermore, Joffe omitted all reference to China's rights in this matter, giving the impression, perhaps unintentionally, that Russia was the *only* government with a major interest in the railroad.

The strong Soviet protest continued with a list of measures to be taken by China, including the arrest of Ostroumov and the temporary appointment of a new CER administration "in agreement with Russia" which would completely replace the Russo-Asiatic Bank. In case China balked at admitting Russian participation in the railroad's management, Joffe closed with a mixture of demands and implied threats: "The action of the Chinese Government at this juncture will have an important bearing on the policy which the Russian Government will pursue in regard to the CER at the forthcoming negotiations and may, indeed, prove the decisive factor."

As if Joffe thought his Chinese protagonists might have missed the implications of his remarks, an explicit statement on the celebrated Karakhan manifestoes was made on November 5, worth quoting extensively because of its completely unconciliatory tone:

Notwithstanding the fact that the non-fulfillment by the Chinese Government of the conditions stipulated in these Declarations could, in all right and justice, free Russia from the promises she had given in the same, the Extraordinary Plenipotentiary Envoy of the RSFSR to the Republic of China deems it necessary, with a view to avoiding all possible misunderstanding, once again to emphasize that the Workers' and Peasants' Government still takes its stand on the basis of these Declarations in general and in the question of the CER in particular.

However, with a view, again to avoiding any misunderstanding whatsoever . . . deems it necessary at the same time to stress that, on the one side, it was quite wrong to draw this inference from these Declarations, that Russia renounces all her interests in China. By these Declarations Russia had renounced the predatory and violent policy of the Tsar's Government and promised to renounce those rights which had accrued to Russia from this policy. But firstly, until all these questions shall have been settled on a free accord between Russia and China, Russia's rights in China will not have lost their strength, and secondly, *these Declarations do not at all annul Russia's legal and just*

*interests in China. In particular, for instance, even if Russia vests in
the Chinese people her title to the CER, this will not annul Russia's
interest in this line, which is a portion of the Great Siberian Railroad*
and unites one part of the Russian territory with another. On the other
hand . . . the promises stipulated in these Declarations of 1919 and
1920, which the Workers' and Peasants' Government still recognizes
as binding it today, cannot after all be valid forever, and that, therefore, *unless the Chinese Government discontinues its ignoring of the
Russian interests, Russia will, perhaps, after all, be obliged to consider
herself free from those promises which she voluntarily gave.*[22]

Thus ran Joffe's "hard" policy toward China. The iron hand
showed bluntly through the seams of the velvet glove.

If Russia thought that its correct legalistic interpretations of
the Karakhan declarations would panic Peking into immediate
negotiations, it was mistaken. Wellington Koo had no intention
of giving up the situation in Outer Mongolia without a struggle,
nor did Joffe's points on the CER escape his attention. A reply
to both notes was dispatched on November 11, promising an in-
vestigation of Ostroumov's actions but refusing any demand for
joint "temporary" administration of the line.[23] Joffe's interpretations of the status of the 1919 and 1920 declarations were confusing and unacceptable in principle, according to Koo, and
further clarification was requested. Koo concluded by insisting
that the railroad be turned over entirely to China, asking for a
restatement of Russia's previous pledge to return all rights and
privileges to China without compensation. At last the issue was
to be clarified once and for all.

Joffe did not dodge the point. On November 14, 1922, he categorically denied that the passage in dispute had occurred in either
Karakhan declaration, quoting it from Koo's note: "It is the intention of the Workers' and Peasants' Government to restore to
China without any compensation, all rights, and interests referring to the Chinese Eastern Railway." [24] The Russian envoy was
prepared to go further, denying that *any* specific proposals had
been made in 1919 *or* 1920, except the suggestion that a treaty be
concluded to regulate the Chinese Eastern Railway. Joffe's cate-

gorical statement was wholly at odds with the facts, since the
1920 declaration had not only included specific proposals on
various topics but had listed them in separate articles as a draft
agreement. In conclusion, the note sounded the warning signal
which by now had become customary for Soviet statements in
China, but it rang far more alarmingly than before. After denying rumored concentrations of Russian troops on the Manchurian
border and alleged Red Army preparations to occupy the railroad
zone, Joffe claimed the charges were untrue

for one reason, if for no others, that, in its actual state, the Red Army
needs no preparations to occuy the CER . . . the Russian Government is not taking a single step which might go contrary to the interests of the Chinese people struggling for its freedom, and *will change
this policy only in the event it is forced by the hostile acts of the Chinese Government.*[25]

Thus far Joffe had reserved for the Waichiao Pu his transition
from protests to demands culminating in implied threats of military force. Carried away with confidence, perhaps, he now lifted
the veil from the eyes of many Chinese Russophiles who had followed his public utterances closely. Joffe's protracted illness prevented his appearing at a dinner in Peking given on the fifth
anniversary of the Russian revolution, but one Professor Ivanov
read the prepared speech. While its theme paralleled the barrage
of notes which had assailed the staff of Wellington Koo, its contrast with previous speeches by Joffe caused it to explode with
considerable repercussion among the large group of sympathetic
Chinese liberals and intellectuals. After the standard introduction which compared Soviet Russia's foreign policy favorably
with the aggressive, competitive imperialism of the West, the
speech moved on to consider the touchy issue of Outer Mongolia:

We only wish that all peoples—and even the people of China fighting
for its national freedom—would, in their mutual relations with other
peoples, as, for instance, with the Mongolian people, be as consequent
and as little imperialistic as the Russian people has remained towards
small nations. . . . I have been able to point out repeatedly that the

stationing of Russian troops in Mongolia concerns Chinese interests no less than Russian interests, and while, in the name of my people and government, I reject energetically the demand for their withdrawal from Urga, the only reason is that I am totally convinced that not only would this be impossible from the viewpoint of Russian interests but that it would be impossible also from the viewpoint of real Chinese national interests, rightly understood [*sic*]—let alone the interest of the people of Mongolia still energetically demanding the Russian forces be left in Outer Mongolia. . . . On the other hand, I have had the opportunity to declare repeatedly that under no circumstances does Russia wish to force her will upon China.[26]

Joffe was dealing with an explosive issue, one which Soviet Russia had already settled to China's displeasure. His tortured statement may merely have been intended to make the best of the situation. No such dilemma arose over North Manchuria, however. Joffe's remarks on this problem did little to enhance his prestige among his Chinese listeners:

. . . Not only is Russia willing to forebear entirely from the violent and imperialist policy of the Tsarist Government—a government hostile to China—but she claims nothing from China. As I had already pointed out, the only question wherein Russia has all reason and full right to expect from the Chinese people that it will understand and satisfy her rightful interests is that of the CER: indeed, this line, which crosses Chinese territory, unites two parts of Russian territory, and as the Russian people, exhausted as they are by their sacrifice in the world war and in the struggle against imperialist intervention, lack the means to build just now a new railroad branch in Russia's own territory, it must inevitably accept this only heritage of the Tsar's regime, which is gone forever. But in this issue also, all that Russia hopes for is that her interests in the question of the Chinese Eastern Railway will be understood and satisfied by China, and that necessary guarantees will be given.

Joffe's address went far to make Russia's "interests" better "understood" in China, but hardly in the manner Joffe anticipated. His explanation of Russian aims and actions was poorly drafted, considering the serious nature of the problems at hand. It accomplished nothing positive in this politically sophisticated audience. China had suffered for too long from similar paternal-

ism to overlook the familiar words and phrases which traditionally presaged another loss of China's power.

Joffe's November 7 address was widely reprinted, as were his
official notes to the Waichiao Pu which eventually found their
way into the Peking press. Chinese reaction was immediate, dis-
persing the goodwill which Joffe had won initially. Typical was
an open letter to the Russian diplomat from a leading professor
of National University.[27] The writer spoke of Soviet pride in its
marked differences with bourgeois diplomacy and then compared
Soviet objections to Japanese troops in northern Sakhalin with
the presence of Red troops in Outer Mongolia. The issue of Urga
had now progressed to the point publicly where the Chinese
Foreign Office felt it could not back down, even had it the desire.
In a counter thrust, it noted an increasing number of border
violations by Red gunboats on the Heilunkiang River and by
Red troops in the Three Eastern Provinces. Refusing to accept
Joffe's charges of Chinese-sponsored White Guard activity, the
Waichiao Pu faced the difficult situation in Urga firmly, declaring: "The withdrawal of Russian troops from Outer Mongolia is
a separate question, which should never be mixed up with the
questions of the navigation rights of the Heilungkiang River and
of the settlement of the CER." [28]

These countercharges from China might have been insignificant in the years of civil war in Russia, for such border crossings
were inevitable with the thousands of miles of unmarked frontier. Coupled with other evidence, however, they suggest that at
the very least, a calculated campaign was under way to throw
alarm into the Chinese negotiators. At the very most, an ex-
tremist group in the Narkomindel may have contemplated a
sudden military move at this time against the Chinese Eastern
Railway administration. Certainly Joffe's notes as examined earlier
support the idea that something was in the air. Moreover, Po-
godin, speaking for the Far Eastern Republic, warned that orders
to disarm White Guards were being disobeyed in China and that

"attacks from one country on the territory of another constitute a *casus belli*." [29] Chinese protests over a raid at Djalanor on December 3 were rebuffed by Joffe with the rejoinder that the raid was made, not by Red troops, but by White Guards disguised as Soviet forces, "possible only because the Chinese authorities do not put a stop to their formation in Manchuria." [30] On December 21, he returned to this ominous theme, warning that "the presence of White bands in China . . . is a constant menace to Russian-Chinese friendly relations." [31] Meanwhile, another piece in the puzzle was supplied in an inflammatory speech by General Uborevich, relayed by Rosta from China: "Another task which has been set upon us we shall also accomplish—that is, to liberate the Russian workers in Manchuria, where the White Guards and the counterrevolutionaries are in full control of a railroad built by the hands and with the means of Russian toilers." [32] Although the news agency later explained that the general had intended to say "redemption" of the CER, instead of "liberation," this hardly removed the significance of the other remarks as far as Chinese readers were concerned.

Joffe hammered relentlessly at the volatile situation in Manchuria. Knowing full well that as long as Wu Pei-fu controlled Peking and Chang Tso-lin held the Three Eastern Provinces, the Waichiao Pu was powerless to act in that area, he continued to attack it for its failure to take punitive measures against border violations, explaining that "up to the present, peace can not be restored along the Russian-Chinese frontiers . . . the numerous official communications on this matter to the Chinese Government . . . are being left unheeded, and today, as heretofore, the CER is freely controlled by the criminal White Guardists." [33]

Old grievances were aired anew as Joffe stepped up his attack. On January 9, 1923, he rejected Koo's demand for compensation to China for services rendered White refugees, ridiculing the contention that China had remained neutral during the civil war. Joffe wrote: "The Chinese Government had also ranked, as is known, among the foreign governments that . . . had carried on a bloody intervention." [34] This was the most violent of his notes, concluding assertively:

From the viewpoint of the Workers' and Peasants' Government, they [China's actions toward White Guards] certainly are characteristic of downright and irreconcilable hostility toward her. . . . The Workers' and Peasants' Government hope that the Chinese Government will alter its hostile position vis-à-vis itself [*sic*], that it will finally make its choice between Reds and Whites, while desisting from its unacceptable policy of being "neutral" between both, and that it will at last cease its propaganda inimical to Russia.

The war of nerves continued as infrequent reports of Russian troop movements along the northern borders continued to filter into Peking. While some of these were undoubtedly inspired by anti-Soviet sources, there was no question of the authenticity of the Far Eastern troops who held an impressive review on Fifth Red Army Day, February 23, 1923.[35] By now, however, the crisis had passed. Joffe had attempted to bring matters to a head with his charges of "downright and irreconcilable hostility." When the bluff was called, his departure from Peking, ostensibly for reasons of health, was the only alternative left to Russia, other than an open use of force. China's position remained firm on Outer Mongolia and the Chinese Eastern Railway. In view of Joffe's insulting notes, it could hardly be expected that negotiations would continue fruitfully, much less that Peking would back down on its declared position.

It is, of course, impossible to evaluate the Narkomindel's responsibility for this "hard" policy or to say precisely how far it was originally intended to go. Undoubtedly elements in the Red Army were anxious to duplicate their success in Outer Mongolia, and Peking's hand was definitely weakened without the support of Japan. However, the situations in the two outlying areas of the Chinese Empire were not analogous. Outer Mongolia had been the base of full-scale attacks upon the Russian Far East. Baron Ungern von Sternberg had been a threat to the peace of the entire area, to Mongols and Russians alike. Whatever pin-pricks may have been felt along the Manchurian border, they could hardly have served as a pretext for armed Soviet interven-tion in the affairs of the Chinese Eastern Railway. Furthermore, in Urga the Reds could count on a large sector of the populace which hated the Chinese and which would welcome a "national-liberation movement." No such unrest could be exploited in the Three Eastern Provinces. These were the reasons which probably stayed the hand that rattled the sword. Unfortunately for Joffe, though, the toughening Soviet attitude toward North China only served as an aid to the many groups which, for a variety of reasons, violently opposed any agreement with the Bolsheviks. Other Chinese, normally favorably disposed toward the "new" diplomacy of Soviet Russia, shifted to an attitude of suspicious concern, motivated by the extremely sensitive nationalism sweep-ing China which Soviet analysts themselves had dissected so penetratingly.[36]

Just as in Outer Mongolia, Soviet pressure in the area of Man-churia coincided with revealing statements in the Russian press which explained Russia's interests more thoroughly than did Joffe's speeches and notes. An unsigned *Izvestiia* article gave a detailed discourse on the Chinese Eastern Railway in which the economic importance of the line was notably diminished, and correspondingly, the political importance was remarkably in-creased—the familiar story of competition with Japan for a sphere of influence in the Far East:

Manchuria is the alpha and omega of Japanese imperialist policy on the Asiatic continent . . . but what profits Japan is unprofitable to China, the United States, and Russia. . . . As for Soviet Russia, it is presently interested in the Manchurian question in two relations. First, interest of security of its borders in the Far East urgently dictates wip-ing out the White-Guardist danger on the side of Manchuria, which for the duration of five years of Russian Revolution was in fact a hor-net's nest of counter-revolution, from which the Russian Far East more than once received a traitorous stab in the back. Horvath, Semenov, Dietrich—all came from Harbin, main center of the Manchurian counter-revolutionary dust-bin. Second, Russia is materially interested in settling the question of the CER which has cost Russia almost 500,-000,000 gold rubles. In the past, the CER was a costly and criminal adventure. Now the CER is a sad heritage of Tsarism, which involves not only the outlay of money for equipment, rolling stock, etc., but also hundreds of thousands of Russian colonists in Manchuria, who serve the needs of the CER and to whose future and interests Soviet Russia can not at all be indifferent.

. . . Soviet Russia stands on the viewpoint of recognizing the full sovereignty of China in Manchuria; it is opposed to Manchuria returning to the arena of international adventurism, directed against China and her independence. Soviet Russia continues to stick to the viewpoint of the necessity of settling the question of the CER to the interests both of China and Soviet Russia, because only from the same point of view can the most expedient solution of the question of the CER lead to equal and normal Russian-Chinese relations in Manchuria.[37]

This analysis spoke for itself, only it took many words to do it. Far more succinct was the presentation in mid-1924 by Vilensky, who was supposedly explaining why Japan and America were so concerned with Manchuria but whose reasons certainly were applicable to Soviet Russia as well:

Manchuria—vast and remarkably weakly populated part of China. Possessing vast natural resources in the form of coal and iron, Manchuria is also a fertile country, capable of producing great surplus of cotton. But most important—that, naturally, is the strategic position of Manchuria, lying on the meeting point of Japan, Soviet Russia, China, and Mongolia.[38]

Thus the wheel had come full circle, from tsars to commissars. Whatever good intentions may have prompted the revolutionary foreign policy of self-denial in 1917 and 1918, by 1923 Soviet Russia was looking at the Far East exactly as had Tsarist Russia. It was an area of immediate concern politically, not only because of Japan's strength, but also because of China's weakness. It was an area of ultimate concern economically, offering raw materials and foodstuffs which might possibly build Russia in Asia as Russia was being built in Europe. The means used to gain these ends embodied not only most of those used by the predecessors of Lenin, Trotsky, and Chicherin but also new ones of propaganda for separatist movements, support of the radical forces in China, and finally open intimidation and threat.

Prior to January, 1923, and Joffe's departure from Peking, the Narkomindel had conducted itself quite properly with respect to the southern government in Canton. Except for private letters of Chicherin to Sun Yet-sen, the revolutionary regime which claimed to be the *de jure* Republic of China was quietly ignored as Soviet representatives tried to negotiate a treaty of recognition with officials in Peking. The first half of this study illustrated the lengths to which Soviet writers were willing to go in order to justify an agreement with Wu Pei-fu in terms of Marxism-Leninism. What the Comintern did was ostensibly its own business; the Narkomindel was negotiating with Peking, not Canton.

Suddenly this careful policy went through an abrupt reversal. Some hint of things to come was carried in two articles written by Joffe especially for Russian consumption. The first, sent from Peking on December 12, 1922, devoted unexpected attention to the Kuomintang as the organization closest to being a genuine political party in China, serving as the meeting point for nationalism and revolution.[39] As if to warn his readers that all was not well with Sino-Soviet negotiations in Peking, Joffe claimed that the individual ties of Wu Pei-fu or Chang Tso-lin were really not very important, that *"dictators come and go, but the masses remain,* and just as in China there has already been born a mass, national-revolutionary movement, so, on it depends the fate of China."* This explanation for his failure in the North concluded by saying that if the possible entente between Wu and Sun materialized, so much the better, but in any case, Russia stood for support of the national revolutionaries.

The Narkomindel conversion to Canton was rather abrupt; perhaps *Izvestiia* editors found the change a little too sudden for their readers, for Joffe's second article was not published for five weeks after its writing. It merits consideration at this point as an expression of his views in January, 1923.[40] Reiterating his previous point on the problems inherent in Peking, Joffe charged that Wu's anti-Sun campaign together with world imperialism formed the two major obstacles to unification of China. He referred to Sun with high esteem, even crediting the Kuomintang leader with exercising an influence over General Chang Tso-lin! Sun Yat-sen was no temporary or accidental phenomenon, but, according to Joffe, personified the Chinese revolution. The inevitable joining together of the Kuomintang and the Communist movements in China would build the mass party necessary to unite China and to oust foreign imperialism. This article illustrates the difficulty of keeping the Narkomindel and Comintern channels wholly separate. Joffe's writing seemed designed for *Kommunisticheskii Internatsional* rather than for *Izvestiia*.[41]

Only the first of these two articles prepared Russian readers in any way for the sudden conclusion of an entente between Adolf A. Joffe and Dr. Sun Yat-sen, on January 26, 1923; the second article did not appear until one month later.[42] Soviet Russia's outstanding diplomat met in Shanghai with the recognized leader of the Chinese revolution and drew up a statement which carried deep significance for their two countries, if not for the entire world. Both parties showed considerable realism in their action. Sun had already written to Chicherin in August, 1921, requesting aid and advice from the Bolsheviks. The West was obviously reluctant to pour the necessary capital into China for developing his grandiose scheme of railways and electrification. Much to Sun's anxiety, Russians had been dickering with Sun's hated rivals in Peking for almost three years and success on their part would mean further problems for him. On the other side, Joffe knew full well the weaknesses of Sun's regime. He undoubtedly had contact with Vilensky, whose knowledge of China was accurate and reliable. Yet he also saw the advantage of winning a handclasp from the respected Dr. Sun in case the Kuomintang should eventually win power. It would serve as a symbol for the Kuomintang-Communist link, even then being urged by the Third International, as well as for Sino-Soviet friendship. Moreover, Joffe may have seen significance in this move for future negotiations with forces in Peking who feared any strengthening of the southern government. Finally, Sun Yat-sen was too dependent on outside help to make any strenuous objections to Soviet troops in Outer Mongolia and Russia was anxious to get any Chinese acquiescence, regardless of how indirect it might be, to its actions in Urga.[43]

Four basic points emerged from the agreement. First, both parties held that "the Communistic order or even the Soviet system cannot actually be introduced into China, because there do not exist here the conditions for the successful establishment of either Communism or Sovietism." [44] Second, Joffe reaffirmed his country's readiness to negotiate with China on the basis of the 1920 Karakhan declaration, renouncing all Tsarist treaties and providing for a new management of the Chinese Eastern Railway. The importance of the CER was underlined in the third point, which stipulated Sun's acceptance of a *modus vivendi* to "temporarily reorganize" the line's management under Chinese-Russian agreement. However, it was specified that this "temporary" arrangement would not prejudice the interests of either party in the final settlement. Fourth and last, Joffe maintained that Soviet Russia had no imperialistic designs in Outer Mongolia nor did it intend to "cause it to secede from China." On his part, Sun accepted Joffe's assurance at face value, refusing to "view an immediate evacuation of Russian troops from Outer Mongolia as either imperative or in the real interest of China." This last point struck an ironic note for those who remembered that it was the Kuomintang which had raised the political storm in 1912 when Russia signed a pact recognizing Mongolian autonomy without consulting China, forcing the ultimate tripartite treaty of Kiakhta in 1915.

It would be difficult to say which party felt more gratified over the entente. Certainly Joffe was fortunate to have partially recouped, in one move, his losses of the previous six months, reestablishing Russia's battered prestige in an important sector of Chinese opinion. He had no intention of dropping talks with the North, as will be seen shortly, although they were to be taken up by his subordinate, M. Davtian. However, Joffe and his Narkomindel cohorts faced some difficulty in reconciling this open agreement with revolutionary circles in South China and their avowed intention of pursuing proper diplomatic procedure in the North. This may well be the reason that, for all its importance, the Sun-Joffe entente received slight attention in Soviet writings, then or later. While the statement won wide publicity in China, it was published in Russia only as a press release. Never was it mentioned in the pages of the Narkomindel, Comintern, or Profintern journals. Furthermore, while the Rosta dispatch in *Izvestiia* and *Pravda* agreed substantially with the version circulated in China, the key phrase in the first point concerning the inadvisability of "Communism or Sovietism" in China was omitted! Considering the theoretical importance of the point as revealed in the first half of this study on Comintern and Profintern debates, the omission appears to be intentional, especially since a reliable authority has shown that a correct version *with* this phrase was received by the Narkomindel in 1923.[45]

In the Far East, Joffe's tactics were by no means exhausted. From Shanghai he moved on to Tokyo to negotiate with one of the very "imperialists" he had just joined Sun in damning as blocks to China's unity. The familiar tactic of playing off South and North China was paralleled by his attempt to play off Japan and China. Joffe's trip to Japan was allegedly for reasons of health, and indeed he had been seriously ill for some time after his September visit to Changchun. However, *Izvestiia* reprinted a small item from the *North China Star* speculating suggestively that only the naive would accept this "excuse" and praising Joffe's trip to Tokyo as another example of shrewd diplomacy.[46] No sooner had Joffe's intended trip been made known than Davtian took up the abandoned post in Peking and, on January 31, proposed that the talks be shifted to Moscow.[47] This was quickly rejected by the Waichiao Pu, which could see little to be gained by traveling the long distance to a capital which initially had sent emissaries to Peking, hat in hand, seeking recognition from China. Davtian quickly assured Koo that his suggestion had been merely intended to speed up negotiations and promised·that they would be resumed as soon as Joffe's health permitted.[48]

Joffe continued to find the Japanese climate more beneficial than that of China. Although his talks with Viscount Goto had been completely unofficial, rumors of an impending alliance between Tokyo and Moscow alarmed China sufficiently to cause the Peking government to appoint Dr. C. T. Wang as head of the Russian Affairs Department in March. Hoping to demonstrate China's increased willingness to negotiate, Wang held a press conference at which he revealed a marked departure from Peking's former intransigent attitude toward Outer Mongolia:

It is China's intention to restart the Russian-Chinese negotiations on Mr. Joffe's return to Peking from Tokyo. . . . I will pay a visit to Marshal Chang Tso-lin. The agenda of the Russian-Chinese conference will be questions regarding Urga, the Chinese Eastern Railway, and the resumption of trade between China and Russia and a few other important questions. *As for the point whether or not trade will be resumed after the question regarding the evacuation of Urga has been settled, or the question of trade be discussed and solved, independent of the question of evacuation, China has not yet come to a decision.* During my present visit, I will carefully study the conditions covering the CER, and acting on the result attained will draw up China's policy vis-à-vis the line.[49]

This position was far removed from the ouster both of Yurin, who sought only a commercial understanding, and of Paikes's "trade delegation" because of Red troops in Outer Mongolia. Evacuation was no longer a prerequisite for negotiations but was relegated to the agenda for future discussion. Some relaxation of China's former stand on the CER was also implicit in Wang's remarks, although this was not stressed so clearly as was Outer Mongolia.

China's concession did not bring Joffe back from Japan where, on April 24, 1923, he was informed by Goto that the Nippon government had decided for a third time to attempt a settlement of the thorny problems of Sakhalin and the Nikolaievsk massacre.[50] Joffe's trip to Japan had lengthened into a six-month visit. By now, Peking had "face" to consider as its patience wore thin. On June 1 it issued a semiofficial statement to the effect that no immediate prospect of Sino-Soviet negotiations existed so long as Russia preferred to conclude an agreement with Japan. Davtian hastened to deny that any such intention was held by Soviet Russia: "Russia will never conclude an agreement violating in any way the interests of China." [51] In view of the Soviet-Mongolian pacts of 1921 and 1922, this reassurance from Joffe's second-in-command carried little weight with the Waichiao Pu.

Meanwhile, the Russian press made no mention of Sino-Soviet negotiations in the six-month period except for one article quoting the position of Li Yuan-hung, president of the Chinese Republic:

China should receive guarantees of the evacuation of Russian troops from Outer Mongolia and send its own troops there. As for the Chinese Eastern Railway, there we are both necessarily first shareholders but the territory through which the CER runs belongs to us . . . I do not propose sending an entire army to Urga, but only a strong guard. In any case, Chinese troops should be there. We intend to act seriously and judiciously in the question of the CER. The Soviet Government will not have any basis to be dissatisfied with our policy, which recognizes all its legitimate requirements.[52]

Vilensky followed the quotation with a cynical remark on Li's impotent position resulting from China's internal dissension and disorder, concluding:

As for Russian-Chinese relations, unfortunately we must state that the unsettled state of these relations, just as the dragging out of the Russian-Chinese negotiations, are the responsibility entirely of the president of the Chinese Republic, Li Yuan-hung.[53]

This assertion was completely refuted by the events since the previous August. Russian-Chinese relations were definitely on the upswing when Joffe won the support of vocal groups shortly after his arrival. Using tactics better adopted for Prussian conference halls than for Chinese tea sessions, however, he had dissipated his strength in bluster and bluff, covering obvious moves of intimidation with thinly veiled rationalizations and accusations. Fortunately for him, Joffe was able to capitalize on the previous relationship between Sun and Chicherin as well as on Sun's growing willingness to work with the Chinese Communists in order to offset his loss of power in Canton. Although the Sun-Joffe entente of January, 1923, boosted Joffe's prestige in China, he decided to improve his position elsewhere, settling in Japan for an indefinite period. A return to Peking at this time might well have brought about the culmination of talks in treaty form, so anxious was Peking to offset a Russian *rapprochement* with either Canton or Tokyo. Joffe played his hand in a different manner, however, prolonging his stay in Japan to the point where Peking had no choice but to declare the mission at an end. In conclusion, it should be noted that even in Japan he was unable to come to a final agreement at this time, although the air was cleared by his talks with Goto so that a settlement of long-standing issues could be foreseen.

All in all, Joffe had only partially understood the atmosphere of the Orient. The Sun-Joffe entente was his main achievement, but his success of Rapallo was not duplicated in China. To accomplish Narkomindel aims, still another effort was to be made, this time directed by the Bolshevik most fully identified with Russia's early policy of friendship and support in China—Leo Karakhan.

XI

The Sino-Soviet Treaty of May 31, 1924

LEO KARAKHAN received his new assignment in late July and on August 2, 1923, left Moscow on the long journey across Siberia to the Middle Kingdom.[1] His name had preceded his person to China by some three years, thanks to the fame of the 1919 and 1920 declarations bearing his signature. Much had happened in the Far East since China had first learned of the Karakhan manifestoes. No longer was the Far Eastern Republic available to sound out opinion semiofficially for Russia. It had been incorporated into the Soviet state in November, 1922, as its buffer service became unnecessary with Japanese evacuation of the Maritime Province. This did not mean that all was well with Russo-Japanese relations. Soviet writers charged that Nippon's exploitation of the South Manchurian Railway had built up the port of Dairen, leaving Vladivostok to die of disuse.[2] Russian economists demanded that the Chinese Eastern Railway be so utilized as to "allow Russia to occupy a position in the Manchurian market commensurate with her international role." [3] Yet by August, 1923, almost 90 percent of all North Manchurian exports were moving over the South Manchurian Railway.[4] Meanwhile, in Tokyo, talks between Joffe and Kawakami had reached an impasse over northern Sakhalin.

China presented a more promising picture to Karakhan, but one that was just as perplexing. The struggle for power between

Peking and Canton remained unresolved. Sun Yat-sen's return to Canton after his enforced sojourn in Shanghai brought no startling changes in the fortunes of the Kuomintang. In accordance with previous missions, Karakhan's destination was Peking, where he had instructions to seek recognition from the government controlled by Wu Pei-fu. Yet much had happened since Wu had assumed power, not the least of which was his shooting of the railroad strikers in February, 1923. Those who had hoped that his ideas on centralized government would bring marked improvements found greater bribery and corruption in Parliament than ever before. Throughout the countryside, lawlessness and looting were increasing month by month. Most dramatic of such incidents was the wrecking of the Pukow-Tientsin express in May, 1923, accompanied by robbing and mishandling of many passengers.[5] Fifteen world powers immediately dispatched demands for stricter order by the central government, showing that foreign intervention was not a dead issue in twentieth-century China. These chaotic conditions had stymied less talented Soviet negotiators, but Karakhan was prepared to seek gains for Russia from Wu's desperate straits. The Chinese general needed outside support and recognition to bolster his tottering regime. A successful conclusion of the long-standing negotiations with Russia was one possible solution to his problems, depending upon the degree of foreign opposition against such a move. Peking had already indicated its willingness to modify its position on Outer Mongolia, while Joffe was sounding out prospects in Japan. Perhaps even the CER could be settled to Moscow's satisfaction as well. It was in this general atmosphere that Karakhan set out to succeed where his three predecessors had failed.

The Deputy Commissar for Foreign Affairs was called upon to display his ingenuity at the very start of his trip. On August 1, Chang Tso-lin's plans for seizing the Chinese Eastern Railway Land Office became known in Moscow. Immediately, Karakhan penned a protest to Chang demanding that the *status quo* remain unchanged until the forthcoming Sino-Soviet conference.[6]

He did not waste his words on Peking in the vain hope that the Waichiao Pu could discipline Chang. Karakhan was determined to get concrete solutions to long-standing problems. If Mukden and not Peking controlled Manchuria, he would deal directly with the famous war lord. Before leaving Moscow, therefore, he held his first press interview, at which he declared:

The main task of my mission is the settlement of the important question of our relations with China. In first place stands the settlement of the question of the CER, which belongs to the workers of Russia but on which, up to now, have subsisted remnants of the White Guard armies of Kolchak and Semenov, using the railroad as a base for adventurist attacks against Soviet Russia.

The second exceptionally important question is the settlement of the rights of the Russian citizens in China. And finally, thirdly, we hope to settle questions creating conditions which might be favorable for developing trade and economic relations between China and Soviet Russia, bringing both countries together.[7]

His omission of Outer Mongolia was not accidental. Karakhan was anxious to deal with first things first. His note to Chang combined with his interview to underscore the importance he attached to the Chinese Eastern Railway. Outer Mongolia could be discussed later.

Despite the sizable anti-Bolshevik colony in Harbin, that city gave an official welcome to the Russian representative on August 11.[8] This was surpassed by the warm reception he received in Mukden on August 18,[9] a promising token of Chang Tso-lin's position. Karakhan's Manchurian trip answered the comment in *Izvestiia* describing the chaos in China on his departure from Moscow: "With whom shall we negotiate?"[10] He would negotiate with those who had the power to carry an agreement into effect, regardless of whom they might be.

Chang Tso-lin intended seizure of the CER Land Office on the grounds that it had been subleasing land for purposes other than strict maintenance of the railroad. Clearly this was a legal excuse to strengthen the war lord's hand along the strategic and valuable railway zone. However, Karakhan made no blustering accusations such as had studded Joffe's notes. He tactfully avoided any criticisms which might have implied that Chang's actions were unfriendly to Russia. In an interview of August 10, he simply reiterated the Soviet position that all Tsarist agreements concluded with China were still in effect, asserted Russia's ownership of the CER until a new agreement was concluded, and attacked Ostroumov and his "White Guard" cohorts for their illegal and "criminal actions." [11] Such tact was to serve him well a year later in his dealings with the Manchurian war lord.

Leo Karakhan understood, perhaps better than any other individual in the Narkomindel, China's needs and aspirations. A lesser figure might have been unable to overcome the unpleasant recollections of Joffe's fiasco that lingered on in the Peking press. He might well have concluded that since public opinion in China was governed primarily by the views of a small but vocal group of literati and by occasional mass demonstrations whipped up under student agitators, no hope or certainty could lie in appealing to this aspect of Chinese society. However, Karakhan recognized that Joffe's errors lay not in his emphasis upon public relations but in his mishandling of those relations. Accordingly, the new mission kept a careful watch on the reaction to its many statements, discerning the appeal that rang loudest the bell of Chinese nationalism. On his arrival in Peking, Karakhan gave a dramatic comparison of the differences between Soviet foreign policy as embodied in his own declarations of 1919 and 1920 and imperialistic foreign policy as evidenced by the attempt of the West to keep China "the Sick Man" of Asia.[12] Avoiding Paikes's blunder of making specific commitments, he added: "At the same time the USSR does not renounce its rights in relations with China in so far as these rights do not violate the sovereignty and interests of the Chinese people."

After this interview of September 2, Karakhan was feted with banquets, receptions, and speeches. Dr. C. T. Wang prodded him at a dinner on September 5, remarking that China had acquired the friendship of the United States, which had refused to accept the Boxer Indemnities; now China hoped for similar consideration from Soviet Russia. Karakhan met this squarely in his reply: "I absolutely refuse to follow the steps of America in its Chinese policy. The USSR first refused indemnities for the Boxer uprising; others followed its example in order not to discredit themselves." [13] It was not difficult to see that America's prestige in China was markedly higher than that of the other great powers, and Karakhan's mission labored steadily on its propaganda to the effect that only Soviet Russia could help an independent China guarantee peace in the Far East. By carefully distinguishing between the "friendly people" and the "hostile ruling-class," he softened the violent accusations which Joffe had leveled indiscriminately in his protests. Karakhan declared that anti-Soviet actions in China were merely the by-product of foreign intervention, not reflections of the true sentiments of the Chinese people. Typical of the change from Joffe's attitude was Karakhan's comment, "Nothing pleased me more during my recent stay in Harbin than the fact that I saw a Chinese administration, Chinese laws, and the realization of Chinese sovereignty." [14] If by this he meant that Chinese rule was more "pleasing" than Japanese administration, he certainly spoke truthfully. The contrast with remarks made only eight months earlier was almost too great. Peking watched respectfully but carefully for further developments from the new envoy. Meanwhile, *Izvestiia* reported the first concrete improvement in relations with the creation of a Russian-Chinese commission to settle frontier incidents along the Manchurian border. [15]

Karakhan soon dispensed with preliminary niceties and proceeded to assail his objective directly. On September 7 the Narkomindel representative informed Wellington Koo that Soviet Russia required formal *de jure* recognition before negotiations could proceed on any of the outstanding problems. [16] Peking promptly rejected this new demand, whereupon a flirtation with Japan was reportedly tried by Karakhan, though apparently nothing came of it. [17] Readers of *Izvestiia* scanned its columns for the entire month following this flurry of activity without finding a word on negotiations in China. The news blackout contrasted ominously with the fanfare of publicity which had accompanied Karakhan's public appearances in Peking. Pessimism was encouraged by an account on October 24, 1923, which told of Karakhan's protest to the Chinese Foreign Office, accompanied by reports of incidents in Harbin. *Izvestiia* continued to print small items on alleged Chinese provocations throughout the winter of 1923–24, while Karakhan increased his pressure on Peking.

Karakhan's first protest, on October 10, concerned a group of Russian ships which had fled Vladivostok after the collapse of the White government and which China now refused to hand back to Russia.[18] On October 22 he dispatched a second note over an incident that interfered with a mail train on the Chita railroad, declaring: "I have every basis to assert that this shocking incident was possible only because the customs administration and railroad gendarmerie at Manchuli station are in the hands of foreigners hostile in relations with the Soviet republic, and of Russian White Guards."[19] Similar language was used in his protest of October 26 citing a number of alleged border violations by China as well as "intolerable and barbarous outrages" committed against Russian citizens in border areas.[20] All these messages concluded with fresh demands for corrective measures.

Suddenly friction in Manchuria flared anew as hostility between Russians and Chinese reached a new peak. Only a month previously, in its new announcement of the mixed border commission, *Izvestiia* had commented favorably on relations in Harbin. Now the semiofficial Bolshevik organ in that Manchurian city lashed out at the Chinese authorities for alleged arbitrary arrests of Bolsheviks and Russians, concluding: "It suffices to walk through the streets of Harbin to note that the Chinese Authorities are rather bent upon rendering the lives of the 300,000 Russians confided to their care as disagreeable and inconvenient as possible."[21] *Izvestiia* followed with a vivid account of a riot of

October 28 where Chinese mobs killed one Russian and injured several others, aided and abetted by Chinese police who were instrumental in breaking up a meeting of Young Pioneers.[22] Further trouble occurred on November 7 when a meeting of Russian workers to celebrate the Russian revolution was fired on by police, injuring four persons. Reportedly the workers had secured prior official permission to hold the rally.[23]

While Karakhan protested the Manchurian incidents in several notes and the events received a prominent position in the Moscow press,[24] Vladimir Vilensky reopened the issue of Outer Mongolia. Writing in *Izvestiia* and summarizing the background of the Mongolian Revolutionary Government, the Narkomindel commentator spoke belligerently of Peking:

. . . Chinese imperialists continue to regard independent [sic] Mongolia as their territory, expressing dissatisfaction with Mongolian democracy. The Mongolian People's Party theoretically agreed to a federation of all peoples of China but under indispensable conditions of freedom from the imperialists, establishing workers' authority, and full equality of Mongolia. Until that time, since China is the tool of imperialists and herself conducts a hypocritical policy, Mongolia will remain fully independent. On this matter is a characteristic speech by the head of the government, Tseren-Dirjun, at a meeting of the People's Party at Urga. On the question of immediate negotiations with China through the mediation of the USSR minister, he replied:

"In China there is now no single government, and it is not known with whom to conduct negotiations. In general, Mongolia will try to obtain independence and if China henceforth wishes to enslave Mongolia, then we will fight."

The words of the president received a vociferous reception from members of the meeting.[25]

It is interesting that the "president" of the new government was quoted as having said that Mongolia would "try to obtain independence," apparently admitting that thus far the international position of Outer Mongolia was still somewhat dubious. His remark on "fighting" China if resistance to Mongolian aspirations were encountered carried no immediate threat, since the few hundred Russian troops supposedly in Urga were no formidable force, nor was the Outer Mongolian army very strong in view of the internal revolts which had shaken the regime in late 1922. However, the reprinting of Tseren-Dirjun's remarks in *Izvestiia* coupled with Vilensky's pointed comments suggested Soviet sanction, if not encouragement, of Mongolian intransigence. Back in Peking, rumors of Red troop concentration along the northern border were denied by Karakhan. There is no indication that these stories had the substance of those a year previous.[26] Russia was certainly not compelled to move belligerently, for opportunities still presented themselves for strengthening its position among the Chinese people.

On November 13, the directors of eight major Chinese educational institutions wrote a joint letter to Karakhan urging that the Boxer Indemnity funds be used for the maintenance of these institutions. His reply of November 15, claiming that Soviet Russia had no intention of accepting the indemnity payments but denying that China had any right to dispose of the funds unilaterally, went to the Chinese Foreign Office, as well as to the petitioners.[27] Although Russia had already insisted that no money go to White Guards or former Tsarist officials, Peking's attitude on this matter was "verging on hostility to the USSR." Karakhan's choice of words prodded the Waichiao Pu into the somewhat specious argument that since it had recognized Karakhan's 1919 declaration renouncing the indemnity, it had the power to assign the funds of its own free choice.[28] The Russian diplomat's rejoinder conceded that he had renounced the funds earlier but correctly claimed that China had not only ignored his declaration in 1919 but had even continued military intervention against Soviet Russia.[29]

This war of words continued in a lengthy correspondence between Leo Karakhan and C. T. Wang in which both sides probed for weak points and possible compromises. On November 30, a Russian note opened with a general résumé of Soviet efforts to reach an understanding with Peking, asserting confidently: "There is no honest Chinese loving his mother country who does not believe today but that friendship with the USSR is actually the main object of the policy of China." [30] Karakhan repeated his earlier demand, insisting that recognition be granted prior to any negotiations as proof that China had ceased its hostile attitude and was willing to function independently of the great powers. This came as a clear rebuff to Wang's proposal of November 28 in which the Chinese negotiator had suggested an agreement on general principles which would cover recognition, the Chinese Eastern Railway, and other matters. Karakhan refused to consider this, probably realizing that evacuation of Outer Mongolia might be made a *quid pro quo* for recognition. He wanted to use his trump card in Urga quite differently, in return for concessions along the CER. In preparation for this, he made an explicit statement concerning the railroad:

Never and nowhere could I have said that all the rights on the CER belong to China. . . . On the assumption that rights of property on the railway as a commercial enterprise belong to the [Soviet] Union, I am willing to discuss at the Conference any proposition of yours, including the proposition that all the rights [of] the line should pass over to China, on conditions to be discussed and decided at the Conference. But even now I can confirm what was said four years ago, namely that the sovereignty of China in the territory of the railway is fully recognized by us, and that we shall not insist on any one of these privileges which the Tsarist government had, and which the other foreign powers still have today in the Railway Zone.[31]

The over-all tone of Karakhan's letter was too hostile for the closing words concerning the CER to be taken at face value. Wang's stàted position was that the fate of the railroad had already been settled by the manifestoes, and all that a conference could discuss profitably would be the necessary guarantees to Russia that no foreign power would have greater privileges than did the USSR. December passed as the Waichiao Pu prepared its next move, and on January 9, 1924, Wang finally replied to Karakhan. In a minor parry he noted that whereas the Russian had reiterated his desire to negotiate on the basis of his earlier declarations, there seemed to be a serious discrepancy in the text of the 1919 manifesto as submitted by the present Soviet mission and the text as received by Peking, "signed and certified as a true copy by Mr. Yanson." [32] This was a lost cause, however. The issue of the disputed passage had long since lost its importance with the previous assertions of Joffe and Karakhan on the "erroneous version." Far more crucial was Wang's comparison of Soviet words with Soviet actions:

> In your opinion the Union of Soviet Russia [*sic*] has by its declarations of 1919 and 1920 shown its complete friendliness to China. In the opinion, however, of the Chinese people this friendliness still leaves something to be desired, since the troops of your Government are still stationed in Chinese territory, namely in Outer Mongolia.
>
> To sum up. When two nations desire to maintain friendly relations with each other it is essential that a formal agreement shall first be signed by them which may be capable of mutual observance. If, on the other hand, only the normal relations are resumed while outstanding questions are to be left for settlement at a future date, how can the Chinese people be expected to be satisfied therewith? [33]

The situation had been summed up completely. With this impasse, negotiations broke down and the Peking *pourparlers* remained quiescent for some time.

Curiously enough, the Narkomindel appears to have made a belated effort to take some action in Urga which would reassure Peking. Despite the obvious wording of the 1921 treaty recognizing the People's Revolutionary Government as "the sole legal Government of Mongolia" and remarks by such leading writers as Vilensky concerning "independent Mongolia," Russia now hedged on its interpretation of Mongolia's status. Vasiliev, Soviet minister to Urga, presented his credentials in January, 1924, stating:

> I will say definitely that present conditions do not permit of our speaking or referring to the "independence" of Mongolia; the only thing referred to is "autonomy" for your country. But here it is important to emphasize that the difference between the two is more apparent than

real. . . . Even if you have merely autonomy, your allegiance will be but nominal. You should be strong enough to insist on being allowed to go you own way along the road to progress and freedom.[34]

This juggling of words was probably intended more for Peking's benefit than for Urga's, but such statements were rather belated. Furthermore, Kalinin, as head of the Soviet government, received the credentials of the Mongolian representative on January 11, 1924. The ceremonies included many references to Soviet help and much stress on Soviet-Mongol relations, but not a word concerning China.[35] Only Vasiliev continued the cautious policy, as shown by his remarks at a dinner given in his honor. In reply to a question from a Mongolian general on the necessity of "giving an armed blow to the aggressive intentions of the Chinese," he explained that the USSR opposed forcing events which would sharpen relations between Mongolia and China, "and in general [is] against rattling arms." [36]

Karakhan may have sensed the impending break in the discussions, but his actions prior to Wang's January letter revealed no anxiety. On December 21 he attacked an alleged order by the governor of Kiangsu province which interfered with trade rights of Russian citizens. His strongly worded note threatened to terminate trade relations with all who supported the Peking regime if no remedial action were taken.[37] Again, on January 8, the Narkomindel official repeated his charge that the illegal sale of Russian ships which had fled Vladivostok indicated White Guard influence over Peking.[38] This protest of Karakhan's was the last item about his activities to appear in *Izvestiia* for over six weeks, reflecting the suspension of negotiations between Wang and Karakhan.

Khodorov provided readers of the Narkomindel magazine, *Mezhdunarodnaia Zhizn'*, with another of the many shifts in Soviet foreign policy interpretation. In a detailed analysis of the economic significance of the Chinese Eastern Railway, no support was given the earlier demand that China understand "the political side of the question." On the contrary, he declared that in appreciation of Russia's strategic and *economic* position, all powers should be excluded from the area except Russia and China:

It is self-evident that in establishing full clarity in the mutual relations between Russia and China in the questions of the CER, it is necessary to remember that the USSR does not lay claim to political rights in the railway zone, acknowledging, not by words, but by acts, the sovereign rights of China. It is a matter of the utilization of the economic significance of the CER, equally necessary for Russia and China.[39]

This reversal of position may have been intended to placate Waichiao Pu sensitivity concerning Chinese sovereignty, paralleling the belated effort to substitute the word "autonomous" for "independent" with reference to Outer Mongolia.

February 2, 1924, brought good news for the Narkomindel, for on that date Great Britain accorded Soviet Russia *de jure* recognition. An unmistakable breach in the anti-Soviet coalition, this action would now permit China to follow suit, to "follow the tendency of her Allies," as Peking had stated it. Vladimir Vilensky waxed optimistic in an article discussing the probable impact of this event on the Far East. In 1919, he had speculated on Sino-Soviet relations from the viewpoint of Russia's dire need of an alliance with China. In 1924, he was concerned primarily with the advantage such an alliance would bring to China, deciding that it was up to Soviet Russia to "grant" it to Peking:

China—the nearest neighbor of the USSR. Having almost 10,000 versts of common border, China is exceptionally interested in establishing normal relations with the USSR—not only politically but economically. Suffice to show that unsettled Russian-Chinese relations reflect unfavorably on the tea industry of China—one of the means of welfare for millions of Chinese people. Another point—the Manchurian problem. The economic development of Manchuria is closely tied to the Chinese Eastern Railway which belongs to the Soviet republic [*sic*] but the question of which remains unsettled between China and the USSR.[40]

Thus in five years the roles had been completely reversed. The shift of power had strengthened Moscow and weakened Peking.

While the Bolsheviks had successfully wiped out foreign inter-
vention and civil war and had finally won recognition from
Great Britain and Italy, the Peking rulers were faced with the
announced coalition of Kuomintang and Communist forces in
Canton, carrying implications of help for Canton from the Third
International.

The years of procrastination were past. The Narkomindel decided to move swiftly in China now that its position elsewhere
had been consolidated. The six-week silence in *Izvestiia* concerning China was broken at the end of February, 1924, with the
report of a sharp note from Karakhan to the Chinese Foreign
Office.[41] He warned that no action on the CER could be taken
without the approval of Soviet Russia and that the *status quo*
must be scrupulously observed because "insignificant changes
might have most serious consequences for China." This dispatch
was followed by Vilensky's most violent attack to date against
the Chinese authorities. In a front-page essay, "Chinese Aggressiveness," he lumped Chang Tso-lin together with the authorities
in Peking, summarizing point by point Karakhan's many protests.[42] Vilensky minced no words in threatening the end of negotiations in China should Peking not comply with Soviet demands
immediately. The length of the article precludes quoting it entirely, but the following excerpts are characteristic of its general
tone:

> . . . [The] hostile actions of the Chinese administration in relation
> to the Russian citizens and the interests of Soviet Russia in the Far
> East . . . cannot be termed other than Chinese aggression against the
> interests of Soviet Russia. . . . The Manchurian administration, evi-
> dently in agreement with the Peking government . . . in every way
> acts contrary to the interests of Soviet Russia and of the entire Russian
> population.
> . . . Soviet Russia has never, in any declaration, renounced its in-
> terests nor the principle of reciprocity, and even less did she think of
> giving anyone a right to unilateral action. Soviet Russia has shown
> much patience in its peaceful policy. China therefore cannot complain
> of Soviet impatience. Suffice to say that we already have our fourth

diplomatic mission in China. One can wait a long time, but even patience has its limits, especially when Chinese officials misinterpret our patience. One of two things: either the present rulers of China actually strive for friendship with Soviet Russia, then they should renounce the anti-Soviet policy in Manchuria; or, official China wishes to prolong this aggressive policy, then it must say this openly.

Peking could afford to wait no longer. If Soviet troops were still in Urga, the best would have to be made of a bad situation. Negotiations were resumed between Karakhan and Wang, despite the official protests of the French Minister, de Fleurian. On March 12, de Fleurian warned that unless the Russo-Asiatic Bank were consulted, "serious consequences" might result from any agreement between China and Russia concerning the Chinese Eastern Railway.[43] This warning was politely but firmly rejected by the Waichiao Pu, unwilling any longer to bow to pressure from Paris.[44] On March 14, 1924, the representatives of China and Russia signed an agreement on general principles for the settlement of questions at a forthcoming conference.

The Wang-Karakhan agreement was immediately hailed in a two-column, page-one *Izvestiia* editorial entitled "Soviet-Chinese Friendship."[45] From the Russian viewpoint, it was a clear diplomatic victory, inasmuch as the agreement specified:

Immediately upon the signing of the present Agreement, normal diplomatic and consular relations between the two Contracting Parties shall be established. The Government of the Republic of China agrees to take the necessary steps to transfer to the Government of the Union of Soviet Socialist Republics the Legation and Consular buildings formerly belonging to the Tsarist Government.[46]

Thus Moscow had won *de jure* recognition from Peking without giving in return anything of strategic importance, and most significantly, without making any serious compromise on Outer Mongolia. Article V covered the situation in Urga:

The Government of the USSR recognizes that Outer Mongolia is an integral part of the Republic of China and respects China's sovereignty therein.

The Government of the USSR declares that as soon as the conditions for the withdrawal of all the troops of the USSR from Outer Mongolia—namely, as to the time-limit of the withdrawal of such troops and the measures to be adopted in the interests of the safety of the frontiers—are agreed upon at the Conferences as provided in Article II of the present Agreement, it will effect the complete withdrawal of all the troops of the USSR from Outer Mongolia.

The conference referred to was to meet within a month, but it was clear from Article V that considerable freedom remained for Russia in defining the necessary "conditions" for evacuation. Although the Red troops had numbered several thousand in 1921 and since had decreased to only a few hundred men,[47] the injury to Chinese sensitivity and sovereignty remained. The first sentence of this article failed to remedy the damage. While it "recognized" Chinese sovereignty over Urga, Karakhan did not bind his country to renounce the treaty of November, 1921, by which Russia had recognized the People's Revolutionary Government as "the sole legal Government" of Mongolia. To be sure, when China agreed, in Article IV, to renounce "all treaties, agreements, etc. concluded between China and any third party or parties affecting the sovereign rights or interests of the USSR," Russia reciprocated by declaring void all treaties concluded "between the *Tsarist* government and any third party or parties." However, nothing was said about treaties concluded by the Bolsheviks injurious to Chinese sovereign rights or interests! This article stood as a sweeping victory for Karakhan's mission.

Karakhan was similarly successful with the Chinese Eastern Railway issue. Article III carried his oft-repeated promise that all treaties between Tsarist Russia and China were to be annulled and/or replaced at the forthcoming conference. The teeth of the proviso was found in Article IX, however, which dealt at length with the strategic railway, over which so much ink had been spilled for the previous seven years:

The CER is a purely commercial enterprise. . . . With the exception of matters pertaining to the business operations which are under the direct control of the CER, all other matters affecting the rights of the National and the Local Governments of the Republic of China— such as judicial matters, matters relating to civil administration, military administration, police, municipal government, taxation, and landed property (with the exception of lands required by the said Railway) —shall be administered by the Chinese Authorities.

The Government of the USSR agrees to the redemption by the Government of the Republic of China, with Chinese capital, of the CER, as well as all appurtenant properties, and to the transfer to China of all shares and bonds of the said Railway. . . . The future of the CER shall be determined by the Republic of China and the USSR to the exclusion of any third Party or Parties. . . . Until the various questions relating to the CER are settled at the Conference . . . the rights of the two Governments arising out of the Contract of August 27, 1896 . . . which do not conflict with the present Agreement . . . and which do not prejudice China's right of sovereignty, shall be maintained.

Not only was China to pay redemption for the railway but the conditions of payment were left unspecified. The clause excluding all other powers from any future role in the CER was as important to Peking in its application to Chang Tso-lin as it was to Soviet Russia in its application to Japan. However, this did not stop Russia from settling accounts on the CER separately with the Manchurian war lord in 1924, nor from selling its share in the line to Japan in 1935, despite angry protests from Peking on both occasions.

The remainder of the agreement disposed of the pledges which Soviet Russia had made, renouncing special rights and concession privileges (Article X), the Boxer Indemnity (Article XI), and extraterritoriality (Article XII). After agreeing to conclude a commercial treaty (Article XIII), the document ended: "The present Agreement shall come into effect from the date of signature." Around this simple sentence turned a dispute that almost shattered the endless efforts of both sides to reach an understanding. The Peking cabinet refused to ratify the agreement, informing Karakhan that Wang had exceeded his powers by attempting to make the agreement effective upon signature. It seems incredible that so experienced a negotiator as Dr. Wang could have made such a basic error, although several explanations were advanced to support this accusation made by government officials.[48] It is probable that Wang was made the scapegoat for errors of judgment within the Waichiao Pu. Certainly the terms of the agreement were not uniformly calculated to enhance Peking's prestige. It had given way in Outer Mongolia with nothing to show but a written pledge to respect China's sovereignty. Before the Chinese Eastern Railway became Chinese property, it would have to be redeemed—not an easy task in view of China's depleted treasury. At the same time, American, French, and Japanese representatives were applying heavy pressure against conclusion of so far-reaching a pact with Soviet Russia.[49] This last point is often overstressed in Western commentaries, but undoubtedly a complex of internal and external pressures prompted the cabinet to take so hazardous a step as refusing ratification.

Karakhan's reaction was no better advised, if more justified. On March 16, he sent a stern letter to Wang, giving a three-day ultimatum for ratification of the agreement, after which time Soviet Russia "will hold responsible for the breaking-off of the negotiations and the breaking-up of the agreement the Government of the Republic of China alone, and will also lay on it the responsibility for all the ensuing consequences." [50]

An ultimatum at this point only added fuel to the fire. Receiving a negative reply from the Chinese government, Karakhan handed an emphatic note of March 19 to Minister of Foreign Affairs Wellington Koo, stating that the USSR

considers the negotiations with the official delegate of the Chinese Government as concluded . . . rejects absolutely any attempt at reverting to the discussion of agreements as already arrived at and signed . . . warns the Chinese Government against committing an irretrievable mistake which will not be without a bearing on the future mutual relations between the USSR and the Republic of China . . . does not consider itself bound by the conditions of the Agreements signed on the 14th of March, and will reserve its full right of freely establishing the conditions of future treaties with China; and . . . [declares that] the Chinese Government will not be able to resume negotiations until it will have without any agreements and unconditionally established normal official relations with the Government of the USSR.[51]

Meanwhile, in Moscow, events took an interesting turn as a result of the situation in Peking. Li Chia-ao had arrived from the Chinese capital as "diplomatic representative" in anticipation of the imminent *de jure* recognition of Soviet Russia by his country, but with the unforeseen impasse he was left in an anomalous position. Chicherin handled him harshly, warning of "the most serious consequences, the responsibility for which falls on the Chinese Government." [52] When Li attempted to parry with the issue of Outer Mongolia, he was immediately rebuffed on two counts. First, Chicherin maintained that the signed agreement should be recognized and that no reconsideration of it was possible, and second, he refused to discuss matters further with Li on the basis that parallel discussions in Moscow could only confuse matters in Peking.[53] Li attempted to make the best of a difficult situation. In a press interview he repeated several times his assurance that all would end well since both countries were friends; this present problem was merely "an incident." [54] Li held that China was only exercising its sovereign right in checking on the agreement and insisted that Wang had misunderstood his instructions. The sixty-two-year-old Chinese delegate emphasized his own sincerity, noting his unwillingness to have made the long journey across Siberia had he not been absolutely certain of eventual Sino-Soviet understanding and agreement.

Vilensky, writing in the same issue of *Izvestiia* carrying Li's apologia, took some of the onus of blame from China and placed it on the ruling circles of France, Japan, and America.[55] Charging that international capitalism was responsible for the temporary setback in Sino-Soviet relations, he asserted confidently that Chinese public opinion would force a restoration of relations between the two great neighbors. Vilensky hit close to the mark. Without any scientific measurement of the *vox populi* of Peking, the reaction from the provinces suggested the Waichiao Pu's stand on the Wang-Karakhan agreement was an unpopular one.[56] Some Chinese, tiring of the five-year lapse since Soviet Russia had made its first stirring proposal to China, demanded that Peking recognize that half a loaf was quite acceptable when nothing but crumbs were offered China elsewhere. In 1924, the many privileges and rights renounced by Russia were perhaps of slight value to the Bolsheviks, but they meant much to a China obsessed with the desire to shake loose from the stifling bonds of nineteenth-century imperialism. Some Chinese supported the Wang-Karakhan understanding for the simple reason that the long-pending Russo-Japanese *rapprochement* would inevitably work to China's disadvantage if the line to Moscow were broken at this point. Finally, there were the scattered but vocal elements of liberal and radical belief who saw their champion in the Russian revolution and were willing to give up an ephemeral hold on Outer Mongolia in return for support and strength from the new force in world affairs—Soviet Russia.

On March 20, 1924, Dr. C. T. Wang was replaced by Dr. Wellington Koo. The next day Koo explained to Karakhan that Wang had exceeded his powers but that if Moscow would drop its ultimatum demanding full restoration of normal diplomatic relations *before* negotiations, Peking would resume discussions gracefully. Karakhan remained adamant; Wang's misdemeanors were no concern of his.[57] If the Chinese Foreign Office did not meet Russia's demands, it would pay the consequences when the Chinese people learned who was to blame for the impasse. Meanwhile, Wang had carried his case to the public forum, insisting that he had acted correctly throughout negotiations. As the controversy raged in the press of both capitals, Peking endeavored to explain its position on March 20 in a circular wire to the provinces. Here was the most concise statement of the official reasons for rejecting the Wang-Karakhan agreement, quite apart from Wang's alleged infraction of protocol. The Waichiao Pu called attention to the inconsistency of "recognizing the sovereignty of China" in Outer Mongolia with the "keeping in force of Mongolian-Soviet treaties and the maintenance of a Russian Minister in Urga." [58] It continued: "The invasion of Russian troops is an act against China's sovereignty, and the troops should be withdrawn immediately, with no conditions to follow." Finally, the wire expressed fear that the transferal of former Russian property in China to the Soviet government might set a precedent interfering with the selling and buying of property held by foreigners in China. It was only on this last point, least important of all, that China was to win any concession from Russia.

Karakhan waited until April 1 before receiving a reply to his second note demanding recognition before negotiation and denying responsibility for the termination of negotiations. The Waichiao Pu on that date emphasized that all contacts between Wang and Karakhan had been in the nature of informal conversations, "as Mr. Karakhan had insisted on avoiding all formal negotiations." [59] Referring to the Russian's letter of March 24 alleging that the three-day limit was not to terminate negotiations but rather to hasten them, Peking remarked:

. . . It is most surprising that the Soviet Envoy, after having set the time-limit, should turn around and blame China for not having asked an extension thereof. . . . It was a mistake on the part of the Soviet Envoy to have set a time-limit at all, for it appears to be an unprecedented procedure for one party to set a time-limit to the other in the nature of a threat when both are engaged in the common task of establishing friendly relations. The Chinese Government did not ask to prolong it, because they could not recognize that the Soviet Envoy had any right to impose a time-limit on the Chinese Government.

With this reaffirmation of its authority to move freely, the Waichiao Pu proposed three modifications of the draft agreement: renunciation of Mongol-Soviet treaties, withdrawal of Red troops immediately and unconditionally, and nonassumption of Russian property rights. Particular importance was placed on the specific demand that *all* treaties violating the sovereignty and interests of either party be renounced. As for Karakhan's insistence on prior recognition of Soviet Russia, the note referred to the first article of the draft agreement:

. . . The completion of the draft agreement, with the proposed modifications and by formal signature of duly authorized representatives, would at once achieve the object which Mr. Karakhan has most in view, and which the Chinese Government are equally desirous to see fulfilled. The inauguration of such relations is not an end in itself. The essential point is that such relations should be re-established on a sound basis of friendliness and good understanding.[60]

Suddenly a curtain of silence surrounded the participants in the discussions and nothing more could be learned for almost two months. Rumors filled the press, and once again warnings to the Chinese officials came from the French and American legations.[61] These admonitions to break all contact with Russian representatives substantiated Koo's fear of foreign intervention and gave emphasis to his plea to Karakhan that all contact be kept completely confidential pending final agreement.[62] Meanwhile, in Moscow the fiction was maintained that all talks had been discontinued. Davtian commented sharply upon his arrival in the Russian capital: "We are not obligated to China; they are obligated to us." [63] He lashed at Koo as a tool of the imperialists, giving as evidence the fact that not only had Koo been educated in the United States but he could read and write English fluently. The writer ignored the fact that Karakhan also could read and write English! Somewhat cryptically, Davtian closed with an assurance to his audience that some agreement would be reached in the future between the two powers.

Realizing the futility of further delays, Peking capitulated. To the dismay of the foreign representatives, the Sino-Soviet treaty of recognition was concluded on May 31, 1924, between M. L. Karakhan and Dr. Wellington Koo. The secrecy of the previous two months had been well justified, for a storm of criticism from the diplomatic colony immediately broke upon the Chinese foreign office. However, support among the native populace was widespread. China had at last come of age in the modern world, negotiating a wholly new treaty with a major power on a basis of equality.

In essence, the treaty was very similar to the preliminary text agreed to three months earlier between Karakhan and Wang. It provided for the establishment of diplomatic relations, cancellation of Russian extraterritoriality, removal of concession privileges, and renunciation of Tsarist treaties. China again refused to recognize any treaties concluded by Soviet Russia which affected "the sovereign rights and interests of the Republic of China," but Soviet Russia did not express its support of this section of the treaty, thus leaving untouched the Soviet-Mongolian treaty of 1921.[64]

China's expressed concern over the problem of Russian property was to be discussed at the forthcoming conference, transfer to the USSR to be determined in accordance with Chinese law. The Boxer Indemnity was to be used solely for the promotion of education in China, and China agreed not to transfer any of the renounced rights or privileges of Russia to a third party or foreign organization.

In view of the furore over the earlier agreement and the official objections voiced in the wire to the provinces, some basic change might have been expected in the two sections of the treaty referring to Outer Mongolia and the Chinese Eastern Railway. The Waichiao Pu had taken a calculated risk in its handling of Wang; some improvement in its position must have been anticipated. Such was not the case, however. On the first problem, Outer Mongolia, the phrases read approximately as before except that the word "questions" was substituted for the word "conditions" in discussing the evacuation of Red troops from Urga:

The Government of the USSR declares that as soon as the questions for the withdrawal of all the troops from Outer Mongolia—namely, as to the time-limit of the withdrawal of such troops and the measures to be adopted in the interests of the safety of the frontiers—are agreed upon at the Conference . . . it will effect the complete withdrawal of all the troops of the USSR from Outer Mongolia.[65]

It is difficult to see what importance Peking attached to the change in wording. The fact remained that China still had not won its minimum demand of immediate evacuation of Russian soldiers from an area recognized in the same treaty as being under the sovereign rule of China.

In addition to the provisions for the Chinese Eastern Railway, already cited in connection with the abortive March agreement, Koo and Karakhan included plans for a provisional management of the railway, recognizing that

inasmuch as the Chinese Eastern Railway was built with capital furnished by the Russian Government and constructed entirely within Chinese territory, the said Railroad is a purely commercial enterprise and that, excepting for matters appertaining to its own business operations, all other matters which affect the rights of the Chinese National and Local Governments shall be administered by the Chinese Authorities.[66]

Soviet strategy was cleverly implemented in the details for this provisional management. A Board of Directors of five Russians and five Chinese was established, one of the latter being appointed as both president of the Board and director-general of the railroad. However, this did not assure the Chinese administrators unhampered control of the line, since all decisions required six votes to be binding, giving the Russians veto power. More important, the vital post of manager of this railway "entirely within Chinese territory" was to be in the hands of a Soviet national, while his two assistants equally represented the two signatories to the 1924 treaty. Lesser posts were similarly divided between China and Russia. When the Board of Directors became deadlocked on any matter, the two governments were to have jurisdiction. The Board was instructed "as soon as possible . . . and in any case, not later than six months" from its inception, to revise the 1896 treaty.

While on paper China appeared to have regained control of the Chinese Eastern Railway, it had already encountered serious limitations. Actually, Peking's victory was more meagre than even this cursory examination would reveal. With an eye to the *Realpolitik* of power divisions in North China, Karakhan supervised negotiations with General Chang Tso-lin, negotiations which had been kept in the background since his visit to Mukden in August, 1923. On September 24, 1924, plenipotentiaries from the Soviet Union and the Three Eastern Provinces concluded an agreement similar to that of May 31, 1924. Aside from a few minor details, it duplicated the arrangement providing for joint Sino-Soviet administration of the Chinese Eastern Railway. Although Peking protested that this pact violated the sovereignty of the central government over the CER zone, the treaty remained in force for both parties. The Narkomindel considered itself fortunate to have won recognition of Russian interests in Manchuria from all parties concerned in North China. It was loath to slight one in favor of the other when the ultimate victor was still in doubt.

China's difficulties did not end here. The Russian members of the Board absented themselves sufficiently to make a quorum of seven impossible, allowing full control to pass into the hands of the Soviet manager. The line was the scene of full-scale warfare between Russian and Chinese troops in 1929 when Chang Tso-lin decided to test Russian determination to remain in Manchuria. Finally, Moscow sold its interests outright to Japan in 1935, in full violation of the 1924 treaties and over strong protests from Peking.

The other problems which had plagued Soviet negotiators for so many years were to have been settled in detail at a major conference of Chinese and Russian representatives, this conference having been agreed upon in the 1924 treaties. Here again China experienced prolonged frustration and disappointment, though the responsibility lay less with Soviet Russia than with chaotic conditions in Peking. The initial meeting of the plenipotentiaries was delayed by minor difficulties, not the least of which was the unstable political situation culminating in a *coup d'état* by General Feng Yu-hsiang. The year 1925 saw efforts by both

Russians and Chinese to agree on preconditions for the conference, and finally it convened in August of that year. However,
the ferment in China was too great for any lasting obligations to
be assumed by Peking, and in 1926 the conference adjourned
without reaching any agreement. Civil war erupted anew. Rus-
sian-supported Kuomintang armies drove northward from South
China in successive sweeps against the war-lord armies of Central
and North China. Thus what were originally designed in 1924
as general points of agreement, to be settled definitively at a
later conference, turned out to be the final written bases of relations on major issues in Sino-Soviet affairs. Not until the Sino-
Soviet Treaty of Friendship and Alliance of August, 1945, were
these points to be re-examined in treaty form.

On the two major issues, the Chinese Eastern Railway and
Outer Mongolia, Soviet Russia succeeded in advancing her interests despite China's repeated objections. Bolshevik commentators
made no effort to conceal their satisfaction with Russia's new
position in the Far East. D. Bukhartsev, writing in 1925, struck
a note of triumph:

The completion of our diplomatic victories in China lies in the transference to the USSR of the Chinese Eastern Railway. This is our big
victory, both politically and economically. For political relations, the
transference to us of the CER means a new victory of our diplomacy
in the East and together with this a defeat of American-European diplomacy. For economic relations, the transference to the USSR of the
railroad means a development of our foreign trade with Manchuria,
increasing our national wealth, a step forward in the task of collecting
the property of the peoples of the USSR, separated in the time of imperialist and civil war.[67]

Bukhartsev's words bore little resemblance to the Karakhan manifestoes of 1919 and 1920, much less to Chicherin's munificent
address of 1918.

Less explicit were Soviet writings on Outer Mongolia, yet
here, too, little effort was made to conceal Russian intentions in
an area recognized in the 1924 treaty as lying within China's

sovereign territory. Symbolic of the deeper issue was the presence of Red Army troops long after the initial provocation of Ungern's attack had passed. Writing in 1923, one Soviet commentator referred directly to the possibility of renewed Chinese expansion into Outer Mongolia, giving this as sufficient reason for keeping Russian troops in Urga. His concluding words clearly indicated that these troops were not primarily intended for the protection of the Mongol people, however. As he put it: "The political effect of the military achievement and the revolutionary events of 1921 will be zero unless quick and decisive steps are taken to strengthen economically the Russian political success." [68] No concern existed here for *Mongolian* political success. Succeeding pages in the same journal spelled out in detail how "to strengthen economically" the Bolshevik position in Urga. Russian trade was to be increased by linking Mongolia and Siberia in an extensive railroad network.[69] The writer expressed hopes of increasing Russian investment opportunities in the nomadic area but showed little interest in how these measures would affect the Mongol economy or raise the living standards of the native population.

It appeared at first that the Koo-Karakhan agreements had met China's wishes in Outer Mongolia more fully than had the earlier agreements concluded under Tsarist Russia. The earlier treaties had only acknowledged Chinese suzerainty over the Mongols, whereas the new pact recognized Chinese sovereignty in the area. Examination of Soviet statements reveals, however, that the spirit, if not the letter, of this provision was seldom observed. Contemporary Russian summaries of the treaty contents omitted any reference to the clause whereby China refused to acknowledge any treaties concluded by Soviet Russia which affected her "sovereign rights," including by implication the Soviet-Mongol pact of 1921. Immediately after conclusion of the Sino-Soviet agreement, *Izvestiia* gave prominent notice to the statement of a Mongol delegate to the Thirteenth Congress of the Russian Communist Party claiming that future relations between Mongolia

and China remained to be settled at a conference. He pledged
that his people would "fight in the most insistent manner for the
status quo." [70] These defiant words preceded the delegate's confident statement that Soviet Russia would act as a friendly intermediary at such a conference, siding with Mongolia's claims.
Elsewhere in this issue of *Izvestiia* readers learned of the establishment of a central bank for trade and industry in Urga whose
main shareholders were "the Mongolian Government and the
Far Eastern Bank of the USSR." [71]

Recognition of China's sovereignty in Outer Mongolia brought
no change in Soviet-Mongol relations. Not until January 24, 1925,
did Chicherin notify Urga that the Soviet Union was ready to
withdraw its troops.[72] Between the signing of the Sino-Soviet
treaty and this date had come the formal establishment of the
Mongolian People's Republic, complete with constitution modeled
on that of the RSFSR. In Peking, Ambassador Karakhan notified
the Chinese government on March 10, 1925, that the withdrawal
of troops had been completed, adding that he hoped the conditions which had necessitated the sending of troops initially "will
not be repeated," and advising China to hereafter use peaceful
means in its relations with the Mongols—implying that the Red
Army's intervention had been directed against China from the
start.[73]

At almost the same time, Commissar Chicherin declared before the Congress of Soviets: "We recognize this republic [Mon-
golia] as part of the Chinese Republic, but we also recognize its
autonomy as sufficiently wide to preclude any interference in the
internal affairs of Mongolia on the part of China, and to permit
independence in its foreign policy. . . . In Mongolia we have a
government completely directing its policy along the line of close
rapprochement with the USSR." [74] It was clearly impossible to
reconcile Chinese sovereignty with an explicit prohibition against
interference in Mongolia's internal *and* external affairs. Coupled
with the Karakhan refusal to repudiate the Soviet-Mongol pact
of November 21, 1921, these statements could only indicate Mos-

cow's determination to exclude China from Outer Mongolia by all means.

Such were the consequences of Peking's years of protest and procrastination in the two most important areas of Sino-Soviet friction. Karakhan had indeed performed his mission well, saving Peking's prestige on paper and Moscow's gains in practice.[75] Less dramatic during the course of negotiations but more far-reaching in its impact was the last area in which the terms of the Koo-Karakhan agreement were to be violated by the Bolsheviks—China's internal political order. For that we must turn to the history of Soviet contacts with the Chinese Communists and the Kuomintang and to Karakhan's role in the swift-moving climax of these contacts in the winter of 1923–24.

XII

Soviet Policy in the Chinese Revolution

KARAKHAN'S mission bore twofold significance for China's future. Not only did he accomplish Moscow's long-desired aim of winning recognition in Peking while preserving positions of power in Manchuria and Outer Mongolia, but in addition, he bore directives destined to carry Russia's influence to the heart of the Chinese revolution in Canton, the stubborn refuge of the Kuomintang. Although it is impossible to detail the history of Communist activity in China at this point, a brief review of the years prior to Karakhan's arrival illustrates the course of events which gradually moved toward an alliance of the Chinese and Russian revolutions.[1]

Translations of Marxist texts such as the *Communist Manifesto* and Karl Kautsky's *Class Struggle* had sparked Chinese discussion groups as early as 1919 and 1920.[2] Leading Chinese reformists became radical organizers under the combined impact of events in Russia and growing Chinese resentment against foreign intervention. Influential scholars such as Ch'en Tu-hsiu, dean of the College of Letters at Peking University, and Professor Li Ta-chao, of the same institution, wove new patterns of Marxism from remnants of traditional Confucian principles mixed with threads of Western radicalism. Although materials on this early period are fragmentary to the point of inconclusiveness, it seems apparent that prior to 1920 Chinese Marxism developed as a spontaneous, indigenous movement. Accounts written many years later tell of Comintern efforts in 1920 to build Communist nuclei in China, particularly around the loosely organized following of Ch'en Tu-hsiu.[3] Certain it is that in this year a Chinese Socialist Youth Corps was formed in Shanghai, while Chinese such as Li Li-san and Chou En-lai organized a Chinese Communist Youth Corps in Paris. So far as is known, neither group had representatives at the Second Comintern Congress, but its resolutions undoubtedly became known to them inasmuch as the Comintern journal reporting the Congress was widely distributed in Russian, German, French, and English editions.

Prominent among Comintern members experienced in the Far East was Maring, whose efforts in Java had won him attention at the 1920 Congress. In 1921, he traveled widely in China, meeting Sun Yat-sen in Kwangsi province and attending the formal inauguration of the Chinese Communist Party at its First Congress, held in Shanghai on July 1.[4] His mission was apparently no more than one of surveying the situation and establishing friendly contact with all sources of revolutionary activity. Comintern criticism both of the Kuomintang and of "intellectual Marxists" followed Maring's trip, but already the ties linking Moscow with Shanghai and Canton had pulled Chinese and Russian radicals toward a common goal: the building of a new China.

The year 1922 proved to be pivotal in the development of the Chinese Communist Party, although it is impossible as yet to write a definitive account of the Party's relations with the Comintern. Within China, it moved from intellectual discussion to proletarian organization, taking an active part in the momentous Hong Kong seamen's strike in January and playing a leading role in the First Congress of the All-China Labor Federation in May, meeting in Canton. Chang Kuo-t'ao, one of the founders of the Chinese Communist Party, attended the Congress of Toilers of the Far East in Moscow, held in January, and it is probable that he conferred with Comintern executives at this time concerning the correct policy for his newly founded party. Whatever the sequence of events, in May the Chinese Communist Party made its first bid to the Kuomintang for a joint program and in June published an explicit declaration favoring a "democratic united front" in China.[5] Both in this document and in the manifesto drawn up at the Second Congress of the Chinese Communist Party in July, Lenin's theses as well as those of Roy found implementation, with all of the contradictions implicit therein.[6] They clearly established the separation between the Communist and Kuomintang parties, leaving no doubt as to the shortcomings of the Kuomintang and the "vanguard" role of the Communists. At the same time, they called for a "united front," aiming to link the Chinese Communists with "the most revolutionary elements" of the Kuomintang.

So far the Chinese Communist Party appeared to be following the Comintern's lead, at least as well as could be interpreted from the Comintern resolutions. It should be remembered that Safarov, at the Congress of Toilers in January, had roundly castigated the Kuomintang delegates and made no secret of his hostility to working with them, necessary as it might be. His remarks were seconded by Chinese Communists present. Suddenly Maring, in the role of Comintern representative, reinterpreted policy to the Chinese Communists with consequences vital for future events. At a special plenum of the central committee of the Chinese Communist Party, called in August, 1922, apparently on his initiative, Maring interpreted "united front" to include the tactic of individual Communists joining the Kuomintang as members, while keeping their separate Communist Party membership and Communist discipline.[7] Ch'en Tu-hsiu seems to have led considerable opposition to this on the logical Marxist ground that it would violate the class character of the two parties. A "bloc within" was quite different from a "bloc without." Any form of united front appeared difficult to accept, as shown by the controversy around Lenin's theses in 1920 and the Comintern writings since that date. This form seemed doubly damned by Marxist theory, which allocated separate parties to separate classes. However, by the time Maring left the conference, his point had been accepted.

Some explanation of this twist to the united front policy may lie in Sun's behavior, although there is as yet no complete account of his activity at this time. As indicated earlier, his letter to Chicherin welcomed Soviet advice and aid, but he was not yet ready to form a coalition with the Chinese Communists, particularly in view of their avowed disrespect for the Kuomintang principles. However, simultaneously with his ousting from Canton in 1922 by General Ch'en Chiung-ming, Sun again came into contact with Comintern representatives, including Maring.[8] Sun was in no position to refuse help from any quarter, and he acknowledged his willingness to work with the Communists on a strictly informal basis, permitting them membership in the Kuomintang so long as they supported Kuomintang principles but not committing himself to any joint party action. Li Ta-chao became the first Communist to join the Kuomintang under the new policy advocated by Maring and accepted by Sun.

The arrangement met the immediate requirements of Moscow and Canton. Sun's renewed Russian interest was shown in a letter of August 30, 1922, written to Chiang Kai-shek: "Recently a letter came from a special envoy sent to enquire about the Far Eastern situation and the means of solving it. I have given him my replies in detail and kept in touch with him, and we may easily consult him on various matters as they arise. I hear that he will bring a military officer with him and I have asked him to send this officer to Shanghai as soon as possible."[9] Sun's dealings with Russian and German advisers became generally known in late 1922 when Ch'en Chiung-ming published seized documents referring to Sun's secret correspondence. Close on the heels of these disclosures came the dramatic Sun-Joffe entente, concluded in January, 1923. Peking had ample justification for concern over the prospect of increased Soviet support to the Chinese revolutionaries in Shanghai and Canton, although it should be stressed that all of these maneuvers which took place before Karakhan's arrival were purely preliminary and explorative in nature. Moscow had not yet committed itself irrevocably in South China, nor had anything materialized in the projected Chinese Communist Party-Kuomintang alliance.

After the Fourth Comintern Congress, with its reiteration of the necessity for support of Asian "national-revolutionary" movements, the Executive Committee of the Comintern passed a resolution binding the Chinese Communist Party to closer collaboration with the Kuomintang. Because of its intricate wording, reflecting the essential dilemma of such a tactic, the resolution bears quoting at length:

(1) The only serious national-revolutionary grouping in China is the Kuomintang Party, basing itself partly on the liberal-democratic bourgeoisie and petit-bourgeoisie, and partly on the intelligentsia and workers. (2) Since the independent workers' movement in the country is still weak and since the central problem for China is the national revolution against the imperialists and their internal feudal agents . . . the Executive Committee of the Communist International considers it necessary to co-ordinate activity between the Kuomintang Party and the young Chinese Communist Party. (3) Therefore under these conditions it is expedient for the members of the Chinese Communist Party to remain within the Kuomintang Party. (4) But this must not be purchased at the cost of destroying the specific political aspect of the Chinese Communist Party. The party must preserve its own organization with a strictly centralized apparatus. In important specific problems, the Chinese Communist Party should organize and educate the working mass, forming trade unions in the aim of preparing a basis for a strong mass Communist Party. In this work the Chinese Communist Party must advance under its own flag, independent from any other political group, however, avoiding, in this, conflicts with the national-revolutionary movement. (5) In the sphere of foreign policy, the Chinese Communist Party should oppose any flirtations of the Kuomintang Party with capitalistic powers and agents, Chinese military governors, or enemies of proletarian Russia. (6) On the other hand, the Chinese Communist Party should influence the Kuomintang in the idea of uniting its force with the forces of Soviet Russia for a mutual struggle against the European, American, and Japanese imperial-

ists. (7) Supporting the Kuomintang Party in all campaigns on the national-revolutionary front, so long as it follows an objectively correct policy, the Chinese Communist Party nevertheless must not fuse with it and during these campaigns must not furl its own flag.[10]

Comintern headquarters did not rest content with this directive. At first glance fully compatible with Lenin's 1920 theses, it nevertheless overlooked China's basic problem, the peasantry. Consequently another resolution of the Executive Committee of the Comintern appeared in May, 1923, timed to coincide with the Third Congress of the Chinese Communist Party. Too long for complete quoting here, its references to the Kuomintang bear repeating because of their treatment of Sun Yat-sen and his followers:

. . . (5) . . . The first responsibility of Communists is to strengthen the Communist Party, turning it into a mass party of the proletariat. . . . (6) . . . Our basic demand in relations with the national-democratic Kuomintang Party must include the *unconditional support of the working movement* in China. . . . (8) The Communist Party is bound to continually push the Kuomintang Party to the side of agrarian revolution. In areas occupied by troops of Sun Yat-sen it is necessary to strive so that confiscation of land . . . will be conducted. . . . (9) On the other hand, we in every way must struggle within the Kuomintang against the fighting combination of Sun Yat-sen and the *militarists,* who are agents of foreign capitalism, hostilely inclined against Soviet Russia. . . . This combination threatens the Kuomintang movement with degeneration . . . which will lead not only to the catastrophic splitting of the national front but also to the abandonment of workers' organizations and the Communist Party, since they at the present time are closely linked with the Kuomintang Party in the struggle against the imperialists and their agents in China. (10) With the aim of avoiding such a trend of the Kuomintang (and especially of Sun Yat-sen) the Chinese Communist Party must demand that a Congress of the Kuomintang Party be called as soon as possible at which the question of creating a broad national-democratic movement must be central.[11]

This Comintern directive is exceptionally interesting because, other than that made by Lenin in 1920, it is the first full-bodied statement of China's peasant problem and its role in the Chinese revolution. Its flat assertion that "the central problem of all politics [in China] is precisely the *peasant problem*" gave an additional jolt to orthodox Marxists in China who now were ordered not only to join a bourgeois party but to transfer their attention from the proletariat to the peasantry. The directive's additional importance lies in its reassertion of the united front policy, spelling out in detail the recognized dangers and attempting to plot the path of the Chinese comrades in each of the various problems which might confront them. It is not a naive statement; in one sense its forebodings of "militarists" proved justified in later events, although not for the reasons given. It stands as the most detailed exposition of Lenin's 1920 theses embodied in directives to the Chinese Communist Party prior to 1924. Its adoption did not necessarily still the differing voices within Comintern or within China, any more than the adopting of Lenin's and Roy's theses in 1920 had ended debate.[12] However, it clearly aimed at eliminating whatever reservations might lie within the Chinese Communist Party concerning the terms of the united front project and its prospects.

Crucial to this project was Sun's attitude, yet his mercurial decisions remained characteristic of his behavior to the very end. His many pleas for help had carried him to Japan during World War I, to Western capitalism in 1920. In 1921, he hoped to defeat Wu Pei-fu by joining hands with Chang Tso-lin; in 1922, he considered arriving at an understanding with Wu against Chang. One of his Western biographers has asserted that even after concluding the Sun-Joffe entente, the Chinese revolutionary leader approached American Ambassador Jacob Gould Schurman. Sun's scheme allegedly proposed five-power armed intervention to pacify China internally, followed by a central administration under foreign tutelage to build the new Republic of China.[13] In view of his past record, it is not surprising that many observers were inclined to dismiss Sun's pro-Russian orientation as merely another minor flirtation, even when Sun's trusted follower, Liao

Chung-kai, accompanied Joffe to Japan during the Russian's protracted recuperation.

Unlike Sun's other efforts, however, his Russian soundings found an encouraging response. In mid-1923, he dispatched the young but promising Chiang Kai-shek to Moscow with instructions to ascertain Bolshevik motivations in the Chinese revolution. Following letters of introduction from Sun to Lenin, Trotsky, and Chicherin, Chiang's arrival in Moscow received favorable treatment, convincing him of the wisdom in a Bolshevik entente.[14]

With Sun's knowledge of Comintern efforts to bring the Chinese Communists to a more cooperative position in relation to the Kuomintang and his steadily increasing contact with Russian representatives, Karakhan's task of establishing rapport with Canton was considerably simplified. Many problems remained to be clarified, in particular the touchy problem of negotiating a treaty of recognition with the Peking government, pledging not to interfere with the internal affairs of China, while maintaining cordial relations with the Canton regime, preparing it for revolutionary victories in the future. Shortly after his arrival in the Chinese capital, Karakhan sent cordial greetings to Sun, remarking: "I count on your support, Dr. Sun, old friend of new Russia, in my responsible task of establishing close contact between our two peoples." [15] Sun's reply to Karakhan of September 17, 1923, summarized recent developments and, in discussing Chiang Kai-shek's mission to Moscow, made a significant reference to future military plans:

What follows is rigidly *confidential*. Some weeks ago I sent identical letters to Comrade Lenin, Tchitcherin [*sic*], and Trotsky introducing General Chiang Kai-shek, who is my chief of staff and confidential agent. I have dispatched him to Moscow to discuss ways and means whereby our friends there can assist me in my work in this country. In particular, General Chiang is to take up with your government and military experts a proposal for military action by my forces in and about the regions lying to the Northwest of Peking and beyond. General Chiang is fully empowered to act in my behalf.[16]

Nothing better illustrated Sun's illusions of grandeur than his discussion of military campaigns "to the Northwest" of Peking, meaning Mongolia, while the Kuomintang remained bottled up in the Canton hinterland, its armies primarily composed of unreliable or poorly trained troops. His scheme was to be handled brusquely by Chicherin later, but for the moment Karakhan's primary concern was to shift the burden of coordinating Soviet strategy from the shoulders of the Peking mission. Accordingly, on September 23, 1923, he sent the following letter to Sun, notifying him of the most important step to date taken to solidify the Moscow-Canton entente:

Dear Dr. Sun,

The absence in Canton of a permanent and responsible representative of our government has long been keenly felt at Moscow. With the appointment of M. M. Borodin, an important step has been taken in this direction. Comrade B. [sic] is one of the oldest members of our party, having worked for a great many years in the revolutionary movement of Russia. Please regard Comrade B. not only as a representative of the Government but likewise my personal representative with whom you may talk as frankly as you would with me. Anything he says, you may rely upon as if I had said it to you personally. He is familiar with the whole situation and besides, before his leaving for the South, we had a long talk. He will convey to you my thoughts, wishes, and feelings.

Hoping that with the arrival of Comrade B. in Canton things will be pushed ahead much more speedily than, to my sincerest regret, it was possible till now, and heartily wishing you success in your work, I remain with friendly regards,

Yours,

[signed] L. Karakhan

PS: I thank you very much for your telegram. It has inspired me with great faith in our common cause in China.[17]

Karakhan's letter is the only known source of the authorization given Michael Borodin to act as an official representative of Moscow in advising the Kuomintang. Assertions that he carried papers from the Executive Committee of the Comintern or from the

Politburo of the Russian Communist Party remain unproved in the face of the evidence.[18] The importance of Borodin's appointment not as a Comintern or Communist Party agent but as a "representative of the Government" lies in its verification of the two-pronged policy of Karakhan and the Narkomindel at this time. While negotiating a treaty of recognition in the North, Soviet Russia officially strengthened a rival regime in the South. Borodin was to become the architect of a new Kuomintang, streamlined in aims and method along the pattern of the Russian Communist Party. Perhaps more than any other single person, he was responsible for the successes of the Chinese revolution from 1924 to 1927. Yet his "appointment" was never mentioned in the Russian press, and no publicity attended his activity in China. Again, as in the case of the Sun-Joffe entente, the most signal victories in China went publicly unhailed in Russia because the fictitious distinction between revolutionary and diplomatic activity was maintained, regardless of the actions of representatives abroad. Throughout the winter of 1923–24, Borodin conferred daily with Sun and other leading Kuomintang officials, but not a word appeared in *Izvestiia* or *Pravda* about his work. Only the Peking activity of Karakhan won recognition in publicity and analysis. The most important story went unreported.

Sun's letter to Karakhan mentioning plans for military action "Northwest" of Peking eventually found its way to Chicherin. The implications of such action for Soviet control of Urga were obvious. Having eliminated Chinese competition from this area, Russia was not anxious to allow the Kuomintang banner to replace the Manchu flag. Commissar for Foreign Affairs Chicherin wrote to Dr. Sun on December 4, 1923:

Dear Comrade:
I thank you very much for your kind letter and for the good feelings transmitted through your delegates. We are all very glad that your delegates have come and we are sure of the beneficial results of their visit. . . .
We think that the fundamental aim of the Kuomintang Party is to

build up a great powerful movement of the Chinese people and that therefore propaganda and organization on the biggest scale are its first necessities. Our example was significant: our military activities were successful because a long series of years had elapsed during which we organized and instructed our following, building up in this way a great organized party throughout the whole land, a party capable of vanquishing all its adversaries. The whole Chinese nation must see the difference between the Kuomintang, a popularly organized mass party, and the military dictatorship of the various parts of China. *The fraternal nations, such as the Mongolian people, the Tibetans, the various races of Western China, must clearly understand that the Kuomintang supports their right of self-determination. Their territories therefore cannot be used for your armed forces.* These are some of the ideas which I now nourish in these questions. We must continue our exchange of ideas and discuss the matter further. When we reach a full agreement, everything will go on much better.[19]

More than Narkomindel concern over Russian hegemony in Urga prompted this advice. The Kuomintang's troubles had resulted largely from Sun's reliance upon purely military action, ignoring completely the important activities of propaganda and agitation among the masses. The criticisms of the Kuomintang in this respect were well taken. However, in view of the 1918–20 invasion of the Ukraine and areas of Central Asia by Red troops, against the will of the inhabitants and in full contradiction of the principle of self-determination, Chicherin's advice to Sun could hardly be taken at face value with respect to Outer Mongolia. Russia was not wholly disinterested in Mongolia's "right of self-determination."

Meanwhile, Borodin worked diligently in Canton, reorganizing Sun's party. Ultimately he managed to forge the varying elements that composed the Kuomintang into a fighting force with a discipline and organization unknown in revolutionary China. The story of Borodin's impact upon the Chinese revolution is another study in itself. Here it can merely be noted that by mid-1924, the influence of the Russian advisers in Canton reached its ascendancy. The First Kuomintang Congress in January, 1924, marked not only the full joining of the Chinese Communist Party and the Kuomintang movement but also the emergence of a new spirit of anti-imperialism coupled with proletarian and peasant participation in the political and military apparatus. Karakhan took this opportunity to send another congratulatory letter to Sun, but the Chinese leader's reply of February showed his anxiety over the negotiations in Peking.[20] As "President of the Chinese Republic," Sun pointed out that since Russia now enjoyed *de jure* recognition from Great Britain, it no longer needed to be satisfied with the "non-representative, anti-nationalistic, and pro-foreign capitalist body" in Peking. The best course for Karakhan to follow would be to establish formal relations with Canton. Such was not the design of the Narkomindel strategist, however. Peking was still available to sign away China's interests in Outer Mongolia and Manchuria, and it was to be utilized accordingly. The Sino-Soviet treaty of May 31, 1924, was the result.

One final event marks January, 1924, as a proper point to close the first chapter of Sino-Soviet relations. On January 21, 1924, Lenin died. Despite illness which had lasted for several years, his death came as a deep shock in China as well as Russia. Sun Yat-sen paid special tribute to the Bolshevik leader at the First Kuomintang Congress. Lenin's death at this turning point in the Chinese revolution was indeed a significant event. The brilliant strategist who for so long had constantly reminded his colleagues of Asia's importance failed to see the fruits of his policy. He was not to witness the dramatic announcement of the Koo-Karakhan pact in the face of united opposition from the foreign powers in China. He was not to see the anti-imperialist slogans he had urged become the battle cry in Shanghai, Canton, Hong Kong, and Hankow. He died with the knowledge that his disputed program of cooperation with the bourgeoisie was finally in actual practice in China, although ignorant of the severe convulsions within the Chinese revolution which were to tear apart such cooperation within three years. Lenin's death coincided with the close of the first phase of Sino-Soviet relations.

XIII

In Conclusion

IN examining Sino-Soviet relations from 1917 to 1924, it is evident that there was not one Soviet policy but several. Various factions within the Communist International penned interminable polemics, arguing the means of adapting Marxist theory and Leninist tactics to turbulent, peasant-dominated China. Profintern publicists took a dim view of Asian revolutionary prospects, scorning any dilution of radicalism for the sake of winning friends in the bourgeois-led movements for independence. Meanwhile, the Narkomindel pursued a somewhat zigzag but determined course aimed at establishing Soviet Russia's place in the Far East regardless of the means required. Two fronts of activity in China, the revolutionary and the diplomatic, sometimes worked separately and at cross-purposes, sometimes remained distinct but parallel. Finally, their merger in 1924 placed Soviet Russia in an ascendant position in the Chinese revolution.

Taking the more exposed front first, that of diplomatic activity, one is struck by the sharp contrast afforded by comparing Soviet foreign policy statements of 1917 and 1918 with the march of events of 1923 and 1924. Bolshevik rule began with an avowedly revolutionary, nonimperialistic foreign policy. It repudiated secret treaties concluded by the Tsarist government carving China into spheres of influence. In 1918, Commissar of Foreign Affairs Chicherin outlined a program of self-denial, offering to return the

Chinese Eastern Railway as well as all concessions taken from China by "unequal treaties." In 1919, the dramatic Karakhan Manifesto embodied these generous proposals in a sweeping statement of sympathy for a new China struggling to cast off the shackles of Western imperialism. Within weeks of drafting, however, the manifesto was rewritten; the offer to return the Chinese Eastern Railway without compensation was deleted. As Red Army troops rolled across Siberia in pursuit of fleeing White Russian armies, Soviet policy concerning China underwent the first of several changes. The changes varied only in degree. Basically their similarity lay in the stiffening attitude toward the Middle Kingdom wrought by the transformation of Narkomindel strategists from revolutionary propagandists to Russian statesmen.

From deletion of the CER offer in 1919 it was but a step in 1920 to infrequent references to "Russia's financial and economic interests" in North Manchuria. By 1922, Joffe's statements included outright demands that "necessary guarantees" be given to safeguard Russian interests in the railway zone. Accompanying his demands were violent charges of counterrevolutionary activity in Harbin, rumors of Red Army movements on the Manchurian border, and inflammatory statements by officials of the Far Eastern Republic. Although Leo Karakhan eschewed such belligerent methods, he insisted categorically that Soviet Russia had never intended to give up its position on the strategic line. Both in the final Sino-Soviet treaty and in Soviet implementation of its provisions, China was accorded a secondary place in the management of the important railroad which cut through much of her richest area. Not until December, 1952, did the Chinese Eastern Railway come under full control of a China then ruled by a friendly Communist regime.

Similarly, Bolshevik steps in Mongolia moved antithetically to Chinese interests, although the details differed somewhat from those in Manchuria. Mongolia had long been a buffer area between Russia and China, closer to Peking in many respects than to St. Petersburg. When the Manchu dynasty upset this arrangement near the end of its life by fostering Chinese colonization, Tsarist Russia reacted accordingly and, with the collapse of the Manchus, strengthened its influence in the nomadic region. The November revolution brought a similar opportunity to China, but the predatory actions of Chinese representatives widened the already deep gulf which existed between Mongols and Chinese. Once the area became the scene of White Guard activity, it was to be expected that Soviet moves would be made at the first provocation. Not only could an immediate counterrevolutionary threat be liquidated but possible repetition of Chinese hegemony, or even Japanese influence, could be thwarted.

The significance of the Mongolian episode in Sino-Soviet relations lies not so much in the initial Bolshevik reaction, as with the Karakhan Manifesto, but in the subsequent chain of events. Whereas in 1920 Moscow notified Peking of its willingness to take part in the ousting of hostile elements from Urga, in 1921 Red troops assisted in establishing the Mongolian People's Republic without prior consultation with Chinese authorities. Existence of a treaty concluded in that year between Moscow and Urga was flatly denied by the Soviet envoy in Peking, Alexander Paikes. Russian troops remained in the region until 1925, despite repeated protests by the Waichiao Pu. Soviet spokesmen carefully avoided speaking of full-fledged independence for the Mongolian government but systematically excluded China's political, economic, and military influence. By the Koo-Karakhan agreements, China was to enjoy full sovereignty in the area, yet Soviet statements made clear that this was simply a face-saving clause submitted to for the sake of securing a treaty of recognition.

Thus Soviet Russia resorted to intimidation, intrigue, and invasion to achieve its ends in Outer Mongolia, raising Russian influence far above the level enjoyed by its Tsarist predecessors. By refusing to give Urga *de jure* recognition, the Bolsheviks prevented other powers, principally Japan, from sending emissaries into this strategic territory. By providing the sole military and financial support for the fledgling regime, Russia assured itself of a loyal area on its vastly extended, poorly protected Asian flank.

Reference to the strategic implications of Mongolia's position invites comparison of the Soviet interests in the two key areas of Sino-Soviet tension. In terms of economic factors, there is little doubt that the Chinese Eastern Railway played a vital role in the well-being of the Russian Far East. From a military standpoint, its possession by Japan or any other hostile power would doom Vladivostok, if not all of the Far Eastern provinces. Politically there is much to support the Bolshevik charge that Harbin was a center of anti-Red forces, though it is doubtful how much danger remained to Russia from this area after 1921. By contrast, Mongolia played little if any part in the economic livelihood of the adjacent Russian territory. Its military threat terminated with the execution of Ungern and the smashing of the pan-Mongol movement.[1] Politically its future under an unstable China promised to be of little consequence as far as Moscow was concerned. What little Japanese influence might penetrate through militant religious sects or sporadic arms-smuggling could hardly warrant the safeguards adopted by Moscow during this period.

Measured in these terms, the solutions which Soviet Russia applied to the problems existing along its extensive border can only be characterized as imperialistic in aim, for they sought to establish Russian power in areas recognized as lying under Chinese sovereignty. That this policy was largely a reaction against threats to Russian security from White Russian and Japanese forces does not alter the fact that Soviet intentions in 1917 and Soviet pledges in 1919 proved inoperative once Russian power became established in the Far East.

To be sure, Moscow renounced many privileges vested in earlier treaties, including the Boxer Indemnity, consular guards, and extraterritoriality. However, the substance of these concessions weighed far less in the scales of power than did the gains in Manchuria and Mongolia. Renunciation of extraterritoriality, for example, particularly suited Russia's purpose of embarrassing the Western powers while preserving her own interests. Inasmuch as Soviet trade proceeded entirely as a state monopoly, Russian agents abroad enjoyed privileges arising from their diplomatic status and therefore had no need for extraterritoriality.

In this sense, a qualitative change in Narkomindel policy is marked in the transition from the stirring declarations of 1917, proclaiming a new era in international relations, to the threatening notes of Joffe and the ultimata of Karakhan, insisting that China admit Russian hegemony within her historical borders. Long before Lenin's death, Bolshevik foreign policy completed its evolution from advancing world revolution to advancing Russia's interests, should there be any conflict between the two aims. In China, the conflict between a radical hands-off, anti-imperialist policy and a traditional interventionist policy asserted itself almost from the very start. Re-emergence of the latter in conformity with Russia's historic policy can be traced consistently from the revision of the Karakhan Manifesto of July 25, 1919, to the Sino-Soviet treaty of May 31, 1924.

These questions naturally arise: How was Russia successful in pursuing a policy of self-interest in China while gaining a reputation in both Peking and Canton of being a close ally of new China? Why did Peking rejoice over a treaty which strengthened Russia's hold in areas traditionally part of China? Setting aside for a moment Soviet moves on the second front, that of revolutionary activity with its attendant emotional impact on the Chinese revolution, the answer to these questions is threefold. In the first place, Russia asserted its power only in the peripheral areas of China. With regard to the immediate, tangible issues, Russia acted in a careful, friendly manner. Renunciation of extraterritoriality provided proof positive to those distrustful of all foreign barbarians that at least one country accepted China as an equal member in international society. This concession may have been under consideration in other world chancelleries, but Moscow moved first, winning for itself the title "friend of new China." Removal of consular guards from the streets of Peking and Shanghai made the uniforms of other Western powers more conspicuous than ever. Appointment of Leo Karakhan as the first fully accredited ambassador to Peking placed him over the ministers representing all other major powers. This implied tribute to China's status in the family of nations outweighed Karakhan's earlier notes to the Waichiao Pu attacking it for Chang Tso-lin's activities in Manchuria. It softened the memory of his three-day ultimatum threatening China with serious "consequences" should his demands be refused. Even in regaining control of the Chinese Eastern Railway, the Soviets moved in a manner calculated to convince the Chinese intellectual that the days of sphere-of-influence diplomacy were past. The mysteries of the 1919 manifesto were forgotten with the 1924 treaty. Far removed from the man in the street, learning of China's "restored rights" in the Three Eastern Provinces, the Harbin headquarters of the "temporary administration" provided welcome privacy for Russian maneuvers aimed at stymieing Chinese officials.

In short, what Russia wanted most mattered least to new China, intent on removing the symbols of inferiority embodied in Boxer Indemnity payments and consular guards. Outer Mongolia and North Manchuria lay well beyond the Great Wall, that physical barrier which still figured as a psychological demarcation of Peking's immediate concern. They appeared still more distant to the revolutionaries of Canton, faced with hostile elements throughout the mainland of China proper. Conversely, the Chinese *idée fixe* of abolishing extraterritoriality concerned an issue of scant importance to Russia. China's ports lay within range of British, French, Japanese, and American gunboats; Russia's stakes had never been high in this area of activity. Coupled with this balance of interests was a clash of interests, to be sure. However, Sino-Soviet relations did not move in a vacuum. An all-pervasive upheaval, evident since the Taiping Rebellion but fast moving to a dramatic and crucial climax, placed all foreign powers on examination in new China. If the Russian policy caused alarm and resentment in some circles, it enjoyed comparison with policies pursued by other world powers. Versailles and Washington epit-

omized the West's inability to cope with this upheaval, to overcome traditional prejudices, and to scrap vested interests in favor
of a new, dynamic approach to China. It is true that Soviet errors brought both the Paikes and Joffe missions to failure, but
Russia was not the only power to err in China. British and French
intervention in Peking's problems somewhat offset the *faux pas*
of Narkomindel negotiators, while Japanese designs on North
China remained highly suspect. Only the United States enjoyed
a favorable position among the Western powers, yet even this
remained somewhat in eclipse by American reluctance to set aside
legal niceties when dealing with China's demands for equal rights
and privileges. American exclusion of Orientals further diminished the admiration of the land of vaunted democracy and equality. Viewed against this background, the 1924 Sino-Soviet pact
takes on added merit as China's first postwar treaty negotiated
with a major power.

A second factor which enabled Soviet diplomatic activity to
proceed along traditional lines of self-interest without embarass-
ing unduly its propaganda appeal to Chinese revolutionaries lay
in the complexities of contemporary communication. Hindsight
has the luxury of time and research to bolster its analyses. Peking
had no large staff of translators and analysts to pour over the
Russian press for clues to Soviet goals. Had it enjoyed such
facilities, it might have seen how in 1919 China was portrayed
as a necessary ally to the young Soviet state, but how by 1924 it
was Russia who was shown as a necessary support for a divided,
chaotic China. Peking might better have understood the Bolshevik use of the traditional divide-and-rule technique as applied
to Mongol against Chinese, China against Japan, and Asia against
the West. Finally, Peking's understanding of Bolshevik intentions
in Canton, as well as Canton's realization of its ultimate fate in
a Kuomintang-Communist coalition, might have emerged from
perusal of the lengthy speeches and articles contained in Comintern publications.

Even had the rulers of Peking gathered complete knowledge of

Soviet means and ends in the Far East, however, they would have had little choice of action before them. This third factor, the political dilemma of North China, has been least examined by Western scholars but is of utmost importance for comprehending the dilatory tactics of the Waichiao Pu during the years' 1920 to 1924. Peking was the capital of China, so recognized throughout the world, yet it was unable to drive Ungern out of Urga, just as it was unable to discipline Chang in Mukden. Its leadership was as bankrupt as its treasury. Young China explored the ideas of Bertrand Russell, John Dewey, and Karl Marx, searching in vain for a solution to the problems which lay everywhere at hand. War lords, corrupt bureaucrats, and monarchists were to be driven out of the Middle Kingdom. What was to replace them, once the Augean stables had been cleaned? A dozen answers came from the intellectuals and politicos who argued and debated in the large metropolitan centers. Russia was apparently pulling herself up by her own bootstraps, but could China? The evidence of 1911 to 1924 stood to the contrary. Russia could proceed with its policy in China, secure in the knowledge that although it was not offering the Chinese people the best of all possible worlds, its offer had yet to be matched by any other power. China could not afford to stand alone.

These three points indicate that Soviet diplomacy in China succeeded in 1924 because of factors other than the influence of Communism and its appeal for Chinese radicals. This is not to say that Soviet strategy ignored the ideological factors involved in the more obscure front, that of revolutionary activity. On the contrary, although the most dramatic aspects of Comintern policy evolved in China after Lenin's death, the groundwork was laid during the years 1917 to 1924. As early as 1919, Chicherin was in correspondence with Dr. Sun, leader of the Kuomintang party, which hoped to overthrow the recognized Peking government. In the same year, the First Congress of the Communist International admitted a Chinese spokesman to its rostrum. Both events had little significance at the time, but they proved manifestations of important trends to follow. Chicherin's correspondence with Sun, intermittent but friendly, strengthened Sun's hopes that his frustrated ambitions could find sympathetic support from Moscow. The Soviets did not need to smash their way into the Chinese revolution; they received specific invitation to participate by no less a figure than Sun himself. His letter of 1921 requesting aid and advice, his entente with Joffe in 1923, his dispatching of Chiang Kai-shek to Moscow later that same year all underscored the Chinese revolutionary's keen interest in the Bolshevik experiment.

Simultaneously with this establishment of a Moscow-Canton line, Soviet leaders worked to organize a Chinese Communist Party in Shanghai, amenable to directives from Comintern spokesmen in Russia. Slow to start, clandestine activity in China increased in 1922–23 as prospects of revolution in Europe faded. Whereas the first months of the Bolshevik regime saw all hopes placed in Europe, the gradual stabilization of European capitalism turned Comintern attentions to the East. In 1920, despite heated debates over the tactics to be employed in colonial and semicolonial countries, die-hard revolutionaries looked to Europe and particularly to Germany for immediate success.. By 1922, Karl Radek was able at the Fourth Comintern Congress to second M. N. Roy's insistence that more fruitful ventures lay in Asia. There great masses of discontented populations might be aroused in a struggle for liberation from native and foreign exploitation. Maring, presenting the official line from Moscow, succeeded in bringing pressure upon the Chinese Communists to infiltrate the Kuomintang. Within a year, the two streams of activity, Narkomindel and Comintern, had merged to carry Russia's prestige to new heights in China. Appointment of Michael Borodin as adviser *extraordinaire* to Sun Yat-sen coincided with implementation of the united front policy, allying the Chinese Communist Party with the Kuomintang. Soviet Russia had entered the mainstream of the Chinese revolution.

It would be fallacious to suppose that Russia's success on this

second front was merely the consequence of personal ties between Chicherin and Sun or of secret activities by Comintern
agents. Far more basic was the dramatic promise embodied in
the Bolshevik ideology, not to mention its accomplishments in the
brief span of seven years. The heady Communist draught with its
potent mixture of anti-imperialism, rampant nationalism, and fervent optimism worked well among the oppressed peoples of Asia,
mired in backward agrarian misery and smarting under the indig-
nities of Western domination. If Russia could cast out foreign
intervention, conquer civil unrest, and raise high the new standard of a workers' and peasants' government, might not China do
the same? One did not need to pursue Marxism through its maze
of economic analysis to understand Bolshevik success or to emu-
late Bolshevik practices. As Sun Yat-sen phrased it on the eve of
the First Kuomintang Congress:

Because we had no model or precedent before us, we were unable to
carry on a well-organized, systematic and disciplined struggle. Now
we have a good friend, Mr. Borodin, who came from Russia. . . . The
Russian Revolution succeeded, because the Communists struggled
strenuously. . . . If we want to achieve success in our revolution we
must learn the Russian method, organization, and training. . . . So I
ask Mr. Borodin to be the educator of our party to train our comrades.
He has had much experience in party organization. I hope that our
comrades will give up their prejudices and faithfully learn his method.[2]

Herein lies a major clue to understanding the success enjoyed
by Soviet activity in China: it ignored no area of promise, confusing and contradictory as such a policy might appear. In Peking,
Narkomindel emissaries sent an endless barrage of notes to the
Waichiao Pu, seeking recognition of Russia's interests in China.
At the same time, they held press conferences, attended banquets,
and systematically built up Russia's prestige among the small but
pivotal group of scholars and officials. In Shanghai, Comintern
envoys provided funds and advice to an amalgam of Chinese
radicals, grouped together under the banners of Marx and Engels,
seeking to expand the minuscule Chinese proletariat into a new

ruling class. In Canton, Russian representatives wooed Sun Yat-sen and rebuilt the ideological foundation as well as the organizational superstructure of the Kuomintang, hoping thereby to direct the new force which might one day unify China and expel all non-Russian influence.

More than one pitfall lay in such a policy. Most obvious of the dilemmas facing those willing to risk such diversified action was the fact that Russian interests and Communist interests sometimes proved incompatible. No figure personified this dilemma better than that of Leo Karakhan. The manifesto bearing his name lost much of its punch because of the decision to make Russian interests paramount to Communist interests. Similarly, his mission to Peking in search of recognition did little to enhance Russian prestige in Canton. As Russians, all could applaud his skill in strengthening Moscow's control in Mongolia and North Manchuria. As Communists, few could condone working with Wu Pei-fu's minions, especially after their demonstrated antiproletarian attitude, while the revolutionary base cried for help in Canton.

In the long run, however, this dilemma was not to prove as explosive as that stemming from the inability of Soviet leaders to agree on what to do with their newly won position in the Chinese revolution. Given the prominence of theory in the Marxist frame of reference, it was of utmost importance that agreement on basic principles be arrived at among those responsible for directing events in distant Peking, Shanghai, and Canton.

As early as 1912, Lenin had formulated the barest outline of his eventual policy in China when he wrote in praise of Sun Yat-sen's "bourgeois-reformist" platform. During World War I he moved to a complete break with European Marxists like Rosa Luxemburg in advocating support for national-liberation movements in colonial and semicolonial countries such as Persia, India, and China. Scattered throughout his articles and speeches of the period were repeated pleas for greater study of Asian revolutions, but not until the Second Comintern Congress did Lenin attempt a systematic formulation of his ideas on tactics to be employed in such revolutions. His timing had little relation to the situation in Asia; it was connected wholly with his reflections upon recent Bolshevik successes in Russia's own revolution. Herein lay another problem to plague Communist leaders directing strategy in China: theories and directives formulated in Moscow often failed to fit the actual situation in Peking, Shanghai, and Canton. To be sure, Lenin had learned his lessons in the bitter but successful struggles of 1917 to 1920, and he felt justified in applying them elsewhere. The fact remains that the 1920 theses adopted by the Comintern had nothing to do with the experience of such Chinese radicals as Sun Yat-sen or Ch'en Tu-hsiu. M. N. Roy, alone among those promulgating a program for the Far East, had extensive experience in Asia, yet his point of departure was India, not China.

Disagreement between Lenin and Asian radicals arose over the fundamental question of relations with the bourgeois leaders of Asian liberation movements. De-emphasizing the role of the proletariat, virtually nonexistent in much of the Far East, Lenin advocated bringing the peasantry into the struggle and allying with the native bourgeoisie. On the first point he received support; on the second he was adamantly opposed. In the Second Comintern Congress, Roy voiced his opposition in a rival set of theses which Lenin managed to soften somewhat before they were submitted to the Congress, but differences of emphasis remained between the two sets of theses. In China, the Chinese Communist Party was loath to accept Maring's advice to infiltrate the Kuomintang, and considerable disagreement appears to have existed within the party on the precise nature of the united front adopted with the Kuomintang in 1924. Unlike Russia, where Bolshevik and Menshevik factions could enjoy limited but fruitful cooperation for the purpose of overthrowing the old order, reformist groups in China were indissolubly wed to the landed interests, and cooperation with Communist forces, bent on land reform, could only lead to strife. As Lenin himself admitted at one point,

orthodox texts of Marxism would be of little service in guiding
Communist parties in the Far East. He might well have said the
same of the verbose yet vague resolutions enacted at successive
meetings of the Communist International. Efforts by Roy and
Lenin to bridge differences of tactic failed. Adoption of their
conflicting sets of theses highlighted this problem but did not
solve it, for it was incapable of solution, given the vast differences
in basic social, economic, and political conditions found in Russia
and China.

A further complication evident in the interminable pages of
debate and controversy during the early twenties was the lack
of agreement within the Soviet elite and the consequent diver-
gence of opinion expressed within the various Bolshevik organizations. Lenin, seconded by the Narkomindel writers, continually
warned of Japanese imperialism. Zinoviev, together with his Comintern associates, constantly stressed the anti-British struggle in
China. Lenin's appeal for cooperation with nationalistic-bourgeois
movements was countered by Zinoviev's vehement antibourgeois
speeches. Despite its adoption of Lenin's theses in 1920, the Comintern continued to place primary emphasis on the Chinese proletariat, ignoring the peasantry and attacking the bourgeoisie. Its
most vitriolic attacks struck at Sun Yat-sen for his "utopian" aspirations and at Wu Pei-fu for his antiproletarian demonstrations.
In sharp contrast, Narkomindel writers wrote glowingly of the
immediate future when China's bourgeoisie would unite China
and drive out foreign influences. To be sure, the militaristic Wu
Pei-fu won the Narkomindel's attention when negotiations went
favorably in Peking, whereas the idealistic Sun Yat-sen received
more praise when relations with Peking became strained. According to the Narkomindel analysis, however, both represented the
most promising force in China, the bourgeoisie, contrary to the
opinion of the major Comintern authors. Finally, the Profintern
took an entirely independent line, castigating Wu Pei-fu for his
violent strike-breaking activities, chiding Sun Yat-sen's compromise tactics, and generally discouraging any emphasis upon the

Chinese proletariat as a hopeful revolutionary base. Indeed, of all the groups writing on world revolution, the Profintern remained most adamant in its insistence upon concentrating Communist activity in the highly industrialized area of western Europe.

Such differences of opinion did not, in and of themselves, doom Soviet policy to failure. Conceivably they might have strengthened policy by bringing healthy criticism and enlightened reinterpretations of doctrine to the fore. On the contrary, however, they ran afoul of several obstacles, some indigenous to twentieth-century Marxist circles, some common to all political organizations. First, these varying analyses were heavily influenced by a priori considerations of how the class struggle *should* develop in Asia, rather than by a careful examination of the manner in which the so-called national-liberation movement was actually evolving. Of the three principal groups under study, the Profintern proved least susceptible to wishful thinking. Its well-informed articles on the nascent state of the Chinese proletariat stood as a challenge to those who permitted Marxist enthusiasm to overlook or to distort facts, but it wielded less influence than either the Comintern or the Narkomindel. When its influence widened somewhat, its deviation from the general Asian line was considered of sufficient importance for Vilensky to administer a sharp rebuke to the Profintern, illustrating the difficulty of developing a factually based policy which conflicted with politically biased, a priori decisions.

Further obstacles to the shaping of a cohesive, realistic policy lay in the personal struggles for power which silenced criticism or magnified insignificant errors of judgment. One such instance was the Serratti incident at the Second Comintern Congress, when the Italian delegate pointed out inconsistencies between Lenin's and Roy's theses but was accused of "counterrevolution" for his remarks. These conflicts did not disappear with the death of Lenin. On the contrary, given the articles and debates of the 1920 to 1924 period, it was to be expected that the removal of the leader would precipitate further conflict and struggle. An additional complication, tending to make such debate politically explosive, was the predilection of Bolsheviks to fit all colonial struggles under one slogan, one tactic, be it an "anti-British" or a "united front" slogan. Once the line was set, any criticism, debate, or deviation was interpreted as hostile to the decision-makers and examined for its intent, rather than for its content. The consequences of these shortcomings in Soviet policy formulation with respect to the Chinese revolution did not become evident until the climactic years of the Kuomintang-Communist alliance, from 1924 to 1927. However, their patterns were discernible when the foundations for such policy were laid, from 1920 to 1924.

In retrospect, the importance of early Soviet policy in China looms large. The positive features of the Karakhan manifestoes, the dramatic propaganda of the Comintern congresses, the personal ties between Chicherin and Sun Yat-sen, and the persistent efforts of Narkomindel and Comintern representatives in China to build up Russian prestige and influence in a backward, chaotic country all combine to throw new light on the manner in which Soviet Russia became the principal ally of new China. Certain consequences of Soviet policy in China as initiated and carried out during the early 1920's have shaped the histories of both countries, as well as of the entire world.

APPENDICES

Appendix A: Chronology

1917 November   Bolsheviks seize power in Petrograd.

December   Disturbances on Chinese Eastern Railway put down by Chinese troops.

1918 March   Japanese-Chinese agreement to manage CER jointly.

April   Russo-Asiatic Bank breaks with Petrograd; reconstitutes bank in Paris.

July   Commissar for Foreign Affairs Georgi Chicherin makes first public official statement of policy in China, renouncing special privileges and returning CER for partial compensation.

August   Chicherin addresses letter to Sun Yat-sen expressing mutual interests.

1919 January   Inter-Allied Technical Commission takes over CER.

March   First Congress of Communist International.

May   Demonstrations in China against Versailles agreement.

July   First Karakhan Manifesto to China, restates policy of renouncing special privileges, Boxer Indemnity, and offers to return CER without compensation (in one version).

August   Declaration to Mongolia, renouncing Russian rights and offering diplomatic relations.

November   Mongolian princes denounce all previous treaties guaranteeing autonomy, under pressure of Chinese occupation troops.

1920 March   Peking receives Karakhan Manifesto via Irkutsk with CER offer included.

      April   Far Eastern Republic officially constituted.

      May   Ten Resolutions of I Ning City, Ili, concluded between authorities in Sinkiang and Russian Turkestan.

      July   Second Congress of Communist International.

                  Anfu clique ousted from Peking; replaced by Chihli coalition of Tsao K'un, Chang Tso-lin, and Wu Pei-fu. New Cabinet suspends payment of Boxer Indemnity funds to Tsarist representatives.

      August   M. I. Yurin, Far Eastern Republic representative, arrives in Peking.

      September   Peking ratifies Ten Resolutions concluded at Ili in May; withdraws recognition from Tsarist representatives in China.

                  General Chang Shih-lin arrives in Moscow, claiming to represent Peking.

                  Second Karakhan Manifesto issued, restating former offer but not specifying terms on CER.

      October   Peking concludes supplementary agreement with Russo-Asiatic Bank on CER.

                  Chicherin dispatches letter to Sun suggesting trade relations.

                  Baron Ungern von Sternberg attacks Urga.

      November   Chicherin orders Red troops into Mongolia, together with Far Eastern Republic troops and Mongol revolutionaries; cancels order before troops cross border when Ungern defeated by Chinese.

1921 February   Ungern captures Urga.

      April   Sun elected "constitutional" President of China in Canton.

                  Tientsin Conference commissions Chang Tso-lin to oust Ungern.

                  Yurin wins draft agreement from Waichiao Pu on Far Eastern Republic-Chinese Relations.

      June   Chicherin notifies Peking Red Army, Far Eastern Republic troops, and Mongol revolutionaries cross border. Third Comintern Congress.

      July   Urga falls to revolutionary armies.

Provisional Government of Mongolia appeals to RSFSR not to evacuate troops.

First Profintern Congress.

First Congress of Chinese Communist Party.

August   Yurin leaves Peking without agreement.

Ungern captured and executed.

Chicherin agrees to leave Red Army in Mongolia.

September   Former Mongol princes abdicate in favor of new regime.

October   Alexander Paikes leaves Moscow to conclude trade agreement in Peking.

Soviet-Mongol conference opens in Moscow.

November   Soviet-Mongol treaty concluded.

Washington Conference opens.

December   Paikes arrives in Peking.

1922   January   First Congress of Toilers of the Far East.

May   Wu Pei-fu defeats Chang Tso-lin; wins control of Peking government.

Waichiao Pu breaks off negotiations with Paikes upon receipt of news confirming Soviet-Mongol treaty of November, 1921.

Lenin suffers serious stroke.

Soviet-Mongol treaty on property.

Chinese Communist Party issues statement calling for limited cooperation with Kuomintang.

June   Ch'en Chiung-ming ousts Sun from Canton.

August   Maring sees Sun in Shanghai; Maring convenes special plenum of Chinese Communist Party and wins acceptance of united front tactic whereby Chinese Communists join Kuomintang as individuals.

Adolf Joffe arrives in Harbin en route to Peking for new negotiations.

September   Joffe leaves Peking temporarily for conference with Japan at Changchun; returns to Peking after failure to win agreement.

November   Fourth Congress of Communist International.

1923   January   Sun-Joffe entente concluded in Shanghai; Joffe leaves for Japan.

Comintern directive to Chinese Communist Party endorsing united front tactic.

May	Third Congress of Chinese Communist Party; Comintern re-emphasizes importance of united front. Sun back in Canton.
August	Leo Karakhan leaves Moscow; confers with Chang Tso-lin in Mukden. Chiang Kai-shek sent to Moscow on behalf of Sun to survey Bolshevik proposals.
September	Karakhan arrives in Peking; notifies Sun of appointment of Michael Borodin to Canton.

1924 January	First Congress of Kuomintang; formal announcement of Chinese Communist Party-Kuomintang united front. Lenin dies. Soviet Union and Mongolia exchange diplomatic representatives.
March	Wang-Karakhan agreement signed; repudiated by cabinet; Karakhan suspends negotiations.
May	Sino-Soviet treaty signed and ratified.

Appendix B: Karakhan Manifesto,
July 25, 1919

ORIGINAL Russian text from V. Vilenskii, *Kitai i Sovetskaia Rossiia* (China and Soviet Russia), pp. 14–16; translation from Jane Degras, ed., *Soviet Documents on Foreign Policy*, I, 158–61. Italicized portion translated by the writer directly from Vilenskii's Russian version; italics added.

DECLARATION TO THE CHINESE NATION AND THE GOVERNMENTS OF SOUTHERN AND NORTHERN CHINA.

At a time when the Soviet troops, having defeated the army of the counter-revolutionary despot Kolchak, supported by foreign bayonets and foreign gold, have entered Siberia in triumph and are marching to join with the revolutionary people of Siberia, the Council of People's Commissars addresses the following brotherly words to all the peoples of China:

After two years of struggle and incredible effort, Soviet Russia and the Soviet Red Army are marching across the Urals to the East, not to coerce, not to enslave, not to conquer. Every Siberian peasant and every Siberian worker already knows this. We bring to the peoples liberation from the yoke of foreign bayonets and the yoke of foreign gold, which are stifling the enslaved peoples of the East, and particularly the Chinese people. We bring help not only to our own labouring classes, but to the Chinese people too, and we once more remind them of what they have been told ever since the great October revolution of 1917, but which was perhaps concealed from them by the venal press of America, Europe, and Japan.

As soon as the Workers' and Peasants' Government took power into its own hands in October, 1917, it addressed all the peoples of the world, in the name of the Russian people, with the proposal to establish a firm and lasting peace. The principle on which this peace was to be established was the renunciation of any seizure of foreign territory, the renunciation of any coercive annexation of foreign nationalities, and of any indemnities. Every people, whether great or small, wherever it dwelt, whether up to then it had lived an independent life or was included against its will as a constituent part of another state, should be free in its internal life, and no Government was to keep it by force within its frontiers.

Immediately after this the Workers' and Peasants' Government proclaimed that all the secret treaties concluded with Japan, China, and the former Allies were annulled; these were treaties by which the Tsarist Government, together with its Allies, by force and bribery enslaved the peoples of the East, and in the first place the people of China, in order to provide profits for Russian capitalists, Russian landlords, and Russian generals. The Soviet Government then proposed to the Chinese Government that they start negotiations to annul the treaty of 1896, the Peking protocol of 1901, and all agreements concluded with Japan between 1907 and 1916; that is, to return to the Chinese people everything that was taken from them by the Tsarist Government independently, or together with the Japanese and the Allies. Negotiations on this question were continued up to March, 1918. Suddenly, the Allies seized the Peking Government by the throat, showered gold on the Peking mandarins and the Chinese press, and forced the Chinese Government to refuse to have any relations with the Russian Workers' and Peasants' Government. Anticipating the return to the Chinese people of the Manchurian Railway, Japan and its allies seized it themselves, invaded Siberia, and even forced Chinese troops to help them in this criminal and unparalleled robbery. But the Chinese people, the Chinese workers and peasants, could not even learn the truth, could not find out the reason for this invasion by the American, European, and Japanese robbers of Manchuria and Siberia.

Now we again address the Chinese people, in order to open their eyes.

The Soviet Government has renounced the conquests made by the Tsarist Government which deprived China of Manchuria and other areas. Let the peoples living in those areas themselves decide within the frontiers of which State they wish to dwell, and what form of government they wish to establish in their own countries.

The Soviet Government returns to the Chinese people without compensation of any kind the Chinese Eastern Railway, and all mining concessions, forestry, and gold mines which were seized from them by the government of Tsars, that of Kerensky, and the outlaws Horvath, Semenov, Kolchak, the Russian generals, merchants, and capitalists.

The Soviet Government renounces the receipt from China of the 1900 Boxer rebellion indemnity, and it is obliged to repeat this a third time because, according to the information reaching us, this indemnity, despite our renunciation, is being exacted by the Allies to pay the salaries and to satisfy the whims of the former Tsarist ambassador to Peking and the former Tsarist consuls in China. All these Tsarist slaves have long been deprived of their powers, but they continue at their posts and deceive the.Chinese people with the help of Japan and the Allies. The Chinese people should know of this and should expel them from their country as imposters and rogues.

The Soviet Government abolishes all special privileges and gives up all factories owned by Russian merchants on Chinese soil. Not one Russian official, priest, or missionary shall be able to interfere in Chinese affairs, and if he commits a crime, he should be subject to the justice of the local courts. In China there should be no authorities and no courts except the authorities and courts of the Chinese people.

In addition to these principal points, the Soviet Government is ready to discuss all other questions with the Chinese people represented by their plenipotentiaries, and to wipe out once and for all the acts of coercion and injustice committed in regard to China by former Russian Governments jointly with Japan and the Allies.

The Soviet Government is well aware that the Allies and Japan will again do everything possible to prevent the voice of the Russian workers and peasants from reaching the Chinese people, that the return to the Chinese people of what was taken from them requires first of all putting an end to the robber invasion of Manchuria and Siberia. Therefore it is now sending the news to the Chinese people, together with its Red Army, which is marching across the Urals to the East to help the Siberian peasants and workers, to liberate them from the bandit Kolchak and his ally Japan.

If the Chinese people wish, like the Russian people, to become free and to avoid the fate which the Allies prepared for them at Versailles, a fate designed to turn China into a second Korea or a second India, they must understand that their only allies and brothers in the struggle for freedom are the Russian workers and peasants and their Red Army.

The Soviet Government proposes to the Chinese people, in the person of their Government, that they enter right away into official relations with us and send their representatives to meet our army.

Deputy People's Commissar for Foreign Affairs
L. KARAKHAN

25 July 1919
Moscow

Appendix C: Karakhan Manifesto,
September 27, 1920

Based on a translation in V. Yakhontoff, *Russia and the Soviet Union in the Far East*, pp. 284–87; and *China Year Book, 1924*, p. 870, "as published by the Soviet mission." For full Russian text see V. Savvin, *Vzaimootnosheniia tsarskoi Rossii i SSSR s Kitaem* (Relations of Tsarist Russia and the USSR with China), pp. 128–29.

TO THE MINISTRY OF FOREIGN AFFAIRS OF THE CHINESE REPUBLIC.

More than a year ago, on July 25th, 1919, the People's Commissar for Foreign Affairs of the Russian Socialist Federated Soviet Republics made known a declaration addressed to the Chinese people and to the Governments of Northern and Southern China. By this the Russian Government, being ready to renounce all the previous treaties concluded with China by the Tsar, and to restore to the Chinese nation all that has been taken from it by force and expropriated by the Tsar's Government and the Russian bourgeoisie, proposed to the Government of China to enter into official negotiations for the establishment of friendly relations.

Now we have information to the effect that our appeal has been received by the Chinese Government, and that the various strata of the Chinese people and divers organizations are expressing their sincere desire to see the Chinese Government enter into negotiations with us in order to establish friendly relations between China and Russia.

The Government of the Chinese Republic has delegated to Moscow a military-diplomatic mission headed by General Chang Shih-lin. We welcome with the greatest joy the arrival of the Chinese Mission to Moscow and hope that through direct negotiations with your representatives we shall establish a mutual understanding of the common interests binding China and Russia. We are convinced that there are no problems between the Russian and the Chinese peoples which cannot be settled for the common good of both peoples. We are aware that the enemies of the Russian and the Chinese peoples are attempting to hinder our friendship and rapprochement, realizing that the friendship of these two great nations and their mutual assistance will strengthen China to such an extent that no foreign nation will be able to keep in bonds and to plunder the Chinese people, as is the case at present.

Unfortunately there is something that prevents a speedy establishment of friendly relations between China and Russia. Your mission, which had opportunity to be convinced in our sincere and friendly attitude towards China, has not received as yet the necessary instructions to start the molding of the friendship between the two nations.

Regretting that the rapprochement is delayed, and that therefore certain important political and commercial interests of both countries do not reach realization, the People's Commissar for Foreign Affairs, in his desire to render service to the issue and to hasten the establishment of friendship between the two nations, declares that he will still adhere invariably to the principles stipulated in the appeal of the Russian Soviet Government of July 25th, 1919, and will apply them on the basis of a friendly agreement between China and Russia.

In elaboration of the principles of the above mentioned appeal the People's Commissar for Foreign Affairs deems it necessary for the good of the two Republics to suggest to the Ministry for Foreign Affairs of the Chinese Republic the following basic points for the agreement.

I

The Government of the Russian Socialist Federated Soviet Republics declares as void all the treaties concluded by the former Government of Russia with China, renounces all the annexations of Chinese territory, all the concessions in China, and returns to China free of charge, and forever, all that was ravenously taken from her by the Tsar's Government and by the Russian bourgeoisie.

II

The Governments of the two Republics shall apply all the necessary means as to immediate establishment of regular commercial and economic relations. Eventually a special treaty shall be concluded, involving the principle of most favored treatment for both contracting parties.

III

The Chinese Government undertakes:
1. Not to render any assistance to private persons, groups or organiza-

tions of the Russian counter-revolutionaries, and not to tolerate their activities on its territory.

2. To disarm, intern and deliver to the Government of the RSFSR all the troops and organizations fighting the RSFSR or its allies, and found on the territory of China at the moment of the signing of the present treaty, and to hand to the Government of the RSFSR all their arms, provisions and property.

3. The Government of the RSFSR undertakes similar obligations in regard to persons or organizations carrying on mutinous activities against the Chinese Republic.

IV

All citizens of Russia residing in China must abide by all the laws and regulations in force in the territory of the Chinese Republic and shall not enjoy any rights of extraterritoriality whatever; Chinese citizens, residing in Russia, must similarly abide by all the laws and regulations in force on the territory of Russia.

V

The Government of the Chinese Republic undertakes:

Immediately upon the signing of the present treaty to discontinue relations with the individuals claiming for themselves the titles of diplomatic and consular representatives of the State of Russia and having no credentials from the Government of the RSFSR and to deport them from China.

To return to the State of Russia, as represented by the Government of the RSFSR all the buildings of the Embassy and consulates belonging to Russia in the territory of China as well as other property and archives of the Embassy and the consulates.

VI

The Government of the RSFSR declines to receive any compensation, payable by China for the Boxer Rebellion, provided that the Government of the Chinese Republic will not distribute the said payments to the Russian consuls or any other persons or Russian organizations unlawfully claiming them.

VII

Immediately upon the signing of the present treaty reciprocal diplomatic and consular representation of the Chinese Republic and the RSFSR shall be established.

VIII

The Russian and the Chinese Governments agree to conclude a special treaty as for the rules and regulations of exploitation of the Chinese Eastern Railway for the needs of the RSFSR. In the making of said treaty, besides China and Russia, the Far Eastern Republic shall also participate.

The People's Commissariat for Foreign Affairs, communicating the above enumerated basic points, has in mind the possibility of amicable discussion of them with your representatives in order to introduce such changes as the Chinese Government may deem necessary for the common good.

The relations between the two great nations are not completely covered by the above stipulated agreement and the delegates of both the countries shall eventually adjust by special agreements other problems of commerce, frontiers, customs, etc.

We shall take all the measures for the establishment of the most sincere friendship between the two parties; and we hope that the Chinese Government in its turn will issue without delay similarly sincere proposals; and so a start towards the conclusion, as speedily as possible, of a treaty of friendship will be made.

Deputy People's Commissar for Foreign Affairs
L. KARAKHAN

27 September 1920
#63737/2 Moscow

Appendix D: Sino-Soviet Treaty
and Declarations, May 31, 1924

Text as given in *Treaties and Agreements with and concerning China,
1919–1929*, pp. 133–39. For text of the agreement for the provisional
management of the Chinese Eastern Railway, with declaration, see
ibid., pp. 141–44.

AGREEMENTS ON GENERAL PRINCIPLES FOR THE SETTLEMENT OF THE QUES-
TIONS BETWEEN THE REPUBLIC OF CHINA AND THE UNION OF SOVIET SOCIALIST
REPUBLICS, WITH SIX DECLARATIONS, 31 MAY 1924.

The Republic of China and the Union of Soviet Socialist Republics, desiring
to re-establish normal relations with each other, have agreed to conclude an
Agreement on general principles for the settlement of the questions between
the two countries, and have to that end named as their Plenipotentiaries,
that is to say:

His Excellency the President of the Republic of China:

Vi Kyuin Wellington Koo,

The Government of the Union of Soviet Socialist Republics:

Lev Mikhailovitch Karakhan,

Who, having communicated to each other their respective full powers,
found to be in good and due form, have agreed upon the following articles:

Article I. Immediately upon the signing of the present Agreement, the
normal diplomatic and consular relations between the two Contracting
Parties shall be re-established.

The Government of the Republic of China agrees to take the necessary
steps to transfer to the Government of the USSR the Legation and Consular
buildings formerly belonging to the Tsarist Government.

Article II. The Governments of the two Contracting Parties agree to hold,
within one month after the signing of the present Agreement, a Conference

which shall conclude and carry out detailed arrangements relative to the questions in accordance with the principles as provided in the following articles.

Such detailed arrangements shall be completed as soon as possible and, in any case, not later than six months from the date of the opening of the Conference as provided in the preceding paragraph.

Article III. The Governments of the two Contracting Parties agree to annul at the Conference, as provided in the preceding article, all Conventions, Treaties, Agreements, Protocols, Contracts, etc., concluded between the Government of China and the Tsarist Government and to replace them with new treaties, agreements, etc., on the basis of equality, reciprocity and justice, as well as the spirit of the Declarations of the Soviet Government of the years 1919 and 1920.

Article IV. The Government of the USSR, in accordance with its policy and Declarations of 1919 and 1920, declares that all Treaties, Agreements, etc., concluded between the former Tsarist Government and any third Party or Parties affecting the sovereign rights or interests of China are null and void.

The Governments of both Contracting Parties declare that in future neither Government will conclude any treaties or agreements which prejudice the sovereign rights or interests of either Contracting Party.

Article V. The Government of the USSR recognizes that Outer Mongolia is an integral part of the Republic of China and respects China's sovereignty therein.

The Government of the USSR declares that, as soon as the questions for the withdrawal of all the troops of the USSR from Outer Mongolia—namely, as to the time-limit of the withdrawal of such troops and the measures to be adopted in the interests of the safety of the frontiers—are agreed upon at the Conference as provided in Article II of the present Agreement, it will effect the complete withdrawal of all the troops of the USSR from Outer Mongolia.

Article VI. The Governments of the two Contracting Parties mutually pledge themselves not to permit, within their respective territories, the existence and/or activities of any organizations or groups whose aim is to struggle by acts of violence against the Governments of either Contracting Party.

The Governments of the two Contracting Parties further pledge themselves not to engage in propaganda directed against the political and social systems of either Contracting Party.

Article VII. The Governments of the two Contracting Parties agree to redemarcate their national boundaries at the Conference as provided in

Article II of the present Agreement, and, pending such redemarcation, to maintain the present boundaries.

Article VIII. The Governments of the two Contracting Parties agree to regulate at the aforementioned Conference the questions relating to the navigation of rivers, lakes and other bodies of water which are common to their respective frontiers, on the basis of equality and reciprocity.

Article IX. The Governments of the two Contracting Parties agree to settle at the aforementioned Conference the question of the Chinese Eastern Railway in conformity with the principles as hereinafter provided:

(1) The Governments of the two Contracting Parties declare that the Chinese Eastern Railway is a purely commercial enterprise.

The Governments of the two Contracting Parties mutually declare that, with the exception of matters pertaining to the business operations which are under the direct control of the Chinese Eastern Railway, all other matters affecting the rights of the National and the Local Governments of the Republic of China—such as judicial matters, matters relating to civil administration, military administration, police, municipal government, taxation and landed property (with the exception of lands required by the said Railway)—shall be administered by the Chinese Authorities.

(2) The Government of the USSR agrees to the redemption by the Government of the Republic of China, with Chinese capital, of the Chinese Eastern Railway, as well as all appurtenant properties, and to the transfer to China of all shares and bonds of the said Railway.

(3) The Governments of the two Contracting Parties shall settle at the Conference, as provided in Article II of the present Agreement, the amount and conditions governing the redemption as well as the procedure for the transfer of the Chinese Eastern Railway.

(4) The Government of the USSR agrees to be responsible for the entire claims of the shareholders, bondholders and creditors of the Chinese Eastern Railway incurred prior to the Revolution of March 9, 1917.

(5) The Governments of the two Contracting Parties mutually agree that the future of the Chinese Eastern Railway shall be determined by the Republic of China and the USSR to the exclusion of any third Party or Parties.

(6) The Governments of the two Contracting Parties agree to draw up an arrangement for the provisional management of the Chinese Eastern Railway pending the settlement of the questions as provided under Section (3) of the present article.

(7) Until the various questions relating to the Chinese Eastern Railway are settled at the conference as provided in Article II of the present Agreement, the rights of the two Governments arising out of the Contract of

August 27, 1896, for the construction and operation of the Chinese Eastern Railway, which do not conflict with the present Agreement and the Agreement for the Provisional Management of the said Railway and which do not prejudice China's rights of sovereignty, shall be maintained.

Article X. The Government of the USSR agrees to renounce the special rights and privileges relating to all Concessions in any part of China acquired by the Tsarist Government under various Conventions, Treaties, Agreements, etc.

Article XI. The Government of the USSR agrees to renounce the Russian portion of the Boxer Indemnity.

Article XII. The Government of the USSR agrees to relinquish the rights of extraterritoriality and consular jurisdiction.

Article XIII. The Governments of the two Contracting Parties agree to draw up simultaneously with the conclusion of a Commercial Treaty and the Conference as provided in Article II of the present Agreement, a Customs Tariff for the two Contracting Parties in accordance with the principles of equality and reciprocity.

Article XIV. The Governments of the two Contracting Parties agree to discuss at the aforementioned Conference the questions relating to the claims for the compensation of losses.

Article XV. The present Agreement shall come into effect from the date of signature.

In witness whereof the respective Plenipotentiaries have signed the present Agreement in duplicate in the English language and have affixed thereto their seals.

Done at the City of Peking this Thirty-First Day of the Fifth Month of the Thirteenth Year of the Republic of China, which is the Thirty-First Day of May One Thousand Nine Hundred and Twenty-Four.

(*seal*) V. K. WELLINGTON KOO

(*seal*) L. M. KARAKHAN

DECLARATION I

The Government of the Republic of China and the Government of the USSR declare that immediately after the signing of the Agreement on General Principles between the Republic of China and the USSR of May 31, 1924, they will reciprocally hand over to each other all the real estate and movable property owned by China and the former Tsarist Government and found in their respective territories. For this purpose each Government will furnish the other with a list of the property to be so transferred.

In faith whereof the respective Plenipotentiaries of the Governments of the two Contracting Parties have signed the present Declaration in duplicate in the English language and have affixed thereto their seals.

Done at the City of Peking, etc.

DECLARATION II

The Government of the Republic of China and the Government of the USSR hereby declare that it is understood that, with regard to the buildings and landed property of the Russian Orthodox Mission, belonging as it does to the Government of the USSR, the question of the transfer or other suitable disposal of the same will be jointly determined at the Conference provided in Article II of the Agreement on General Principles between the Republic of China and the USSR of May 31, 1924, in accordance with the internal laws and regulations existing in China regarding property-holding in the inland. As regards the buildings and property of the Russian Orthodox Mission belonging as it does to the Government of the USSR at Peking and Patachu, the Chinese Government will take steps to immediately transfer same as soon as the Government of the USSR will designate a Chinese person or organization, in accordance with the laws and regulations existing in China regarding property-holding in the inland.

Meanwhile the Government of the Republic of China will at once take measures with a view to guarding all the said buildings and property and clearing them from all the persons now living there.

It is further understood that this expression of understanding has the same force and validity as a general declaration embodied in the said Agreement on General Principles.

In faith whereof, etc.

DECLARATION III

The Government of the Republic of China and the Government of the USSR jointly declare that it is understood that with reference to Article IV of the Agreement on General Principles between the Republic of China and the USSR of May 31, 1924, the Government of the Republic of China will not and does not recognize as valid any treaty, agreement, etc., concluded between Russia since the Tsarist regime and any third Party or Parties affecting the sovereign rights and interests of the Republic of China. It is further understood that this expression of understanding has the same force and validity as a general declaration embodied in the said Agreement on General Principles.

In faith whereof, etc.

DECLARATION IV

The Government of the Republic of China and the Government of the USSR jointly declare that it is understood that the Government of the Republic of China will not transfer either in part or in whole to any third Power or any foreign organization the special rights and privileges renounced by the Government of the USSR in Article X of the Agreement on General Principles between the Republic of China and the USSR of May 31, 1924. It is further understood that this expression of understanding has the same force and validity as a general declaration embodied in the said Agreement on General Principles.

In faith whereof, etc.

DECLARATION V

The Government of the Republic of China and the Government of the USSR jointly declare that it is understood that with reference to Article XI of the Agreement on General Principles between the Republic of China and the USSR of May 31, 1924:

(1) The Russian share of the Boxer Indemnity which the Government of the USSR renounces will, after the satisfaction of all prior obligations secure thereon, be entirely appropriated to create a fund for the promotion of education among the Chinese people.

(2) A special Commission will be established to administer and allocate the said fund. This Commission will consist of three persons, two of whom will be appointed by the Government of the Republic of China and one by the Government of the USSR. Decisions of the said Commission will be taken by unanimous vote.

(3) The said fund will be deposited as it accrues from time to time in a Bank to be designated by the said Commission.

It is further understood that this expression of understanding has the same force and validity as a general declaration embodied in the said Agreement on General Principles.

In faith whereof, etc.

DECLARATION VI

The Government of the Republic of China and the Government of the USSR agree that they will establish equitable provisions at the Conference as provided in Article II of the Agreement of General Principles between the Republic of China and the USSR of May 31, 1924, for the regulation of the situation created for the citizens of the Government of the USSR by the relinquishment of the rights of extraterritoriality and consular juris-

diction under Article XII of the aforementioned Agreement, it being understood, however, that the nationals of the Government of the USSR shall be
entirely amenable to Chinese jurisdiction.

In faith whereof, etc.

Appendix E: Major Documents

June 25, 1919—Obrashchenie Kitaiskomu narodu k pravitel 'stvam iuzhnogo i severnogo Kitaia (Declaration to the Chinese People and to the Governments of Southern and Northern China); in V. Vilenskii, *Kitai i Sovetskaia Rossiia* (China and Soviet Russia), p. 15.

August, 1919—Appeal to the Mongolian People; in V. Vilenskii, "Sovetskaia Rossiia i Mongoliia" (Soviet Russia and Mongolia), *Izvestiia*, No. 245 (1092), November 20, 1920, p. 1; also Doksom, "Istoricheskie uroki 15 let revoliutsii" (Historical Lesson of Fifteen Years of Revolution), *Tikhii Okean*, No. 3 (9), July-September, 1936.

May 27, 1920—Ten Resolutions of I Ning City, Ili; in *Treaties and Agreements with and concerning China, 1919–1929*, p. 23.

September 27, 1920—Karakhan statement to the Ministry of Foreign Affairs of the Chinese Republic; in V. P. Savvin, *Vzaimootnosheniia tsarskoi Rossii i SSSR s Kitaem* (Relations of Tsarist Russia and the USSR with China), p. 128.

November 10, 1920—Chicherin statement on intended intervention of Soviet troops in Outer Mongolia; in *Pravda*, No. 256, November 14, 1920, p. 2.

November 27, 1920—Chicherin statement canceling Soviet intervention in Outer Mongolia; in *Pravda*, No. 269, November 30, 1920, p. 2.

June 15, 1921—Chicherin statement on entry of Soviet troops into Outer Mongolia; in *North China Herald*, July 9, 1921, p. 87.

August 10, 1921—Chicherin reply to appeal from People's Revolutionary Government of Mongolia for retention of Soviet troops in Outer Mongolia; in *Izvestiia*, No. 177 (1320), August 12, 1921, p. 2.

September 14, 1921—Chicherin reply to appeal from Mongolian People's Republic for aid in Mongol Chinese relations; in *Izvestiia*, No. 207 (1350), September 17, 1921, p. 3.

November 5, 1921—Soglashenie ob ustanovlenii druzhestvennykh otno-shenii, Sovetskaia Rossiia i Mongoliia (Agreement to Establish Friendly Relations, Soviet Russia and Mongolia); in *Sbornik deistvuiushchikh dogovorov, soglashenii, i konventsii zakliuchennikh s inostrannymi gosudarstvami* (Collection of Operative Treaties, Agreements, and Conventions Concluded with Foreign Governments), II, 29.

May 31, 1924—Agreement on General Principles for the Settlement of the Questions between the Republic of China and the USSR; in *Treaties and Agreements with and concerning China, 1919–1929*, pp. 133–39.

NOTES

Notes

INTRODUCTION

1. *The Second Congress of the Communist International, Stenographic Report*, prefatory page. Full identification of all works referred to in the present study will be found in the Bibliography.

2. E. H. Carr, *The Bolshevik Revolution, 1917–1923*, III, vii.

CHAPTER I *Before November: Lenin on China*

1. V. I. Lenin, *Sochineniia* (Works), 2nd ed., XXVI, 135. The editors note that Lenin was probably referring to an article by Sun Yat-sen, "The Social Significance of the Chinese Revolution," printed in *Nevskaia Zvezda*, No. 17, July 15, 1912. In Lenin's *Tetradi po imperializmu* (Notes on Imperialism), some indication of his interest in China is given in a vehement attack upon Baron von MacKay's *China, die Republik der Mitte* (Berlin, 1914). While excerpting a map from the work as well as statistics on railroad concessions in China held by foreigners, Lenin called it a "false and reactionary" study. A bibliography on China is appended, although the lack of comment makes it unclear whether it was taken from MacKay's work or whether these were other books on China which Lenin consulted: J. Kentley and S. Johns, *Sun Yat-sen and the Awakening of China* (London, 1913); Fosberg-Rekov, *Revolution in China* (Berlin, 1912); I. Schoen, *Aims of Russia in China* (Vienna, 1900); M. Brandt, *East Asiatic Problems* (Berlin, 1897); W. Schiller, *An Outline of Modern Chinese History* (Berlin, 1913); see *Tetradi*, pp. 501–4.

2. V. I. Lenin, *Collected Works*, 2nd ed., IV, 60–61; from *Iskra*, No. 1, December 1, 1900.

3. V. I. Lenin, *Sobranie sochinenii* (Complete Works), 1st ed., XI, Part 1, 100–101; from *Proletarii*, No. 33, July 23, 1908.

4. The Conference proclaimed "the world significance of the revolutionary struggle of the Chinese people, bearing the liberation of Asia and undermining the hegemony of the European bourgeoisie. The Conference, manifesting the deep enthusiasm and fullest sympathy with which the proletariat of Russia follows the successes of the revolutionary peoples of China, greets the revolutionary-republicans of China and brands the misbehavior of Russian liberalism which supports the policy of Tsarist seizures." Lenin, *Sobranie sochinenii*, XII, Part 1, 32; from the resolutions of the Paris Conference of the Russian Social Democratic Workers' Party, January, 1912.

5. Lenin, *Sochineniia*, 3rd ed., XVI, 26–31; from *Nevskaia Zvezda*, No. 17, July 15, 1912.

6. The use of the term *feudalism* in this study will reflect Bolshevik references only. In this sense it does not carry the traditional Western implications of large latifundia, rigid socio-economic relationships, etc. It more generally is used in opposition to *capitalism;* for China, *precapitalist relations* closely approximates its meaning.

7. Lenin, *Sochineniia*, 3rd ed., XVI, 29. Italics in original.

8. *Ibid.*, p. 30.

9. Lenin, *Sobranie sochinenii*, 1st ed., XIX, 22; from *Pravda*, No. 163, November 8, 1912. Italics in original.

10. Lenin, *Sochineniia*, 3rd ed., XVI, 395; from *Pravda*, No. 113, May 18, 1913.

11. Lenin, *Collected Works*, XIX, 55; from *Vorbote*, No. 2, April, 1916. Italics in original.

12. Lenin, *Sochineniia*, 3rd ed., XVI, 26; from *Nevskaia Zvezda*, No. 17, July 15, 1912.

13. Lenin, *Sobranie sochinenii*, 1st ed., XIX, 20; from *Pravda*, No. 163, November 8, 1912.

14. Lenin, *Sochineniia*, 2nd ed., XVII, 436; from "On the Right of Nations to Self-Determination." Italics in original.

15. Lenin, *Collected Works*, XVIII, 358; from *Sotsial-Demokrat*, No. 47, October 13, 1915.

16. *Ibid.*, XIX, 204–6; from "The Pamphlet by Junius," August, 1916. Italics in original.

17. *Ibid.*, XIX, 55.

18. Lenin, *Sobranie sochinenii*, 2nd ed., XVII, 430–31.

19. V. I. Lenin, *Imperialism, the Highest Stage of Capitalism*, p. 82.

20. *Ibid.*, p. 119. Italics in original.

21. *Ibid.*, p. 96.

22. Lenin, *Collected Works*, XIX, 254; written in October, 1916.

23. *Ibid.*, XIX, 402–3; from a lecture on the 1905 revolution delivered in January, 1917.

24. G. Zinoviev, *Voina i krizis sotsialisma* (War and the Crisis of Socialism), 2nd ed., pp. 125 ff.; written before September, 1916.

25. Lenin, *Sobranie sochinenii*, 3rd ed., XVI, 26.

CHAPTER II   *Revolution and Foreign Policy: 1917–1920*

1. E. H. Carr, *The Bolshevik Revolution, 1917–1923*, III, 16.

2. *Pravda*, No. 213, December 26, 1917, p. 3.

3. *Izvestiia*, No. 253, December 16, 1917, p. 5.

4. The Russo-Chinese treaties of 1896, 1898, and 1901 established the Chinese Eastern Railway Company, administered by a Russo-Chinese Bank. Shareholders could be only Russian or Chinese, although the money supplied by the Tsarist treasury came from loans floated in France. The Russo-Chinese Bank later merged with the Banque du Nord to become the Russo-Asiatic Bank.

5. U.S. Department of State, *Papers Relating to the Foreign Policy of the United States, 1918: Russia*, II, 3–5.

6. *Millard's Review*, January 15, 1918, p. 169.

7. *Pravda*, No. 16, February 3, 1918, p. 3.

8. *Ibid.*, No. 20 (247), February 8, 1918, p. 3. "The Chinese Mission officially notified the NKID that the Government of the Chinese Republic has now decreed to revoke the prohibition of export of foodstuffs from Manchuria and Vladivostok. By this act the Chinese Government expresses the hope that all of these foodstuffs will be used exclusively for the population of the Russian Republics and will not fall into the hands of hostile elements."

9. *Ibid.*, No. 17 (244), February 5, 1918, p. 3; No. 38 (264), March 1, 1918, p. 3.

10. *Ibid.*, No. 29 (256), February 19, 1918, p. 4.

11. *Ibid.*, No. 31 (258), February 21, 1918, p. 3.

12. *Ibid.*, No. 69 (295), April 11, 1918, p. 3. Chicherin also announced the appointment of Y. D. Yanson as Commissar for Foreign Affairs of Eastern Siberia.

13. *Izvestiia*, No. 138 (402), July 5, 1918, p. 7; Address to Fifth Congress of Soviets, July 4, 1918.

14. In the protocol providing for the construction and operation of the Chinese Eastern Railway, concluded in 1896 together with a treaty of alliance between China and Russia, China was given the right to "buy back this line upon repaying in full all capital involved as well as all the debts

contracted for this line, plus accrued interest . . . at the expiration of thirty-six years from the day on which the line is finished and traffic is in operation." See J. V. A. MacMurray, ed., *Treaties and Agreements with and concerning China, 1894–1919*, I, 84.

15. Vladimir Vilenskii (Sibiriakov) was born in Siberia and grew up in Far Eastern revolutionary movements. A Menshevik from 1912 to 1917, he was elected deputy to the All-Siberian Congress of Soviets after working at Yakutsk. He joined the Bolsheviks in Irkutsk and was elected to the central committee at the Second All-Siberian Congress in February, 1918, becoming Commissar for Supply in the Siberian Sovnarkom at the same time. With the fall of the revolutionary government, he escaped to Moscow in April. In July and August, 1919, he worked on a Sovnarkom commission for Siberian affairs and wrote for *Izvestiia*. After taking part in the Red defeat of Kolchak, he headed the RSFSR Sovnarkom mission for foreign affairs in Siberia. From 1920 to 1922, he traveled between Moscow and the Far East, taking part in negotiations with Japan and China. In late 1922, he became secretary to the editor of *Izvestiia*, writing extensively on Far Eastern affairs. See *Deiateli revoliutsionnogo dvizheniia v Rossii* (Participants in the Revolutionary Movement of Russia), pp. 816–71. Vilenskii's writings are an exceptionally important source for the study of Sino-Soviet relations from 1917 to 1924.

16. *Izvestiia*, No. 163 (715), July 26, 1919, p. 1.

17. V. Vilenskii, *Kitai i Sovetskaia Rossiia* (China and Soviet Russia), p. 15. For comment on this source see my article, "The Soviet Offer to China of 1919," *Far Eastern Quarterly*, X (August, 1951), 355–64. The pamphlet bears the official markings certifying to its authenticity and was one of a series by Vilenskii dealing with the situation in the Far East.

18. *Izvestiia*, No. 188 (740), August 26, 1919, p. 1; *Pravda*, No. 188, August 26, 1919, p. 1. Although it was customary for Sovnarkom materials to be printed as an official release, the Karakhan Manifesto was included in a routine news story summarizing speeches at a meeting of Chinese workers in Moscow on August 24, 1919.

19. The wire was in French, from Yanson, representative for Foreign Affairs of the Peoples of Siberia and the Far East, at Irkutsk, "signed by Karakhan as a true copy certified." *China Year Book, 1924*, p. 870. For immediate reaction in China see *Millard's Review*, March 27 and April 10, 1920. The "first" full translation appeared in *Millard's Review*, July 5, 1920. This includes the CER offer, as does a version in the *North China Herald*, December 1, 1923, p. 590.

20. This phrase came in the sentence immediately preceding the CER statement: "Let the peoples residing in these regions decide for themselves

within the boundaries of which State they desire to live, *and the form of government which they desire.*" The italicized portion is found in the Vilenskii pamphlet and in the Irkutsk wire but not in the Russian newspaper versions. Inasmuch as "these regions" referred to Manchuria and "other regions" of China, it may have been felt indiscreet to suggest revolutionary activity in a note aimed at bettering Sino-Soviet relations. No subsequent attention was drawn to this part of the manifesto.

21. *Millard's Review*, June 5, 1920, p. 25. The Anfu clique then in power was inclined to treat with disfavor any *rapprochement* with Soviet Russia, and it is interesting to note that no subsequent Chinese statements prior to 1924 questioned the authenticity of this text publicly.

22. *Hsin ch'ing nien*, No. 6, May, 1920, translated the manifesto, accompanied by declarations of praise reflecting many shades of political opinion, including tributes from deputies of the National Assembly, the All-China Student Federation, etc.; summarized in Benjamin I. Schwartz, *Chinese Communism and the Rise of Mao*, p. 214, n. 44.

23. Karakhan's position was unequivocal: "Never and nowhere could I have said that all the rights of the Chinese Eastern Railway belong to China." *China Year Book, 1924*, p. 875, from his letter to C. T. Wang, November 30, 1923.

24. A. Antonov-Ovseenko, "Soglashenie o KVZhD" (Agreement on the CER), *Izvestiia*, No. 132 (2167), June 12, 1924, p. 2. He incorrectly cites the number and date of the original *Izvestiia* article containing the text of the manifesto without the CER offer. His appointment to the Narkomindel came in February, 1924; see *Deiateli revoliutsionnogo dvizheniia v Rossii*, pp. 117–18.

25. V. P. Savvin, *Vzaimootnosheniia tsarskoi Rossii i SSSR s Kitaem* (Relations of Tsarist Russia and the USSR with China), p. 97.

26. *Pravda*, No. 181, August 16, 1919, p. 1.

27. Leang-li T'ang, *The Inner History of the Chinese Revolution*, p. 138.

28. A. Voznesenskii, "Rossiia i Kitai" (Russia and China), *Izvestiia*, No. 53 (605), March 9, 1919, p. 1; letter of Chicherin to Sun, August 1, 1918. Voznesenskii headed the Eastern section of Narkomindel at this time. In his article he mentioned having met Sun in Nanking, sometime during 1912–13. There is doubt over the fate of Chicherin's letter. Sun declared in 1921 that he had received no letter from Chicherin prior to one dated October 31, 1920; see *Bol'shevik*, No. 19, October 15, 1950, pp. 46–48.

29. *Izvestiia*, No. 260 (524), November 28, 1918, p. 2. The same article noted the formation of a propaganda bureau for Asia sponsored by the executive committee of the Moscow section of the Russian Communist Party. According to a contemporary pamphlet, whose author claimed personal ac-

quaintance with Sun Yat-sen, the program of the Union for Liberation of the East ranked China second only to Japan as the "most advanced" Asian countries. China's place was accorded it on somewhat misleading premises —its allegedly having "one language, one government, one religion"; see K. Troianovskii, *Vostok i revoliutsiia* (The East and Revolution).

30. Rosta wireless dispatch of January 8, 1919, as quoted by A. L. P. Dennis, *The Foreign Policies of Soviet Russia*, pp. 314–15.

31. *Pervyi kongress Kominterna* (First Comintern Congress), p. 161. Chang Yun-kwei and Lao Hsiu-chao were the two Chinese spokesmen. Lao spoke at the Second Comintern Congress in 1920, but otherwise appears to have played no part in the Comintern. His name does not appear in Western studies on the Chinese Communist Party. Chicherin, reporting for the credentials committee, referred to Asian representatives as "emigrant groups of Chinese and Korean workers living in Russia"; *ibid.*, p. 49.

32. *Ibid.*, pp. 242–43. Lao spoke in Chinese and Russian, *ibid.*, p. 148. The speech was reported in *Izvestiia*, No. 51 (603), March 6, 1919, p. 2, and *Pravda* of the same date.

33. *Pervyi kongress Kominterna*, p. 207; the "socialist character" in these areas was certainly "less" rather then "more" clearly expressed.

34. A. Voznesenskii, "Revoliutsionnyi pozhar na Vostoke" (Revolutionary Conflagration in the East), *Izvestiia*, No. 204 (756), September 14, 1919, p. 2.

35. At least three "All-Russian Congresses of Chinese Workers" were held in Moscow. Many Chinese took part in the civil war in Siberia and the Far Eastern provinces; *Izvestiia*, No. 188 (740), August 26, 1919, p. 1.

36. V. I. Lenin, *Sobranie sochinenii* (Complete Works), 1st ed., XVI, 390; speech at Second All-Russian Congress of Communist Organizations of Peoples of the East, from *Izvestiia*, December 20, 1919.

37. Lenin, *Sobranie sochinenii*, XVI, 391. Italics added.

38. *Ibid.*, XVII, 6; speech of January 26, 1920.

39. *Ibid.*, p. 34; speech of March 1, 1920.

40. *Lenin i Vostok* (Lenin and the East), pp. 60–64, a collection of essays, including "an unpublished interview"; see also K. Fuse, *Soviet Policy in the Orient*, p. 2, translated into English from the Japanese.

CHAPTER III   *The Second Comintern Congress*

1. V. I. Lenin, *Selected Works*, X, 231–38.

2. E. H. Carr, *The Bolshevik Revolution, 1917–1923*, I, 70 ff. The revisions and implementations of the principle of self-determination in Bolshevik theory are traced particularly well here, pp. 253 ff.

3. Lenin, *Selected Works*, X, 243–44. Italics added.

4. *Vtoroi kongress Kominterna; stenograficheskii otchët* (Second Comintern Congress; Verbatim Report), p. 138.

5. Although "socialism in one country" was not an issue until the hopes of revolution elsewhere had been snuffed out by the stabilization of capitalism in the mid-twenties, the debate at that time drew heavily on Lenin's revision of 1920. Particularly was this true with reference to the possibility of by-passing capitalism in backward areas on the strength of Russian Socialism alone.

6. Lenin, *Selected Works*, X, 242.

7. For a detailed examination of Marx's strictures against the peasantry, see David Mitrany, *Marx against the Peasant* (Chapel Hill, 1951). Speaking of the French peasant, Marx termed this class that which "represents barbarism within civilization"; see Karl Marx, *The Class Struggles in France, 1848–1850*, from Marx-Engels, *Selected Works* (Moscow, 1951), I, 159. Lenin's shift in emphasis from "neutralizing the peasantry" in 1917 to making the peasantry central in the first stage of Asian revolution was to provide the necessary link in Marxism-Leninism whereby Chinese Communists could be "Marxists" while pursuing a wholly agrarian program in the late 1930's.

8. *The Second Congress of the Communist International as Reported and Interpreted by the Official Newspapers of Soviet Russia*, pp. 133–34; speech to the Third All-Russian Congress of Chinese Workers, quoted from *Izvestiia*, June 22, 1920. Italics in original. According to *Pravda*, No. 141, June 30, 1920, the Congress heard speeches by Kalinin, Chicherin, Voznesenskii, and Lao Hsiu-chao. Considerable emphasis was given the prospects of Sun Yat-sen in Lao's remarks. Resolutions adopted centered on organizing Chinese workers in Russia, evacuating Chinese from Russia to their homeland, demanding immediate diplomatic relations from Peking, and organizing a "school" for Chinese workers.

9. Lenin, *Selected Works*, X, 236.

10. *Vtoroi kongress*, p. 122. In his proof sheets, Lenin remarked, "particularly necessary to exert all efforts to apply the fundamental principles of the Soviet system to countries in which precapitalist relations predominate by creating 'Toilers Soviets,' etc."; see Lenin, *Selected Works*, X, 236.

11. V. I. Lenin, *Left Wing Communism: An Infantile Disorder* (Moscow, 1950), p. 8.

12. *Protokoly kongressov Kommunisticheskogo Internatsionala, vtoroi kongress* (Proceedings of Congresses of the Communist International, the Second Congress), p. 498.

13. *The Second Congress . . . as Reported*, p. 135; from Pak Dinshun, "The Revolutionary East and the Immediate Problems of the Communist

International," *Petrogradskaia Pravda,* July 27, 1920. Such agreement by Roy and Pak seems accurately reported, if reluctantly expressed, since the minutes of the Congress show heated debate on many points, some of which was directed at Lenin. However, agreement within the halls of the Comintern did not signify acceptance by Asian Communists generally in 1920. An examination of the early activities of the Chinese Communist Party, particularly from 1921 to 1925, reveals little attention to peasant problems and a familiar emphasis upon the proletariat as the "vanguard of revolution." See, for instance, Conrad Brandt, John K. Fairbank, and Benjamin I. Schwartz, *A Documentary History of Chinese Communism,* pp. 51–77, wherein the manifestoes of the first four congresses of the Chinese Communist Party fail to reflect Lenin's stress upon peasant tactics as presented in 1920. It should be noted that the early history of the Chinese Communist Party shows varying degrees of responsiveness to Comintern debates and directives. Where accord was reached, it was often by means of Comintern couriers who interpreted directives and persuaded Party leaders to comply; see Harold R. Isaacs, *The Tragedy of the Chinese Revolution,* pp. 58–59, and Benjamin I. Schwartz, *Chinese Communism and the Rise of Mao,* pp. 37–45, for an examination of the role played by Maring in bringing the Chinese Communist Party to a policy of active collaboration with the Kuomintang. As is evident in the Comintern's debates and its publications, sharp disagreements and differing interpretations existed throughout these years. It may be that Lenin's words had little or no impact in China at this time because they were unpalatable to proletarian-minded Marxists and hence were quietly ignored.

14. Lenin, *Selected Works,* X, 236.

15. *Ibid.,* p. 237. Italics added.

16. Marx-Engels, *Sochineniia,* VII, 489; quoted in E. H. Carr, *op. cit.,* I, 13.

17. *Vestnik 2-go kongressa Kommunisticheskogo Internatsionala* (Herald of the Second Congress of the Communist International), No. 1, July 27, 1920.

18. *Ibid.,* p. 2.

19. In a private interview with Robert C. North on October 15, 1950, Roy discussed this difference of opinion and remarked that he thought it was no more than one of degree. Roy's remarks, while interesting, were based on his personal recollection of events thirty years previous. No available documentary evidence substantiates his analysis. Summary of interview was placed at disposal of the author by R. C. North.

20. Lenin, *Selected Works,* X, 241.

21. *Ibid.,* p. 240.

22. *Vtoroi kongress,* pp. 184–85; for a personal but highly partisan account, see Anzhelika Balabanova, *My Life as a Rebel,* p. 275.

23. *Vtoroi kongress,* p. 138.

24. *Ibid.,* p. 164.

25. *Ibid.,* p. 146.

26. *The Second Congress . . . as Reported,* p. 136. Italics in original.

27. *Vestnik,* No. 1, July 27, 1920.

28. *Ibid.,* p. 2. In Roy's interview with North, mentioned previously, he denied that Lenin resisted Roy's formulation of the revolutionary process in East and West. This is not supported by the contemporary accounts of the meeting. Roy's claim that Lenin's rebuke of "going too far" referred to another matter is not in accordance with the available materials. At one point, Lenin flatly asserted that "Comrade Roy's remarks are without sound basis." *Vestnik,* p. 2.

29. *Protokoly kongressov,* pp. 496–98; as Roy read them to the Congress before final revision, see *Vtoroi kongress,* p. 122.

30. *The Second Congress of the Communist International, Stenographic Report,* p. 578.

31. *Vtoroi kongress,* p. 188.

32. *Ibid.,* pp. 184–85. In *Vestnik,* No. 2, July 29, 1920, Serratti is quoted as abstaining because he believed that "socialist revolution could and must exist without helping so-called national-democratic parties."

33. For the incorrect Russian version, see *Vtoroi kongress,* pp. 603–6; *Vestnik,* Nos. 6–7, August 7–8, 1920; *Resoliutsii i ustav Kommunisticheskogo Internatsionala* (Resolutions and Statutes of the Communist International); *Kommunisticheskii Internatsional,* No. 13, pp. 2430–34; Bela Kun, ed., *Komintern v dokumentakh* (Comintern in Documents), pp. 95–97; Bela Kun, ed., *Kommunisticheskii Internatsional v documentakh, resheniia, tezisy, i vosvaniia kongressov Kominterna i plenumov IKKI* (The Communist International in Documents, Decisions, Theses, and Appeals of the Comintern Congresses and Plenums of the ECCI), pp. 130–32; V. I. Lenin, *Sochineniia* (Works), 2nd ed., XXV, 573–75. These are all in precise agreement with the German versions; see *Leitsätze zum II. Kongress der Kommunistischen Internationale,* pp. 101–6; *Die Kommunistische Internationale,* No. 13, pp. 2487–90; *Der Zweite Kongress der Kommunistischen Internationale, Protokoll der Verhandlungen,* pp. 145–50; *Leitsätze und Statuten zum II. Kongress der Kommunistischen Internationale,* pp. 66–70.

The correct Russian version appears in *Protokoly kongressov,* pp. 496–98, and G. Kara-Murza and P. Mif, eds., *Strategiia i taktika Kominterna v natsional'no-kolonial'noi revoliutsii, na primer Kitaia* (Comintern Strategy and Tactics in the National-Colonial Revolution, For Example, China), pp. 40–43.

34. *Protokoly kongressov,* p. xii: "In one instance, it happened that almost an entire document was translated anew; we refer to the supplementary theses on the national-colonial question, which were published in Russian in translation from German, while the German text was in its turn translated from English, and moreover translated entirely incorrectly." A careful check of the French and English versions supports this explanation. For the most authoritative English text, see *The Second Congress of the Communist International, Stenographic Report,* pp. 576–79. Correspondence between M. N. Roy and the author of this study in 1950 failed to throw any additional light; Roy had no text at hand and seemed unaware of the Comintern's error. See *II-e Congrès de la III-e Internationale Communiste, compte-rendu stenographique,* p. 151; *Statuts et résolutions de l'Internationale Communiste,* pp. 90–94; *Theses and Statutes of the Third (Communist) International,* pp. 70–74. These three versions are identical with the Russian of 1934, except that the French omits the sentence, "For the overthrow . . . ." *The Communist International,* No. 13, pp. 2415–18, is not in agreement with any other text, borrowing from every version, apparently, including Roy's speech to the Congress.

35. *Vtoroi kongress,* p. 146.

36. This word appears as *gosudarstvennost'* in *Vtoroi kongress,* p. 148, or *Staatlichkeit* in *Der Zweite Kongress,* p. 175. It appears that Lao spoke twice, once within the commission and once before the Congress, on July 28 and July 30; see *The Second Congress . . . as Reported,* p. 45. This may explain the slight difference between two German versions paralleled by exactly the same difference between the two Russian editions of 1921 and 1934. Instead of *Staatlichkeit,* a later German version reads *bürgerlichen Demokratie;* see *Berichte zum Zweiten Kongress der Kommunistischen Internationale,* p. 240; for the corresponding Russian, see *Protokoly kongressov,* p. 123. The original word, *Staatlichkeit,* was more anarchistic than its successor.

CHAPTER IV   *The Chinese Puzzle*

1. For a general survey of conditions in Chinese factories and the obstacles to trade union activity, see Nym Wales, *The Chinese Labor Movement.*

2. Ta Chen, "The Labor Situation in China," *Monthly Labor Review,* No. 6, December, 1920, p. 207.

3. *Ibid.,* p. 209. For detailed tables on five Chinese cities, see *Monthly Labor Review,* No. 2, August, 1921, pp. 3–15.

4. J. B. Tayler and W. T. Zung, "Labor and Industry in China," *International Labor Review*, No. 1, July, 1923, pp. 5–10; written in November, 1922.

5. "Labor Conditions in China," *International Labor Review*, No. 6, December, 1924, pp. 1011–18; summary of Report of Child Labor Commission appointed by Shanghai Municipal Council.

6. Ta Chen, "Labor Unrest in China," *Monthly Labor Review*, No. 6, December, 1920, p. 23.

7. Ta Chen, "The Labor Movement in China," *International Labor Review*, No. 3, March, 1927, pp. 351 ff. Wales, *op. cit.*, estimates that 6,500 took part in strikes in 1918 and 91,500 in 1919, but gives no sources.

8. Ta Chen, "The Shipping Strike in Hong Kong," *Monthly Labor Review*, No. 3, March, 1922, pp. 9–15.

9. Accounts disagree as to the casualties suffered in the clashes between soldiers and workers. Ta Chen reports that three workers were killed and forty were wounded; see his article "The Labor Movement in China," *International Labor Review*, No. 3, March, 1927, p. 356. N. Wales, *op. cit.*, p. 215, claims that well over fifty were killed and several hundred wounded.

10. The best account of the complex political picture is found in *China Year Book* for 1921 and 1924.

11. L. L. T'ang, *The Inner History of the Chinese Revolution*, p. 138.

12. *Ibid.*, pp. 152–53.

CHAPTER V *Congress of Toilers of the Far East: 1922*

1. V. Alekseev, "Ocherki sovremennogo Kitaia" (Essay on Contemporary China), *Vostok*, No. 2, 1923, pp. 105–17. Most of his material came from *China Year Book, 1921*.

2. *Pervyi s'ezd narodov Vostoka, Baku, stenograficheskii otchët* (First Congress of Peoples of the East, Baku, Verbatim Report), p. 40. Only eight Chinese were present; one was appointed to the propaganda bureau.

3. G. Safarov, "Vostok i revoliutsiia" (The East and Revolution), *Kommunisticheskii Internatsional*, No. 15, 1921, pp. 3127–40.

4. *Ibid.*, p. 3136. Italics in original.

5. *Protokoll des III. Kongresses der Kommunistischen Internationale*, p. 1018. In view of Roy's usual long-winded orations, such a procedure may have been dictated by sheer expediency.

6. *III. kongress Kominterna*, p. 140; it is extremely doubtful that Chang represented any formal group, since the Chinese Communist Party was not formed until after the Third Congress had convened. The First National Congress of the Chinese Communist Party was held July 1, 1922; Benjamin I. Schwartz, *Chinese Communism and the Rise of Mao*, p. 205.

7. *Protokoll des III. Kongresses,* p. 1035.

8. L. Trotsky, *The First Five Years of the Communist International,* pp. 223, 237.

9. *Izvestiia,* No. 216 (1063), September 29, 1920.

10. *Izvestiia,* No. 168 (1311), August 2, 1921, p. 1.

11. No explanation for Narkomindel's modified policy appeared in the Soviet press. It is probable that Vilenskii's proposal would have proved impractical, since China did not recognize Soviet Russia and the only participants would have been the Far Eastern Republic and the Mongolian government, hardly an auspicious gathering compared with that at Washington. Furthermore, the role of the Far Eastern Republic delegation at Washington proved nettlesome to the Japanese, in keeping with Soviet interests.

12. This Congress is known in Russian by this name as well as by the title "Congress of Revolutionary Organizations of the Far East." For the most complete account, verbatim in many instances, see *The First Congress of Toilers of the Far East* (Petrograd, 1922). Use of this record in preference to other editions, particularly the German, is based on the adoption of Russian and English as official languages at the Congress itself; *ibid.,* p. 174. However, for minor improvements in translating speeches by Russian delegates, the highly abridged version, *Pervyi s'ezd revoliutsionnykh organizatsii dal'nego Vostoka* (First Congress of Revolutionary Organizations of the Far East) has been helpful. In addition, the Congress was reported at considerable length in the current issues of *Izvestiia.*

13. The problem of identifying Chinese who attended early Soviet meetings is complicated by the practice of assuming pseudonyms and by the varying transliterations of Chinese names into Russian. According to *The First Congress,* Li-Kieng [*sic*], Tao, and Wang were named to the presidium. Only Wang is identified, representing a women's delegation and member of the Canton Parliament. In *Izvestiia,* No. 16 (1455), January 22, 1922, p. 2, the only Chinese allegedly placed on the presidium are identified as Chang Pen-ya and Liao [*sic*]. According to Conrad Brandt, John K. Fairbank, and Benjamin I. Schwartz, eds., *A Documentary History of Chinese Communism,* p. 30, Chang Kuo-t'ao, one of the founders of the Chinese Communist Party, attended the Congress. No reference to him by this name is made in the Russian materials.

14. The Chinese delegation, second largest present, held 37 deciding votes and 5 consultative votes. The breakdown of 39 persons in this group, including 2 additional delegates from the Communist University of Far Eastern Workers, in Moscow, indicates that 30 were under thirty years of age; 20 were intellectuals, 9 were workers, 9 were peasants, and 1 is enigmatically identified as "other"; 14 were Communists, 11 belonged to

the Young Socialist League, and 14 were "non-Party"; 9 had higher education, 26 had intermediate schooling, and 4 had only attended elementary
grades; see *The First Congress*, p. 239. It should be noted that not all of
the delegates may have come from China, since the credentials committee
admitted persons without credentials, "considering the conspirative conditions of delegates," *ibid.*, p. 237. For a later account of how the delegation
was recruited in China, see *Brief History of the Chinese Communist Party*
(mimeographed, Columbia University, n.d.), translated from documents
seized from the Soviet Embassy by Chang Tso-lin's forces in 1927. Internal
evidence supports the authenticity of these records.

15. A. Tivel, *Piat' let Kominterna* (Five Years of Comintern), p. 68. No
other reference has been found for the "Congress of Toiling Women of the
Far East" although Tivel includes a manifesto issued by this group; the
youth meeting was reported in the Moscow press.

16. *The First Congress*, p. 25; *Pervyi s'ezd revoliutsionnykh*, pp. 12–13.

17. *The First Congress* translated the last part of this sentence ". . . assistance to Mongolia."

18. *Ibid.*, pp. 31–32; the last part of the sentence in Russian reads,
"Kakoi meroi vy merite, toi zhe otmeritca i vam," *Pervyi s'ezd revoliutsionnykh*, p. 20.

19. *Pervyi s'ezd revoliutsionnykh*, p. 26.

20. *Pravda*, No. 17, January 24, 1922, p. 2. Danzan was one of the
Mongolian signatories to the November 5, 1921, treaty.

21. Although a member of the presidium was also named Tao, it seems
certain from the record that he was another Chinese and not the Kuomintang delegate.

22. *The First Congress*, p. 61; these remarks are deleted from Tao's
speech in *Pervyi s'ezd revoliutsionnykh*, p. 199, nor was this speech carried
in *Pravda* or *Izvestiia*.

23. *The First Congress*, p. 108.

24. *Ibid.*, pp. 153–54.

25. *Pervyi s'ezd revoliutsionnykh*, pp. 58–59.

26. *Ibid.*, p. 60.

27. *The First Congress*, p. 177.

28. *Ibid.*, p. 182; the English version refers to the Kuomintang as the
"Homindan." Certainly Tao was on firm ground so far as the single-tax
proposal was concerned, and some of Sun's ideas bore more resemblance to
the soviet system than to that of parliamentary government.

29. *Ibid.*, pp. 184 ff. None of this was reported in the contemporary
press or in the Russian version.

30. *Ibid.*, p. 192; *Izvestiia*, No. 25 (1464), February 2, 1922; speech of

January 27, 1922. The Russian version omits a phrase, "In dealing with you, followers of the Kuomintang, as with our allies, friends, and comrades . . . ." This seems too extreme a phrasing, even for Safarov, and may have been distorted in the English translation.

31. This was in contradiction with Safarov's earlier statements that "the first problem is ousting the foreigner . . . China is not faced with . . . rapid sovietization." *The First Congress*, p. 167.

32. *Ibid.*, p. 199.

33. A. Bolgar, "The Far East," *International Press Correspondence*, II, No. 78, 583.

34. Until research in Chinese sources can reveal Tao's authorization, it may be presumptuous to consider him an official Kuomintang spokesman, but with one possible exception, his remarks did not run counter to the radical wing of the Kuomintang. Only on Mongolia does Tao seem to have taken a position more extreme than might have been warranted; even Sun was unwilling to speak so unequivocally of Mongolia's separation from China in his conversations with Adolf Joffe, one year later.

35. According to *Brief History*, other points of tension fragmented the Chinese delegation, among them being disillusionment over famine conditions prevailing in Russia at that time.

36. This was the only reference to China in the plenums from July 13, 1921, to March 4, 1922.

37. Before an article by Chen Po, editor of a magazine translated as *Social*, the editors felt constrained to note his "individualistic tone" which obstructed the "necessary clarity and Marxist precision"; they included the article because of its "factual material," referring to the abundance of statistics. Of the sixty pages devoted to China, this article had the most laudatory remarks for Sun and the Kuomintang and had no reference to Communism in China; see *Pervyi s'ezd revoliutsionnykh*, pp. 153–63.

CHAPTER VI *Comintern Comments on China: 1922–1924*

1. G. Maring, "Revoliutsionnoe dvizhenie v iuzhnom Kitae" (The Revolutionary Movement in South China), *Kommunisticheskii Internatsional*, No. 22, 1922, pp. 5803–16.

2. In a personal interview with Harold Isaacs in 1935, Maring told of a visit with Sun in Kwangsi in 1921; Harold I. Isaacs, *The Tragedy of the Chinese Revolution*, p. 62. A Japanese source puts Maring at the First Congress of the Chinese Communist Party in July, 1921; see Conrad Brandt, John K. Fairbank, and Benjamin I. Schwartz, eds., *A Documentary History of Chinese Communism*, p. 30. In August, 1922, Maring attended a special plenum of the central committee of the Chinese Communist Party at Hang-

chow, as Comintern representative. Isaacs probably errs in claiming the article discussed above was Maring's report, written after the plenum, since the issue of the magazine is dated September 13, 1922, and it is highly doubtful that he could have returned to Moscow in time. Furthermore, all articles in *Kommunisticheskii Internatsional* which bore date lines in 1922 appeared two to six months after writing; see, for instance, V. Vilenskii, "Politicheskie gruppirovki i partii v Kitae" (Political Groupings and Parties in China), dated August 9, 1922, but not published in *Kommunisticheskii Internatsional* until November 1, 1922, No. 22, pp. 6077–6104.

3. Roy, in his interview with R. C. North, many years later, placed considerable emphasis on Maring's role as interpreter of Comintern policy to the Chinese Communist Party. As noted above, the 1921–25 program of the Chinese Communist Party gave little emphasis to the peasantry but increasingly stressed collaboration with the bourgeoisie.

4. There seems little to support Isaacs's account, other than his interview with Maring in 1935, to the effect that the Comintern was divided regionally, with a so-called Irkutsk line arguing support for Wu Pei-fu and Maring reversing this line in mid-1922. Nor has any source been found for E. H. Carr's suggestion that Zinoviev supported this "line" at the Congress of Toilers of the Far East; see Isaacs, *op. cit.*, p. 59, and E. H. Carr, *The Bolshevik Revolution, 1917–1923*, III, 533–34. Carr's analysis at this point draws heavily on Isaacs, who, in turn, does not distinguish clearly in his text between what Maring told him and what is included in Leang-li T'ang, *The Inner History of the Chinese Revolution*. The difficulty in verifying Isaacs's and T'ang's accounts stems from their reliance upon personal recollections, admittedly of those intimately involved, more than upon contemporary documents. However, additional problems arise from the ambiguity of such terms as "Soviet policy" and "Moscow" when it is not clear whether the term means a monolithic decision-making center or a particular group within the Comintern or perhaps in the Narkomindel. As will be seen in Chapter VII when Vilenskii's articles are reviewed in detail, Narkomindel writings continued to give Wu Pei-fu a favorable slant long after his smashing of the February, 1923, railroad strike. Comintern writers, on the other hand, generally lashed out violently at the northern militarist, before, as well as after, the strike.

5. "The Situation in China and Japan," *International Press Correspondence*, No. 72, August 25, 1922, p. 542. In view of the obvious parallels between this report and Maring's article, it is probable that he was its author.

6. I. Maiskii, "Present Day China," *International Press Correspondence*, No. 76, September 5, 1922, p. 570.

302   *Notes*

7. G. Voitinskii, "Bor'ba Kitaiskogo proletariata" (Struggle of the Chinese Proletariat), *Novyi Vostok*, No. 2, 1922, pp. 341–50; also *International Press Correspondence*, No. 98, November 13, 1922, p. 874. Voitinskii served as Comintern agent in China and headed the Far Eastern Bureau of the Third International.

8. A contradictory analysis from the Chinese Communist Party on June 10, 1922, declared: "The Canton government has not been restricting the labor movement"; from "First Manifesto on the Current Situation," Brandt, *op. cit.*, p. 58. This manifesto appeared in full translation in *Novyi Vostok*, No. 2, 1922, pp. 606–12.

9. Carr, *op. cit.*, Vol. I, Chapter VIII, discusses this in detail.

10. Louis Fischer, *The Soviets in World Affairs*, I, 462; Fischer bases his account on a personal interview with Chicherin.

11. No Comintern congress convened in 1923.

12. *IV. vsemirnyi kongress Kommunisticheskogo Internatsionala, izbrannye doklady, rechi, i rezoliutsii* (Fourth World Congress of the Communist International, Selected Reports, Speeches, and Resolutions), p. 18. A. Tivel, *Piat' let Kominterna* (Five Years of Comintern), p. 48, gives the membership of the Chinese Communist Party as 500, but all other Communist sources contradict this. Tivel's handbook is a useful guide, but its many statistics must be carefully checked for accuracy.

13. *Protokoll des vierten Kongress der Kommunistischen Internationale*, p. 634. Liu Jen-ching was one of twelve present at the First Chinese Communist Party Congress, in July, 1921; Brandt, *op. cit.*, p. 30.

14. *IV. vsemirnyi kongress*, p. 45.

15. *Ibid.*, p. 49; the section concerning the antibourgeois program was omitted from the *Izvestiia* account of his speech as was his remark concerning "the struggle against the capitalistic regime" in backward areas; *Izvestiia*, No. 255 (1694), November 11, 1922, p. 2. Both parts were reported correctly in *Pravda*, No. 255, November 11, 1922, p. 3.

16. *IV. vsemirnyi kongress*, p. 194.

17. *Ibid.*, p. 204.

18. *Ibid.*, p. 265.

19. *Ibid.*, p. 239.

20. *Protokoll des vierten Kongress*, p. 615.

21. B. Schwartz, *Chinese Communism and the Rise of Mao*, pp. 37–45; for a different interpretation, see Isaacs, *op. cit.*, pp. 58–59.

22. *IV. vsemirnyi kongress*, p. 270.

23. *The Fourth Congress of the Communist International* (London, 1922), p. 221, as quoted in B. Schwartz, *op. cit.*, p. 37.

24. *Izvestiia*, No. 266 (1705), November 24, 1922, p. 3.

25. *Ibid.*, p. 3.

26. G. Kara-Murza and P. Mif, eds., *Strategiia i taktika Kominterna v natsional'no-kolonial'noi revoliutsii, na primer Kitaia* (Comintern Strategy and Tactics in the National-Colonial Revolution, For Example, China), p. 46.

27. *Ibid.*, p. 48.

28. *Ibid.*, p. 51. Italics added.

29. G. Maring, "Krovarnyi epizod v istorii Kitaiskogo rabochego dvizheniia" (Bloody Episode in the History of the Chinese Labor Movement), *Kommunisticheskii Internatsional*, Nos. 26–27, 1923, pp. 7455–66. An unusual footnote by editors Zinoviev and Radek claimed "disagreement" with Maring on "several points," but did not enumerate the specific disagreements. Maring referred favorably to Sun Yat-sen's labor relations in this article, consistent with his earlier views.

30. C. Brike, "Natsional'nye i klassovye perspektivy bor'by Kitaiskogo proletariata" (The National and Class Outlook for the Struggle of the Chinese Proletariat), *Pravda*, No. 50, March 6, 1923, p. 1.

31. Musin, "Kitaiskoe rabochee dvizhenie i fevral'skaia zheleznodorozhnaia zabastovka" (The Chinese Labor Movement and the February Railroad Strike), *Novyi Vostok*, No. 4, 1923, pp. 129–50.

32. Musin, "Kratkii obzor rabochego dvizheniia v Kitae za 1922 g." (Brief Survey of the Labor Movement in China in 1922), *Kommunisticheskii Internatsional*, No. 25, 1923, pp. 7071–78.

33. *Ezhegodnik Kominterna* (Comintern Yearbook), p. 743.

CHAPTER VII   *Other Voices: Narkomindel and Profintern*

1. V. I. Lenin, *Sobranie sochinenii* (Complete Works), XXV, 509; speech of November 26, 1920.

2. V. I. Lenin, *Sochineniia* (Works), 3rd ed., XXVII, 293.

3. *Ibid.*, 2nd ed., XXVII, 415; from *Pravda*, No. 49, March 4, 1923.

4. Stalin was in Europe only twice, at the Stockholm Congress of the Russian Social Democratic workers' Party in 1906, and for six weeks in early 1913, spent chiefly at Cracow and Vienna; see Issac Deutscher, *Stalin: A Political Biography* (New York, 1949), pp. 82, 115. According to M. N. Roy, Lenin always depended on Stalin whenever a question on Asia arose, but Stalin's knowledge of Asia was based solely on his experience with Georgian minorities; M. N. Roy interview with R. C. North, October 15, 1950. Roy's reference to Lenin cannot be checked, although it seems doubtful in view of the nearly complete absence of China in Stalin's pre-1924 writings.

5. *Pravda*, No. 241, November 6, 1918, p. 3.

6. J. V. Stalin, *Sochineniia* (Works), IV, 171–73; from *Zhizn' Natsional'nosti*, No. 3, November 24, 1918.

7. N. Bukharin, *Krizis kapitalizma i kommunisticheskoe dvizhenie* (The Crisis of Capitalism and the Communist Movement), p. 29; also *Dvenatsatii s'ezd RKP (b)*, p. 245. Zinoviev, opening the Congress in place of Lenin who was indisposed, paid general tribute to "the certain rapprochement . . . between the first victorious country of proletarian revolution—our country on the one hand, and on the other, the awakening East"; *Izvestiia*, No. 84 (1821), April 18, 1923. This was the only meeting of the Russian Communist Party prior to 1924 which dealt with China at any length.

8. Bukharin, *op. cit.*, p. 25.

9. Lenin, *Sobranie sochinenii*, XXVI, 509.

10. For a firsthand account of American intervention in Siberia and its checking of Japanese designs, see W. S. Graves, *America's Siberian Adventure, 1918–1920* (New York, 1931).

11. *Izvestiia*, No. 148 (1587), July 6, 1922, p. 3.

12. V. Vilenskii, "Politicheskie gruppirovki i partii v Kitae" (Political Groupings and Parties in China), *Kommunisticheskii Internatsional*, No. 23, 1922, pp. 6077–6104.

13. Even here Vilenskii was not entirely wrong. During the 1930's, the Nationalist government under Chiang Kai-shek received military aid and advice from Hitler Germany. The Anti-Comintern Pact, linking Germany with Japan, did not come until 1936, and German aid did not cease for well over a year after that.

14. V. Vilenskii, "Oktiabr'skaia Rossiia—maiak dlia narodov Azii" (October Russia—Beacon for Peoples of Asia), *Izvestiia*, No. 252 (1691), November 7, 1922, p. 1.

15. Louis Fischer, *The Soviets in World Affairs*, I, 301; for a fuller study of American policy during this period, see Pauline Tompkins, *American-Russian Relations in the Far East* (New York, 1949), pp. 181 ff., and W. A. Williams, *American-Russian Relations, 1781–1947* (New York, 1952), pp. 177 ff.·

16. V. Vilenskii, "Perspektivy revoliutsionnogo dvizheniia v Kitae" (Outlook for the Revolutionary Movement in China), *Novyi Vostok*, No. 2, 1922, pp. 317–30.

17. *Ibid.*, p. 329.

18. I. Maiskii, "Kitai i ego bor'ba" (China and Her Struggle), *Pravda*, No. 166, 1922; see also Maiskii's article in *International Press Correspondence*, summarized in Chapter VI. He later became Soviet Ambassador to Great Britain.

19. Vilenskii, "Perspektivy revoliutsionnogo," *Novyi Vostok*, No. 2, 1922, p. 329. Italics added.

20. A. Khodorov, "Novyi kabinet v Pekine" (New Cabinet in Peking), *Vestnik Narkomindel*, Nos. 4–5, 1922, pp. 107–16.

21. In light of Ch'en's later *coup d'état* against Sun, it is amusing to see an evaluation of Ch'en as a "convinced Communist," *Vestnik Narkomindel*, Nos. 1–2, 1921, p. 12. A footnote called him "not only a revolutionary general . . . but a brilliant organizer, receiving the sympathies of the masses, popular," etc.

22. A. Khodorov, "Koalitsiia Chang Tso-lina i Sun Iat-sen" (Coalition between Chang Tso-lin and Sun Yat-sen), *Mezhdunarodnaia Zhizn'*, No. 9 (127), July 29, 1922, pp. 41–46.

23. *Izvestiia*, No. 148 (1587), July 6, 1922, p. 3. This was the most favorable reference to Wu Pei-fu in *Izvestiia* which had appeared so far. Contrary to the assertions of most Western writers, Soviet attitudes toward Wu had wavered between caution and hostility. On August 23, 1920, Vilenskii commented in *Izvestiia* that the struggle among northern militarists would be replaced by struggle "between the revolutionary South and the militaristic North." Wu's victory over the pro-Japanese Anfu forces was not "victory of the revolution, but through this victory Chinese society nears the hour of the class struggle." On October 9, 1920, Vilenskii wrote for *Izvestiia* at the time of a Chinese mission to Moscow, noting that Wu Pei-fu had a pro-Russian orientation, since China had to choose Japan or Russia as an ally. Nothing he wrote praised Wu directly. On November 16, 1921, *Izvestiia* ran an unsigned article praising Sun as a "Chinese radical" but describing Wu as "formerly popular in 1920 but now fighting Sun with [help from] Great Britain." While Sun "represents the idea of the national bourgeoisie of China . . . throwing off world capitalism," Wu had "objectively" passed into the hands of "world reaction and Chinese counter-revolution."

24. Vilenskii, "Politicheskie gruppirovki," *Kommunisticheskii Internatsional*, No. 23, 1922, pp. 6077–6104.

25. B. Nikolaevskii, "Revoliutsiia v Kitae, Japoniia, i Stalin" (Revolution in China, Japan, and Stalin), *Novyi Zhurnal*, VI, 1943, 229–57. Nikolaevskii, an émigré authority on Soviet foreign policy, maintains that Stalin's speeches of 1925, particularly to the Fourteenth Party Congress, developed a new theory of revolution based primarily on the army instead of upon the proletariat.

26. V. Vilenskii, "Sovremennyi Kitai" (Contemporary China), *Izvestiia*, No. 180 (1619), August 12, 1922, p. 2.

27. *Ibid.*, No. 181 (1620), August 13, 1922, p. 2.

28. *Ibid.*, No. 182 (1621), August 15, 1922, p. 2.

29. V. Vilenskii, *Izvestiia*, No. 18 (1755), January 27, 1923, p. 3. The Sun-Joffe entente will be discussed in detail later.

30. V. Vilenskii, "Novyi prezident Kitaia" (New President of China), *Izvestiia*, No. 272 (2009), November 28, 1923, p. 2.

31. An interesting, if somewhat confused, account of the Karakhan-Borodin relationship in 1923 was given by M. N. Roy in his interview with R. C. North. Roy asserted that Karakhan started on his mission to win the support of Wu, but he became interested in Canton and fully approved of Borodin's activities there. There is no doubt that Karakhan and Borodin kept in contact with each other, but it is not clear from the scanty evidence how much of their action was directed from Moscow and how much was "played by ear" as Roy indicated.

32. V. Vilenskii, "Za velikoi Kitaiskoi stenoi" (Behind the Great Chinese Wall), *Izvestiia*, No. 212 (1651), September 21, 1922, p. 2.

33. *Ibid.*, p. 3.

34. L. Heller, "Otchët II. kongressa Profinterna o rabochem dvizhenii v Kitae" (Report at the Second Profintern Congress on the Labor Movement in China), *Krasnyi Internatsional Profsoiuzov*, No. 1 (24), January 27, 1923, pp. 132–37.

35. *Ibid.*, p. 135.

36. *Biulleten' Profinterna*, No. 14, p. 1.

37. *Pervaia mezhdunarodnaia konferentsiia revoliutsionnykh professional'nykh i proizvodstvennykh soiuzov, stenograficheskii otchët* (First International Conference of Professional and Industrial Trade Unions, Verbatim Report), p. 10.

38. "Rabochee dvizhenie (Kitai)" (The Labor Movement—China), *Krasnyi Internatsional Profsoiuzov*, No. 11, December 31, 1921, pp. 572–77. Although no author is given, the article is identical with a pamphlet by Kh. Eidus, *Ocherki rabochego dvizheniia v stranakh Vostoka* (Essays on the Labor Movement in Countries of the East). Writing in *Izvestiia*, No. 177 (1320), August 12, 1921, Eidus lamented the deplorable conditions in Asia which permitted the bourgeoisie to expand while suppressing the proletariat. To make matters worse, the proletariat, lacking national consciousness before, now received this stimulus from the bourgeoisie and became hopelessly chauvinistic. Eidus made no direct reference to China in this article.

39. Iu. Smurgis, *Kitai i ego rabochee dvizhenie* (China and Its Labor Movement).

40. *Ibid.*, p. 20.

41. Heller, "Otchët," *Krasnyi Internatsional Profsoiuzov,* No. 1 (24), January 27, 1923, p. 137.

42. *Biulleten' II. kongress Krasnogo Internatsionala Profsoiuzov* (Bulletin of the Second Congress of the Red International of Trade Unions), p. 8.

43. S. Girinis, ed., *Profintern v rezoliutsiiakh* (Profintern in Resolutions), p. 100; see also *Resolutions and Decisions of the Second World Congress of the Red Labor Union International,* p. 37.

44. "Stachenoe dvizhenie v Kitae" (The Strike Movement in China), *Krasnyi Internatsional Profsoiuzov,* No. 2 (25), February, 1923, pp. 294–99.

45. *Pravda,* No. 52, March 8, 1923, p. 2.

46. *Otchët o rabotakh III. sessii tsentralnogo soveta Krasnogo Profinterna* (Report on Work of the Third Session of the Central Council of the Red Profintern), p. 7.

47. L. Heller, *Profsoiuzy na Vostoka* (Trade Unions in the East), p. 18.

48. V. Vilenskii, "Rabochee dvizhenie v Kitae" (The Workers' Movement in China), *Krasnyi Internatsional Profsoiuzov,* No. 12 (35), December, 1923, pp. 613–16.

CHAPTER VIII   *Heritage from the Past: Narkomindel in China*

1. Information on Sino-Russian trade is based on Ping-yin Ho, *The Foreign Trade of China.*

2. The Baikal-Amur line, circumventing Manchuria, was built during the Second Five Year Plan.

3. M. N. Pavlovsky, *Chinese-Russian Relations,* pp. 1–97, gives a lucid, scholarly survey of Mongolia's historic position in this respect.

4. Owen Lattimore, *Manchuria, Cradle of Conflict,* pp. 53–70, contrasts the different social problems facing Chinese emigration to the two areas, Mongolia and Manchuria.

5. Pavlovsky, *op. cit.,* pp. 32–35.

6. I. J. Korostovets, *Von Cinggis Khan zur Sowetrepublik,* p. 175.

7. *Millard's Review,* March 27, 1920, p. 182.

8. *Ibid.,* April 5, 1919, p. 212. The Chinese reply attacked Kudashev's failure to curb Ataman Semenov as Peking had previously requested. The fiction of recognizing an impotent representative of a nonexistent government proved highly convenient.

9. G. M. Friters, *Outer Mongolia and Its International Position,* pp. 188–89. An interesting but highly biased account of a Mongol claims that a separatist movement in Mongolia started at this time; Ho-t'ien Ma, *Chinese Agent in Mongolia,* p. 82.

10. K. S. Weigh, *Russo-Chinese Diplomacy*, pp. 191–93.

11. *Millard's Review*, December 6, 1919, p. 12.

12. For a vivid description of Hsü's excesses, see *Millard's Review*, December 6, 1919, p. 12.

13. *Izvestiia*, No. 245 (1092), November 2, 1920, p. 1. This text of the declaration was embodied in an article by Vilenskii and did not include the last sentence, which is found in a similar version reprinted many years later; see Doksom, "Istoricheskie uroki 15 let revoliutsii" (Historical Lesson of Fifteen Years of Revolution), *Tikhii Okean*, No. 3 (9), July-September, 1936, p. 72. There is no reason to suppose this last sentence not to have been in the original manifesto; its existence was verified verbatim in the official *Diplomaticheskii Slovar'* (Diplomatic Dictionary), II, 714, published in 1950 under the direction of A. Vishinsky. It is interesting to note that the sentence immediately preceding, which reads, "By overthrowing . . . ," is omitted from the Doksom version. In view of official Soviet policy in the mid-thirties to deny Mongolia's independence and thereby deny the right of other nations, particularly Japan, to send emissaries there, this deletion appears intentional. As for dating the manifesto, no accounts agree. V. Vilenskii puts it as August, 1919, while *Diplomaticheskii Slovar'* dates it June 26, 1919. In view of the many chronological inaccuracies in the *Slovar'*, it is probable that Vilenskii's date is correct. A thorough search in the 1919 files of *Izvestiia* and *Pravda* failed to reveal any text other than that offered by Vilenskii in 1920.

14. H. T. Kong, "China, Japan, and the Siberian Question," *Millard's Review*, March 6, 1920, pp. 12–14.

15. *Izvestiia*, No. 91 (938), April 29, 1920, p. 1. According to this dispatch, a "large number" of Chinese traders together with a "military-diplomatic mission" arrived on April 24, concluding an agreement whereby "China recognizes the succession of right on the CER to the new Russian government in Siberia. Occupation by the Chinese troops is only of a temporary nature, prior to completion of establishing of the new government in the Far East." In addition to promising measures against Semenov and opening the Chinese-Russian border for trade, the mission declared China's willingness "to admit consular representatives of Russia." With the exception of the reference to trade, none of these measures could have been concluded at the time, given the anti-Russian orientation of the Peking government. No other reference to these terms was ever made in the Russian press. The article remains, however, as an interesting indication of Bolshevik hopes, particularly with regard to the Chinese Eastern Railway.

16. Although no Russian text was published at the time, a detailed account of the negotiations and a summary of the terms was included in *Dip-*

lomaticheskii Slovar', I, 671 ff. This account claims that contact, established in March, 1918, between local Russians and Chinese, was strengthened by "a special mission of the Narkomindel of the RSFSR sent to Turkestan for negotiations." However, civil war intervened, and no further negotiations took place until the beginning of 1920 when Red Army units reached the Sinkiang border. With the approval of local Chinese officials, according to this account, the Red Army crossed the border in pursuit of White Guard detachments. "At the end of May, 1920, these troops, quickly completing their military operations, were withdrawn from the territory of Sinkiang." Negotiations followed between "commissions of the CEC and the Sovnarkom of the RSFSR in Turkestan" and Chinese officials in Sinkiang. For an English version of the treaty, see *Treaties and Agreements with and concerning China, 1919–1929*, p. 23.

17. *Millard's Review*, July 24, 1920, p. 422.

18. *Ibid.*, June 5, 1920, pp. 24–26.

19. *North China Herald*, August 21, 1920. The delegation included B. L. Simpson, B. Georges Padoux, and Dr. John C. Ferguson. It was appointed by Chang's new regime.

20. *Ibid.*, p. 480.

21. *Ibid.*

22. *China Year Book, 1921*, p. 651.

23. *Millard's Review*, January 1, 1921, pp. 238–39.

24. *North China Herald*, September 9, 1920, p. 806.

25. *Millard's Review*, September 25, 1920, p. 203.

26. *Ibid.*, October 2, 1920, p. 262.

27. *Ibid.*, October 2, 1920, p. 281.

28. V. P. Savvin, *Vzaimootnosheniia tsarskoi Rossii i SSSR s Kitaem* (Relations of Tsarist Russia and the USSR with China), pp. 128–29; a translation appears in V. Yakhontoff, *Russia and the Soviet Union in the Far East*, pp. 384–87. Both writers incorrectly date the document as "October 27, 1920," but this date is not supported by any contemporary Soviet sources. It is probable that Yakhontoff copied his text from Savvin's booklet, which appeared in 1930 and is cited in his bibliography, rather than from Narkomindel archives as Yakhontoff alleges. A correct translation appears in *China Year Book, 1924*, p. 870, "as published by the Soviet mission." Vilenskii referred to the memorandum in *Izvestiia*, No. 225 (1072), October 9, 1920, p. 2, but gave no text.

29. For an explanation of Chang's probable position as a member of the former Anfu government, see R. T. Pollard, *China's Foreign Relations, 1917–1931*, p. 135. In view of Peking's very conservative behavior with respect to the Bolsheviks, it is doubtful that it would have moved so far in

advance of the Allies as to send a formal delegation to Moscow. In Kara-khan's second manifesto, Peking's attention was called to the fact that the mission "has not yet received the necessary instructions to start the molding of friendship between the two nations"; Savvin, *op. cit.,* p. 128. If Chang acted without authority in representing himself to Moscow as an emissary of Peking, he was not without precedent. *Pravda,* No. 94, May 4, 1920, p. 1, reported that a Chinese mission had arrived in Verkhne-Udinsk, intending to go to Irkutsk and eventually to Moscow where it was to "regulate Russian-Chinese relations and to open trade." This may have been Chang's "mission." There is no Russian evidence to support E. H. Carr's assertion that Peking's repudiation of Chang was "a fiction designed to propitiate Western opinion by playing down any relations with Moscow." *The Bolshevik Revolution, 1917–1923,* III, 510, n. 2.

30. *Godovoi Otchët, 1920–21,* p. 53.

31. *China Year Book, 1924,* p. 870.

32. The manifesto was forwarded to Peking, together with a "corrected copy" of the 1919 declaration, by General Chang; it was formally acknowledged in two notes of February 3 and February 11, 1921; *North China Herald,* December 1, 1923, p. 591.

33. *Millard's Review,* January 1, 1921, p. 239.

34. Lyon Sharman, *Sun Yat-sen, His Life and Its Meaning,* pp. 243–44.

35. *Bol'shevik,* No. 19, October 15, 1950, p. 46; full translation in *Current Digest of the Soviet Press,* II, No. 43, 20. This "envoy" was probably Maring; see Harold R. Isaacs, *The Tragedy of the Chinese Revolution,* p. 62, which tells of Maring's visit to Sun "in the spring of 1921."

36. Two Chinese accounts tell of efforts by Voitinsky in 1920 to see Li Ta-chao in Peking and Ch'en Tu-hsiu in Shanghai, after which Ch'en organized a "Chinese Socialist Youth" group; see *Chia I-chun, Chung-hua Min-kuo Shih* (Peiping, 1930), p. 176; and *Chung-kuo Ko T'ang P'ai chih Shih Liao yü P'i P'an* (Peiping, 1947), p. 310. The latter asserts that Voitinsky gave $5,000 in gold to Ch'en and urged that a Communist Party be formed in China. Maring's activities are described in Edgar Snow, *Red Star Over China,* p. 156, wherein he is identified as "M. Marlin."

CHAPTER IX   *First Attempts: The Yurin and Paikes Missions*

1. *Millard's Review,* October 23, 1920, p. 398.

2. *Ibid.,* December 11, 1920, p. 99.

3. *Ibid.,* December 25, 1920, p. 213.

4. *Ibid.,* January 1, 1921, pp. 238–39.

5. *Ibid.;* see also *Godovoi Otchët, 1920–21,* p. 35.

6. *Millard's Review,* November 6, 1920, p. 550.

7. V. Vilenskii, "Sovetskaia Rossiia i Mongoliia" (Soviet Russia and Mongolia), *Izvestiia*, No. 245 (1092), November 2, 1920.

8. *Pravda*, No. 256, November 14, 1920, p. 2; this incorrectly dates the note as November 10. The date was corrected in the next NKID announcement. This text had not been found when the manuscript was made available to E. H. Carr, hence his erroneous comment, "The Soviet note of November 10, 1920, has apparently not been published," *The Bolshevik Revolution, 1917–1923*, III, 513, n. 2.

9. *Pravda*, No. 269, November 30, 1920, p. 2.

10. *Izvestiia*, No. 3 (1146), January 5, 1921, p. 1; Chinese Foreign Office wire to the Chinese ambassador in London, received by L. Krassin.

11. For details on the contacts in Urga, see Carr, *op. cit.*, p. 512, quoting from the unpublished memoirs of the Dilowa Hutukhtu, and G. M. Friters, *Outer Mongolia and Its International Position*, pp. xxvi–xxviii.

12. *Godovoi Otchët, 1920–21*, p. 56. In *Diplomaticheskii Slovar'* (Diplomatic Dictionary), II, 714, this appeal is quoted in part as reading, "We request help of the Great Soviet Russia. We want to make our country independent."

13. *Izvestiia*, No. 10 (1153), January 16, 1921, p. 2; Narkomindel note No. 574.

14. A subsequent Russian dispatch from Urga found conditions there quite satisfactory among the Russian populace and characterized Chinese administration as wholly proper; *Izvestiia*, No. 26 (1153), February 6, 1921, p. 2. This dispatch was filed prior to Ungern's capture of the city on February 2.

15. *Izvestiia*, No. 32 (1175), February 13, 1921; *China Year Book, 1924*, p. 576.

16. *Izvestiia*, No. 68 (1211), March 30, 1921; *China Year Book, 1924*, p. 576.

17. *Izvestiia*, No. 250 (1393), November 6, 1921, p. 2. Here Chicherin, in a review of recent events entitled "God vostochnoi politiki Sovetskoi vlasti" (One Year's Policy of Soviet Power), remarked: "Already in the time of Ungern's hegemony, a people's revolutionary government of Mongolia was formed, an army created on Russian territory." See also I. Maiskii, *Vneshnaia politika RSFSR, 1917–1922* (The Foreign Policy of the RSFSR, 1917–1922), p. 169; *Godovoi Otchët, 1920–21*.

18. K. S. Weigh, *Russo-Chinese Diplomacy*, pp. 200–214. See also *Letters Captured from Baron Ungern in Mongolia*, published by the Far Eastern Republic commission to the Washington Conference, for Ungern-Chang references; also *Conference on Limitation of Armaments*, p. 1398, for alleged Japanese ties.

19. *North China Herald,* June 4, 1921, p. 652; interview of May 25, 1921. The Soviet press featured rumors of the Chinese press concerning an imminent pact in Peking; *Izvestiia,* No. 112 (1255), May 25, 1921, p. 2, noted the publication of the Anglo-Soviet trade treaty in Chinese and quoted the Chinese Minister of Foreign Affairs reassuringly on an immediate settlement of Far Eastern Republic-Chinese relations. In this sense, Carr's statement that Yurin's conversations "led to no result" is misleading; Carr, *op. cit.,* p. 511. Yurin at least won counterproposals from the Waichiao Pu which he took back to Chita for consultation.

20. *Izvestiia,* No. 160 (1303), July 19, 1921, p. 1.

21. *North China Herald,* July 9, 1921, p. 87; italics added. No Russian text appeared in the Moscow press, although this was allegedly a Rosta dispatch from Moscow.

22. *Ibid.,* p. 92.

23. *North China Herald,* July 30, 1921, p. 312; italics added. *Pravda,* No. 179, August 14, 1921, p. 3, quoted Yurin similarly in a much-delayed report from Novo Nikolaievsk.

24. *North China Herald,* August 6, 1921, p. 386.

25. *Izvestiia,* September 1 and 9, 1920; see also Yanson's article, *Izvestiia,* No. 247 (1094), November 4, 1920, p. 2.

26. *Izvestiia,* No. 252 (1099), November 9, 1920, p. 1.

27. *Ibid.,* No. 60 (1203), March 20, 1921, p. 1.

28. A. E. Khodorov, *Mirovoi imperializm v Kitae* (World Imperialism in China), pp. 30 ff.; although this booklet was published in 1922, it was written in the latter part of 1921.

29. *Ibid.,* pp. 34, 50.

30. I. Maiskii, *Sovremennaia Mongolia* (Contemporary Mongolia).

31. *Ibid.,* p. 329. Italics in original.

32. G. Chicherin, "God vostochnoi politiki Sovetskoi vlasti, *Izvestiia,* No. 250 (1393), November 6, 1921, p. 2. Chen is identified as a "consul" although his precise status is unclear.

33. *Ibid.*

34. *Izvestiia,* No. 257 (1400), November 16, 1921, p. 2.

35. *Ibid.,* No. 175 (1318), August 10, 1921, p. 1.

36. *Ibid.,* No. 177 (1320), August 12, 1921, p. 2. Italics added.

37. *Ibid.,* No. 223 (1366), October 6, 1921, p. 2.

38. *Ibid.,* No. 205 (1348), September 15, 1921, p. 1.

39. *Ibid.,* No. 207 (1350), September 17, 1921, p. 3.

40. Friters, *op. cit.,* pp. 102–6.

41. *Izvestiia,* No. 207 (1350), September 17, 1921, p. 3.

42. M. N. Pavlovsky, *Chinese-Russian Relations,* pp. 51–53, gives a vivid

description of the sudden furor in Peking when news was received of the treaty.

43. *North China Herald,* December 24, 1921, p. 824.

44. H. T. Kong, "Soviet Mission in Peking," *Millard's Review* (title changed at this time to *China Weekly Review*), December 31, 1921, p. 190.

45. *Izvestiia,* No. 253 (1396), November 11, 1921, p. 1; *Pravda,* No. 254, November 11, 1921, p. 1. Carr, *op. cit.,* pp. 530–31, is technically correct but misleading in saying: "The Soviet-Mongolian treaty of November 5 was not yet known to the world. . . . In April, 1922, the publication of the . . . treaty. . . ." It is important to establish the announcement of the treaty, at least in the Russian press, as preceding the arrival of Paikes in Peking, because of Paikes's denial that any such treaty existed.

46. International lawyers may find interesting the Soviet versions of this particular section of the treaty. In both *Izvestiia* and *Pravda,* the phrase "edinstvennim zakonnim pravitelstvom" was used. When the full text of the treaty appeared in *Sbornik deistvuiushchikh dogovorov, soglashenii, i konventsii zakliuchennikh s inostrannymi gosudarstvami* (Collection of Operative Treaties, Agreements, and Conventions Concluded with Foreign Governments), II, 29–31, it quoted the RSFSR as recognizing the Mongolian regime as "edinstvennim Zakonnim Pravitelstvom" while the Mongolian regime acknowledged the RSFSR as "Edinstvennoi Zakonnoi Vlastiiu Rossii." Note the difference in capitalization as well as wording. To add to the confusion, when the second edition of *Sbornik* was published in 1928, the RSFSR recognized the Mongolian regime as "edinstvennim zakonnim pravitelstvom" while the Mongolian regime acknowledged the RSFSR as "edinstvennoi zakonnoi vlastiiu rossii" (pp. 77–79). There is no way of ascertaining the original text of the treaty until a more authoritative version is available. The remainder of the treaty does not differ from edition to edition, and stands essentially as summarized in the contemporary press.

47. In *Diplomaticheskii Slovar',* II, 708, V. Molotov, writing on Soviet-Chinese treaties, refers to the Mongolian regime of 1921 as "the government of independent Outer Mongolia." In the same work, an article on Soviet-Mongol relations states: "Mongolia was the first country in the Far East with whom Soviet Russia established diplomatic relations." The 1921 treaty "established mutual recognition," *ibid.,* II, 714.

48. *China Year Book, 1924,* p. 582.

49. *North China Herald,* December 24, 1921, p. 824.

50. *Ibid.,* December 31, 1921, p. 887; *China Weekly Review,* December 31, 1921, p. 190.

51. As proof that the Narkomindel's position on the CER had not

changed, reference should be made to Chicherin's circular note to the countries assembled at the Washington Conference, terming the railway a problem "which concerns exclusively Russia and China." He continued: "Although the Russian Government expressed its readiness to transfer said railroad into the hands of the Chinese authorities, under condition that China give certain guarantees necessary for this transfer, the latter has not yet occurred, and the rights of Russia on this railroad remain in full force. Only at that moment, when agreement is reached on this question between the Russian delegation, which is charged with solving this problem, and the Chinese Government, will the change in Russian rights on this railroad be in force. . . . But until then these rights remain and will remain exactly as they were until now." Narkomindel note to Great Britain, France, Japan, United States, Belgium, Italy, copy to China, December 8, 1921; from *Izvestiia*, No. 278 (1421), December 10, 1921, p. 1.

52. *China Weekly Review*, December 21, 1921, p. 215; see also *Izvestiia*, February 16, 1922, where the Chinese press is quoted as insisting that "the Peking government, ignoring the decision of the Washington Conference on the question of the CER, *immediately open negotiations on this question with the Soviet mission.*" (Italics in original.)

53. R. T. Pollard, *China's Foreign Relations, 1917–1931*, pp. 244 ff.

54. *Izvestiia*, No. 75 (1514), April 2, 1922, p. 2.

55. *China Year Book, 1924*, p. 857.

56. *Izvestiia*, No. 120 (1559), June 1, 1922, p. 1.

57. *Ibid.*, No. 119 (1558), May 31, 1922, p. 1.

58. For text of a Soviet-Mongolian treaty of May 31, 1922, on ownership of property, see *Treaties and Agreements with and concerning China, 1919–1929*, p. 102.

59. I. Maiskii, "Mongoliia" (Mongolia), *Novyi Vostok*, No. 1, 1922, pp. 154–83.

60. *Ibid.*, p. 168.

61. S. Kotliarevskii, "Pravovye dostizheniia Rossii v Azii" (Russian Legal Attainments in Asia), *Novyi Vostok*, No. 1, 1922, pp. 34–43.

62. E. H. Carr, *German-Soviet Relations Between the Two World Wars, 1919–1939* (Baltimore, 1951), gives an excellent summary of the clandestine relations of this early period.

CHAPTER X *The Joffe Mission*

1. A. Ivin, "Sovremennyi Kitai" (Contemporary China), *Novyi Vostok*, No. 2, 1922, pp. 552–59.

2. *China Year Book, 1924*, p. 858.

3. *Ibid.; North China Herald,* August 19, 1922, p. 512; *ibid.,* September 9, 1922, pp. 716–17.

4. *Izvestiia,* No. 207 (1647), September 16, 1922, p. 1, reported that conversations between the two diplomatic representatives were held on August 23, 30, and 31, 1922.

5. *Ibid.*

6. *China Weekly Review,* September 9, 1922, p. 67. Italics added.

7. *Izvestiia,* No. 207 (1647), September 16, 1922, p. 1.

8. *Ibid.,* No. 215 (1654), September 24, 1922, p. 1.

9. *Ibid.*

10. "Problemy dal'nego Vostoka" (Problems of the Far East). *Izvestiia,* No. 178 (1617), August 10, 1922, p. 2.

11. V. Vilenskii, "Za velikoi Kitaiskoi stenoi" (Behind the Great Chinese Wall), *Izvestiia,* No. 185 (1624), August 18, 1922, p. 3.

12. Paikes's statement of December 10, 1921, concerning the CER was never reported in the Moscow press.

13. M. Kazanin, "Pekin i problemy dogovora" (Peking and Treaty Problems), *Mezhdunarodnaia Zhizn',* No. 14, October 31, 1922, pp. 26–32.

14. *Ibid.,* p. 28.

15. *Ibid.,* p. 32.

16. J. Hart, "Mr. Yoffe and the Failure of Chinese-Russian Negotiations," *China Weekly Review,* January 27, 1923, p. 340.

17. *Ibid.*

18. *China Year Book, 1924,* p. 859.

19. *Ibid.,* p. 860; note of October 14, 1922.

20. *Ibid.,* p. 860.

21. *North China Herald,* November 18, 1922, p. 426; *Izvestiia,* No. 255 (1694), November 11, 1922, p. 1.

22. *North China Herald,* November 18, 1922, p. 421; *Izvestiia,* No. 255 (1694), November 11, 1922, p. 1. Italics added.

23. *North China Herald,* November 18, 1922, p. 426.

24. *China Year Book, 1924,* p. 862; *Izvestiia,* No. 261 (1700), November 18, 1922, p. 4.

25. *China Year Book, 1924,* p. 862; *Izvestiia,* No. 261 (1700), November 18, 1922, p. 4. Italics added.

26. *Living Age,* CCCXVI, 73–76; *North China Herald,* November 18, 1922; *Izvestiia,* No. 255 (1694), November 11, 1922, p. 1; only parts were carried in the Russian press.

27. *China Year Book, 1924,* p. 862.

28. *North China Herald,* November 18, 1922, p. 431.

29. *China Year Book, 1924,* p. 861.

30. *China Weekly Review,* January 27, 1923, pp. 339 ff.

31. *Ibid.*

32. *Ibid.*

33. *Ibid.*

34. *Ibid.*

35. *China Weekly Review,* March 24, 1923, p. 115.

36. For an extended analysis of Chinese reactions to Joffe, see J. Hart, "Mr. Yoffe and the Failure of Chinese-Russian Negotiations," *China Weekly Review,* January 27, 1923, pp. 339–41.

37. "Sovetskaia Rossiia i Mandzhurskaia problema" (Soviet Russia and the Manchurian Problem), *Izvestiia,* No. 295 (1734), December 28, 1922.

38. *Izvestiia,* No. 112 (2147), June 18, 1924, p. 1.

39. A. Joffe, "Kitaiskii kavardak" (Chinese Puzzle), *Izvestiia,* No. 3 (1740), January 5, 1923, p. 2.

40. A. Joffe, "Nachalo" (The Beginning), *Izvestiia,* No. 40 (1777), February 22, 1923, p. 2.

41. The Comintern journal made no reference to Joffe's mission.

42. *Pravda,* No. 17, January 26, 1923, carried a five-line dispatch from Chita to the effect that on January 17 Joffe had arrived in Shanghai "where he conversed with Sun Yat-sen. Public opinion in China is favorable toward Comrade Joffe." Telling of Ch'en Chiung-ming's expulsion from Canton, the item concluded: "Sun Yat-sen remains in Shanghai with the aim of uniting China."

43. While both Benjamin I. Schwartz and Harold R. Isaacs link the Sun-Joffe entente with Comintern efforts to form a united front in China, the available materials do not wholly support this analysis. Joffe went to China as a Narkomindel representative, and he turned to Sun in Shanghai only when his Peking mission was stalemated. It is clear that Narkomindel and Comintern interests included such an entente; this does not, however, prove that the Comintern participated in directing Joffe's activity.

44. *China Year Book, 1924,* p. 863; this version checks completely with a Chinese translation made at the time and published in *Tung-fang tsa-chih,* Vol. XX, No. 2.

45. The Rosta version published in the Moscow dailies read: "Comrade Joffe emphasized that in his opinion the most urgent task for China is its unification and its attainment of full independence. He informed Sun Yat-sen that China enjoys the warmest sympathies of the Russian people and can count on their help"; *Izvestiia,* No. 22 (1759), February 1, 1923, p. 2; *Pravda,* No. 22, February 1, 1923, p. 2. The unpublished Russian version reported that Dr. Sun did not think the Soviet system could be introduced

in China "because the conditions do not exist here for the successful establishment of Communism or Socialism [*sic*]. Mr. Joffe absolutely agrees with this view and, furthermore, submits that the chief and immediate aim of China is the achievement of national union and national independence. Mr. Joffe informed Dr. Sun that in the solution of this great problem, China would find the warmest sympathy of the Russian people and could depend on the aid of Russia"; translated from the fortnightly bulletin of the Soviet political representative in Peking, February 1–15, 1923, in the archives of the Narkomindel, by Louis Fischer; see Louis Fischer, *The Soviets in World Affairs*, II, 540–41. In view of Joffe's suicide in November, 1927, and his established sympathies with Leon Trotsky (see Louis Fischer, *Men and Politics*, pp. 95 ff.), it is no surprise that later Soviet histories avoid his role in the Sun-Joffe entente. Thus *Diplomaticheskii Slovar'*, II, 780, in a biography of Sun Yat-sen, notes: "In 1923, while living in Shanghai, Sun made contact with diplomatic representatives [*sic*] of the USSR, who at that time were conducting negotiations with the Peking government." The summary of the entente omits any reference to the statement concerning the inadvisability of Communism in China.

46. *Izvestiia*, No. 20 (1757), January 30, 1923, p. 1.

47. *China Year Book, 1924*, p. 864.

48. *Ibid.*

49. *China Weekly Review*, April 21, 1923, p. 290.

50. Fischer, *The Soviets*, II, 553.

51. *China Year Book, 1924*, p. 865.

52. *Izvestiia*, No. 70 (1807), March 30, 1923, p. 2.

53. *Ibid.*

CHAPTER XI   *The Sino-Soviet Treaty of May 31, 1924*

1. *Izvestiia*, No. 173 (1910), August 3, 1923, p. 1.

2. A. E. Khodorov, "Rossiia i dal'nyi Vostok" (Russia and the Far East), *Torgovlia Rossii s Vostokom*, No. 1, June, 1923, pp. 4–6.

3. *Ibid.*, p. 5.

4. G. Dikii, "Mandzhurskii rynok i russkaia promyshlennost'" (The Manchurian Market and Russian Industry), *Torgovlia Rossii s Vostokom*, Nos. 3–4, 1923, p. 17.

5. R. T. Pollard, *China's Foreign Relations, 1917–1931*, p. 179.

6. *Izvestiia*, No. 175 (1912), August 5, 1923, p. 2.

7. *Ibid.*, No. 173 (1910), August 3, 1923, p. 1.

8. *Ibid.*, No. 183 (1920), August 17, 1923, p. 2.

9. *Ibid.*, No. 190 (1927), August 25, 1923, p. 1; *China Weekly Review*, August 25, 1923, p. 446.

10. *Izvestiia,* No. 174 (1921), August 4, 1923, p. 1.

11. *Ibid.,* No. 177 (1916), August 10, 1923, p. 1.

12. *Ibid.,* No. 201 (1938), September 7, 1923, p. 2; *China Weekly Review,* September 15, 1923, p. 102.

13. *Izvestiia,* No. 202 (1939), September 8, 1923, p. 2.

14. *China Year Book, 1924,* p. 866.

15. *Izvestiia,* No. 216 (1953), September 25, 1923, p. 2.

16. *China Year Book, 1924,* p. 866.

17. *Ibid.*

18. *Ibid.,* p. 867.

19. *Izvestiia,* No. 243 (1980), October 24, 1923, p. 2.

20. *China Year Book, 1924,* p. 867.

21. *Ibid.,* p. 866.

22. *Izvestiia,* No. 249 (1986), October 31, 1923, p. 2.

23. *Ibid.,* No. 258 (1995), November 11, 1923, p. 2.

24. *Ibid.,* No. 259 (1996), November 13, 1923; *ibid.,* No. 269 (1997), November 14, 1923.

25. V. Vilenskii, "Mongoliia protiv iga imperialistov" (Mongolia against the Imperialistic Yoke), *Izvestiia,* No. 251 (1988), November 2, 1923, p. 3.

26. *China Year Book, 1924,* p. 867.

27. *Ibid.,* p. 867; *Izvestiia,* No. 266 (2003), November 21, 1923, p. 1.

28. *China Year Book, 1924,* p. 873; as noted previously, Peking had merely acknowledged receipt of the two declarations in 1921.

29. *Ibid.,* p. 873.

30. *Ibid.,* p. 874.

31. *Ibid.,* p. 876.

32. *Ibid.,* p. 878.

33. *Ibid.,* p. 878.

34. G. M. Friters, *Outer Mongolia and Its International Position,* p. 127.

35. *Izvestiia,* No. 10 (2045), January 12, 1923, p. 2.

36. *Ibid.,* No. 16 (2051), January 19, 1924, p. 4.

37. *Ibid.;* No. 294 (2031), December 23, 1923, p. 2.

38. *Ibid.,* No. 8 (2043), January 10, 1924, p. 1.

39. A. E. Khodorov, "KVZhD" (CER), *Mezhdunarodnaia Zhizn',* No. 1, 1924, p. 33.

40. V. Vilenskii, "Iaponiia, Kitai, i voprosy priznavaniia SSSR" (Japan, China, and the Question of Recognizing the USSR), *Izvestiia,* No. 34 (2069), February 10, 1924, p. 1.

41. *Izvestiia,* No. 50 (2085), February 29, 1924, p. 1.

42. V. Vilenskii, "Kitaiskaia agressivnost' " (Chinese Aggressiveness), *Izvestiia,* No. 54 (2086), March 1, 1924, p. 1.

43. *Izvestiia,* No. 63 (2098), March 16, 1924, p. 1; *China Year Book, 1924,* p. 879.

44. *Izvestiia,* No. 86 (2121), April 13, 1924, p. 1.

45. *Ibid.,* No. 63 (2098), March 16, 1924, p. 1.

46. *China Year Book, 1924,* p. 880; quoting Rosta News Agency of March 21, 1924.

47. *North China Herald,* November 24, 1923, p. 526.

48. A. K. Wu, *China and the Soviet Union,* pp. 152–55, gives an interesting account in support of the cabinet's action, based upon an interview with Wellington Koo in 1939. However, the evidence he presents is biased and inconclusive.

49. Louis Fischer, *The Soviets in World Affairs,* II, 545; Pollard, *op. cit.,* p. 186.

50. *China Year Book, 1924,* p. 879.

51. *Izvestiia,* No. 64 (2099), March 18, 1924, p. 1; *ibid.,* No. 66 (2101), March 21, 1924; *China Year Book, 1924,* p. 880.

52. *Izvestiia,* No. 66 (2101), March 21, 1924, p. 1. Li was the alleged source of the Peking report in March, 1920, claiming that Bolshevik authorities had repudiated the Irkutsk text of Karakhan's 1919 manifesto.

53. *Ibid.*

54. *Ibid.*

55. *Ibid.*

56. *North China Herald,* April 5, 1924, p. 2; see also K. S. Weigh, *Russo-Chinese Diplomacy,* p. 298.

57. *Izvestiia,* No. 67 (2102), March 22, 1924.

58. *China Year Book, 1924,* p. 883.

59. *Ibid.,* p. 885.

60. *Ibid.,* p. 887.

61. Pollard, *op. cit.,* p. 189; *North China Herald,* April 12, 1924, p. 42; *North China Herald,* May 17, 1924; *China Weekly Review,* May, 1924, p. 153.

62. L. Fischer, *op. cit.,* II, 546.

63. *Izvestiia,* No. 101 (2136), May 6, 1924, p. 2.

64. *China Year Book, 1924,* p. 1197. The May 31, 1924, decisions were embodied in an "Agreement on General Principles" which included fifteen articles, an "Agreement for the Provisional Management of the CER" of eleven articles, and seven Declarations. China's denunciation of Soviet treaties was part of an article in the main "agreement" signed by Wang and Karakhan. In May, it was removed from "Declaration III" but therein stated to have "the same force and validity as a general declaration embodied in the said Agreement on General Principles." For full text of the relevant doc-

uments, see Appendix C of this study. In view of the Soviet refusal to renounce the pacts which China would not recognize, it is interesting that in
none of the Bolshevik commentaries or summaries of the May, 1924, agreement is Declaration III included or summarized. See I. V. Kliuchnikov and
A. Sabanin, eds., *Mezhdunarodnaia politika noveishego vremeni v dogovorakh, notakh, i deklaratsiiakh* (International Politics of Our Times in Treaties, Notes, and Declarations), III, 310–12; V. P. Savvin, *Vzaimootnosheniia
tsarskoi Rossii i SSSR s Kitaem* (Relations of Tsarist Russia and the USSR
with China), pp. 128–30; also *Diplomaticheskii Slovar'*, II, 708. The original text of the 1924 treaty was in English. For complete Russian translation,
including the Chinese denunciation of Soviet treaties in Declaration III, see
*Sbornik deistvuiushchikh dogovorov, soglashenii, i konventsii zakliuchen-
nikh s inostrannymi gosudarstvami* (Collection of Operative Treaties, Agreements, and Conventions Concluded with Foreign Governments), 2nd ed.,
pp. 30–37 and pp. 327–29.

65. *China Year Book, 1924,* p. 1103.

66. *Ibid.,* p. 1194.

67. D. Bukhartsev, *Sem' let nashei vneshnei politiki* (Seven Years of Our
Foreign Policy), p. 27.

68. G. Dikii, "Sblizhenie Rossii s Mongoliei" (Rapprochement of Russia
and Mongolia), *Torgovlia Rossii s Vostokom,* No. 1, 1923, p. 8.

69. V. Slepchenko, "Puti soobshcheniia s Mongoliei i v Mongolii" (Means
of Communication with Mongolia and in Mongolia), *Torgovlia Rossii s Vostokom,* No. 1, 1923, pp. 23–27.

70. *Izvestiia,* No. 126 (2161), June 4, 1924, p. 1.

71. *Ibid.,* p. 3.

72. Doksom, "Istoricheskie uroki 15 let revoliutsii" (Historical Lesson of
Fifteen Years of Revolution), *Tikhii Okean,* No. 3 (9), July-September,
1936, pp. 73–74, gives the full text of Chicherin's note as well as an un-
dated reply from the Mongolian government agreeing to his proposal.
According to *Pravda,* No. 59 (2990), March 12, 1925, p. 1, this reply was
given in early March.

73. *Pravda,* No. 59 (2990), March 12, 1925, p. 1.

74. *Ibid.,* No. 54 (2985), March 6, 1925, p. 5.

75. Karakhan was executed for alleged treason in the purges of December, 1937. *Diplomaticheskii Slovar',* II, 708, consequently makes no mention
of him and explains the conclusion of the 1924 treaty as being the result
of "the demands of the Chinese people" for better relations with Russia. In
connection with this claim of universal support in China for the 1924 treaty,
it is interesting to note an analysis by Voitinskii revealing considerable op-

position in Canton. Writing in 1925, he recalled his last visit with Sun in Canton, shortly after the Sino-Soviet accord: "Even Kuomintang members were dissatisfied. It seemed to them that to conclude this treaty was to act unfaithfully in relations with the Southern government of Dr. Sun. Canton found itself in hostile relations with Peking but we concluded a treaty with Peking. They did not understand that . . . in concluding a treaty with the North, we were thereby lessening the danger for the South. Sun completely rejected this [hostile] point of view, showing that he well understood the meaning of the treaty between the Soviet Union and the Chinese government, the significance of this for the interests of the Chinese people." G. Voitinskii, "Moi vstrechi s Sun Yat-senom," *Pravda*, No. 61 (2992), March 15, 1925, p. 2.

CHAPTER XII   *Soviet Policy in the Chinese Revolution*

1. Several scholarly studies provide excellent accounts of the formative years of Chinese Communism. Benjamin I. Schwartz, *Chinese Communism and the Rise of Mao*, pp. 7–37, discusses the intellectual ferment as well as the history of the Chinese Communist Party from a thorough study of Chinese and Japanese sources. Less detailed but handy for reference is the "Chronology of the Communist Movement in China, 1918–50," contained in Conrad Brandt, John K. Fairbank, and Benjamin I. Schwartz, eds., *A Documentary History of Chinese Communism*, pp. 29–31. For an examination of the important figures of the period, see R. C. North, *Kuomintang and Chinese Communist Elites*.

2. V. Vilenskii, "Kitaiskaia Kommunisticheskaia Partiia" (The Chinese Communist Party), *Novyi Vostok*, No. 2, 1922, pp. 604–12; see also Mao Tse-tung's autobiography in Edgar Snow, *Red Star over China*, p. 139.

3. Brandt, *op. cit.*, p. 29; see also two Chinese sources, *Chia I-chun, Chung-hua Min-kuo Shih* (Peiping, 1930), p. 176; and *Chung-kuo Ko T'ang P'ai chih Shih Liao yü* (Peiping, 1947), p. 310. G. Voitinski, writing on the occasion of Sun's death in March, 1925, told of a visit with Sun in the fall of 1920, arranged through "Comrade Ch.," probably Ch'en Tu-hsiu. Sun allegedly inquired as to how "the struggle in South China" and that in Russia might be linked, lamenting: "The geographical position of Canton gives us no possibility of establishing contact with Russia." According to Voitinskii, Sun asked if a "powerful radio station in Vladivostok or Manchuria" might not facilitate contact between Petrograd and Canton. G. Voitinskii, "Moi vstrechi s Sun Yat-senom," *Pravda*, No. 61 (2992), March 15, 1925, p. 2.

4. Brandt, *op. cit.*, p. 30. Harold R. Isaacs, *The Tragedy of the Chinese*

Revolution, p. 62, claims that Maring visited Sun in the early spring of 1921 but gives no other information on this trip. Leang-li T'ang, *The Inner History of the Chinese Revolution,* p. 155, claims that "Mahlin [*sic*] first met Wu Pei-fu in the North and then went South to see Sun Yat-sen . . . secretly organized the Chinese Communist Party, and on his return to Moscow recommended that the Third International should enter into relations both with Sun Yat-sen and Wu Pei-fu." It is impossible to give a precise record without more immediate sources than these.

5. V. Vilenskii, "Kitaiskaia Kommunisticheskaia Partiia" (The Chinese Communist Party), *Novyi Vostok,* No. 2, 1922, prints the full text of the June declaration, translated by Khodorov. This is the only instance where Vilenskii linked himself approvingly in print with the Chinese Communist Party, probably because of his long advocacy of support to bourgeois groups and to Sun which at this point was accepted by the Party.

6. Brandt, *op. cit.,* pp. 51 ff. gives analysis and translation of these documents.

7. Although all accounts agree as to Maring's tactic, there are differences about the degree of pressure he applied to win acceptance of this policy. Schwartz, *Chinese Communism and the Rise of Mao,* pp. 36–45, concludes after careful examination of Chinese and Japanese materials that Maring invoked Comintern discipline; Isaacs, *op. cit.,* pp. 58 ff., accepts Maring's disclaimer of carrying "orders." M. N. Roy, *Revolution and Counterrevolution in China,* p. 534, notes that there was opposition in the Chinese Communist Party but that "the original negative attitude of the Communist leaders was an ultra-left stupidity . . . corrected under the guidance of the Communist International."

8. Schwartz, *Chinese Communism and the Rise of Mao,* p. 40, tells of a meeting with Dallin, cited in a later document by Ch'en Tu-hsiu. Isaacs, *op. cit.,* p. 58, relates Maring's meeting with Sun.

9. Stephen Chen and Robert Payne, *Sun Yat-sen, a Portrait* (New York, 1946), p. 197.

10. G. Kara-Murza and P. Mif, eds., *Strategiia i taktika Kominterna v natsional'no-kolonial'noi revoliutsii, na primer Kitaia* (Comintern Strategy and Tactics in the National-Colonial Revolution, For Example, China), p. 112, translated in full; adopted on January 12, 1923.

11. *Ibid.,* pp. 114–16. Italics in original. P. Mif, *Kitaiskaia revoliutsiia* (The Chinese Revolution), p. 6, prints an abbreviated version omitting entire sections.

12. Its acceptance by the Chinese Communist Party was formalized in another manifesto calling for a congress under Kuomintang auspices for the

purpose of building a "people's government" and launching a "united national front" against the Peking regime; Manifesto of the Chinese Communist Party, July, 1923, in *Novyi Vostok*, No. 4, 1923, pp. 282–86. In an introduction, Voitinskii welcomed this as evidence of Party understanding "that in the present historical moment it cannot yet claim the role of the single liberator of its people . . . but it knows, better than all other political groupings, by what paths national liberation must go." As for Sun, Voitinskii noted that "Dr. Sun Yat-sen, at the present, undoubtedly has posed much more clearly to himself the meaning of the political propaganda of his slogans which he proposed in the revolution of 1911, far from the limits of that territory which he now occupies. On the other hand, an understanding of the role of world imperialism in the destiny of peoples of the Far East, and particularly of China, has come to him now as never before."

13. Lyon Sharman, *Sun Yat-sen, His Life and Its Meaning*, p. 250. No record of this conversation has found in published papers of the State Department.

14. Shih-i Hsiung, *The Life of Chiang Kai-shek*, pp. 178–79. Later Soviet accounts ignore Chiang's role although sometimes they refer generally to his mission. In E. M. Zhukov, ed., *Mezhdunarodnoe otnoshenie na dal'nem Vostoke, 1870–1945 g.* (International Relations in the Far East, 1870–1945), p. 363, a "diplomatic mission" of Sun's is dated as 1923, but no further information is given nor is any reference made to the Sun-Joffe entente. In *Diplomaticheskii Slovar'*, II, 916–19, a lengthy biography of Chiang omits mention of his Moscow journey.

15. Louis Fischer, *The Soviets in World Affairs*, II, 634.

16. Typed copy of original file of Sun-Karakhan correspondence in the personal collection of Louis Fischer; this as well as the following documents were received by Fischer from Karakhan personally. Italics in original. Voitinskii, *Novyi Vostok*, No. 4, 1923, p. 281, cited Sun's telegram to Karakhan as "clearly evident that he [Sun] really understands in which country's interest coincide the interests of the revolutionary movement of China."

17. *Ibid.*

18. Isaacs, *op. cit.*, p. 63, claims that Borodin was "delegated by the Politbureau of the Communist Party of the Soviet Union" but offers no source for this statement.

19. Fischer file of Sun-Karakhan correspondence. Italics added.

20. This letter is dated February 2, 1924, but was probably written shortly thereafter, inasmuch as the British decision to recognize Russia was made known officially on February 2.

CHAPTER XIII   *In Conclusion*

1. Later Soviet accounts agree that the military problem ended in late 1921. *Diplomaticheskii Slovar'*, II, 714, for instance, says: "By the end of 1921, Mongolia was completely freed of White Guards." It appears that the Red Army remained solely for the purpose of safeguarding the pro-Russian orientation of the country; see G. M. Friters, *Outer Mongolia and Its International Position*, p. 126.

2. Shu-chin Tsui, "The Influence of the Canton-Moscow Entente on Sun Yat-sen," *The China Social and Political Review*, XX (1936), 102; speech of Sun Yat-sen of December 1, 1923.

BIBLIOGRAPHY

Bibliography

Abramson, M. "Politicheskoe obshchestvo i partii v Kitae" (Political Society and Parties in China), *Novyi Vostok*, No. 1, 1922.

Alekseev, V. "Ocherki sovremennogo Kitaia" (Essays on Contemporary China), *Vostok*, No. 2, 1923.

Antonov-Ovseenko, A. "Soglashenie o KVZhD" (Agreement on the CER), *Izvestiia*, No. 132 (2167), June 12, 1924.

Antropov, P. Bibliografiia Azii (Bibliography on Asia). Moscow, 1929.

Balabanova, Angelica. My Life as a Rebel. New York, 1938.

Bau, Mingchien J. China and World Peace. New York, 1928.

Bibliografiia Vostoka (Bibliography on the East). Moscow–Leningrad, 1937.

Blanchard, P. "Bolshevism in China," *The Nation*, September 23, 1925.

Bolgar, A. "The Far East," *International Press Correspondence*, Vol. II, No. 78.

Borkenau, Franz. World Communism, a History of the Communist International. New York, 1939.

Brandt, Conrad, John K. Fairbank, and Benjamin I. Schwartz, eds. A Documentary History of Chinese Communism. Cambridge, Mass., 1952.

Brief History of the Chinese Communist Party (mimeographed, Columbia University, n.d.).

Brike, C. "Natsional'nye i klassovye perspektivy bor'by Kitaiskogo proletariata" (The National and Class Outlook for the Struggle of the Chinese Proletariat), *Pravda*, No. 50, March 6, 1923.

Bukharin, N. Krizis kapitalizma i kommunisticheskoe dvizhenie (The Crisis of Capitalism and the Communist Movement). Moscow, 1923.

Bukhartsev, D. Sem' let nashei vneshnei politiki (Seven Years of Our Foreign Policy). Moscow, 1925.

Carnegie Endowment for International Peace. Division of International Law. Treaties and Agreements with and concerning China, 1919–1929. Washington, 1929.

Carr, E. H. The Bolshevik Revolution, 1917–1923 Vols. I–III, New York, 1950–53.

Chen, Pan-tsui. "Reminiscences of the First Congress of the Communist Party of China," *The Communist International*, No. 13, 1936.

Chen, Stephen, and Robert Payne. Sun Yat-sen, a Portrait. New York, 1946.

Chicherin, G. "God vostochnoi politiki Sovetskoi vlasti" (One Year's Policy of Soviet Power), *Izvestiia*, No. 250 (1393), November 6, 1921.

China Year Book, 1921. Tientsin, 1923.

China Year Book, 1924. Tientsin, 1926.

Comintern. [Communist International.]

——Pervyi kongress Kominterna, mart, 1919 g. (First Comintern Congress, March, 1919). Moscow, 1933.

——Vtoroi kongress Kominterna; stenograficheskii otchët (Second Comintern Congress; Verbatim Report). Moscow, 1921.

——Protokoly kongressov Kommunisticheskogo Internatsionala, vtoroi kongress (Proceedings of Congresses of the Communist International, the Second Congress). Moscow, 1934.

——Der Zweite Kongress der Kommunistischen Internationale, Protokoll der Verhandlungen (The Second Congress of the Communist International, Record of Proceedings). Hamburg, 1921.

——Berichte zum Zweiten Kongress der Kommunistischen Internationale (Reports to the Second Congress of the Communist International). Hamburg, 1921.

——Leitsätze zum II. Kongress der Kommunistischen Internationale (Theses of the Second Congress of the Communist International). Petrograd, 1920.

——Leitsätze und Statuten zum II. Kongress der Kommunistischen Internationale (Theses and Statutes of the Second Congress of the Communist International). Hamburg, 1921.

——II-e Congrès de la III-e Internationale Communiste, compte-rendu stenographique (The Second Congress of the Third Communist International, Verbatim Report). Petrograd, n.d.

——Statuts et résolutions de l'Internationale Communiste (Statutes and Resolutions of the Communist International). Petrograd, 1920.

——Theses and Statutes of the Third (Communist) International. Moscow, 1920, reprinted by the United Communist Party of America, n.d.

——The Second Congress of the Communist International, Stenographic Report. Moscow, 1920.

——The Second Congress of the Communist International as Reported and Interpreted by the Official Newspapers of Soviet Russia. Washington, 1920.

——Vestnik 2-go kongressa Kommunisticheskogo Internatsionale (Herald of the Second Congress of the Communist International). Moscow, July–August, 1920.

——Resoliutsii i ustav Kommunisticheskogo Internatsionala (Resolutions and Statutes of the Communist International). Petrograd, n.d.

——III. kongress Kominterna (Third Comintern Congress). Moscow, 1921.

——Protokoll des III. Kongresses der Kommunistischen Internationale (Proceedings of the Third Congress of the Communist International). Hamburg, 1921.

——Theses and Resolutions Adopted at III World Congress of the Communist International. Moscow, 1921.

——IV. vsemirnyi kongress Kommunisticheskogo Internatsionala, izbrannye doklady, rechi, i rezoliutsii (Fourth World Congress of the Communist International, Selected Reports, Speeches, and Resolutions). Moscow, 1923.

——Biulleteni IV. kongressa Kominterna (Bulletins of the Fourth Comintern Congress). Moscow, November–December, 1922.

——Protokoll des vierten Kongresses der Kommunistischen Internationale. Hamburg, 1923.

——Pervyi s'ezd narodov Vostoka, Baku, stenograficheskii otchët (First Congress of Peoples of the East, Baku, Verbatim Report). Petrograd, 1920.

——Pervyi s'ezd revoliutsionnykh organizatsii dal'nego Vostoka (First Congress of Revolutionary Organizations of the Far East). Petrograd, 1922.

——The First Congress of the Toilers of the Far East. Petrograd, 1922.

Condliffe, J., ed. Problems of the Pacific, 1927. Chicago, 1928.

Conolly, Violet. Soviet Economic Policy in the East. London, 1933.

—— Soviet Trade from the Pacific to the Levant. London, 1935.

Dallin, David. Soviet Russia and the Far East. New York, 1948.

Degras, Jane, ed. Soviet Documents on Foreign Policy. Vol. I, 1917–1924. London, 1951.

Deiateli revoliutsionnogo dvizheniia v Rossii (Participants in the Revolutionary Movement in Russia). Moscow, 1931.

Dennis, Alfred Lewis P. The Foreign Policies of Soviet Russia. London, 1924.

Dikii, G. "Mandzhurskii rynok i russkaia promyshlennost'" (The Manchurian Market and Russian Industry), *Torgovliia Rossii s Vostokom,* Nos. 3–4, 1923.

—— "Perspektivi Rossisko-Mandzhurskoi torgovli" (The Outlook of Russo-Manchurian Trade), *Torgovliia Rossii s Vostokom,* Nos. 5–6, 1924.

—— "Sblizhenie Rossii s Mongoliei" (Rapprochement of Russia and Mongolia), *Torgovliia Rossii s Vostokom,* No. 1, 1923.

Diplomaticheskii Slovar'. See Vyshinskii, A., ed.

Doksom. "Istoricheskie uroki 15 let revoliutsii" (Historical Lessons of Fifteen Years of Revolution), *Tikhii Okean,* No. 3 (9), July–September, 1936.

Eidus, Kh. Ocherki rabochego dvizheniia v stranakh Vostoka (Essays on the Labor Movement in Countries of the East). Moscow, 1922.

Ezhegodnik Kominterna (Comintern Yearbook). Moscow, 1924.

Far Eastern Republic. Letters Captured from Baron Ungern in Mongolia. Washington, 1922.

Fischer, Louis. Men and Politics. New York, 1941.

—— The Soviets in World Affairs. Vols. I–II, Princeton, 1951.

—— Unpublished private papers containing typed copy of Karakhan-Sun correspondence, obtained from L. Karakhan.

Friters, Gerard M. Outer Mongolia and its International Position. Baltimore, 1949.

Fuse, K. Soviet Policy in the Orient. New York, 1927.

Girinis, S., ed. Profintern v rezoliutsiiakh (Profintern in Resolutions). Moscow, 1928.

Grierson, Philip. Books on Soviet Russia, 1917–1942. London, 1943.

Hart, J. "Mr. Yoffe and the Failure of Chinese-Russian Negotiations," *China Weekly Review,* January 27, 1923.

Heller, L. "Otchët II. kongressa Profinterna o rabochem dvizhenii v Kitae" (Report at the Second Profintern Congress on the Labor Movement in China), *Krasnyi Internatsional Profsoiuzov,* No. 1 (24), January 27, 1923.

—— Profsoiuzy na Vostoka (Trade Unions in the East). Moscow, 1923.

Ho, Ping-yin. The Foreign Trade of China. Shanghai, 1935.

How, Julie. "The Development of Ch'en Tu-hsiu's Thoughts, 1915–18." Unpublished M.A. thesis, Columbia University, 1949.

Hsiung, Shih-i. The Life of Chiang Kai-shek. London, 1948.

Isaacs, Harold K. The Tragedy of the Chinese Revolution. Stanford, 1951.

Ivin, A. "Sovremennyi Kitai" (Contemporary China), *Novyi Vostok*, No. 1, 1922; No. 2, 1922; No. 3, 1923; No. 4, 1924.

Joffe, A. "Kitaiskii kavardak" (Chinese Puzzle), *Izvestiia*, No. 3 (1740), January 5, 1923.

―――― "Nachalo" (The Beginning), *Izvestiia*, No. 40 (1777), February 22, 1923.

―――― "Russian Policy in China," *Living Age*, January 12, 1923.

Kara-Murza, G. "Kitai v 1918–24 godakh" (China in the Years 1918–24), *Istorik-Marksist*, Nos. 5–6.

Kara-Murza, G., and P. Mif, eds. Strategiia i taktika Kominterna v natsional'no-kolonial'noi revoliutsii, na primer Kitaia (Comintern Strategy and Tactics in the National-Colonial Revolution, For Example, China). Moscow, 1934.

Kazanin, M. "Pekin i problemy dogovora" (Peking and Treaty Problems), *Mezhdunarodnaia Zhizn'*, No. 14, October 31, 1922.

Kerner, Robert J. Northeastern Asia, a Selected Bibliography. Berkeley, 1939.

Khodorov, A. E. "KVZhD" (CER), *Mezhdunarodnaia Zhizn'*, No. 1, 1924.

―――― "Koalitsiia Chang Tso-lina i Sun Iat-sen" (Coalition between Chang Tso-lin and Sun Yat-sen), *Mezhdunarodnaia Zhizn'*, No. 9 (127), July 29, 1922.

―――― "Lenin i natsional'nyi vopros" (Lenin and the Nationality Question), *Novyi Vostok*, No. 5, 1924.

―――― Mirovoi imperializm v Kitae (World Imperialism in China). Shanghai, 1922.

―――― "Novyi kabinet v Pekine" (New Cabinet in Peking), *Vestnik Narkomindel*, Nos. 4–5, 1922.

―――― "Rossiia i Dal'nyi Vostok" (Russia and the Far East), *Torgovliia Rossii s Vostokom*, No. 1, 1923.

―――― "Sovetskoe predstavitel'stvo v Kitae" (Soviet Representation in China), *Izvestiia*, No. 226 (1665), October 7, 1922.

Kliuchnikov, I. V., and A. Sabanin, eds., Mezhdunarodnaia politika noveishego vremeni v dogovorakh, notakh, i deklaratsiiakh (International Politics of Recent Times in Treaties, Notes, and Declarations). Moscow, 1925–28.

Komintern. See Comintern.

Kong, H. T., "China, Japan, and the Siberian Question," *Millard's Review*, March 6, 1920.

―――― "Soviet Mission in Peking," *Millard's Review*, December 31, 1921.

Korostovets, I. Von Cinggis Khan zur Sowetrepublik (From Genghis Khan to Soviet Republic). Berlin, 1926.

Kotliarevskii, S. "Pravovye dostizheniia Rossii v Azii" (Russian Legal Attainments in Asia), *Novyi Vostok*, No. 1, 1922.

Kun, Bela, ed. Komintern v dokumentakh (Comintern in Documents). Moscow, 1926.

—— Kommunisticheskii Internatsional v dokumentakh; resheniia, tezisy, i vozzvaniia kongressov Kominterna i plenumov IKKI, 1919–1932 (The Communist International in Documents, Decisions, Theses, and Proclamations of the Comintern Congresses and Plenary Meetings of the E.C.C.I, 1919–1932). Moscow, 1933.

"Labour Conditions in China," *International Labor Review*, No. 6, December, 1924.

Lattimore, Owen. Manchuria, Cradle of Conflict. New York, 1932.

Lenin i Vostok (Lenin and the East). Petrograd, 1925.

Lenin, V. I. Collected Works. New York, 1927–45.

—— Imperialism, the Highest Stage of Capitalism. New York, 1939.

—— Left Wing Communism: An Infantile Disorder. Moscow, 1950.

—— Selected Works. Moscow, 1946.

—— Sobranie sochinenii (Complete Works). Moscow, 1919–20.

—— Sochineniia (Works). 2nd ed., Moscow, 1926–32.

—— Sochineniia (Works). 3rd ed., Moscow, 1926–46.

—— Tetradi po imperializmu (Notes on Imperialism). Moscow, 1939.

—— Vostok i revoliutsiia (The East and Revolution). Moscow, 1924.

Lobanov-Rostovsky, Andrei. Russia and Asia. New York, 1933.

Loewenthal, Rudolf. Bibliography of Russian Literature on China and Adjacent Countries, 1931–1936. Cambridge, 1949.

Lozovskii, A., ed. Rabochii Kitai (Workers of China). Moscow, 1925.

Ma, Ho-t'ien. Chinese Agent in Mongolia. Baltimore, 1949.

MacMurray, John V. A., ed. Treaties and Agreements with and concerning China, 1894–1919. Vols. I–II, Washington, 1919.

Maiskii, I. "Kitai i ego bor'ba" (China and Her Struggle), *Pravda*, No. 166, 1922.

—— "Mongoliia" (Mongolia), *Novyi Vostok*, No. 1, 1922.

—— "Present Day China," *International Press Correspondence*, No. 76, September 5, 1922.

—— Sovremennaia Mongoliia (Contemporary Mongolia). Irkutsk, 1921.

—— Vneshnaia politika RSFSR, 1917–1922 (The Foreign Policy of the RSFSR, 1917–1922). Moscow, 1923.

Maring, G. "Krovarnyi epizod v istorii Kitaiskogo rabochego dvizheniia" (A Bloody Episode in the History of the Chinese Labor Movement), *Kommunisticheskii Internatsional*, Nos. 26–27, 1923.

—— "Revoliutsionnoe dvizhenie v iuzhnom Kitae" (The Revolutionary

Movement in South China), *Kommunisticheskii Internatsional,* No. 22, 1922.

Mif, P. Kitaiskaia revoliutsiia (The Chinese Revolution). Moscow, n.d.

Musin. "Kitaiskoe rabochee dvizhenie i fevral'skaia zheleznodorozhnaia zabastovka" (The Chinese Labor Movement and the February Railroad Strike), *Novyi Vostok,* No. 4, 1923.

—— "Kratkii obzor rabochego dvizheniia v Kitae za 1922 g." (Brief Survey of the Labor Movement in China in 1922), *Kommunisticheskii Internatsional,* No. 25, 1923.

Nikolaevskii, B. "Revoliutsiia v Kitae, Japoniia, i Stalin" (Revolution in China, Japan, and Stalin), *Novyi Zhurnal,* No. 6, 1943.

—— "Vneshnaia politika Moskvi" (The Foreign Policy of Moscow), *Novyi Zhurnal,* Nos. 1–8, 1942–44.

Norins, Martin R. Gateway to Asia, Sinkiang. New York, 1944.

North, Robert C. Unpublished memorandum of private interview with M. N. Roy, October 15, 1950.

North, Robert C., and I. de S. Pool. Kuomintang and Chinese Communist Elites. Stanford, 1952.

Norton, Henry K. China and the Powers. New York, 1927.

—— The Far Eastern Republic of Siberia. London, 1923.

Pasvolsky, Leo. Russia in the Far East. New York, 1922.

Pavlovich, M. P. Voprosy kolonial'noi i natsional'noi politiki i III¹ Internatsional (Questions of Colonial and National Policy and the Third International). Moscow, 1920.

Pavlovsky, Michel N. Chinese-Russian Relations. New York, 1949.

Pollard, Robert T. China's Foreign Relations, 1917–1931. New York, 1933.

Potemkin, V. P., ed. Istoriia diplomatii (History of Diplomacy). Vols. I–III, Moscow, 1945.

"Problemy dal'nego Vostoka" (Problems of the Far East), *Izvestiia,* No. 178 (1617), August 10, 1922.

Profintern. [Red International of Trade Unions.] Pervaia mezhdunarodnaia konferentsiia revoliutsionnykh professional'nykh i proizvodstvennykh soiuzov, stenograficheskii otchët (First International Conference of Professional and Industrial Trade Unions, Verbatim Report). Moscow, 1921.

—— Vtoroi kongress Krasnogo Internatsionala Profsoiuzov (Second Congress of the Red International of Trade Unions). Moscow, 1923.

—— Biulleten' II. kongress Krasnogo Internatsionala Profsoiuzov (Bulletin of the Second Congress of the Red International of Trade Unions). Moscow, n.d.

—— Resolutions and Decisions of the Red Labor Union International. New York, 1921.

Profintern (*continued*)

———— Resolutions and Decisions of the Second World Congress of the Red Labor Union International. Chicago, n.d.

———— Otchët o rabotakh III. sessii tsentral'nogo soveta Krasnogo Profinterna (Report on Work of the Third Session of the Central Council of the Red Profintern). Moscow, 1923.

"Rabochee dvizhenie (Kitai)" (The Labor Movement—China), *Krasnyi Internatsional Profsoiuzov*, No. 11, December 31, 1921.

Radek, K. Piat' let Kominterna (Five Years of Comintern). Moscow, 1924.

———— Razvitie mirovoi revoliutsii (Development of the World Revolution). Moscow, 1920.

Red International of Trade Unions. See Profintern.

Safarov, G. "Vostok i revoliutsiia" (The East and Revolution), *Kommunisticheskii Internatsional*, No. 15, 1921.

Savvin, V. P. Vzaimootnosheniia tsarskoi Rossii i SSSR s Kitaem (Relations of Tsarist Russia and the USSR with China). Moscow, 1930.

Sbornik deistvuiuschchikh . . . s inostrannymi gosudarstvami. See USSR NKID.

Schwartz, Benjamin I. Chinese Communism and the Rise of Mao. Harvard, 1951.

Sen, Chih-yuan. "Sino-Soviet Relations." Unpublished M.A. thesis, Columbia University, 1932.

Sergeev, G. Lenin i Stalin o razdele Kitaia (Lenin and Stalin on the Division of China). Moscow, n.d.

Sharman, Lyon. Sun Yat-sen, His Life and Its Meaning. New York, 1934.

Shumiatskii, B. "S'ezd trudiashchevsia dal'nogo Vostoka" (Congress of Toilers of the Far East), *Izvestiia*, No. 15 (1454), January 21, 1922.

"The Situation in China and Japan," *International Press Correspondence*, No. 72, August 25, 1922.

Skachkov, P. Bibliografiia Kitaia (Bibliography on China). Moscow, 1930.

———— "Lenin o zarubezhnom Vostoke" (Lenin on the East beyond the Border), *Bibliografiia Vostoka*, 1932.

Slepchenko, V. "Puti soobshcheniia s Mongoliei i v Mongolii" (Means of Communication with Mongolia and in Mongolia), *Torgovliia Rossii s Vostokom*, No. 1, 1923.

Smurgis, Iu. Kitai i ego rabochee dvizhenie (China and Its Labor Movement). Moscow, 1922.

Snow, Edgar. Red Star over China. New York, 1937.

"Sovetskaia Rossiia i Mandzhurskaia problema" (Soviet Russia and the Manchurian Problem), *Izvestiia*, No. 295 (1734), December 28, 1922.

"Stachenoe dvizhenie v Kitae" (The Strike Movement in China), *Krasnyi Internatsional Profsoiuzov*, No. 2 (25), February, 1923.

Stalin, J. Sochineniia (Works). Moscow, 1947.

Sukhotin. "Sovetskaia Rossiia na Vostoke" (Soviet Russia in the East), *Mezhdunarodnaia Zhizn'*, No. 15, November 7, 1922.

Ta Chen. "The Labor Movement in China," *International Labor Review*, No. 3, March, 1927.

———— "The Labor Situation in China," *Monthly Labor Review*, No. 6, December, 1920.

———— "Labor Unrest in China," *Monthly Labor Review*, No. 2, August, 1921.

———— "The Shipping Strike in Hong Kong," *Monthly Labor Review*, No. 3, March, 1922.

T'ang, Leang-li. The Inner History of the Chinese Revolution. New York, 1930.

Taylor, J. B., and W. T. Zung. "Labour and Industry in China," *International Labor Review*, No. 1, July, 1923.

Tivel, A. Desiat' let Kominterna v resheniiakh i tsifrakh (Ten Years of Comintern in Decisions and Figures). Moscow, 1929.

———— Piat' let Kominterna (Five Years of Comintern). Moscow, 1924.

Treaties and Agreements with and concerning China, 1919–1929. See Carnegie Endowment for International Peace.

Troianovskii, K. Vostok i revoliutsiia (The East and Revolution). Moscow, 1918.

Trotsky, L. The First Five Years of the Communist International. New York, 1945.

———— Piat' let Kominterna (Five Years of Comintern). Moscow, 1924.

Tso, Lein-en. The Chinese Eastern Railway, an Analytical Study. Nanking, 1930.

Tsui, Shu-chin. "The Influence of the Canton-Moscow Entente on Sun Yat-sen," *The China Social and Political Review*, Vol. XX, 1936.

USSR NKID Sbornik deistvuiushchikh dogovorov, soglashenii, i konventsii zakliuchennykh s inostrannymi gosudarstvami (Collection of Operative Treaties, Agreements, and Conventions Concluded with Foreign Governments). Vols. I–III, Moscow, 1921; 2nd ed., Vols. I–VIII, Moscow, 1928.

U.S. Department of State. Papers Relating to the Foreign Policy of the United States, 1918: Russia. Vols. I–II, Washington, 1932.

Vilenskii, V. "Iaponiia, Kitai, i voprosy priznavaniia SSSR" (Japan, China, and the Question of Recognizing the USSR), *Izestiia*, No. 34 (2069), February 10, 1924.

———— Kitai (China). Moscow, 1923.

———— Kitai i Sovetskaia Rossiia (China and Soviet Russia). Moscow, 1919.

———— "Kitaiskaia agressivnost'" (Chinese Aggressiveness), *Izvestiia*, No. 50 (2086), March 1, 1924.

Vilenskii, V. (*continued*)

—— "Kitaiskaia Kommunisticheskaia Partiia" (The Chinese Communist Party), *Novyi Vostok*, No. 2, 1922.

—— "Mongoliia protiv iga imperialistov" (Mongolia against the Imperialistic Yoke), *Izvestiia*, No. 251 (1988), November 2, 1923.

—— "Novyi prezident Kitaia" (New President of China), *Izvestiia*, No. 272 (2009), November 28, 1923.

—— "Oktiabr'skaia Rossiia—maiak dlia narodov Azii" (October Russia— Beacon for Peoples of Asia), *Izvestiia*, No. 252 (1691), November 7, 1922.

—— "Perspektivy revoliutsionnogo dvizheniia v Kitae" (Outlook for the Revolutionary Movement in China), *Novyi Vostok*, No. 2, 1922.

—— "The Political Situation in China," *International Press Correspondence*, No. 24, March 8, 1922.

—— "Politicheskie gruppirovki i partii v Kitae" (Political Groupings and Parties in China), *Kommunisticheskii Internatsional*, No. 23, 1922.

—— "Rabochee dvizhenie v Kitae" (The Labor Movement in China), *Krasnyi Internatsional Profsoiuzov*, No. 12 (35), December, 1923.

—— "Sovetskaia Rossiia i Mongoliia" (Soviet Russia and Mongolia), *Izvestiia*, No. 245 (1092), November 2, 1920.

—— "Sovremennyi Kitai" (Contemporary China), *Izvestiia*, No. 180 (1619), August 12, 1922; No. 181 (1620), August 13, 1922; No. 182 (1621), August 15, 1922.

—— "Za velikoi Kitaiskoi stenoi" (Behind the Great Chinese Wall), *Izvestiia*, No. 185 (1624), August 18, 1922; No. 197 (1636), September 3, 1922; No. 212 (1651), September 21, 1922.

Voitinskii, G. "Bor'ba Kitaiskogo proletariata" (Struggle of the Chinese Proletariat), *Novyi Vostok*, No. 2, 1922.

—— "Moi vstrechi s Sun Yat-senom," *Pravda*, No. 61 (2992), March 15, 1925.

—— "Proletariat i natsional'noe dvizhenie v Kitae" (The Proletariat and the National Movement in China), *Novyi Vostok*, No. 4, 1923.

Voznesenskii, A. "Revoliutsionnyi pozhar na Vostoke" (Revolutionary Conflagration in the East), *Izvestiia*, No. 204 (756), September 14, 1919.

—— "Rossiia i Kitai" (Russia and China), *Izvestiia*, No. 53 (605), March 9, 1919.

Vyshinskii, A., ed. Diplomaticheskii Slovar' (Diplomatic Dictionary). Vols. I–II, Moscow, 1948–50.

Wales, Nym. The Chinese Labor Movement. New York, 1945.

—— Red Dust. Stanford, 1952.

Weigh, K. S. Russo-Chinese Diplomacy. Shanghai, 1928.

Woo, T. C. The Kuomintang and the Future of the Chinese Revolution. New York, 1938.

Wu, A. K. China and the Soviet Union. New York, 1949.

Yakhontoff, Victor A. Russia and the Soviet Union in the Far East. New York, 1931.

Zhukov, E. M., ed. Mezhdunarodnoe otnoshenie na dal'nem Vostoke, 1870–1945 g. (International Relations in the Far East, 1870–1945). Moscow, 1951.

Zinoviev, G. Sochineniia (Works). Leningrad, 1924.

———— Voina i krizis sotsialisma (War and the Crisis of Socialism). Petrograd, 1920.

The following periodicals and newspapers have been examined for the date indicated. Full reference to specific articles quoted from them will be found in the notes.

Biulleten' NKID. Moscow. 1920–24.

Bol'shevik. Moscow. 1924.

Chinese Social and Political Science Review. Peiping. 1936.

Communist International. Leningrad, London, New York. 1919–24.

Communist Review. London. 1921.

Far Eastern Quarterly. Menasha, Wis. 1951.

Godovoi Otchët NKID. Moscow. 1918–24.

International Labor Review. Geneva. 1921–27.

International Press Correspondence. Vienna, London. 1921–24.

Istorik-Marksist. Moscow. 1926.

Izvestiia. Moscow. 1917–24.

Kommunisticheskii Internatsional. Moscow. 1919–24.

Die Kommunistische Internationale. Leningrad, Hamburg, Basel. 1919–24.

Krasnyi Internatsional Profsoiuzov. Moscow. 1921–24.

Mezhdunarodnaia Zhizn'. Moscow. 1920–24.

Millard's Review, later Weekly Review, China Weekly Review. Shanghai. 1917–24.

Monthly Labor Review. Washington. 1920–22.

North China Herald. Shanghai. 1917–24.

Novyi Vostok. Moscow. 1922–24.

Novyi Zhurnal. New York. 1942–44.

Pravda. Moscow. 1917–24.

Tikhii Okean. Moscow. 1934–38.

Torgovliia Rossii s Vostokom. Moscow. 1923–24.

Vestnik Narkomindel. Moscow. 1919–22.

Vostok. Leningrad. 1922–25.

INDEX

Index